RING

RING

A Biography of

Ring Lardner

by
Jonathan Yardley

ROWMAN & LITTLEFIELD PUBLISHERS, INC.
Lanham • Boulder • New York • Oxford

Published in the United States of America by Rowman & Littlefield Publishers, Inc.
4720 Boston Way, Lanham, Maryland 20706
www.rowmanlittlefield.com
12 Hid's Copse Road
Cumnor Hill, Oxford OX2 9JJ, England
Distributed by National Book Network
Copyright © 1977 by Jonathan Yardley
First Rowman & Littlefield edition 2001

British Library Cataloguing in Publication Information Available
A previous edition of this book was cataloged as follows by the Library of Congress:
Yardley, Jonathan. Ring. Includes Index.   1. Lardner, Ring Wilmer, 1885–1933—Biography.
2. Authors, American—20th century—Biography.
PS3523.A7Z9   818'.5'209   77-1661
ISBN 0-7425-1160-X (pbk. : alk. paper)
Printed in the United States of America

♾ ™ The paper used in this publication meets the minimum requirements of American National
Standard for Information Sciences—Permanence of Paper for Printed Library Materials,
ANSI/NISO Z39.48-1992.

Grateful acknowledgment is made to the following for permission to reprint previously published material:

Ring Lardner, Jr., for permission to reprint excerpts from his parents' letters and various public writings by his father.

Chicago Tribune: Various excerpts from news stories and columns written by Ring Lardner, published in the *Chicago Tribune.*

Harcourt Brace Jovanovich, Inc., The Hogarth Press Ltd. and the Literary Estate of Virginia Woolf: Excerpts from the essay, "American Fiction," by Virginia Woolf, reprinted from *The Moment and Other Essays,* by Virginia Woolf.

Harper & Row Publishers, Inc.: Excerpts from *The Lardners,* by Ring Lardner, Jr. (1976).

Farrar, Straus & Giroux, Inc.: Excerpts from *The Twenties,* by Edmund Wilson, edited with an Introduction by Leon Edel. Copyright © 1975 by Elena Wilson, Executrix of the Estate of Edmund Wilson. Introductory material Copyright © 1975 by Leon Edel.

Macmillan Publishing Co., Inc.: Excerpts from *The Glory of Their Times,* by Lawrence S. Ritter. Copyright © 1966 by Lawrence S. Ritter.

New Directions Publishing Corp.: Excerpts from "Ring," reprinted from *The Crack-Up,* by F. Scott Fitzgerald. Copyright 1945 by New Directions Publishing Corporation.

The New Yorker: Extracts from writings by Ring Lardner published in *The New Yorker,* reprinted by permission.

Harold Ober Associates, Inc.: Menu from the Hotel Chatham with notations handwritten by F. Scott Fitzgerald and Maxwell Perkins.

Charles Scribner's Sons: Brief excerpts from the following books: *Dear Scott, Dear Max: The Fitzgerald-Perkins Correspondence,* edited by John Kuehl and Jackson Bryer. Copyright © 1971 by Charles Scribner's Sons; *Editor to Author,* by John Hall Wheelock. Copyright 1950 by Charles Scribner's Sons; *Tender Is the*

To My Parents
with gratitude and love

No man but a blockhead ever wrote except for money.

—Doctor Johnson

A Special Acknowledgment

Writing this book would have been a vastly more difficult and prolonged process had it not been for the research assistance given me by Richard Layman of the English Department at the University of South Carolina. Not merely did he make available to me the thousands of photocopies of Lardner work, principally journalism, he had assembled in connection with his doctoral dissertation; he also recopied hundreds of these for me, sparing me more hours than I care to contemplate hunched before a microfilm viewer. He further performed a great array of special services, the most important being tracking down minute details of Lardner's life. He is not to be held to account for any of my interpretations, on some of which we have amicably agreed to disagree.

During 1976 Rick was co-editor, with Matthew J. Bruccoli, of *Some Champions*, a fine collection of previously unassembled Lardner material, and *Ring Lardner: A Descriptive Bibliography*, which, having relied on it daily in the writing of this book, I can recommend as a superb piece of work. These books firmly establish Rick as a Lardner scholar of the first rank. I have no question that others will be, as I most emphatically am, in his debt.

Other acknowledgments will be found on page 395.

Contents

Part One

Frank Chance's Diamond

"He went on to tell me that I was to join the White Sox in the South, travel with them through the rest of their spring tour and, if I made good, Stick With Them All Season! O diary!"

It is an August afternoon in 1910, and the correspondent of the Chicago *Tribune* is sitting in the press box at Comiskey Park. The stadium, a grand construction of steel and concrete, has been open for only two months, and the smell of newness is still in the air. Below the correspondent, on the green field defined as a diamond by brief swatches of brown and sharp lines of white, the game of baseball proceeds at a swift yet stately pace. The sun slowly falls as the afternoon advances, and the shadows steadily lengthen, but there is no score and the innings march past.

The correspondent watches intently. He is, as the young woman he will marry a year from now describes him, "a *very large*, handsome, young man who holds his head very high in the air and looks at the world with very amused and twinkling eyes." He dresses rather sternly, in the fashion of the day: dark suit, dark knit tie, high starched collar, dark-banded straw boater—the darkness relieved only by the bright stripes of his shirt. As he watches the game he keeps meticulous score in a small, neat script. In the ceaseless chatter of the press box he is an oasis of silence; he delights in the noise around him but only occasionally contributes to it, and then in a low, deliberate voice one must strain to hear through the din.

He is only twenty-five years old, but he is as much a professional in his craft as the players before him are in theirs. So when at last the shadows command the field and the umpires end the contest— "Game called on account of darkness!"—he turns with dispatch to the heavy typewriter before him and begins to write. He types with two fingers, the keys clacking along the pages in staccato bursts punctuated by occasional pauses. The words he writes describe vividly and lovingly what he has seen:

Sixteen innings. o to o. That was the way the last game of the series between the Sox and Athletics wound up. People who left the park at the finish, four minutes before 7 o'clock, did not regret the loss of supper half as much as they would have regretted missing that ball game.

Perhaps it was not the best ever played, but don't try to tell anyone who saw it that there have been many better. The book says there was just one longer runless contest in the big leagues and that was the one between Washington and Detroit in July last year. That one lasted eighteen rounds. Most of us missed that one, so we must be content to talk about yesterday's in the years to come.

And when we talk don't let us say that so and so could and should have scored in such and such an inning. Let us remember only that neither side had the shadow of a right to win against such pitching as that of Ed Walsh of Meriden, Conn., and John Coombs of Colby College. And don't let us say that Walsh was better than Coombs, or that Coombs was better than Walsh. They were both just about perfect. Coombs struck out eighteen men. Walsh made up for that with his feat in the first half of the sixteenth inning, when he absolutely refused to allow a Philadelphia run with fast men on second and third, no one out and three of the Athletics' five best batters coming up.

For more than five years—from March, 1908, to June, 1913—Ring Lardner reported the daily events of major-league professional baseball. For many more years than that, baseball was at or very near the core of his existence. As a boy in Niles, Michigan, he played the game with his friends, cheered the local heroes in their contests against neighboring towns, and counted down the days to the baseball excursions he would make once or twice a year with his father and his brother, Rex, to Chicago, ninety miles to the west. As a beginning reporter in South Bend, Indiana, he heightened his understanding of the game by covering the Central League, a minor league in which many outstanding players of the day refined their skills to major-league levels. Though he stopped covering baseball regularly in the summer of 1913, it was one of the subjects most frequently discussed in the daily column he wrote for the Chicago *Tribune* until 1919, and he covered almost every World Series until the mid-twenties. His first fiction, published in 1914, had a baseball setting, and he became a national celebrity because of the baseball stories collected under the title *You Know Me Al*. Eventually he wearied of the stupidity of so many of the game's fans, and after the integrity of the game was conclusively undermined by the Black Sox scandal of 1919 he turned, in disgust and sorrow, to other subjects. Yet he never lost his love for baseball as he had once known it, and in the last years of his life he remembered it with deep nostalgic longing.

He was, however, much more than a successful baseball "scribe." He was one of the most respected writers of the twenties, widely discussed and widely imitated. His short stories were read by millions, honored and anthologized, scrutinized and praised by critics. For a time, at least, his name was invariably listed alongside those of the other certifiably "important" writers of the period: Scott Fitzgerald, Ernest Hemingway, John Dos Passos, Thomas Wolfe, Sherwood Anderson. But it was always listed with reservations— with, in baseball's statistical language, an asterisk. And the asterisk was baseball itself. Fitzgerald, who was his devoted friend, summarized the problem in a tribute written shortly after Ring's death in September, 1933:

> The point of these paragraphs is that whatever Ring's achievement was it fell short of the achievement he was capable of, and this because of a cynical attitude toward his work. How far back did that attitude go—back to his youth in a Michigan village? Certainly back to his days with the Cubs. During those years, when most men of promise achieve an adult education, if only in the school of war, Ring moved in the company of a few dozen illiterates playing a boy's game. A boy's game, with no more possibilities in it than a boy could master, a game bounded by walls which kept out novelty or danger, change or adventure. This material, the observation of it under such circumstances, was the text of Ring's schooling during the most formative period of the mind. A writer can spin on about his adventures after thirty, after forty, after fifty, but the criteria by which these adventures are weighed and valued are irrevocably settled at the age of twenty-five. However deeply Ring might cut into it, his cake had the diameter of Frank Chance's diamond.

Fitzgerald's words were both kind and unkind, accurate and inaccurate, selfless and self-serving. He insisted on judging Ring by the standards he had set for himself, and as a consequence he was blind to Ring's ultimate accomplishments. Though Fitzgerald was a person of great kindness, he was not wholly untouched by the jealousies that ran so deeply and thickly through his literary circle, and there is more than a trace of sheer competitiveness in his words. Yet they can be neither slighted nor ignored because they point the way to an understanding of Ring's life and work. Fitzgerald *was* right about one thing: baseball was where Ring Lardner began, and to comprehend Ring Lardner one must look to baseball in the first two decades of the twentieth century.

We begin, then, with Frank Chance's diamond.

THE STAGE CAN BE SET with three anecdotes, three stories that help define the world Ring entered in the spring of 1908:

The first occurred during the World Series of 1909. The competing teams were the Detroit Tigers and the Pittsburgh Pirates, and each had a star of heroic dimensions. The Detroit left fielder was Ty Cobb, twenty-two years old, "The Georgia Peach" to sports writers but a feared and hated opponent to his fellow players. The Pittsburgh shortstop was Honus Wagner, thirty-five years old, stocky and clumsy in appearance but called "The Flying Dutchman" because of his range and speed. It was the first time the two players had met, and a test was mandatory. Cobb reached first base and yelled down to Wagner: "Hey, Krauthead, I'm coming down on the next pitch! Get out of the way or I'll cut you to pieces!" Wagner answered, "I'll be waiting." As the pitcher went into his windup, Cobb dug his spikes into the dirt and headed for second. Wagner covered second base and took the catcher's throw. Cobb came in with his spikes high, but Wagner was ready: he took the ball and slammed it into Cobb's mouth. Cobb left the field, and his cut was closed with three stitches. Supremacy had been established.

The second involves a player named Herman A. Schaefer. He, too, played for the Tigers, but he was Cobb's polar opposite: a pudgy, jolly eccentric known, with real affection, as "Germany." The story was told by a teammate, Davy Jones, to Lawrence S. Ritter, who recorded it for his monumental oral history of early baseball, *The Glory of Their Times*:

> We were playing Cleveland and the score was tied in a late inning. I was on third base, Schaefer on first, and Crawford was at bat. Before the pitcher wound up, Schaefer flashed me the sign for the double steal—meaning he'd take off for second on the next pitch,

and when the catcher threw the ball to second I'd take off for home. Well, the pitcher wound up and pitched, and sure enough Schaefer stole second. But I had to stay right where I was, on third, because Nig Clarke, the Cleveland catcher, just held on to the ball. He refused to throw to second, knowing I'd probably make it home if he did.

So now we had men on second and third. Well, on the next pitch Schaefer yelled, "Let's try it again!" And with a blood-curdling shout he took off like a wild Indian back to first base, and dove in headfirst in a cloud of dust. He figured the catcher might throw to first—since he evidently wouldn't throw to second—and then I could come home same as before.

But nothing happened. Nothing at all. Everybody just stood there and watched Schaefer, with their mouths open, not knowing what the devil was going on. Me, too. Even if the catcher *had* thrown to first, I was too stunned to move. I'll tell you that. But the catcher didn't throw. He just stared! In fact, George Stovall, the Cleveland first baseman, was playing way back and didn't even come in to cover the bag. He just watched this madman running the wrong way on the base path and didn't know *what* to do.

The umpires were just as confused as everybody else. However, it turned out that at that time there wasn't any rule against a guy going from second back to first, if that's the way he wanted to play baseball, so they had to let it stand.

So there we were, back where we started, with Schaefer on first and me on third. And on the next pitch darned if he didn't let out another war whoop and take off *again* for second base. By this time the Cleveland catcher evidently had enough, because he finally threw to second to get Schaefer, and when he did I took off for home and *both* of us were safe.

The third took place in a small town in Wisconsin in the autumn of 1906. The World Series had recently been played, and the nation had paid fascinated attention to one of the most celebrated contests in baseball history: the victory of the Chicago White Sox, the "Hitless Wonders," over their neighbors and competitors, the Chicago Cubs, whose record of 116 victories in the regular season of that year has never been surpassed. As was the custom in baseball's early years, the White Sox were capitalizing on their success by making a barnstorming tour of the provinces. The small Wisconsin town in question awaited their visit with all the excitement due a papal audience, and when their train pulled in, a little boy rushed up to see his heroes. He looked, then turned and said, "Why, they're only *men*, aren't they!"

IT WAS A TOUGH GAME played by tough men, yet for all its rudeness it also had humor and innocence. Its players had been raised on Georgia farms, in Pennsylvania coal towns and Chicago alleys, and they brought the individual character of their backgrounds to the game. There was no sameness, no conformity, and in its diversity baseball was, if not an exact microcosm of pre–World War I America, a reasonably faithful representation of a young nation still too close to its frontier to have lost its rough edge or its folk heritage. It was a nation of 90 million people but only four hundred major-league ballplayers, and to the 90 million, the four hundred were demigods; not until the nation learned that the 1919 World Series had been fixed would everyone understand that the four hundred were "only *men*."

The game was still very young. It had been "founded"—to the extent that its origins can be confirmed—less than half a century before Ring saw his first game. The formative game of what we know as baseball is said to have been organized on a meadow in New York City in the spring of 1845, by a surveyor named Alexander J. Cartwright. Professional baseball did not begin until 1869, when the Cincinnati Red Stockings were put together by Harry Wright, a jeweler, whose famous team took the baseball message around the country while running up a record of fifty-six victories, one tie and no defeats. The National Association of Professional Base Ball Players, now the National League, was formed two years later, and it had the field pretty much to itself until the American League came along in 1901. After two years of expensive and generally fruitless competition, the two leagues united in 1903 and played the first World Series that fall.

So when Ring headed South for spring training in 1908, there had been only five seasons of what is called baseball's "modern era." The game was so young, in fact, that the ink was still fresh on its birth certificate. In 1905 a special commission had been formed to investigate its origins and produce an official account. Such was the gravity of the question that the six-man board included two United States senators and four men "high in the councils of the game itself," and such were the fears that "an English origin" might be discovered that an academic observer was moved to write: "It [baseball] was a development, not an invention; and from the evidence at hand we only know that America and baseball met each other when they were young and grew up together. The commission will decide; and let us hope that when our base-ball doctrine is handed down the game will not be in any way beholden to any Foreign Power." His fears were groundless. After two years of study and some rather elaborate invention, the commission weighed in with the "doctrine" that baseball had been founded by a Union general named Abner Doubleday in 1839 in the pleasant upstate New York lakeside hamlet of Cooperstown—a pure fiction, to be sure, but a charming one that the nation eagerly embraced and has never quite repudiated.

Young though it was, the game was, in the words of the baseball historian Harold Seymour, "ingrained in the American psyche." Its rhythms, alternating between prolonged quiet and intense activity, were those of a nation still predominantly rural yet clamoring with urban vigor. Perhaps even more important, it was, uncertainty over its origins notwithstanding, indisputably American, and to a nation seeking both identity and distinctiveness it was visible evidence that it need be beholden to no "Foreign Power" for sport, diversion or, presumably, anything else. So it quickly became the "national pastime," and its affairs assumed such importance that Ring was a long way from joking when he described its annual championship as the "World's Serious."

For a game that was "national," it had some distinctly parochial limits. The sixteen teams in the two leagues were east of the Mississippi and north of the Mason-Dixon line, and would remain that way until the removal in 1958 of the Brooklyn Dodgers to Los Angeles and the New York Giants to San Francisco; Boston was its city farthest north and east, and St. Louis was farthest south and west. The national population center was moving inexorably westward—it had reached southern Indiana by 1910—but baseball would not follow it until the cities of the West were large and wealthy enough to support the game.

Baseball was also a white man's game. It tolerated Indians (whom it usually called "Chief," as in Chief Bender and Chief Meyers) and light-skinned Cubans, but black Americans were systematically barred. In 1901 John J. McGraw, the manager of the Baltimore club in the new American League, attempted to sneak a talented black player named Charlie Grant into the league by disguising him as an Indian named "Charlie Tokohama," but Charles A. Comiskey of the White Sox identified the interloper as "the crack Negro second baseman from Cincinnati, fixed up with war paint and a bunch of feathers," and he was quickly exiled. A similar fate awaited William Clarence Matthews five years later; he was a Negro shortstop for Harvard who wanted to play professional ball but was excluded and turned instead to the law, at which he became quite successful. For other blacks with fewer alternatives, it was the emerging Negro leagues, or the barnstorming Negro teams, or nothing. It remained that way until 1947, when Jackie Robinson joined the Brooklyn Dodgers and, it can be argued, initiated the climactic phase of the civil rights revolution.

Despite its geographical and racial restrictions, baseball was growing rapidly and healthily. Seymour, in his definitive *Baseball: The Golden Age*, points out that "external influences—the expanding economy, growing population and urbanization, technological innovation and improvement—provided a generally beneficial climate for professional baseball." It seized the opportunity. A National Commission was organized to govern the game (its members were the presidents of the two major leagues and a chairman chosen by them) and the groundwork for prosperity was laid. A schedule of 154 games was established, and in those cities that had two teams (Boston, Chicago, St. Louis, New York and Philadelphia) schedules were coordinated to avoid direct competition. The wooden ball parks of the late nineteenth century were replaced by steel-and-concrete structures: Sportsman's Park in St. Louis in 1902; Shibe Park in Philadelphia and Forbes Field in Pittsburgh in 1909; League Park in Cleveland and Comiskey Park in Chicago in 1910; Ebbets Field in Brooklyn, the Polo Grounds in New York and Griffith Stadium in Washington in 1911; Fenway Park in Boston, Crosley Field in Cincinnati and Tiger Stadium in Detroit in 1912; Weeghman (now Wrigley) Field in Chicago in 1914; and Braves Field in Boston in 1915. The parks were privately financed and owned, but they were the Colosseums of the New World and the sources of enormous pride for the cities lucky enough to have them. Ring was in Pittsburgh for the opening of Forbes Field, and his uncharacteristically breathless account suggests the excitement and civic hoopla of the occasion:

Before the biggest crowd that ever saw a ball game the world's champion Cubs beat Fred Clarke's Pirates on Pittsburgh's beautiful new field this afternoon, 3 to 2. A throng of 30,338, or ninety-one more than the former record, paid their good money to Messrs. Dreyfuss and Murphy, and there were at least 5,000 more who came in on invitations from the president of the Pittsburgh club. . . .

The women came dressed as if for the greatest society event of the year, and perhaps it was for Pittsburgh's year. Gorgeous gowns, topped by still more gorgeous hats, were in evidence everywhere. Most of the gowns were white and formed a pretty combination with the prevalent green of the stands.

Beyond the outfield fences Schenley park and some of the handsomest buildings of the Carnegie Institute were visible. The stands, themselves constructed almost entirely of Pittsburgh steel and concrete, completely surrounded the field and yet were not big enough to hold the mammoth crowd. . . .

Policemen were scarce, but the throng, disappointed though it was by general appearance and the final outcome of the game, was a peaceable assemblage and was just as polite as it looked. When most of Pittsburgh's inhabitants and excursionists from the surrounding cities and villages had found seats either in boxes or stands or on mother earth, Prof. Nerillos' military band began attracting much attention to itself by parading toward the home bench. There the usual line of athletes was formed and the procession started for the home plate.

At that point the Cubs themselves, officers and magnates of the two big leagues, including President Pulliam and Acting President Heydler of the National League, President Dreyfuss of the Pittsburgh club, and President Ben Shibe of the Philadelphia Athletics, who came over to see whether or not Barney had anything on him in the way of a ballyard, joined the crowd and started for the flag pole. There, without any of the usual accidents, the stars and stripes were hoisted with a pennant bearing the words "Forbes Field" trailing a little below.

When the ceremonies at the flag pole had been completed the procession came back to the playing field and the two teams took their fielding practice amid more noise than ever has been heard in Pittsburgh or the adjacent locality. When the gong rang for the beginning of the game, John Morin, director of public safety, which in English means chief of police, appeared in the middle of the diamond and looked bashfully up at the third deck of the box seats. There was seated Mayor Magee, and he threw the first ball on to the field. Director Morin caught it neatly and journeyed to the pitchers' mound. From the slab the strong arm of the law hurled it almost over the plate and into the waiting hands of Catcher Hackenschmidt Gibson. After that all human obstacles disappeared from view and the battle was on.

The battle was fought with a five-ounce ball, three inches in diameter; it had a rubber core surrounded by three layers of tightly wrapped woolen yarn, all of it covered with a hand-stitched horsehide cover. The ball stayed in play no matter how much punishment it took, with two fairly predictable results: it got pounded out of shape ("I've caught many a ball in the outfield that was mashed flat on one side," one oldtimer has recalled) and base hits were hard to come by. By 1910 it was obvious that action had to be taken. Baseball is a game in which the balance between offense and defense is especially delicate, and it can be thrown off—or deliberately altered—by remarkably slight changes in equipment or the conditions of play. The change the National Commission decided to make was to replace the rubber core with a cork center. It did so in the 1911 season, and the results were precisely what the commission wanted. Here is how Ring described the change in a May, 1911, letter to his fiancée, Ellis Abbott:

> I know you're not interested in baseball, but I am, in one particular phase of it. They are using a new ball this year. It's livelier and that means more hitting, and more hitting means longer games, and that's the devil. It appears to be impossible to finish a game in less than two hours. It's bad enough now, but it's going to drive me crazy when it keeps me away from my own home.

The change was not actually quite as dramatic as Ring, contemplating the prospects of mournful hours away from his future bride, imagined it to be. The overall major-league batting average rose a mere nine points, from .250 to .259, in the 1911 season. The results were far more evident—and far more heinous in Ring's view—when the so-called jackrabbit ball was introduced in the twenties and the age of the home run was ushered in. The change of 1911 was merely a piece of delicate tinkering, and it permitted baseball to enjoy an artistically successful decade.

Batters were helped almost as much by the gloves of the opposition as by the livelier ball. When oldtimers talk about the differences between the game then and now, the one they seem to stress most frequently is the change in gloves. Today's fielders wear huge leather contraptions belted together with thick webbing, gloves so large that in the hands of one as skilled as Brooks Robinson they virtually shut off a whole area of the field to the offense. By contrast, the fielder's glove of the pre–World War I era was a mere slice of leather barely larger than the player's hand. It had no webbing and, for that matter, no pocket. It gave no aid to a bad fielder, and a good one had to strain his resources to get any real use out of it other than self-protection.

Fielders were placed at an additional disadvantage by the playing surfaces, which were rough and unpredictable, and by the uniforms they wore. They were made out of eight-ounce flannel, an oppressively heavy material that gained five or ten pounds of sweat on hot, humid summer days. The players' knickerbockers often flopped around their legs (they usually bought the uniforms too big, to account for shrinkage) and thus further hampered free and easy movement. The large, flapping shirt collars must have provided further distraction, and vision in a bright sun could not have been helped by the tiny brims on their caps.

The players got to show off their raiment—some of which was bright even by the standards of the multicolored uniforms allegedly pioneered by Charles O. Finley in the late nineteen-sixties —in a pregame ritual known as the "tally-ho." Jimmy Austin, a ballplayer of the time, describes it:

> . . . when I first came to the big leagues they didn't have clubhouses in most parks, especially not for the visiting team. We'd get into uniform at the hotel and ride out to the ball park in a bus drawn by four horses. They used to call it a tally-ho in those days. We'd sit on seats along the side and ride, in uniform, to the ball park and back.
>
> That ride was always a lot of fun. Kids running alongside as we went past, and rotten tomatoes once in a while. Always lots of excitement when the ball club rode by, you know, with plenty of yelling back and forth, as you can well imagine.

With the construction of the new ball parks the visiting teams got clubhouses and the tally-ho vanished, a lamentable victim of the age of concrete and steel. Horse-drawn buses, too, were replaced by trolleys and subways, and mass transit made the games more accessible to more people. Canny owners recognized the possibilities such conveniences offered, and took advantage of them. Charles Comiskey of the White Sox, for example, posted a blunt announcement on wooden signs in subway and trolley stations:

BASE
BALL
TODAY

Game time in Chicago was 3 P.M., an hour chosen in the hope that it would be equally congenial for working husbands, whose jobs let them off by then, and their wives, who wanted to have dinner on the table by six. Admission prices, according to Seymour, were "25 cents, 50 cents, 75 cents, and a dollar, depending on whether they were for bleacher, grandstand, pavilion, or box seats." He has calculated the average admission price from 1909 to 1916 at 66 cents. That bargain did not, however, include balls hit into the seats. Spectators were expected to return them, and there were frequent battles between fans trying to sneak out with forbidden souvenirs and stadium police assigned to retrieve them.

The concession stands sold much the same fare available in ball parks today (a new invention, Coca-Cola, was an immediate and particular favorite) and much of it was sold by Harry M. Stevens, whose huge firm still does ball-park business around the country. The big difference between then and now was that until 1917, you could buy hard liquor under the stands; a "partial inventory" of early twentieth-century ball-park equipment assembled by Seymour includes "390 beer mugs, 108 beer flips, 92 whiskey glasses, 40 ginger ale glasses, 17 claret glasses . . . 2 strainers, 7 corkscrews, 6 toddy spoons, 6 lemonade spoons . . . 3 beer vents . . . 2 ice coolers, 2 awnings, 2 mops, 3 brooms, 19 large wooden tubs."

The fans did not need Demon Rum, however, to work themselves into high baseball spirits. Though Ring used a gentle coinage, "pastiming," to describe the game, "war" was often a more fitting description of what took place when the Cubs, then on the West Side, met the South Side's White Sox in a World Series or a City Series. Emotions were so high that the entire city was swept up, as witness this account of Chicago during the great World Series of 1906:

. . . it may be imagined what happened when a city was proudly divided against itself, and that city Chicago. The parks could not hold Chicago, naturally. The streetcars were held back by crowds watching the bulletins. The theaters were packed with audiences who watched newspaper reports; everywhere were crowds watching imaginary base-ball because they could not get in. At the final contest there were 23,627 who managed to get in; the rest stretching away for blocks. Early in the morning they had come and got into line with their lunches in boxes and the pink or green supplements of newspapers,—willing to stand and eat dinner afoot on the mere chance of getting in. Chicago was "base-ball crazy."

The "imaginary base-ball" to which the writer referred took various forms. The most famous probably was the diagram of a diamond mounted prominently in Times Square by the *New York Times*, by which thousands in the pre-radio years followed World Series scores sent in by telegraph and posted on the diamond. In Chicago, the *Tribune* took over Orchestra Hall and advertised a "Big Electric Scoreboard," and when the Cubs went to Philadelphia for two games of the 1910 World Series, fans were advised that "you can see every play and every inning of 'em, clearly and comfortably *right here in Chicago.*" Seats, it warned, were *"going like hot cakes."*

So were seats in the ball parks. Though gate admissions dropped sharply in 1917 and 1918, due primarily to a wartime 130-game schedule, the overall picture in the first two decades of the century is of vigorously increasing attendance: from about 4¾ million in 1903 to over 9 million in 1920, with a few peaks and valleys in between. Comparisons with nineteen-seventies attendance, which has averaged over 30 million a year, must be qualified on several counts: there are half again as many teams now, the schedule has been increased to 162 games, the majority of games are at night, ball-park capacity is vastly larger, and so is the population.

All things considered, the comparisons indicate that baseball before World War I was doing very well at the box office—and it had to do well because there were no radio or television fees to bail out marginal operations. The owners, who in their group photographs look like delegates to a convention of walruses, all decked out in bowlers and Chesterfields, with fat black cigars stuck in their mouths, had to scramble to pick up a profit. Some of their methods were questionable: in the game's earlier years there were instances of interlocking ownerships, or "syndicate ball," but that was barred because it radiated an unpleasant possibility of rigged games. More typically, the "magnates" involved themselves in elaborate player transactions and kept sharp eyes on the ebb and flow of pennies in their treasuries.

Player trades and sales became particularly complicated in 1914 and 1915, when Organized baseball was briefly challenged by the Federal League. Like the American Football League a half-century later, it offered dizzying bonuses and salaries to established players and sent the owners into a panic. One of the ways in which they attempted to fight back was a public relations crusade depicting players who jumped to the new league as money-hungry turncoats deserting loyal fans and teammates. But the campaign backfired in the winter of 1915, when Connie Mack sold off the stars of his great Philadelphia Athletics rather than give in to salary demands that had intensified as a result of Federal League competition. One of the players he sold was Eddie Collins, the second baseman, to the Cubs. Even though the sale strengthened one of his favorite teams, Ring reacted to it with a bitter, and penetrating, verse:

> *Players who jump for the dough.*
> *Bandits and crooks, every one.*
> *Base ball's a pleasure, you know.*
> *Players should play for the fun.*

> *Magnates don't care for the mon.*
> *They can't be tempted with gold.*
> *They're in the game for the fun—*
> *That is why Collins was sold.*

On the whole, however, Ring was sympathetic to the owners and their budgetary difficulties. He liked Charles Comiskey of the White Sox and evidently was amused by the flamboyant owner of the Cubs, Charlie Murphy. He never hesitated to accept an owner's offer of a free drink, and he regularly traded hot-stove-league gossip over glasses of whiskey with Comiskey and his close friend Ban Johnson, president of the American League and the de facto ruler of baseball. Ring's sympathy for these men was such that his first published magazine piece, "The Cost of Baseball," which appeared in March, 1912, was a thorough and authoritative explanation of baseball finances. Beginning with spring training, he provided a detailed chart of where a magnate's money went:

Players' salaries	$65,000
Purchase of players	20,000
Transportation	12,500
Rental of park	15,000
Park salaries	6,500
Hotels	8,000
Office expense (including salaries)	5,500
Repairs	4,500
Spring trip	5,000
Players' supplies (uniforms, balls, etc.)	4,000
Park police	1,800
Insurance	1,500
Taxicabs, carriages, etc.	900
League fund	10,000
Trainer	1,500
Scouts	4,000
Sundries (advertising, printing, etc.)	3,300
TOTAL	$169,000

While Ring acknowledged that, after box-office, concessions and other receipts, the owners netted "an annual profit of from $10,000 to $175,000 per magnate," he closed the piece on a note singularly friendly to the men in the counting houses: "Ponder these things, Mr. Fan, and perhaps you will be more content with your own lot, and less envious of the gentleman who gets that dollar or half dollar of yours on a summer afternoon. Perhaps, too, you will feel a touch of sympathy for him when, on a Saturday in July, dark clouds gather above you. He's not going to the poorhouse. No, but the asylum is not so far away."

Much of that profit, need it be said, was made in the manner customary to sports magnates: exploitation of players. Everything is relative, and it must be borne in mind that a rookie's salary of $1,500 to $2,000 for a half year's work looked pretty good to the average American worker, who was hauling in about $525 a year. But as Seymour points out, ballplayers are "a relatively scarce, highly skilled group," and the players of the early years were not rewarded according to their skills or the money they brought in at the box office. If anything, they were taken to the cleaners.

Seymour lists some of the grievances the short-lived Players' Fraternity attempted to remedy in 1913 and 1914: ". . . violations of draft and waiver rules, arbitrary fines and suspensions, pay cuts for men transferred to different teams, failure to provide copies of contracts and to live up to agreements, relegation of veterans to bush leagues, and so forth."

The players, unfortunately, were ripe for such exploitation. It would be difficult to imagine a less sophisticated group of men gathered together in one profession. As Davy Jones described them to Lawrence Ritter: "We had stupid guys, smart guys, tough guys, mild guys, crazy guys, college men, slickers from the city, and hicks from the country. And back then a country kid was likely to *really* be a country kid." Doubtless the preponderance of hayseeds has been exaggerated (in considerable measure by people who have misread Jack Keefe of *You Know Me Al* as a depiction of the typical ballplayer), but essentially it was a country boys' game played by hillbillies and urban rejects. They simply happened to have a talent for hitting a ball with a bat or throwing a curve, and in many cases it was the only talent they had. A few collegians gave a veneer of social respectability to their ranks, but many players were illiterate, coarse and incredibly naïve. A great deal of heavy drinking went on, much of it no doubt induced by the boredom of life on the road and the eagerness of worshipful fans to ply their heroes with hard liquor. It is no wonder that the game "wasn't a very respectable occupation," as Davy Jones recalled it:

> I figured I'd stay in it just a few years, and then go back to the law once I got on my feet financially. To give you an idea about its respectability, I was going with a girl at the time and after I became a professional ballplayer her parents refused to let her see me any more. Wouldn't let her have anything more to do with me. In those days a lot of people looked upon ballplayers as bums, too lazy to work for a living. So Margaret—that was her name—and I had to break up.

Some of them were hard livers in other respects. Seymour reports that difficulties politely known as "social diseases" were an occasional problem; if the press said a player had "malaria" or "rheumatism," it might well be syphilis or gonorrhea. There is much evidence in Ring's letters and published writings, however, to suggest that many of the players were as innocent as he was in play and love. A lot of them were stage-struck, as Ring was, and in the off-season they tried to score in vaudeville as hoofers, comics, actors and singers. Singing, in fact, seems to have been as popular with traveling ballplayers as poker playing. Almost every club had at least one barbershop quartet, and the passion of some players for harmonizing was extraordinary. In one of his early short stories, "Harmony," Ring wrote a gentle spoof about a player who sacrifices his first-string position in order to get a talented singer onto the club.

During the first three and a half seasons he was on the road with baseball teams, Ring conducted a courtship by correspondence as noteworthy for its innocence as for its ardor, and so did many of the "hard-boiled" ballplayers. Much of their time was spent hanging around hotel lobbies waiting for mail call and the arrival—so they devoutly prayed—of their loved ones' latest missives. Some of the game's more celebrated players were thus afflicted, as Ring told Ellis:

Speaking of letters, I have a new job. I don't know what to call it. It consists of standing perfectly still and listening while one or the other of two ball players reads me his latest letter from his girls—from one of his girls, rather. It seems these two—who are Mordecai Brown and Frank Schulte—must confide in some one. The only reason I know of that I am the victim is that they can trust me to keep still. We all came into the hotel together tonight and there was mail for everybody. I took my letter from you and started for my room when Mr. Brown stopped me. He said he wanted to talk to me awhile and I told him I had a letter to read. He said: "You read yours and I'll read mine and then we'll swap." I didn't want to make it look like a one-sided deal, so I told him mine was from my sister and wouldn't interest him. So I had to read his and, as soon as I was through, Schulte gave me a sign that he wanted to see me and there was another one to read. And all the time they were detaining me, I wanted to get away and read your letter again.

Those players who had successfully completed their courtship had other preoccupations:

You ought to hear the athletes discuss the relative merits of their babies. There was an argument in my room last night that was the funniest I ever heard. Mr. Hofman's Mary Jane has two teeth and two others just breaking through. She weighs twenty-five pounds. Mr. Reulbach's Edward has four whole teeth and weighs twenty-six. But Mary Jane can pound her fist on the arms of a chair and laugh at the noise. Yes, but Edward is a boy. Whereupon I told them that my four months old nephew—there isn't any such—could dive from a tower ninety feet high into a dishpan full of salt water without making a splash. I wanted to get them out of the room so I could go to sleep. One of them left a five o'clock call for my room by way of revenge. Whenever they start their debates in Schulte's presence, he quits them by saying. "Wait till you hear what my dog can do."

These Chicago Cubs, worrying over mail call and Mary Jane's teeth, were authentic American heroes—although not heroes of the first stripe. That distinction belonged to the early giants of the game, men whose names are now enshrined in American legend. These were the men Ring watched from the press box, chatted with in the clubhouse, drank with in saloons. There were the great managers: Connie Mack, *né* Cornelius McGillicuddy, of the Athletics; Clark Griffith of the Senators; John McGraw of the Giants. There were the pitchers: Christy Mathewson, Walter Johnson, Cy Young, Grover Cleveland Alexander, Mordecai (Three-Finger) Brown, Rube Marquard, and Big Ed Walsh of the White Sox, whom Ring called "the most willing, tireless and self-confident hurler that ever struck terror to the hearts of his opponents." There were the hitters: Ty Cobb, Honus Wagner, Napoleon Lajoie, Frank (Home Run) Baker, Tris Speaker, Eddie Collins, Wahoo Sam Crawford. There were the clowns and eccentrics: Rube Waddell, Germany Schaefer, Ping Bodie, Artie Hofman. There was a great umpire: Bill Klem, who bore an astonishing resemblance to a catfish and went into a blind rage if a player should suggest as much. And there were three men whose names became inextricably bound together:

> *These are the saddest of possible words—*
> *Tinker to Evers to Chance.*
> *Trio of Bear Cubs and fleeter than birds—*
> *Tinker to Evers to Chance.*
> *Thoughtlessly pricking our gonfalon bubble,*
> *Making a Giant hit into a double,*
> *Words that are weighty with nothing but trouble—*
> *Tinker to Evers to Chance.*

That is the way Franklin P. Adams, columnist and versifier of the New York *World*, described the Cubs' 1906–09 double-play combination of Joe Tinker, Johnny Evers and Frank Chance. The Cubs of that era were one of baseball's first "dynasties" (a term that seems to embrace any team that wins two or three championships in a row), and Adams' little rhyme gave both the team and the three players a permanent place in baseball legend. It was a place earned less by their overall abilities than by the rhythmical sound made by reciting their names. Tinker, the shortstop, had a lifetime batting average of .262 and Evers, the second baseman, batted .270—figures not significantly above the overall average for the period. Ballplayers and journalists who saw them remember them as able but not exceptional. Chance, on the other hand, was a genuine Hall of Famer, with a lifetime average of .296 and an impressive record as player-manager. He was a handsome, intelligent man who evidently had the respect and affection of players, fans and journalists. There was no irony in his nickname, "The Peerless Leader."

These men were heroes, but they were not distant from the ordinary people who elevated them to that exalted station. The nation was still small enough and the game informal enough so that players and fans could fraternize easily. Rube Marquard, as a youth, had been aided in a hard moment by some Chicago firemen, and as a star for the Giants he never forgot them: "And boy, for years after that, whenever the Giants would come to Chicago I'd go out to that firehouse. I'd sit out front and talk for hours. The firemen would have all the kids in the neighborhood there . . . and all the families that lived around would stop by . . . and it was really wonderful. Everybody was so nice and friendly. Gee, I used to enjoy that. It was a great thrill for me." Davy Jones, with his baseball earnings, helped put his brother through pharmaceutical school; the two then went into partnership, opening a drugstore in downtown Detroit: "Well, the thing was a huge success. After a home game I'd join him at the drugstore and jerk sodas and talk about the game. The fans loved it. Business was so terrific that after a while we had *five* stores. I got so I was spending all my free time in the stores, and when we went on the road I took pharmacy textbooks along to study."

Since that time so many sports have come to compete for fans'

attention, and their loyalties are so confused by the tangled overlapping of sports "seasons," that it is difficult to re-create a time
when there was really only one sport and people followed it with
single-minded devotion. Yet that is the kind of grip baseball had,
and the fans submitted to it happily. In the lingo of the day they
were "bugs." Almost all of them were men and boys; photographs
of ball-park crowds reveal scarcely a female. Those photos do, on
the other hand, reveal hats and caps; no one seems to have attended baseball games bareheaded, and most wore suits and ties.
They collected pictures of their heroes, as James T. Farrell recalls:
"In those days, pictures of baseball players, both major- and
minor-league players, came with certain brand packages of cig-
arettes—Piedmonts, Sweet Caporals, and Sovereigns." Most of all,
they fancied themselves experts on the game and they loved to
try to impress each other with their knowledge. Ring, who had
been a "bug" as a youth but had been promoted by virtue of
professional circumstances to "scribe," looked on them with a
mixture of amusement and irritation:

> The man who is on intimate terms with the ball players, who
> calls at their hotel and takes them out in his machine, goes to the
> station with them to see them off, gets letters from them occasion-
> ally, and knows they are just real people, isn't the real "fan" or
> "bug," even if he does have to pay to get into the park.
> The real article is the man who knows most of the players by
> sight, as they appear on the field, but wouldn't know more than
> one or two of them if he saw them on the street, struggles hard to
> keep an accurate score and makes a mistake on every other play,
> or doesn't attempt to score at all, disputes every statement made by
> his neighbors in the bleachers whether he knows anything about
> said statement or not, heaps imprecations on the umpire and the
> manager, thinks something is a bonehead play when it really is
> good, clever baseball, talks fluently about Mathewson's "inshoot,"
> believes that Hank O'Day has it in for the home team and is pur-
> posely making bad decisions, and says "Bransfield is going to bat for
> Moore" when Walsh is sent in to hit for Chalmers.
> He doesn't know it all, but he's happy. He is perfectly satisfied
> when the folks around him believe what he says, and sometimes he
> almost gets to believing it himself. He's having a thoroughly enjoy-
> able afternoon, if his team wins. If it doesn't, he knows just why

and can tell his wife, his brother or his pal, that evening, how the tables could have been turned if only Manager Tenney had used a little judgment.

What the fans most longingly yearned for was what they called "the dope," or "inside baseball," and they looked to the gentlemen of the sporting press to provide it. They were glad to do so—or to attempt to, for in truth many of them were scarcely more knowledgeable than the fans they pretended to educate. Ring was an exception to the rule, being a sports writer who was respected by the players for understanding the intricacies of the game and being able to describe them clearly in his stories. Like virtually all sports writers then and since, Ring got into the business because he was a fan, but by and large he was able from the start to keep in check any hero-worship he might have felt—and eventually he would abandon it almost entirely.

Not so the majority of his colleagues. They were "gee whiz" reporters of the sports scene, and no "aw nuts" school had yet been founded to provide an antidote to their cheerleading. Most of them never ceased to revel in the thrills their jobs provided (thrills summarized by Ring as "brushing majestically past the pass-gate man, strutting along the rear aisle of the stand in the hope that some one will know you are a baseball writer, speaking to a player or two and getting answered, finding your own particular seat in the press box and proceeding to enlighten the absent public regarding the important events on the field, in your own, bright, breezy style") and they were willing to pay the price necessary to keep the thrills coming. That price was: to be an advocate rather than a critic, to tell the good news about the club they covered and to suppress the bad, to humor loutish, hypersensitive players, and to stay out of the manager's way.

There were other reasons why it behooved the "scribes" to toe the line. Many of the teams, Ring wrote in "The Cost of Baseball," " 'pay the freight' for newspaper correspondents." That suited the newspapers for which they worked just fine, as it enabled them to give their readers baseball coverage without having to pay anything for it except telegraph charges and their reporters' insubstantial salaries. A reporter who didn't write what a club liked could get dropped from its retinue—so he faced pressure from his employer as well as the club to write the company line. As if those pressures weren't enough, there was always the fear of physical violence at the hands of an inebriated or pathological (or both) ballplayer offended by a story criticizing his play.

If there was a bit of whorishness in the relationship of these gentlemen to the people they covered, there was a great deal of bad prose in the stories they wrote about them. Sports writing was, like baseball, a relatively new pursuit, and it was still finding its way—for the most part in the wrong directions. To begin with, sports editors felt an obligation to give their readers batter-by-batter, sometimes pitch-by-pitch accounts of the local teams' games, with the result that the stories were interminable and doggedly chronological. That, however, created an obvious problem: the stories tended to be deathly dull. Since circulation wars were virulent—and in Chicago especially so—editors were under pressure to produce sprightly pages, and they in turn pressured their writers to produce sprightly copy. The results suggest that "sprightly" was a synonym for "florid." Until Ring and the generation of sports writers who followed and imitated him changed it, the rule on the sports pages was: Never use one word when two or three will do, and never use a simple word when a sesquipedalian euphemism is handy. So this is what happened: pitchers became "hurlers," outfielders were "gardeners," hits were "stings" and "wallops," bases were "sacks," runners were "nailed at the plate," pennants were "gonfalons." At times the sports pages seemed to be a bad dream by Sir Walter Scott.

To imply that Ring came to the Chicago *Inter-Ocean* in the fall of 1907 and changed all that overnight would be utterly inaccurate. Not only did he come as a fan, but in certain respects he always remained one; in letters to Ellis, for example, he often referred to whichever team he was covering, the Cubs or the White Sox, as "we." He was perfectly capable of slinging sports-page clichés with the worst of them, and the examples quoted in the paragraph above are all from his own stories. His maturation into a reasonably objective, skeptical reporter and commentator took place over several years and was not completed until he had left the regular baseball beat and the pressures attendant thereto.

Ring's own description of his initiation into the fraternity of major-league baseball is testimony enough to the gee-whiz attitude he brought to his first assignment. He had switched from the *Inter-Ocean* to the Chicago *Examiner* in February of 1908, and shortly after his arrival was called to the office of "my sporting editor, Harry Shroudenback." They talked for a while, then:

> He went on to tell me that I was to join the White Sox in the South, travel with them through the rest of their spring tour and, if I made good, Stick With Them All Season! O diary!
>
> Never since' that night have I criticized anyone for fickleness! Happy beyond words, I jumped from the National to the American League, and the Cubs, whom I had idolized all my life, became nonexistent so far as I was concerned. Ed Walsh, formerly an object of hatred, was now my hero and soon to be my friend. Mordecai Brown and Ed Reulbach—theretofore objects of my worship—were suddenly as unimportant as going to bed.
>
> As a matter of fact, I was not being highly honored. The Cubs looked like a cinch to repeat. They deserved an experienced and able historian, and Hughey Fullerton was all of that. The Sox were old and faded out at the heels. If anything happened to Walsh, they would be lucky to finish in organized baseball. In any case, so the *Examiner*, and most Chicagoans, thought, they had all the earmarks of a Class B outfit, and I was a Class B scribe. But what did I care? At least I was through with trying to write hot heads on West Side Y.M.C.A. basket-ball games.
>
> "Will my stuff be signed?" I asked timidly.
>
> "Sure," said Shroudy. "You are James Clarkson now, and don't disgrace that grand old name."
>
> James Clarkson, if you must know, was the *Examiner*'s perennial expert. Hughey Fullerton and Charley Dryden might come and go, but James stayed on forever. I don't know who originated him; I only know his job was safe and that the fans swore by him. And why not? He had been writing baseball day after day, year after year, and how were the fans to guess that he never was the same person two years in succession?

Ring, then, was to begin his career as a correspondent as the author of sports-page prose so faceless and predictable that it could run under a convenience by-line and no one would know the difference. Did that matter to him? If it did, not much. He hopped a train and headed for New Orleans. When he got there he went to the St. Charles Hotel, ran into George Rice of the Chicago *Daily*

News, and got his introduction to the code under which he would be working. Rice introduced him to the manager ("Mr. Jones, christened Fielder by prophetic parents") and this conversation took place:

JONES: I suppose you're just another pest. You'll probably ask a lot of childish questions.

RING: Undoubtedly.

JONES: Well, go ahead and shoot, and let's get it over. But first, where do you come from? I mean where were you born?

RING: Niles, Michigan.

JONES: Have you been working in Chicago long?

RING: Three months and a half.

JONES: How old are you?

RING: Twenty-three. White. Grandparents on both sides lived to be seventy.

JONES: You're fresh, too, aren't you? What I'm trying to get at is, what qualifies you to write about baseball? You couldn't learn it in Niles. I've been through the place. There aren't enough men to make up a ball club.

RING: We were shy one, so we used a woman in center field.

JONES: Niles wit! But I'm serious. Why do metropolitan newspapers hire inexperienced kids like you to report big-league baseball?

RING: I think it's my turn to ask a childish question. Were you a manager the first year you broke into the big league?

JONES: All right, Niles. We'll get along if you don't pester me too much. The boys that drive me crazy are the ones who want to know who's going to pitch tomorrow. If I can't tell them and they guess wrong, they're sore.

RING: I promise never to bother you with a question like that. My paper will be satisfied if I guess right three-quarters of the time. So I'll just stick to Walsh.

And so began a crucial period in Ring's life: he was going on the road. He would stay there for five years, and for the last two or three of them he would be sick of it. But for a long time he delighted in the baseball life he was allowed to enter, the trains that rattled him across the American landscape, the cities he visited and the vistas he saw. A charming and ingenious poem he sent to his family, Ellis Abbott and Wilma Johnson (a Niles girl with whom he was conducting a chatty, nonromantic correspondence) reflects excitement and high spirits. He called it "The Route of Ringlets," noting that it was "Published as a Guide for his genial Correspondents (With Carbon Copies)":

> *On March 18, young Lardner'll go*
> *Down to the city of N.O.*
> *New Orleans is the city's name,*
> *A city not unknown to fame.*
> *From March 19 to March 22,*
> *He'll tarry in New Orleans, Lou.*
> *And then, on March the 23,*
> *He'll sojourn in Montgomery.*
> *From this cute town in Alabam*
> *He'll travel up to Birmingham*
> *And there remain the 24th*
> *Before proceeding farther north*
> *To Nashville up in Tennessee,*
> *And there the next three days he'll be.*
> *On 28 and 29,*
> *In burg of Evansville so fine,*
> *On 30th and 31st*
> *In Terre Haute, of towns the worst.*
> *And on fair April's first two days,*
> *In Indianapolis he stays;*
> *In Cincinnati 4 and 5,*
> *And then, my goodness sakes alive,*
> *To old South Bend he'll go once more,*
> *Renew acquaintance made of yore,*
> *The sixth day of the month he'll spend*
> *Among the ruins of old South Bend.*
> *The next three days in cute Champaign,*
> *Eleventh, twelfth in cute Fort Wayne,*
> *And then back to Chicago go,*
> *To stay about ten days or so.*
> *And through this era, do not fail*
> *As follows to address his mail:*
> *"For Mr. Lardner, in the care*
> *Of the White Sox," and b'lieve me, fair*
> *Young correspondents, large and small,*
> *I'm glad to hear from one and all.*

As Ring traveled this prolonged baseball journey, two crucial developments took place in his professional life. In Pullman smoking cars, hotel lobbies and stadium clubhouses, he listened to the talk of baseball people; occasionally he contributed to it, for despite his silences he was gregarious, but mostly he listened, unconsciously storing it in his memory as the basic resource for the fiction that would come in later years. When he was not talking with baseball people he was watching them at play, and the judgments he reached about the nature of excellence and the search for it would profoundly affect his outlook upon the larger world.

Traveling by rail was fun for the most part, but it had its distinct drawbacks. The advent of air conditioning was a long way off, and a June train ride from Philadelphia to St. Louis, like so many other such jaunts, was "hot, dusty and tedious, and Ohio factories and Indiana corn fields failed to provide a diversion." Ring was nearly six feet, two inches—this at a time when six feet was still considered tall—and he and a Pullman berth had a basic problem:

> When I was twenty-two [*sic*] I began touring the South and the big-league circuits with the White Sox and Cubs. For six years I stuck with one club or the other and, I guess, spent about ninety nights per annum in lower berths. Now a person who is five-feet-ten may be able to get comfortable in a Pullman, but a person who is an inch over that figure must learn to take tucks in himself. As for gents of my royal highness, they can either try to rest on their backs with their feet against the floor of the upper or share the washroom with George and the shoes.

Once he got to a town, Ring headed straight for the hotel to see if any mail from Ellis awaited him, and if he was in luck (as usually he seems to have been) he was exuberant: "It was great to find two letters—one a long one—waiting for me this morning. The one you started Tuesday and finished Wednesday was the most comforting and the dearest letter I ever saw. . . ." There was a scramble to rent a typewriter, portables not having been invented. And then he could lapse into the routine of a baseball day. If he was on a spring-training trip, most of it would be spent at the park —watching practice or the day's exhibition, keeping an eye on the rookies, swapping gossip and "dope."

Ring's second spring-training trip, in 1909, was made with the Cubs, and it had a great influence on him. His own position was far more secure, for one thing: he was a by-lined reporter for the

Chicago *Tribune,* and he was covering the world champions, one of baseball's greatest teams. Though he had become thoroughly entranced with the White Sox the previous year—they confounded the pre-season skeptics and stayed in the pennant race until the last two days of the season—he nonetheless was fulfilling his dream of traveling with the team he had worshiped since boyhood. What was most important about that spring, however, is that he acquired the material for his first systematic writing about ball-players, and he made the friendship of Frank Schulte.

Schulte was two and a half years older than Ring, a native of western New York State who loved horses and picked up the nick-name "Wildfire" because he raced a horse of that name in the off-season. The nickname was also suited to his play, which was energetic and productive; in his best season, 1911, he led the National League in home runs (with 21, a record at the time), runs batted in (107) and slugging percentage (.534). With Jimmy Sheckard and Artie Hofman he formed what Ring nearly two decades later called "the best outfield I ever looked at." What mattered most to Ring about Schulte, however, was that they had in common a mixture of reserve and gregariousness, a taste for doggerel, and a sense of the ridiculous. Schulte was not well edu-cated (though neither, in the formal sense, was Ring), but he had a lively mind and a quick wit, and Ring liked him enormously. By the spring of 1910 Ring was slipping little verses into his news stories and attributing them to Schulte. Probably 90 percent of what Ring credited to Schulte, perhaps more, he had actually writ-ten himself, but there can be no doubt that Schulte's humor sharpened his own.

Readers outside Chicago first encountered both Ring and Schulte in December, 1910. Ring had taken the editorship of the *Sporting News,* "The Bible of Baseball," and had begun a column called "Pullman Pastimes." The column, and Ring's career as an editor, lasted only until mid-February, 1911, but in the ten pieces he wrote Ring gave a preview of what was to come in his later baseball pieces. The columns have little of the amiable skepticism that would mark Ring's "In the Wake of the News" columns a few years later; they are merely amiable, providing a bit of chit-chat for baseball fans. They do, on the other hand, provide an acquaintance with Schulte and the rest of the Cubs, and in all likelihood the mere writing of them helped give Ring the confidence that he could do more than write straight baseball reports —for his journalism took sharp turns in new directions after he left the *Sporting News.*

Ring introduced Schulte to readers of the *Sporting News* right away. In his first piece, after describing the amusingly hyperbolic chatter engaged in by several of the Cubs, he offered an alternative entertainment: "Or you can share Frank Schulte's seat and listen to stories you have heard before but which you must laugh at because he is telling them. Frank takes delight in repeating his stories when he knows he is repeating them. He also has plenty to say that is amusing regarding his teammates' failings, and he isn't afraid to talk when said teammates are listening." Schulte enjoyed baseball but did not think the world hung on the outcome of the games he played: "He likes to win all right, but he doesn't see why defeats should be the cause of tears or post-mortems." He obviously had better things to do:

> . . . In his seat all alone or with a willing listener sits Mr. Schulte:
> "The boys seem to forget there'll be a game tomorrow to play. They act as if this was the last one they ever were going to get into. The pennant is lost now, and there isn't a chance for us to cop that World's Series money. Let's hope the White Sox don't finish first. A city series with them will net the boys enough money to worry through the winter on. They didn't trip us today because they played better ball. Oh, no. There never was a day when any team played better ball than these ten-time champion Cublets. Rigler called everything wrong and the luck was dead against us from the start.
> "You saw Jack Murray hit that one out of the ball yard? Well, that's no credit to Murray. He had his eyes shut or was talking to some one back in the grandstand when he let that one loose. He didn't meet the ball square. Oh, no. The ball hit his little finger nail and bounded off it over the fence. Besides, Edward (that's Reulbach) intended to get him to bite on his fall-away. No, Edward didn't want to get the ball over the plate. No, Edward was blinded by the dust and he pitched within Murray's reach when he really thought he was throwing to catch Doyle off second.
> "Yes, and Schulte played that ball wrong, too. He ought to have left the park and stood on the approach to the elevated station. Then, you know there was a high wind blowing. Otherwise, that

would have been a foul fly that Archer could have eaten up. But the pennant's gone now and we might as well arrange a barnstorming tour of some kind."

Then, if feeling particularly good, Mr. Schulte breaks into song, so softly that he can't be heard more than two seats away:

"Kidney stew and fried pig's feet—

"That's the grub I loves to eat.

"I guess there's no use of our going to Boston at all. The way luck's breaking against us and with all the umpires in the league ordered to give us the worst of it, we haven't a chance to take a game even from the Doves. . . .

"Never mind, boys, There'll be another ball game tomorrow and Schulte will play right field and bat third. Three cheers for the national pastime!"

This is followed by a few moments of staring out of the window into the dark night. Then, if he is in one of his rare poetic moods:

"This base ball season soon will end,
  Or else I am a liar;
  Then I'll go back to Syracuse
  And drive my old Wildfire.
  Against the fastest horses there
  My old Wildfire will go,
  And show his heels to all of them
  Upon the pure white snow.
  How glad I am the time is nigh
  When reins and whip I'll wield;
  'Tis easier to drive a horse
  Than run around right field."

Schulte's irreverence was perfectly suited to Ring's, and doubtless there are contributions from both men in that conversation, recalled as it was a year after the fact. Though Ring did not know it then, Schulte's skepticism was reinforcing his own, and the alibi-dropping ballplayers whom Schulte satirized would emerge three years later as Jake Keefe, and five years later with the name Ring gave to the American language, "Alibi Ike."

In the other "Pullman Pastime" columns Ring gave a full, if uncritical, portrait of the travel activities of the Cubs. Chief among them was "the indoor national pastime," the poker game, or "the P.G.," as Ring often referred to it. It was "a stiff proposition," with limits varying from a quarter to a dollar, the limit being lowered by order of Manager Chance whenever poker-table tensions threatened to disrupt team tranquillity. Occasionally an outsider would slip into an empty seat, with dire results; the players' tolerant attitude toward their fans did not extend to such intrusions, with the result that any such uninvited visitor was "likely to get a trimming" in the pocketbook.

Another way of passing the time was in conversation, and "generally they find diversion in argument and the arguments are all the more interesting in that the points brought out don't have to be even distant cousins to the truth." The players took country people's delight in hyperbole; the point of their arguments was to see who could come up with the most outrageous topper. One dispute involved the nature and location of the Gulf Stream, and even allowing for the intervention of Ring's imagination, it captures the zany flavor of the dialogue:

REULBACH: What makes you think they were Gulf Stream fish?

PFIESTER: Well, for one thing, it was horribly hot. Lundy put his finger in the water and scalded it. And then every fish we caught had a big "G.S." branded on his left side.

STEINFELDT: How did it come we didn't see the fish?

PFIESTER: We sold them for 800 bucks as soon as we got back to New York.

STEINFELDT: Didn't you say it was on Sunday?

PFIESTER: It was Sunday when we started, but we didn't get back till Monday morning. Chance fined us each 100 bucks for staying out all night. So we made only $300 apiece on the deal.

STEINFELDT: Didn't you have to pay the skipper anything?

PFIESTER: Not a cent, but we had to give him a dozen fish. He couldn't catch 'em himself.

REULBACH: Why not?

PFIESTER: 'Cause he was a Swiss and Gulf Stream fish won't bite when they know a Swiss is after them.

STEINFELDT: How do they know when a Swiss is fishing?

PFIESTER: He always uses cheese for bait.

REULBACH: Well, Jack, that proves pretty conclusively that the Gulf Stream is only 18 miles off New York. But it must turn due East there, for it runs right along the coast of Scotland.

STEINFELDT: What makes you think that?

REULBACH: Well, my paternal grandfather was a native Scotchman—

PFIESTER: Yes, Reulbach's a Scotch name, all right.

REULBACH: —and he owned a big estate right on the coast. He used to entertain all his Edinburgh friends there and of course, they used to play games to pass away the time. They had a game called "Knock-the-Ball," and they played it over a course of nine holes. But the course was so close to the ocean that most of the time they drove the ball into the water. I forgot to tell you they used eggs for balls. Anyhow, when they finally recovered the eggs, they were hard-boiled. So they figured they were boiled in the Gulf Stream. On this account, they began to call the game "Gulf" and finally they changed it to "Golf."

TINKER (*from the other end of the car*): Room for one more.

STEINFELDT: That's me. (*Exit.*)

PFIESTER: What did we start to argue about?

REULBACH: I've forgotten. It was something about the heat in Boston and New York.

PFIESTER: Well, you win anyway, with that Golf finish.

It is a short step indeed from that dialogue, whether invented in whole or in part, to the "nonsense plays" of the twenties that gave Ring a reputation among literati (though he scarcely had invited it) as a devotee of Dada and the Theater of the Absurd.

Exaggeration, in one form or another, was everywhere. Players exaggerated the prowess of their babies, they told tall tales, and their practical jokes had a distinctly overblown flair. Jimmy Sheckard, the champion Cub in that regard, once went from berth to berth, awaking each player to ask, "Do you know where Hofman's berth is?"—although, as Ring noted, he "must have known something about the distribution of berths," since he managed not to arouse Chance. Finally he found Hofman, got him out of bed, and murmured an apology:

"I'm sorry I couldn't find you sooner. . . . I just remembered you wanted me to show you my coal warehouse."

"What coal warehouse? I never heard of one," Mr. Hofman said.

"Why the warehouse where I store the coal from my mines. I knew you'd want to see it, but I'm afraid it's too late now, for we've passed it. I was looking out the window about 15 minutes ago, and I couldn't see it, but I could point right at it, for I know just where it is. It's 18 miles North, on this side of the car, and about 10 miles back. I'm sorry I woke you up for nothing, but I knew you'd never forgive me if I didn't let you know about it."

A sweet disposition and weakness resulting from loss of sleep prevented Mr. Hofman from starting a fight. Instead, he just murmured: "All right, you win," and crawled back to bed. This seemed to satisfy Mr. Sheckard, for he refrained from disturbing the peace again that night.

They were in many respects really just big overgrown boys, and Ring loved the ones who were natural, without pretense, hard players on the field and genial companions off it. Utterly without pretensions himself, he naturally gravitated to those players who shared his unaffected ease. The longer he covered baseball regularly, the more he concentrated on the game itself, and the more he tended to focus his attention—and his admiration—on those men who played it as he believed it should be played.

In that regard, it is important to emphasize that although the form of the game and its rules have changed remarkably little over the years, baseball before the introduction in 1920 of what Ring called "Br'er Rabbit Ball" was markedly different in style and execution. A couple of statistics make the point plainly enough: In 1911, home runs were hit at an average of .41 per game for *both* teams; a half-century later, in 1961, the figure was 1.90, an increase of more than four and a half times. By the same token, in 1911 triples were hit at a rate of 1.07 per game; in 1961 the figure was .53, a decrease of almost exactly one half.

The home run is the hallmark of the power game, the triple of the speed game. The home run symbolizes a game dominated by brute force, one in which victory can be won by the proverbial "single swing of the bat." The triple, by contrast, is emblematic of a game in which more complex skills dominate: the skill of the batter in placing hits and his speed in covering the bases, as well as the skill of the fielder in holding the runner to as few bases as possible. Objective students of baseball would say that both the power game and the speed game have their merits, and that the balance between the two that has evolved since 1961—the biggest home-run year in baseball history, and one of the least interesting seasons artistically—has produced a "better" game than ever before. But Ring in this respect was no objective student at all. He had been brought up on "dead-ball" baseball, and he simply would not accept any other kind as a legitimate form of the game.

By the same token, the standards of excellence he came to believe in were shaped by the dead-ball game, and they remained his standards despite the ways in which baseball changed.

Though it would be three more years before he would express his understanding of baseball excellence with absolute clarity, Ring gave a strong indication of the direction in which he was moving in a piece written for the Chicago *Examiner* in August, 1912. He was discussing the White Sox, who were having an indifferent year, and he went to some lengths to single out a player who had gotten little attention:

> Morris Rath, Jimmy Callahan's second baseman, appears to be doomed to go through his baseball career without recognition as a star, and this despite the fact that he is one of the steadiest ball players in the American League.
>
> Rath is referred to by his mates as the brains of the White Sox infield. This title was given him by Matty McIntyre in a spirit of kidding, and yet it is anything but undeserved. Morris is probably no smarter than either of the Sox third basemen, Lord and Zeider, and he is usually so quiet that his headwork goes unnoticed. He seldom is guilty of a foolish play, and his "noodle" is so well thought of by the manager that he is often entrusted with the job of signing for waste pitches, and throws with runners on.
>
> In the International League last season Rath hit well over .300. In fact, his figure was closer to .400. His extra base clouts were few and far between and his record of stolen bases was nothing to boast of. At present, he is a few points below .300, but he has the happy habit of reaching first base oftener than any one else on the team. He is a hard man to pitch to, a man who seldom swings at bad balls.
>
> Rath is shy of bodily strength and ability to steal his way around the paths. Otherwise, he is a mighty good ball player and a man who can be depended on to hold up his end, offensively and defensively.

Everything Ring most admired, and not just in ballplayers, is suggested there. It happens that Rath turned out to be not the ballplayer Ring thought him to be—he played only three more seasons, and those with mixed results—but he helped Ring locate the essence of what he admired. That was: reliability, hard work, "brains," self-improvement, fulfillment of one's abilities whatever their limits, selflessness. Three years later Ring elaborated on the point in four baseball articles he wrote for *American*

Magazine. In effect, he used the four articles to identify his own baseball heroes and to explain why they were heroic. The pieces are written in a strained effort at idiomatic language that is now difficult to read without wincing, but it is worth the effort to gain an understanding of what Ring was saying.

The first piece was a tribute to the Boston Braves of 1914, the "Miracle Braves" who had been led by their manager, George Stallings, from last place in late July to the National League championship and then a shocking World Series victory over the redoubtable Philadelphia Athletics. Ring had sentimental reasons for admiring the Braves—he had covered them for the Boston *American* in 1911 (the year he and Ellis married), when they were hopeless losers known as the Rustlers—but there was no sentimentalism in his assessment of their success. They won, he made clear, because Stallings had goaded them to play at or above their best, and the players were willing to make the effort: "I say the Braves won by hustlin' and fightin' rather than because they was a aggregation o' world-beaters. . . . A club that cops in spite of a few weaknesses has did more than a club that cops because they's no other club in their class. . . . The kind o' men that can do their best in a pinch is the kind that's most valuable in baseball or anywhere else. They're worth more than the guys that's got all the ability in the world but can't find it when they want it." Ring, who knew better than anyone else that his own talents were limited, held in the highest respect those people "that can do their best."

The second article was called "Some Team" and was Ring's "line o' dope," his personal all-star team. Its members were: Nap Rucker of Brooklyn and Willie Mitchell of Cleveland, left-handed pitchers; Walter Johnson of Washington, Grover Cleveland Alexander of the Philadelphia Phillies, Christy Mathewson of the New York Giants and Eddie Cicotte of the White Sox, right-handed pitchers; Jimmy Archer of the Cubs and Ray Schalk of the White Sox, catchers; Jake Daubert of Brooklyn, first base; Eddie Collins of the Philadelphia Athletics, second base; Rabbit Maranville of the Boston Braves, shortstop; Frank Baker of the Athletics, third base; Ty Cobb of Detroit, Tris Speaker of the Boston Red Sox and Joe Jackson of the White Sox, outfielders. As Ring acknowledged, a few of the selections were surprising, notably that of Nap Rucker, but his reasons for choosing Rucker were revealing: ". . . I'm choosin' him because he ain't no flash in the pan, as they say. He's been pitchin' long enough to show that he ain't no accident, and he ain't nowheres near through. . . . Rucker knows what he's out there for. He ain't like a lot o' these pitchers that leaves their brains on the bench." To the reliability for which he had cited Morris Rath, Ring added a further refinement: durability. As for Eddie Cicotte, Ring wrote: "They ain't a smarter pitcher in baseball and they's nobody that's a better all-round ball player, no pitcher, I mean." Still another requirement, then, was added: versatility, the ability to contribute to one's team in more than one way.*

The last two pieces were about Ty Cobb and Christy Mathewson, the individual players Ring most admired. That these were the two he chose was vivid testimony to his refusal to let a player's personality color his evaluation of his performance. Cobb probably was the most hated man ever to play major-league baseball. He was a racist, a bully and a psychopath. He drew no distinction between teammates and opponents; he fought them all, and all of them detested him. Mathewson, on the other hand, was such an upright, kind and selfless individual that some skeptics wondered if he was for real. He was a graduate of Bucknell, he looked like a combination of Dink Stover and Frank Merriwell, and according to Hugh Fullerton, he "specializes in chess and when on the circuit spends his evenings at chess clubs playing the local champions."

All of which made absolutely no difference to Ring. He did make a half-hearted effort to portray Cobb as a decent fellow, but what really mattered to him was Cobb the ballplayer. When Cobb came into the league in 1905, Ring wrote, "he runs bases like a fool," and "he couldn't hit a lefthander very good." Despite these lapses he was a fine, indeed an extraordinary, player, but that wasn't good enough for him:

> That was when he first come up here. But Ty ain't the guy that's goin' to stay fooled all the time. When he wises up that somebody's got somethin' on him, he don't sleep nor do nothin' till he figures out a way to get even. . . . He seen he couldn't hit the curve when

---

* There is a sad footnote to "Some Team." One of the men Ring considered but did not select was Ray Chapman, the young shortstop for the Indians. "Chapman at Cleveland's goin' to be good," Ring wrote, "if he don't have no more accidents." Five years later Chapman was killed by a beanball.

it was breakin', so he stood way back in the box and waited till it'd broke. Then he nailed it. . . .

Cobb was widely accused by jealous fellow players of being "lucky" (as if he had any control over that), but Ring felt that "he makes his own luck" by heady play. Cobb could do his best in a pinch, and so could Mathewson: "They's a flock o' pitchers that knows a batter's weakness and works accordin'. But they ain't nobody else in the world that can stick a ball as near where they want to stick it as he can. . . . I s'pose when he broke in he didn't have no more control than the rest o' these here collegers. But the diff'rence between they and him was that he seen what a good thing it was to have, and went out and got it." One thing Matty had little of, however, was luck. For all his brilliance, for all his 367 victories and his stunning 2.13 lifetime earned-run average, he lost some of the most heartbreaking games in some of the most brutal circumstances. Worst of them all was the seventh game of the 1912 World Series, when his Giant teammate, Fred Snodgrass, made the famous error that led to two unearned Red Sox runs and a crushing loss. Ring was there, and he filed this report:

BOSTON, MASS., Oct. 16—Just after Steve Yerkes had crossed the plate with the run that gave Boston's Red Sox the world's championship in the tenth inning of the deciding game of the greatest series ever played for the big title, while the thousands, made temporarily crazy by a triumph entirely unexpected, yelled, screamed, stamped their feet, smashed hats and hugged one another, there was seen one of the saddest sights in the history of a sport that is a strange and wonderful mixture of joy and gloom. It was the spectacle of a man, old as baseball players are reckoned, walking from the middle of the field to the New York players' bench with bowed head and drooping shoulders, with tears streaming from his eyes, a man on whom his team's fortune had been staked and lost, and a man who would have proven his clear title to the trust reposed in him if his mates had stood by him in the supreme test. The man was Christy Mathewson.

Beaten, 3 to 2, by a club he would have conquered if he had been given the support deserved by his wonderful pitching, Matty tonight is greater in the eyes of New York's public than ever before. Even the joy-mad population of Boston confesses that his should have been the victory and his the praise.

No, Ring didn't let his admiration for Mathewson influence his appreciation for the pitcher's courage, or vice versa, but he did have a special feeling for this great man who had such bad luck. In the fall of 1925 Mathewson died of tuberculosis—the same disease that contributed to Ring's death eight years later—and Ring, despite his normal dislike for such assignments, agreed to be publicity chairman of the Christy Mathewson Memorial Foundation, which was raising funds for a gymnasium and memorial rotunda at Bucknell, and a cross at Saranac Lake, where he died.

Ring may have been thinking about Matty when he wrote, in a 1930 piece on "Br'er Rabbit Ball," that "I have always been a fellow who liked to see efficiency rewarded. If a pitcher pitched a swell game, I wanted to see him win it. So it kind of sickens me to watch a typical pastime of today in which a good pitcher, after an hour and fifty minutes of deserved mastery of his opponents, can suddenly be made to look like a bum by four or five great sluggers who couldn't have held a job as bat boy on the Niles High School scrubs." From the day of its introduction, the lively ball preyed on Ring's mind: it had ruined *his* game. Once, in the late twenties, he dropped into the press box at the Polo Grounds and watched a few innings. When he got up to leave, a reporter pointed to the batter, Chuck Klein, and said, "There's a fellow can hit 'em." Ring replied, "Swings good, but how far do you think he'd hit 'em with the old ball?" In the summer of 1932, when illness forced John McGraw to retire, Ring wrote him a nostalgic letter:

> . . . Baseball hasn't meant much to me since the introduction of the TNT ball that robbed the game of the features I used to like best—features that gave you and Bill Carrigan and Fielder Jones and other really intelligent managers a deserved advantage, and smart ball players like Cobb and Jim Sheckard a chance to *do* things.
>
> You and Bill Gleason and Eddie Collins were among the few men left who personified what I enjoyed in "the national pastime."

What must be stressed, however, because so often exactly the opposite is claimed, is that Ring had not given up on baseball per se. He made his changed attitude quite clear in a column written in 1921: "I got a letter the other day asking why didn't I write about baseball no more and I usen't to write about nothing else, you might say. Well friends, may as well admit that I have kind of lose interest in the old game, or rather it ain't the old game which I have lose interest in it, but it is the game which the magnates has fixed up to please the public with their usual good judgment."

Ring wanted baseball to be what it had been—or what he remembered it as being—when he was young. The game he remembered was clean, honorable, ordered, subtle, intricate, beautiful, somehow *natural*. The game he saw for the last dozen years of his life was, he thought, corrupt, obvious, tainted, graceless, *unnatural* because it did not always appropriately reward the diligent and the lazy. In some measure he was right, in some measure he was merely nostalgic and even sentimental. Yet it is not pure coincidence that the Black Sox Scandal occurred in 1919, that the jackrabbit ball was introduced in 1920. Baseball was not the only American institution that was corrupted in the wake of world war and the beginning of that disastrous experiment in institutionalized morality, Prohibition. It's just that of the institutions that were corrupted, this was the one Ring knew best. It had been too large a part of his life for him to part with it without grief.

Part Two

Beginnings

"All and all I can remember
living back in Niles, Michigan,
30 or 40 yrs. ago and we didn't
have no telephone and neither
did anybody else and those was
amongst the happiest days
of my life."

NILES, MICHIGAN, MAY NOT HAVE BEEN THE QUINTESSENCE OF turn-of-the-century small-town America, but it was close enough so that when Ring later wrote about his boyhood there, or described the customs and mores of the town, millions of readers who had grown up in towns just like it smiled in recognition. Ring was born there on March 6, 1885, and he did not leave it permanently until November, 1907. Like other Midwesterners who moved East in the early decades of the twentieth century, he never quite lost his love for the place of his roots or his sense of being an outsider in the jangling environs of New York. He did not regret the decision to leave ("Small towns are fine to grow up in and a writer finds out a lot of things in small towns he can't learn anywhere else. But it wouldn't be the same as you got older in a small town"), yet he knew that what he had left was lost forever, and at times, particularly in the last years when he was sick and discouraged, he yearned to recapture it. He was well aware how profoundly Niles had shaped him, and he was glad of it.

Niles is just barely in Michigan, five miles north of the Indiana state line and ten miles from South Bend. Lake Michigan is twenty miles to the west. In favorable traffic you can drive to Chicago in a couple of hours, the pollution intensifying with each of the ninety miles. The population now is about 13,000, and Main Street, which slopes through the heart of town down to the St. Joseph River, has the defeated, washed-out look characteristic of today's small-town centers. The action is along U.S. 31, the main road to South Bend. There you can stay at the Holiday Inn or the Golden Eagle Inn, and dine at Burger Chef or McDonald's or Som'Place Else or Kentucky Fried Chicken. In the new library, a handsome building of which the librarians are justifiably proud, there is a small collection of Ring's books, behind glass. At the nearby Fort St. Joseph Museum, there are Ring's mother's books, a letter he wrote to his sister Lena, and a curator who is surprised that anyone asks about Ring Lardner. The house on Bond Street in which Ring was born still stands, and across the street is a marker; the funds to place it there were raised by local high school students after the city fathers failed to come up with the money. The birthplace itself is now a boarding house.

Niles at the turn of the century had a population of about 4,000. Its social structure was both rigid, in that the lines were clearly drawn, and fluid, in that the lines could be reasonably freely crossed for purposes of friendship and sociability. At the top was a small group of Anglo-Saxon families, the local aristocracy; they lived mostly along the east bank of the St. Joseph River and attended Trinity Church. In the middle was a religiously mixed class of shopkeepers and service people. At the bottom, with aspirations of moving into the middle, were the poor; the Irish tended to live on the West Side, across the river, and the Germans in an area called the Dickereel. The town was surrounded by fertile farms, and industry was making increasing contributions to the local economy. Some Niles residents worked in South Bend; they commuted to it on the interurban trolley, which Ring liked to call the "inter-ruben." The aristocracy managed its real-estate investments and watched the money roll in. Some rich people from Chicago had vacation or weekend houses along the river, though they do not seem to have participated much in the life of the town.

But there was plenty of it. Niles ladies held teas and musicales and joined literary societies. There were parties and dinners, at which generous amounts of food and liquor were served, and no one stood very firmly on social ceremony. Entertainment was provided by the traveling shows that passed through town and by various local theatrical organizations, notable among them the American Minstrels. Fathers and sons went to Central League baseball games in South Bend, where they could also see the baseball and football teams of Notre Dame University. Children had piano lessons and dancing lessons, and in school there were debates and recitations and the classics. They rode horses and had picnics on the banks of the river and went skinny-dipping above the French Paper Mill dam.

It was a small town, but it provided an impressive array of shops and services. Clothiers included J. Julius Sons, which advertised as "The Satisfactory Store," and Eaglesfield, which offered "silk and mohair shirt waists, muslin underwear, hosiery in all the newest styles, and ladies' walking shorts." Doctors Z. L. Baldwin and B. D. Giddings saw patients from 8 A.M. to 8 P.M. in their offices over Griffin's Drug Store. Groceries were available at D. H. Bunbury's store, and F. C. Schmidt sold "fresh, salted, dried and smoked meats," as well as "fish and provisions." Horseshoeing and blacksmithing were done by Aldrich & Son, and C. H. Zwergel sold livery. The quick and the dead were served by H. E. Price, a "Dealer in Pictures, Frames, etc.," who also was the local "Undertaker and Embalmer." E. H. Murphy ran a "Tonsorial Parlor," Hing Lee was the proprietor of the Chinese Laundry, C. S. Quimby was the local agent for Rambler Bicycles, Hatch & Hamilton did plumbing, and an alternative to high school was offered by Marshall & Henry, owners of the Palace Billiard Room. The Niles City Bank, with capital of $35,000, promised "Conservative, courteous, prompt and careful attention given to all business entrusted to us," according to Dickson S. Scoffern, Cashier.

The Lardner name is nowhere to be found in business advertisements of the time because the Lardners were above such petty enterprises. Not merely was the family in the top stratum of society, it *was* the top. By virtue of blue blood, established roots and considerable wealth, the Lardners came as close to genuine aristocracy as a small Midwestern town could hope to see.

The blue blood came from Lynford Lardner, who immigrated to Philadelphia from London in 1740 and became a leading citizen of the colony of Pennsylvania. The Niles connection was established in 1836 when Henry Lardner, a physician who never entered practice but made both a profitable marriage and a successful career in various land and timber undertakings, moved to the young town. His only son, Henry, Ring's father, was born in 1839 and educated in Philadelphia. He returned to Niles in 1857, taking over a substantial farm left to him by his father. He also sought and won, in 1861, the hand of Lena Bogardus Phillips.

Lena Lardner was what members of the tribe call a "P.K."—a preacher's kid. Her father, the Reverend Joseph Phillips, was rector of Trinity Church. She was a devout woman who played the church's organ for a half-century, but she also had plenty of the rebelliousness that seems to come with being a preacher's kid. She loved music, the theater and literature, and she was what can only be called a poetess. Her verse, which appeared in various Midwestern newspaper columns of the sort that solicit contributions from readers, was for the most part dreadfully cheerful, or cheerfully dreadful. Two collections of it were published, *Sparks from the Yule Log* and *This Sprig of Western Pine*, and if the titles do not say all that needs to be said, then surely the dedication of the latter volume, to Theodore Roosevelt, does:

> *To our Chief Ruler, firm and good,*
> *(By wise and simple understood,)*
> *I offer—neither rare nor fine—*
> *This simple "spray of Western Pine."*

It would be easy, in fact, to make fun of Lena Lardner, for at first glance she was one of those female eccentrics of whom each small town is expected to have one. Her energies were ferocious, her charities were both infinite and unpredictable, and her indifference to social convention was complete. It is tempting to dress her up in lorgnette and floppy hat, grant her the presidency of the Wednesday Literary Club, and leave it at that. Except for the evidence indicating that, her occasional peculiarities to the contrary, she was a person of formidable and beneficial influence on all her children—considerably more so than their genial but quiet father, who remained much in her shadow.

Henry and Lena Lardner had two sets of children. The first six were born in the early years of their marriage, and three of them survived: William, Henry, Jr., and Lena. Then, when both parents were in their forties, they had three more: Reginald, who was known as Rex; Anna, called Anne; and Ringgold Wilmer. Ringgold was a family name, having become one in honor of a Union admiral bearing the singular monicker of Cadwallader Ringgold; Wilmer was the maiden name of an aunt of Henry Lardner's. The combination, whatever its sources, was deadly, and the family had the good sense—not to mention the kindness—to shorten it quickly to Ring. For the rest of his life he regarded the name with a mixture of vexation and amusement. He kept his middle name such a secret that Ellis Abbott, five weeks before she was to marry him, wrote to ask: "Also isn't your middle name Wilmer? I have to have it for the invitations," to which he replied: "Does 'Wilmer' have to appear? Whether he does or not, please don't put any gold on the end of the Ring. It's bad enough without that." On the other hand, it gave him a small storehouse of material for jokes ("'I did not know you were a candidate,' writes Wilbur Nesbit, 'until I happened into the bath department of the C.A.A. the other night and saw the sign, "Ring for Attendant"'"), and it certainly gave him, in the words of his first biographer, Donald Elder, "the most distinctive *nom de plume* in American letters since Mark Twain."

The setting in which Ring grew up was close to idyllic. The Bond Street house was spacious, and the grounds encompassed several acres. There was a private Lardner baseball diamond, a tennis court, and a small stable with "whitish gray twin mares aptly named Dolly and Polly" and a horse named Fred who "trotted part of the time and paced part of the time," and did either—or neither—according to whim. The lawn rolled down to the street, and across the street a steep bank went down to the river. The tracks of the Cincinnati, Wabash & Michigan ran between the road and the river, and Ring and Rex—who had, as most boys of the day did, a passion for trains—made them a regular hangout. There were animals all over the place, and the house was littered with cats.

As is often the case with the children of middle-aged parents, Rex, Anne and Ring were given every affordable luxury. In their early years, each was provided with his or her private Irish nursemaid, the Irish presumably being both plentiful and cheap. A coachman named Ed Donnelly was on hand to take them wherever they wished to go. But until Ring was eight, he could not go *without* the coachman or another servant. The Lardner children, when they were young, were not allowed to go out into the world; the world was brought in to them. They lived in what amounted to a compound. Children were permitted to visit them, and plenty did, but they were kept isolated from whatever real or imagined evils lurked on the West Side or the Dickereel until they were deemed old enough to cope with them.

Still, they seem to have had lots of fun. Ring was pressed into pumping the bellows on the church organ upon occasion, and he sang in the choir, but he also found time to carve his initials prominently on the altar rail, where they are still clearly visible. He was energetic, even a bit of an exhibitionist, given to taking the most prominent or juiciest roles in family theatricals and engaging in boyish pranks. He was born with a deformed foot, which was corrected surgically. He wore a brace until he was eleven, but that did not prevent him from taking part in games and organizing boys' baseball teams; the only permanent consequence of the deformity was that his left leg was thinner than his right. He went swimming in the St. Joe, as the river was and is universally known in the area, and one riverside picnic produced a Lardner story that probably is apocryphal, though one may be allowed to hope it is not.

According to the tale, the Lardner children were picnicking by the river with some other kids, among them six unruly and somewhat unpopular brothers and sisters by the name of Stone. As a boyhood friend of Ring's recalled the rest of the story,

> One fine picnic day, two Stone kids went over the cliff and rolled promptly down into the St. Joe, which was rather deep at that point. They were pushed or something. . . . Ring Lardner was right there. He saw the two Stone kids go sliding down the cliff, saw their bright red heads bobbing in the St. Joe.
>
> "By gosh," said Ring, "it's true."
>
> "What's that?" somebody asked.
>
> "A rolling stone gathers no moss," returned Ring. Then he promptly slid down the cliff, jumped into the St. Joe and hauled the Stone kids to safety.

The isolation of the three young Lardners extended to their grammar schooling, which was conducted in the Lardner house by a tutor named Harry Mansfield and at times by Mrs. Lardner. Mansfield was a gentle man with a fixation on penmanship, and, as Ring described it many years later:

> . . . We had a private tutor that come to the house every morning at 9 and stayed till noon and on acct. of it taking him 2 and a ½ hrs. to get us to stop giggling, why they was only a ½ hr. left for work and this was genally always spent on penmanship which was his passion.
>
> The rules of penmanship at that time provided that you had to lean your head over to the left, wind up like they was nobody on second base, and when you finely touched pen to paper, your head followed through from left to right so that when you come to the end of the line, your right ear laid flat on the desk.

Little Ring strikes a wistful pose. As is evident, he had good reason for calling himself "Ringlets" in his correspondence with Ellis Abbott.

An early photograph of Ring as a professional journalist. It probably was taken during his first stint with the Chicago Tribune, from 1908 to 1910.

Who the two fellows behind him are is a total mystery, but there seems little doubt that Ring had visited a few saloons before he made it to the photographer's studio.

Above: *A typical baseball crowd during the dead-ball era; the advertiser in the upper left-hand corner obviously knew where his buyers congregated.* Below: *The White Sox strike a formal pose. Ellis and Ring made the Western trip with them, but didn't get into the picture; heaven knows why the little girl did.*

The two ball players Ring most admired. Ty Cobb comes into third base with his customary ferocity (above); Christy Mathewson warms up (left). One was a bully and the other a gentleman, but what mattered to Ring was that both of them developed their great abilities to the fullest degree.

PROMINENT BASEBALL WRITERS OF THE COUNTRY HERE FOR THE SERIES

JOE S. JACKSON
DETROIT FREE PRESS

FRANK B. HUTCHINSON JR.
ASSOCIATED PRESS

R.W. LARDNER
CHICAGO TRIBUNE

GEORGE C. RICE
CHICAGO DAILY NEWS

In October 1909 Ring covered the World Series in Pittsburgh and was carica-
tured by a local newspaper. He sent the results (above) to Ellis, and added his
own editorial emphasis to the headline. The horseman below is Frank Schulte,
Ring's friend and "collaborator," posing with Wildfire, whom he raced on ice
during the off-season.

Ellis and Ring. Where or when the picture was taken is not known, but it was in that time when everything was beautiful and green.

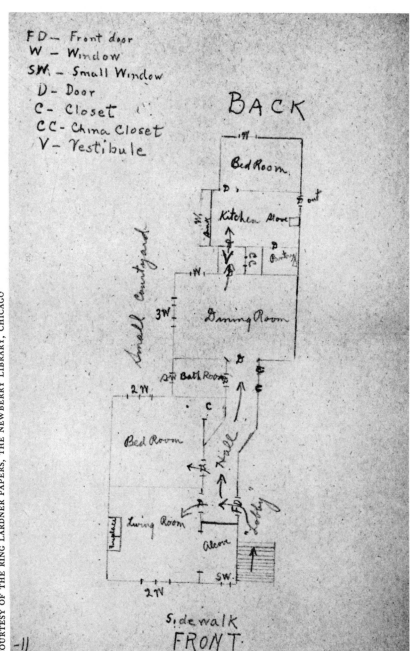

In the spring of 1911, Ring took on the assignment of finding an apartment to settle in with his bride-to-be. The floor plan he mailed her left scarcely a question unanswered; she told him that "I am crazy about it, really." It was at 16 Park Drive in Brookline, Massachusetts.

RING LARDNER, JR.

The best-known photograph of Ring. It was taken around 1913, in the offices of the Chicago Tribune. He was then beginning to write "In the Wake of the News"; the busher stories—and fame—were only months away.

It was really Lena Lardner, however, who determined the kind and quality of education the children received. The Lardners had a fine library ("All the books," according to the Niles *Daily Star*, "were marked with an engraved card on which was the Lardner coat of arms, and the motto in Latin 'Not the Highest but the Best' "), and Mrs. Lardner directed the children to the ones she most loved and admired. These included novels by the Brontës and Dickens, and collections of English poetry. The reading she preferred tended to move the heart rather than the mind, and Ring acquired a similar taste. In 1923 he was asked to name "10 Books I Have Enjoyed Most," and the list he gave (there is absolutely no suggestion that he was pulling anyone's leg, as he often did in such circumstances) has the influence of Lena Lardner all over it: *Alice in Wonderland, Alice Through the Looking-Glass, The Adventures of Sherlock Holmes, The Memoirs of Sherlock Holmes,* Lear's *Nonsense Book, David Copperfield, Oliver Twist, Forty Years a Gambler on the Mississippi, Little Women* and *Alice Adams.* When he grew older he became attached to Dostoyevsky, and he frequently said that *The Brothers Karamazov* was his favorite novel.

Lena Lardner's religious faith had as profound an effect on Ring as her love of literature, though not in the intended way. Because of her vigorous Episcopalianism, Ring came into regular contact— probably daily—with the King James Bible and the *Book of Common Prayer.* No one who has had a prolonged exposure to these two masterpieces comes away from them unaffected. They teach the grace, elegance and nobility of the English language as no textbook can, and Ring learned the lesson. Though his reputation would be earned as a writer of the idiomatic American language, filled to overflowing with slang and illiteracies, Ring's prose when he wrote in his own voice was flawless—and it was precisely because he knew proper English so well that he was able to reproduce improper English so meticulously and accurately.

Music was Lena Lardner's other love; it became Ring's as well. He came to it with a distinct advantage, as he later told an interviewer: "Maybe it's true that my hearing is keener than my other senses. If you play a chord on the piano, I can tell what key it's in, even if I happen to be several rooms away. Musicians tell me it's a pretty rare faculty. They call it having a perfect ear." Such an ear of course can be as perfect for language as for music, and the effect on his writing career of his musical interests is obvious. But Ring gave such considerations little thought. He enjoyed music purely for its own sake, and throughout his life nothing gave him greater pleasure. Apparently he knew classical music well enough (though he detested opera), but his abiding love was the popular music of the time: the "coon songs" made popular by his lifelong idol, the black singer Bert Williams, and the romantic songs young men and women crooned to each other on Moonlight Bay. His musical talents were as substantial as his love for song; he sang a strong baritone as a teenager and bass as an adult, played the piano well enough to provide the accompaniment for late-night singing at parties attended by show-business people, and mastered—or at least got the better of—every musical instrument he tried, and he tried quite a few.

If there is a recurrent theme in the pursuits Lena Lardner enjoyed and passed on to her children, it lies in the word "enjoyed." Notwithstanding her compassion and her strong sense of *noblesse oblige*, at heart she believed that life was supposed to be fun. For Ring, learning this lesson was a mixed blessing. Certainly it helped him maintain a healthy perspective on life; he had a splendid capacity to take things seriously but never solemnly, and his playful spirit brought laughter, warmth and happiness to everyone who knew him even remotely well, not to mention millions of readers. On the other hand, the search for fun—which was at the heart of his quixotic quest for success in vaudeville and the Broadway theater—prevented him from making the kind of wholehearted commitments necessary to the fulfillment of his artistic talents. A principal reason why he never wrote a novel, for example, no matter what justifications he gave in various letters, interviews and private conversations, was that the effort of writing one was more of a commitment than he cared to make to work he basically did not like very much; he was capable of pouring countless hours into disastrous musical comedies which—to what should be his admirers' everlasting gratitude—never saw the light of day, but he simply did not allow himself the time for a sustained effort at serious writing. In that respect, his priorities were somewhat out of kilter. And so, too, were his expectations. Though he was at heart a realist, he never quite lost Lena's firm conviction that life not merely should be but *would be* fun, and there is no question that when life became no fun at all, that was a principal cause of the disillusionment and despair that set in on him.

His mother's insistence on isolating him from the muck and mire as a young boy also had mixed results. His precocity was able to flower in the more or less hermetic atmosphere of the Lardner estate, and he probably paid closer attention to his studies, informal though they were, than many children in the public schools. Most emphatically, it needs to be said on Lena's behalf that none of the children emerged from her cocoon spoiled, willful or intransigent; if anything, their sensitivity to their immediate surroundings seems to have been heightened by the experience. But it was a very narrow upbringing, and its effects cannot be underestimated. Ring gave a clear indication of how profound they were in a 1917 interview in which he was asked if he admired Mark Twain:

> Yes, . . . but I like Booth Tarkington's *Penrod* stories better. I've known Booth Tarkington's boys and I've not known those of Mark Twain. Mark Twain's boys are tough and poverty-stricken and they belong to a period very different from that of our own boys. But we all know Penrod and his friends.

Ring thought he was saying that Twain's boys were of a generation too far removed from his own for him to identify with them. What he was actually saying was that having grown up in a sanitized world, he had no intimate feeling for a "tough and poverty-stricken" world outside his own experience; the comparatively easy, carefree world of Penrod and his friend Sam, on the other hand, was close enough to Ring's own background so that he could identify with it.

This same view was reflected in Ring's attitude toward the poor and members of minority groups. Compassion, when it beats in an aristocratic heart, tends to take one of two forms: compassion for the general but not the specific, or compassion for the specific but not the general. Ring's followed the latter course. He was incapable of unkindness to an individual human being, and it did not make the slightest difference what that person's wealth, social standing, color or religion. When he lived in Great Neck, he shocked and alienated some of his neighbors by having blacks as guests in his house. His friendship with Bert Williams could not be called close, but he certainly treasured it. He moved in the markedly Jewish world of the theater with no discomfort, and he caused none.

Yet he could be as callous toward the mass of "colored" people as he could be sensitive to an individual black. He employed, quite casually, almost all of the racial and ethnic slurs of the time —and since they were very much of his time and place, he should not be held a bigot on account of it. He was guilty, however, of some unconscionable generalizations, no matter how innocently intended. In the thousands of hours he spent on trains he must have encountered thousands of porters, yet he wrote that "every porter's name is George," a comment that is itself beneath comment. He thought it was funny, and probably many of his readers did too, to portray "George" with "his laughable darky dialect, . . . rolling those big eyes and doing the double shuffle." But he reached his personal depths during the Disarmament Conference of 1921:

> . . . the commander in chief of the French Army, who my elevator boy nicknamed Marshall Fox, picked up a couple more degrees yesterday and now it looks like he had pretty near enough to start a fever. Mr. Fox got one of his new ones from Georgetown and the other from Howard University where the colored boys goes to school. Georgetown also presented him with a slight token of their esteem in the form of a sword.
> "Just what I needed," was the Marshall's delighted comment. The Howard students might of give him a razor for all I know.

This attitude is not the legacy of Lena Lardner, but that of the class to which Ring belonged, the time in which he lived, and the small town in which he grew up. It is also less an expression of racial prejudice than a manifestation of the aloofness that was among Ring's singular characteristics, a distance that he kept between himself and the moil of humanity—an aristocrat's reserve made all the greater by a shy and sensitive man's need for protection, for what Sherwood Anderson called his "mask." But no matter what the explanations for it, his unthinking acceptance of racial and ethnic stereotypes was a flaw of character in a man who otherwise had very few.

RING'S ISOLATION CAME TO AN END in the summer of 1897, when he was twelve years old. He seems to have left the cocoon with no regrets, though it was probably his early boyhood to which he referred when he wrote: "All and all I can remember living back in Niles, Michigan, 30 or 40 yrs. ago and we didn't have no telephone and neither did anybody else and those was amongst the happiest days of my life"—a recollection that has to do with much more than the absence of telephones in the Niles of his youth. The isolation ended with his matriculation in Niles High School. All three children took a high-school-equivalency test and all three flunked, but evidently the flexing of a bit of Lardner family muscle persuaded the superintendent of schools to bend the rules in their case. They were admitted provisionally: Rex to the tenth grade, Ring and Anne to the ninth.

As it turned out, they all did well both academically and socially. Ring, who had been a trifle pudgy as a young boy, got tall in a hurry ("When I was born I was about the same height as other people of that age, but when I was thirteen I suddenly began to shoot up, perhaps because I lived near Chicago") and was big enough for football, baseball and general hell-raising, at which he proved himself expert. In his freshman year he studied composition, English literature, beginning Latin, algebra and American history, though he admitted that "most of we boys done our studying at a 10x5 table with six pockets in it," presumably in the establishment run by Messrs. Marshall & Henry. The students were dragged line by line through *The Lady of the Lake* and *The Idylls of the King* and what Ring described as "Milton's and Scott's Best Sellers" and, of course, *The Rime of the Ancient Mariner*:

. . . when we come yawning to recitation the next day they was no way for the teacher to know whether we had spent the night trying to get Coleridge or the 14 ball.

One of the boys or gals would get up and read the first few stanzas followed by questions in regards to same.

TEACHER: Mr. Brown, what is an ancient mariner?

MR. BROWN: Why, let's see, it's a it's a kind of a old sailor.

TEACHER: And what is meant when it says he stoppeth one of three?

MR. BROWN: Well well it means it means he stopped a man. They was three men and he stopped one of them one of the three.

TEACHER: Mr. Starkweather, what is a loon?

MR. STARKWEATHER: It means somebody that is kind of crazy. (*Aside.*) Like a lot of teachers.

(*Laughter from admirers of Mr. Starkweather.*)

TEACHER: Let's have quiet. Now, Miss Millard, explain the line eftsoons his hand dropt he.

MISS MILLARD: It means that pretty soon right away he dropped his hand.

MR. STARKWEATHER (*aside*): He didn't even have a pair.

TEACHER: Let's have quiet.

Ring joked about his schooling in his journalism, but he took it seriously and learned from it, as he acknowledged when he recalled that "we was taught in rhetoric class that the main thing to remember in writing was to be terse and concise and etc. and not use no wds. that was not nessary"—a recollection to which he appended the pointed observation that "I don't know if this teaching is still in vogue, but if so I advice young men who expects to write for a living to forget it as soon as possible a specially if they aspire to membership in the Baseball Writers Assn. of America." He probably learned more from Latin, too, than he admitted —it is a demanding teacher of the weight, value and meaning of words, all of which he knew perfectly—but in any event, he got a grand story out of his sufferings at the hands of the classics: "Caesar would of been kind of tiresome except for the gals. Their system of translating was to first find out the meaning of the wds. and then read from left to right in the order named. Like for inst. 'When Caesar in Gaul hither was as before related he that the Helvetians were in phalanges solid marching heard' and etc. This give it the elements of a puzzle which was lacking when we boys was called on. For we boys had boughten from last yr's sophomores a funny little book which only every other line was latin and the rest English that give you a kind of broad hint as to what was going on."

He got a classic liberal education: in the sophomore year, Caesar, botany, algebra, literature, "higher arithmetic" and rhetoric; in the junior year, Cicero, German, geometry, world history "and 2 other studies which I forget"; in the senior year, Ovid, Virgil, German, Shakespeare, history and physics. He also got an education in the rough ways of the football field, in a game against a rival school: "We had to punt and I started down the field hoping I would not get there first as their punt catcher was a man named Hogan. Well I did not get there first or last neither one as I decided to stop on the way and lay down a wile. This decision was reached immediately after receiving a special message from admirers on the side lines in the form of a stone carefully wrapped up in wet snow. The message was intended for my ear and came to the right address. For the rest of that fall I was what you might term stone deaf on that side."

Niles high schoolers led a lively social life, and Ring was an active participant in it. There were hayrides, sleigh rides, picnics, amateur theatricals, marshmallow roasts, ball games—all of which provided ample opportunity for boys and girls to get together. Youths of high school age not being old enough to begin the formal minuet of courtship, there was a freedom and light-heartedness to these encounters on which Ring seems to have thrived. His friends included Tom Swain, Billy Beeson, Wilma Johnson, Blanche Millard, "Doc" Ostrander, Edith Baumberger, Nannie Bonine and, above all, Arthur Jacks, who would remain a dear friend for life. Ring dated girls, had his share of adolescent infatuations, and once was rescued from a romantic fate worse than death by his horse, Fred, the trotter and pacer:

> . . . one night they was a show in South Bend 10 miles from my home town and I wanted to take a gal to it who I thought I was stuck on and I didn't have no $1.50 to hire a livery rig as we used to call it, so I hitched up Fred and took her over in him and he trotted all the way in fine style, but when we got in the buggy to come home Fred heard the dame make the remark that she had promised her mother to not stay out later than 12:30 so the minute we left the city limits of South Bend Fred began to pace and it was after 12:30 already when we got as far as Notre Dame still 8 miles from home . . .
>
> Well anyway we got to the gal's home at ½ past 3 which was at that time the latest which either she or I or Fred had been up, but mother was still setting up and I tried to tell her the old proverb about how you can trot a horse to South Bend but you can't trot him home but she couldn't hear me on acct. of somebody talking all the time. So that is the last I seen of that special gal except as a friend but afterwards she grew married to another man that couldn't afford livery rigs and she left him flat just like I would of been left only for Fred. . . .

Ring's most serious romantic involvement during the Niles years was with Ethel Witkowsky, a Chicagoan whose family summered at Barron Lake, east of Niles. It is not clear whether the romance broke up for religious reasons—she was Jewish—but it appears to have ended by the time Ring met Ellis Abbott in the summer of 1905 and there is no evidence that its termination had any traumatic effect on Ring; certainly it did nothing to diminish the delight he took in the company of girls.

When Ring was in the company of boys, he spent a good deal of it in the pool hall and in local saloons. Drinking was an accepted part of the life in Niles, and both Ring and Rex took to it early—which they were able to do without difficulty because most saloons in Niles merely winked at the twenty-one-year age requirement. When Ring wrote that by the age of sixteen "I had mastered just enough of one live foreign language to tell Razzle, a gullible bartender, that Ich war ein und zwanzig Jahre alt," he was bending the truth for the sake of a joke. He was much more accurate in describing an establishment called Pigeon's, "where everybody that had a dime was the same age and the only minors was the boys that tried to start a charge acct." Beer was principally what he drank (as he grew older he developed a particular fondness for bourbon whiskey) and it was so cheap that for 20 cents "you could get enough to patrol 4th St. serenading true music lovers of the opposing sex." Any time of day was fine for a drink; the Lardner brothers often stopped by a saloon for an early-morning pick-me-up.

Ring held his liquor exceedingly well; it brought him out, relaxed him, and made conversation easier for him. He started drinking because he liked the taste of beer and liquor, and he liked what alcohol did for him, and for some time he was able to keep his consumption under control. He did, however, establish fairly early a pattern in which a period of very heavy drinking would alternate with a period of abstinence, and when he entered the hard-drinking business of sports writing, the periods of abstinence grew less frequent.

In the spring of 1901, Ring—who was sixteen years old—and Anne graduated from Niles High School; Ring was class poet, producing verse most charitably described as juvenalia. He was offered a scholarship at Olivet College, a small institution sixty miles to the northeast, but he turned it down. He had no idea what he wanted to do, and he had picked a poor time for such indecisiveness. The family fortune, which once had seemed so invulnerable, was vanishing. Ring's older brother William had become a partner in a Minnesota bank which failed; Henry Lardner, unfortunately, had backed his son with large investments in the bank and lost them all. His losses were compounded by another bad investment, in a Canadian mining operation. Between the two, he was forced to sell off most of his property in order to pay off his creditors, which he managed to do.

Life apparently went on pretty much as usual in the Lardner household after these setbacks, though gradually the family's standard of living declined, and it is difficult to ascertain how much Ring was affected by, or even knew the full dimensions of, his father's loss. It is worth noting, however, that later in life he became obsessed with making enough money to give his own wife and children every necessity and luxury they desired—yet at the same time he had an oddly cavalier attitude toward spending money, as though he had a clear notion of the potential evanescence of riches. He also developed an obsession with life insurance, perhaps because he was pained by the reduced circumstances into which his widowed mother eventually was driven; and it is a good thing he did, for it was insurance that made up the bulk of his own estate and enabled Ellis to live reasonably comfortably in widowhood.

There do not seem, in any case, to have been great pressures on Ring to contribute to the family's income. After graduation he went rapidly through a series of somewhat mysterious jobs, including "an office boy's portfolio with the [McCormick] Harvester Company in Chicago" at $4 a week and a similar position with a Chicago real-estate firm, Peabody, Houghteling and Company; each lasted two weeks before he was canned. While in Chicago, he stayed with his friends from Niles, the Jackses, whose earlier move to the big city had caused much grief in the Lardner family: ". . . the Jacks boys were virtually inseparable from the younger Lardners, so that when the Jackses moved to Chicago, the Asmuses, Kaisers, Wolfords and Mantkes, who were employed by the Michigan Central, had a good laugh at the sight of men ranging in age from twelve to twenty frankly shedding tears at a mere parting. As matters turned out, the Jackses, and particularly the Jacks parents, ought to have done all the crying, while the Lardners gave their tribal cheer, for on visits to Chicago during the next ten years the Lardners' hotel was the Jacks domicile, and the rates per day or week, American plan, were nothing."

Ring returned to Niles and got a job at $1 a day as "third assistant freight hustler at the Michigan Central in Niles," which he held until he was dismissed "for putting a box of cheese in the through Jackson car, when common sense should have told me that it ought to go to Battle Creek." At this point his father, perhaps deciding that he was harboring chronic unemployables, sent Ring and Rex to the Armour Institute of Technology in Chicago, with the bizarre notion that Ring should learn mechanical engineering, a career in which he had neither interest nor ability: ". . . I can't think of no walk in life for which I had more of a natural bent unless it would be hostess at a roller rink." He entered in January, 1902, and took up a peculiar curriculum consisting of mechanical drawing, physics, trigonometry, shop and rhetoric:

> Shop work, as its name implies, was all done in the shop and I didn't need to waste no thought on it in what I and my brother laughingly called our room, which was a replica of a telephone booth located in the Armour flats, a bldg. which compared in beauty and cleanliness with a big Four Day coach running between Indianapolis and Benton Harbor. The first assignment I got in the shop was to plane a piece of board about 2 ft. long by ½ feet wide by 2 inches thick. Well, I worked on it a couple of hrs. and turned it in and pretty soon teacher come over and handed it to me and I was surprised and asked him did he mean I was to keep it and he said he thought I might as well and maybe I could manage to put a couple more grooves and humps in it and use it as a back scratcher or a mold for French pastry. . . .
>
> Along in February I recd. a valentine from the dean asking me to call on him on a certain evening at eight, but I didn't want to get into entanglements with a married man and also we had tickets for that night to see Williams and Walker in "The Sons of Ham."
>
> Came spring and examinations, I passed in rhetoric with one of the highest marks in the class and figured that this give me a perfect record as it was the only study I was taking. But came another valentine from the dean containing a few fond words of farewell and congratulating me on having finished at Armour in faster time than any other student in his memory.

So Ring and Rex returned home, presumably to face a perturbed Henry Lardner, who scarcely could afford to fritter away his dwindling resources on two vagabonds. Rex managed to find a job with the Niles *Daily Sun* as a reporter, and eventually he added the duties of Niles stringer for the Kalamazoo *Gazette* and the South Bend *Tribune*. Ring was less fortunate. He spent most of the next year dawdling around the house. In 1903 he did take and pass a civil service examination, and he got odd jobs in the post office, but he reserved much of his energies for the American Minstrels, an organization of thirty young men who put on shows for local audiences. In April, 1903, the Minstrels produced a two-act entertainment called *Zanzibar*, which would have absolutely no significance except that Ring wrote the music and lyrics, and the text was printed by Fred D. Cook, Publisher, of Niles—making the fourteen-page booklet the first known publication to bear the by-line of Ring Lardner. It probably had a fair amount of youthful charm as presented at the Niles Opera House on April 14, but neither Ring's lyrics nor Harry Schmidt's book have weathered the years well. The "argument," or plot, suggests the influence of Gilbert and Sullivan:

> The story opens just after the death of the Sultan of Zanzibar. His son and successor, Seyyid Barghash, has been educated in foreign countries and is expected home to take the throne. Shylock and Padlock, whose former homes were in Buchanan, Mich., appear as valets to two young New Yorkers. Shylock is mistaken for the young Sultan. He at once assumes the throne, but being better acquainted with American government, he changes his title to Mayor, appoints Padlock City Clerk and the members of his court aldermen. In the second act the real Sultan appears and adds complications to the plot. Shylock explains that he was merely keeping the throne warm for the Sultan, and all ends happily.

Ring played Shylock and his friend Tom Swain was Padlock. The city-government scene enabled the Minstrels to spoof the workings of the Niles City Council, and apparently it was the enthusiastic reception this local angle received that persuaded Fred Cook to publish the play. Ring's lyrics included a love song:

> *Ujji, the moon is shining up in the skies,*
> *And stars are winkin' at me from above;*
> *Come, babe, and let me look into your eyes,*
> *Oh, Ujji, my Afcan love!*

IT WAS NOT UNTIL 1904 that Ring got his first taste of steady work. Bascom Parker, Jr., a family friend who owned the Niles Gas Company, took Ring on as a combination meter reader, book-keeper, bill collector, office boy and floor mopper:

> The making out of bills and the keeping of books came under the head of hard labor. The mopping was a kind of game; I used to see whether I could do it today faster than I had done it yesterday. Trying to collect bad debts and get new customers was a set-up; I have always been a person who could take no for an answer. Reading meters was the rub, because meters are usually in dark cellars, where my favorite animal, the rat, is wont to dwell. When I entered a cellar and saw a rat reading the meter ahead of me, I accepted his reading and went on to the next house.

He disliked the job with the gas company, but there is no evidence that he made positive efforts either to get out of it or to find a more congenial line of work. He simply drifted along, enjoying the social life of Niles and the friendship of his contemporaries, basking in the pleasures and relative lack of pressure of small-town life. Given his indifference to the careers available in Niles, it is easy to see him drifting along for the rest of his life, married to a local girl, playing at amateur theatricals, idling at some undemanding occupation, drinking in local saloons and, later, speak-easies. But that accounts neither for happenstance nor for the fierce work energies that waited to be lit in him.

It is the theory of Ring Lardner, Jr., as persuasively advanced in *The Lardners: My Family Remembered*, that his father's "professional life was shaped by accidental circumstances to a much greater extent than by conscious intention." Certainly there can be no argument that he came into journalism entirely by accident. He may, perhaps, have envied Rex the newspaper career he had entered, but there are no reliable reports of any efforts he made to get hired at the Niles paper or anywhere else. He did, however, leap at his first clear opportunity to escape the gas company.

How it came about is the subject of several accounts that differ slightly, but a satisfactory version can be pieced together from them. The stories that Rex was filing to the South Bend *Tribune* caught the admiring attention of the editor of its competitor, the South Bend *Times*. His name was Edgar A. Stoll; his father owned the newspaper. Sometime in the late fall of 1905 Stoll made a trip to Niles especially to see Rex, in the hope of hiring him away as a full-time staffer. As Ring described what followed,

> . . . Mr. Stoll came to Niles and discovered that Rex was on his vacation. His employer did not know where to reach him—or why Mr. Stoll wanted to reach him—but was sure Mr. Stoll could get the desired information from me. Mr. Stoll sought me out and stated his errand, also inquiring whether my brother was tied up to a contract. I said yes, which was the truth. I asked how much salary he was willing to offer. He said twelve dollars a week. Why?
>
> "Oh," I said, "I thought I might tackle the job myself."
>
> "Have you ever done any newspaper work?"
>
> "Yes, indeed," I said. "I often help my brother." This was very far from the truth, but I was thinking of those rats.

The result was that Ring, totally without journalistic experience, was offered the job of "society reporter, court-house man, dramatic critic and sporting editor for the South Bend, Indiana, *Times*." His salary would be $12 a week, a considerable improvement over the $8 he was getting from the gas company, though "other members of my family pointed out that while twelve dollars was four dollars more than eight dollars, transportation on the interurban would amount to $2.40 a week and I would have to pay for bad lunches in cheap restaurants instead of getting good lunches at home, free." But Ring never did care much about food. A job beckoned in which his facility with words could be tested, in which he could join the company of baseball players, and in which he could begin to enter the world on his own. He took it. He was twenty years old.

RING RECEIVED NO BY-LINES during his two years with the *Times* —newspapers had yet to discover that the by-line was a handy device for inflating reporters' egos and diverting their attention from small paychecks—so any discussion of his work in South Bend must be prefaced with the acknowledgment that the work under discussion could be someone else's. But that is highly unlikely. Ignoring Ring's contributions elsewhere in the paper, one can focus on the sports pages confident that he was their principal, probably only, regular local writer. Furthermore, Ring's distinctive approach to sports reporting began to emerge remarkably early in his career, and a thorough search of the South Bend microfilms by

Richard Layman has unearthed a rich supply of material which, in that time and place, could only have been written by Ring Lardner.

To certain circles in Niles, Ring's appointment was big news, and the local paper announced it with a flourish. The story, probably written by Rex, declared that "Mr. Lardner is a recognized local authority on all matters that pertain to legitimate sports, and he is at the same time a writer of ability, having the vernacular of ring, the base ball diamond, the football field and other lines of sport, at ready command, a very essential qualification of one who is to fill the position of sporting man on a city paper, having a sporting page feature. . . . His friends will expect to see him get to the front as a sporting authority, a field that offers as good an opportunity for advancement and remunerative employment as any branch of journalism today."

Ring reported for work in early January, 1906. Then, and for the rest of the time he worked in South Bend, he took the interurban both ways, at a round-trip cost of 40 cents a day, and like most people, he worked a six-day week. He was habitually late getting started in the morning; his sister Lena recalled seeing "his long legs flying down Michigan Street" in a Dagwood Bumstead race for the trolley. If the meals he had to eat in South Bend cafés or saloons disappointed him by comparison with the hearty fare at home, he kept it to himself. He was happy in his job, he worked very hard at it, and he learned a lot.

His true flowering began that April, when he got his first chance to cover baseball regularly. South Bend had a team in the Central League, a Class B minor league that also had clubs in Grand Rapids, Springfield, Canton, Wheeling, Dayton, Evansville and Terre Haute. The 1906 season was the league's fourth, and the first in which South Bend would finish in the second division. But not having a winner to cover didn't seem to bother Ring, and professionally it was good for him—it forced him to develop his own resources for making stories interesting, for holding the attention of readers notwithstanding the dreary succession of losses. The other teams had plenty of good players, many of whom went on to the majors, notable among them Rube Marquard, Donie Bush, John Ganzel and Goat Anderson. The South Bend club was managed by Algernon Grant, "who was as good and smart a second baseman as you ever looked at and whose weakness with the bat was all that had prevented a long and lucrative big-league career." The games were played at Spring Brook Park, where Ring served both as *Times* correspondent and official scorer, at $1 a game.

The latter assignment required Ring to sit at a small table, near both the left-field line and the visitors' bench. It was an exposed position, to say the least, and Ring spent some of his time dodging either foul line drives or various objects hurled in his direction by players irate over scoring decisions. He later remembered how, as he described it, Dan Howley of the Grand Rapids club (who eventually became a big-league manager) protected him from severe injury at the hands of a teammate who was heaving fast balls in Ring's direction; Howley "made a sidewise dive that stopped a shot which would have blown my head clear across the state line."

Ring's first journalistic efforts were tentative, but it did not take long for him to settle upon a style in which he seems to have been comfortable. Much of his prose was overblown, and it would remain that way until he came under tougher and more capable editing in Chicago, but he very early showed that he could do some things unusually well: he could analyze all sports, baseball in particular, knowledgeably and dispassionately; he could brighten straightforward game accounts by centering them around a single individual or event; and he could make people laugh. Any sample of his 1906 prose must be read with the understanding that he was still a beginner, but the signs of what lay ahead were clearly there:

> The 13th of June will be set apart by Mayor Fogarty as a red letter day in the history of South Bend at the next meeting of the common council. This day was marked by three miraculous events, viz., "Tillie" Telinde made two singles, George Hepler's farm near Notre Dame was increased in population by the birth of a three-legged pig and the South Bend team won a base ball game. It would be hard to choose among these events which was the most remarkable and our tired brain has work enough before it without wasting time and gray-matter in a choice, but suffice it to say, that there will never be an exact repetition of all these things in the same day.

As that indicates, Ring was perfectly willing to be fairly blunt about the accomplishments, or lack of same, of the locals; yet he did so in a light-hearted, bantering tone that managed to make the point without offending the players themselves. It was a blend of dispassion and compassion that he refined over the years, and as much as anything else it was what separated him from the "gee whiz" baseball writers who shied away from any form of criticism, no matter how mild.

Though baseball was Ring's chief interest, he covered every sport played in South Bend: boxing matches, bowling leagues, trotting and pacing horse races, and of course Notre Dame football, which was a long way from the glory of the Rockne years but was already of more than local interest. It is safe to say that Ring also did much of the dirty work of a newspaper sports department: putting together box scores, taking high school results over the telephone, rewriting wire-service stories into major-league wrap-ups, and dealing with the endlessly inquisitive public. (No newspaper department, with the possible exception of the city desk, gets more visitors and telephone callers than sports, and none deals with a higher percentage of nuts and bores.) Ring was a fine reporter, accurate and fair, who took on the most routine assignments willingly and made the most of them.

There are only a few advance glimpses of devices Ring later used, but they are worth noting. By July, 1906, he felt comfortable enongh in his job to slip colloquial speech into his stories: "The score at the time was 4 to 2—us had the 4 and them the 2." He made more and more frequent efforts at humor, though most of them were strained and long-winded; he had not yet learned how to deliver a laugh quickly, and the offhanded style that would become his trademark was a long way away. He also tried his hand at doggerel, though not very successfully:

> *Wait till the sun shines, Angus,*
> *And the field is nice and dry,*
> *We'll play two games on Monday,*
> *You and I.*
> *To Springbrook park we'll wander*
> *When Old Sol is high.*
> *Wait till the sun shines, Anguish,*
> *Bye and bye.*

By the time Ring had been on the job a year, he had made impressive progress. At the end of 1906 he wrote a "Résumé of Sport"

—a year's-end review of local athletic activities—that showed the confidence he felt in himself and provided a look at the sports life of a turn-of-the-century American community:

Looking back over the past year local followers of sport have three things to be thankful for. There were no fake fights pulled off in our midst, the high school football team went through the season with no deaths and only one defeat and the South Bend ball club did not run absolutely last. For the first of these sources of gratefulness, let us extend a vote of heartfelt thanks to the local promoters of pugilism, who have booked very few matches; for the second to the high school team itself for its great and successful fight for the sectional championship; and, for the last, to the Terre Haute club, which absolutely refused to give up its hold on the cellar door.

There are also manifold matters of deep regret to the heart of the true sport lover, but these we will pass over in brief, since it is not good for the heart to be sorrowful at the opening of the new year. For one thing, the tennis championship of Navarre Place was never satisfactorily settled. There were innumerable claimants of the honor, as there are of every championship title, but on the showing of all the wielders of the racket north of the bridge, it would be unfair to single out anyone as being superior to his neighbors. The bait casting club has not held its regular meetings for some time and there is really no telling whether or not it has breathed its last. . . .

Rowing races in South Bend are mostly indulged in by teams of opposite sexes, which makes the sport doubly interesting, but precludes the possibility of making public the records. Boat races are numerous on the old St. Joe in the warm summer evenings. . . .

Bowling has made rapid strides during the past twelve-month and is now at its zenith in this city. The formation of the Elks' and Antlers' leagues has done much to bring the sport to its present place of popularity. . . .

Golf has taken its regular place among the summer sports and its advance must be attributed partly to the efforts of Harry S. Turple, who instructs the members of the St. Joseph Valley Country club in the Scotch game. . . .

That chess and checker records are not available is to be regretted. Playing the slot machines was very popular at an earlier season of the year, but has fallen off a trifle within the last two or three weeks. Curling is confined mostly to daintily scented boudoirs, although we have heard some curlers on the street.

The new year Ring thus began was to be among the most important of his life, though there was no sign of impending drama for several months. When it happened, however, it happened fast. In July, Ring attended a marshmallow roast on the banks of the St. Joe, where he met Ellis Abbott, a houseguest of his friend Wilma Johnson. His reaction was immediate and emphatic: "I thought: 'It's my affinity who's seated over there.'" He seems to have known almost from the moment he saw her that he wanted to marry her, and he pursued her with single-minded intensity. The next Saturday she came to a baseball game in South Bend, and he managed to exchange a few words with her; on Sunday he and Rex visited the Johnson house, but Billy Beeson was there and Ring had little chance to further his cause. His big opportunity came a few weeks later when he saw her get off a train at the Michigan Central depot; he angled for a chance to talk with her and succeeded, and "bore her gripsack down" to the Johnsons'.

After that, matters moved swiftly—more swiftly, in all likelihood, than Ellis realized. During her visit they took a nocturnal stroll, and "a few days later, years it seemed," Ring went to a picnic in Ellis' hometown of Goshen, Indiana, twenty-five miles east of South Bend. There they had to say farewell, as Ellis was about to leave for her junior year at Smith College, in Northampton, Massachusetts. Ring undertook almost at once to pursue his courtship by mail, and his correspondence with her began in September.

Ellis was from a background remarkably similar to Ring's, which had nothing to do with the initial attraction but undoubtedly helped as flirtation grew into romance. Her father, Frank Parker Abbott, had a prosperous lumbermill in East Chicago, and her mother, Jeannette Hascall Abbott, was both as doggedly optimistic and as poetically inclined as Lena Lardner. The Abbotts had three sons and five daughters, of whom Ellis was the second oldest. Their house in Goshen was substantial and comfortable, and like the Lardner house, it was the center of the children's lives—though they do not seem to have been quite so rigidly confined as were the young Lardners. The Abbotts also had a vacation cottage at Lake Wawasee, fifteen miles to the south, where they spent their summers.

Ellis was two years younger than Ring and about a foot shorter. She had a lively, lovely face and an appealing figure with, at that time, just a hint of pleasing plumpness. She was bright and fun-loving, but according to Ring Lardner, Jr., she lacked confidence in herself intellectually, even though her Smith education put her several rungs ahead of Ring on that ladder. Her quick mind and sense of humor plainly appealed to Ring as much as her good looks, for their courtship was conducted almost entirely through the mails and a woman of lesser intelligence could not have held his attention for so long.

If Ring had stayed in South Bend, the courtship would have been entirely different, for Ring would have been able to press his case in person during Ellis' vacations. But he did not stay in South Bend because he felt the stirrings of a desire previously undetected in him: ambition. He developed an urge "to quit South Bend and get a job on a paper in Chicago or New York," and he found unexpected assistance in the person of his friend Phil Jacks, Arthur's brother, who somehow knew Hugh S. Fullerton, chief baseball writer for the Chicago *Examiner*.

Fullerton was a good-natured fellow, a bit of a windbag but bearably so, who had achieved a considerable reputation by predicting the outcome of the 1906 World Series. The Cubs were overwhelmingly favored that year against the "Hitless Wonders" of the White Sox, but Fullerton wrote an advance story arguing that the White Sox would win by four games to two; he even named the scores by which he expected the White Sox to win. He was working then for the *Tribune*, and its editors refused to print the story. Fullerton, however, was right about the final outcome if not the precise scores, and at the end of the Series the embarrassed editors printed his story with an apology and an affidavit testifying to the date the story was written. The incident made Fullerton a minor celebrity and, some sports writers have argued, he coasted on it for the rest of his career.

Ring took his vacation in October, during the World Series between the Cubs and the Tigers, and went to Chicago. Phil Jacks took him to the *Examiner*, introduced him to Fullerton and left him to his own devices. Ring was put to the test at once:

> " 'There was a little chicken lived down on the farm.' " Thus Hughey opened on me.
>
> I gazed at him in bewilderment.
>
> 'The next line," he went on, "is 'Do you think another drink would do us any harm.' "

I was going to be careful. "I can't have another, because I haven't had one."

"Don't you ever have one?" asked Hughey.

"No," I said.

"Phil,' said Hughey sadly, "gave me to understand on the phone last night that you wanted to get a job in the sporting department of some paper here."

"I do," said I, "but I guess there isn't much chance."

"I'm afraid not," said Hughey. "There's one opening in town that might lead into a baseball job, but 'Do you think another drink would do us any harm?' "

My slow-motion Michigan mind began to function. "Is there any place we could get one—I mean, in this neighborhood?"

"If there weren't, why would we have our office in this neighborhood?"

So Ring and Fullerton went off to a saloon and Ring, suddenly anxious to demonstrate his prowess at the bar, knocked down a good amount of bourbon, "several big shots in small glasses, straight and neat." The results were felicitous. The whiskey "did away with my innate reticence," and Ring began to talk, "intelligently and in regular baseball idiom, which is the same in a Class B league as in the minors," about the likely major-leaguers then playing in the Central League. Fullerton liked him enormously, took him to the White Sox ball park, and introduced him to Charles A. Comiskey, saying, "I'm going to find a job for this boy in somebody's sporting department. He's been writing baseball on the South Bend *Times* for two years, but he isn't as sappy as that sounds."

Fullerton arranged a seat for Ring in the press box at the West Side Ball Park, where the Cubs then played, and the two ended up spending the entire Series together, traveling by train to Detroit and back:

It was a whole week since I had met Hughey, and all through that week I must have been pretty much of a pest. Not since our first day together had he mentioned "job," and I was growing nervous. But in the rain-soaked, tremulous press coop at Detroit, I was introduced to Frank B.—alias Duke—Hutchinson in the following speeches:

HUGHEY: Here's your man. I turn him over to you.

DUKE: With reluctance?

HUGHEY: With more baseball sense than you've got.

DUKE: That's damning with faint praise. But it isn't important right now. (*To me*): Do you know any football?

ME: I played it in high school, and I've seen it played often by Michigan——

DUKE (*interrupting*): That's enough. (*To Hughey*): Does he know what paper he's going to work for and what salary he's going to get?

HUGHEY: The paper is the *Inter-Ocean* and the salary is eighteen-fifty a week.

Ring pointed out that he was getting $15 in South Bend (the *Times* had given him a raise) but he was not about to haggle over salary. He accepted the position, returned to South Bend and told the Stolls he was leaving. They were not especially eager to see him go, having put considerable time and energy into developing his talents, but there obviously was no way to hold on to him, and they had the consoling presence of J. P. McEvoy, Ring's recently hired assistant, who was able enough to handle the job.

"The real requiem," as Ring recalled it, was held on Bond Street. Lena Lardner knew that unlike Ring's previous forays into Chicago, "this time . . . I was going for good." She put up some resistance, but it consisted primarily of insisting that Ring board with "an eminently respectable Episcopal lady in reduced circumstances" who would feed him nourishing meals and keep him out of mischief. He agreed, though with a palpable lack of enthusiasm. In November he moved to Chicago.

It was a beginning, but inevitably it was also an end. Ring would return to Niles over and over in the years to come, and he would write about it with unflagging affection, but he would never again truly be a part of it. The regularity and insularity of life in a small town are such that once one breaks away from its daily rhythms, a permanent severance is effected. But more than Niles was coming to a close for Ring. A way of life was ending, the gentler life of turn-of-the-century upper-class America. It was a life shaded by parasols, a life lived to the peaceful pace of a paddle-wheel steamer idly inching its way across a lake, a life frozen brightly on a wall by the lamp of a magic lantern.

Ellis knew that life as well as Ring did. One spring evening in

1910 she wrote him a letter which, in a few words casually and hastily set down, somehow summarizes everything that was vanishing:

> Helen and I went on a nice little bat this afternoon. We took a book, a box of strawberries and some sugar and walked way out in the woods, down by the river. Then Helen read out loud while I ate strawberries. Everything is beautiful and green.

Part Three

A Courtship

*"This letter seems to be
nothing but a railroad guide.
If we save all the time tables
we have needed in the last
eight or nine months, we will
have a nice start for a library."*

F

ROM THE FALL OF 1907 TO THE SUMMER OF 1911, RING CARRIED out an arduous and delicate balancing act. On the one hand he was a rising young newspaperman, ambitious and extraordinarily hard-working, on the road much of the time with the baseball and football teams he covered. On the other hand he was conducting, almost exclusively by mail, an increasingly passionate courtship, one with its full share of emotional heights and depths. It is remarkable enough that he managed to pursue both career and romance under such trying circumstances. It is even more remarkable that he emerged from this long trial wholly successful in both endeavors: he acquired a solid record of professional achievement, with a small taste of the national recognition that would later be his, and he got the girl.

The courtship was carried out under the rules of the class and time to which both Ring and Ellis belonged, and those rules were rigid. Each tiny step toward the final goal was taken in a fever of anticipation and a throb of accomplishment. Each smile had its own intonation, each letter's salutation was heavy with meaning, each encounter was measured over and over in retrospect, each glance was weighed for undiscovered gains or losses. These matters took time, so there was nothing especially unusual in the nearly four years that elapsed between the first meeting of Ring and Ellis and their marriage. Whether it was in fact a disadvantage for Ring, the pursuer, to court Ellis largely by mail is by no means certain, for the shyness that steadily crept over him as he grew older was less evident on paper than in the flesh, and he was able to state his ardor in his letters with a passion that cannot but have impressed his intended.

The record of the courtship is voluminous, consisting of some seven hundred letters. The seriousness of Ring's purpose from the outset is emphasized by the doggedness with which he saved all of Ellis' letters, even her most trivial and noncommittal post-cards. Ordinarily Ring saved nothing (when Maxwell Perkins put together Ring's first Scribner short-story collection he had a devil of a time tracking down copies of the stories) but he held on tight to every snippet from Ellis.

There is a distinct and not very surprising pattern to the correspondence, beginning with flirtatious playfulness and becoming more and more serious as each new piece of romantic territory was seized. In the early stages not a great deal seemed to be at stake, and Ring and Ellis attempted to impress each other by amusing each other. Later there were more momentous matters under consideration—a father to be beseeched, a wedding date to be set, an apartment to be rented—and the letters took on a tone of deeper intensity. The early letters, however, are delightful, full of spunk and sass and high spirits.

From the beginning Ellis knew how to get Ring's goat, and she obviously enjoyed doing so. In December, 1907, at home for the holidays, she flung him a hint of the high life she was leading: "This is the very day of our very wonderful dance and, oh, we are *very* busy—even to talk to Ringling any longer." But as the romance grew more serious, she used her skill at teasing to let him know how much progress he was making. A year later he wrote: "And remember, Rabbit, leap year is drawing to a close. Remember, I am as shy as a kitten, but ready and eager to jump at an opportunity when it is presented in the right spirit." She replied: "I am deeply indebted to you for your suggestion or rather caution concerning leap year. Perhaps if you would tell me what the right spirit is I might see that someone presented you with the required opportunity"—a reply which was deliberately coy and evasive, but which also made clear the tantalizing possibility that she really was interested in his advances. Another year later, in a lovely sentence, she granted him still further ground: "Yes, dear, I do mind if you call me dear and I won't have it, dear." Her banter usually focused on their romance, but from time to time she dropped in a wholly irrelevant tidbit that made happily evident why Ring was so taken with her:

   . . . You know I am teaching Sunday school class and I am such a little heathen myself that I am scared to death for fear I'll shatter some of their most particular beliefs. We had a wild discussion, yesterday, about Jesus casting out the evil spirts and their entering into the herd of swine. The only conclusion we came to was that it was an awful waste when pigs are so very, very expensive.

Throughout the correspondence, both Ring and Ellis did their share of complaining. When a romance is carried out by mail, the frequency of letters invariably becomes an issue, and Ring constantly grouched that he was getting the short end of it:

My last letter must have reached you last Tuesday. You answered it Saturday night. You waited five days when you knew two days was or were too long to suit me. You don't show any consideration for me. You needn't tell me the old busy stuff. I know the two reasons you don't write more promptly—1—You don't want to— 2—You know you exasperate me by delaying.

What they complained about most, however, was just plain bad luck. In their efforts to see each other, they were at the mercy of Ring's baseball schedule and the timetables of the various railroads upon which they depended. In June, 1908, for example, there was the possibility of a meeting, as Ring outlined it:

Here are a lot of ifs:
If we get out of New York on a certain train Thursday night and if the said train remains on time, we will arrive in Goshen before six o'clock Friday evening. If we do, I shall get off said train and seek a telephone. If I find one, I shall call up your domicile. If you are away, I shall board the interruben and hasten to Niles. Remember, you are not to change your programme one particle on account of this conditional statement.
The chances are 37 to 1 against the deal's going through according to schedule.

He was right, and a clearly disappointed Ellis saw the missed opportunity as an omen:

. . . Do you know I think you and I are doomed to just miss each other through the rest of life. When I visit Johnny [Wilma Johnson in Niles] this summer you will come home the day I leave and when I am in Chicago you will leave the day I come. Isn't it tragic—and I long to see you so! I have a vision that when you are on your

honeymoon I will dash past you in an automobile and toot my horn.
Will you watch for me?

They saw each other so rarely that even with the pictures they
gazed at daily—pictures wrung from each other after elaborate
negotiations—each must have forgotten what the other looked
like. Telephone conversations were rare, so much so that at one
point Ellis complained: "There! I forgot who I was talking to and
what I was talking about. But, you know, you can't expect one to
keep up a *very* exciting correspondence on one conversation a
year—and *that* over the telephone." By the fall of 1910 Ring felt
as though he had become a prisoner of all the trains that never
seemed to get one or the other of them to the right place at the
right time: "This letter seems to be nothing but a railroad guide.
If we save all the time tables we have needed in the last eight or
nine months, we will have a nice start for a library."

No one who has not courted by mail can fully appreciate all
the excruciating subtleties and nuances involved. The slightest
change in a salutation or conclusion can shake the earth, so it was
with the utmost care that Ring moved from "Dear Rabbit" (Rabbit
being a play on Abbott) to "Bright Cherry Blossom" to "Love of
My Life" to "Possessor of My Soul." The transition from "Yours"
to "As Ever" in Ellis' letters must have thrilled him, for "As Ever"
in those days bordered on an endearment. Not for a moment were
these changes casual; they were undertaken only after the most
deliberate consideration of their potential impact—one must not
seem to rush ahead too hastily, yet neither must one seem laggardly.

But such questions were a long way off in the fall of 1907. Ellis
was busy with her studies at Smith, and Ring was making two
huge adjustments, from Niles to Chicago and from the South
Bend *Times* to the *Inter-Ocean*. It is hard to say which transition
was greater or more difficult, though Ring took both in stride.

CHICAGO IN 1907 WAS A CITY of incredible vigor, wealth, diversity,
filth, poverty, inventiveness and degradation. It was the heart of
the heart of the country, a booming city of nearly 2 million that
was the rail center of the nation. Its slaughterhouses fed America;
a year before Ring's arrival the nation had been shocked by *The
Jungle,* a horrifying depiction of the meat industry by Upton Sinclair, one of the young "muckrakers" who found Chicago an

especially inviting target for investigative reporting. Its architects, notably Louis Sullivan, were developing the first truly American urban style, one that emphasized efficiency, economy and sturdiness of construction but did not slight ornamentation.

Its downtown streets were packed with pedestrians and horses and cable cars and horseless carriages. "The city is fearfully busy at all of its corners," one observer wrote a few years later. "New Yorkers shudder at Thirty-fourth street and Broadway. Inside the Chicago loop are several dozen Thirty-fourth streets and Broadways. . . . It is no laughing matter to folks who have to thread it. Trolley cars, automobiles, taxicabs, the long lumbering 'buses that remind one of the photographs of Broadway, a quarter of a century ago or more, entangle themselves with one another and with unfortunate pedestrians and still no one comes forward with practical relief." To the north of downtown, along the Gold Coast, the widowed Mrs. Potter Palmer held sway over high society; she was a lively Kentuckian with the endearingly folksy name of Bertha. To the southwest another formidable woman was dominant: Jane Addams of Hull House, the conscience of Chicago, the tough reformer who described conditions in the city's slums bluntly and powerfully: "The streets are inexpressibly dirty, the number of schools inadequate, sanitary legislation unenforced, the street lighting bad, the paving miserable and altogether lacking in the alleys and smaller streets, and the stables foul beyond description. Hundreds of houses are unconnected with the street sewer. The older and richer inhabitants seem anxious to move away as rapidly as they can afford it. They make room for newly arrived immigrants who are densely ignorant of civic duties." Only a mile and a half to the southeast of Hull House lay another world, that of the Levee, a sinkhole of crime and political corruption that had as its chief ornament the Everleigh Club, a world-famous whorehouse.

The corruption that permitted the Everleighs to flourish was everywhere; from the bottom of the ward system to the top of City Hall, everything stank. Reform campaigns came and went, and from time to time achieved brief success, but the odor of political thievery remained—providing a never-ending source of news for the city's press, which seized gleefully upon each new outrage. The papers also went gleefully after each other, in some of the most violent circulation wars the country has ever known—

wars which endangered the health and even the lives of distributors, and which placed a primary emphasis in the newsrooms not on depth or accuracy of coverage but on sensation.

In the competition between Chicago's four morning papers—the others were the *Tribune*, the *Record-Herald* and the *Examiner*—the *Inter-Ocean* ran a poor fourth, even though it had a circulation of around 100,000. It had been founded in 1872 as an organ of the Republican Party with the unequivocal slogan, "Republican in everything, independent in nothing." But by 1907 it was in weak financial condition; Ring soon found that "we were on our last limbs, and the issuance of weekly pay checks was always followed by a foot-race downstairs to the bank; the theory being that only the first five or six to reach the paying teller's cage would land in the money." Still, the *Inter-Ocean* gave him a start in Chicago journalism, and in his brief stay there he established himself firmly.

Ring was put right to work, which quickly gave him what he wanted: an excuse to escape the confines of his genteel boarding-house. He went on to a schedule that required him to report to the office in the early afternoon and kept him there "until two or three o'clock in the morning, leaving only for a hurried dinner or to cover an assignment or two." He pointed out to his landlady that he would thus be unable to join her at the dinner table and would be coming in at late hours, whereupon she agreed that he would be better off elsewhere. So he found a room at North State and Goethe, "ate in terrible restaurants," and was much happier. Soon he began to share a room with his colleague Richard G. Tobin, the assistant to the sports editor, and the two became close friends. Ring took Tobin to Niles for a visit, which led to many more: in October, 1908, Tobin married Ring's sister Anne. Ring also apparently persuaded the *Inter-Ocean* to hire Rex, establishing a pattern that would continue throughout his life. Rex, four years older than Ring, was an able journalist—many people in Niles thought he was the one in the Lardner family who would go places—but he did not have much of what is now known as self-starting power, and he followed Ring from job to job with good-natured pliability. Ultimately, when Ring became famous and influential, he was able to help Rex hold responsible magazine positions by selling his own work exclusively to Rex—and if he felt

Rex was mistreated by an employer, he would take his stories, and
Rex, elsewhere.

Ring began by covering Chicago high school football; he also
made a trip to Lake Forest to observe the practices of the most
famous team in college football history, the Carlisle Indians, and
interview their equally famous coach, Pop Warner, who told him
to keep an eye on "a man named Thorpe." That Saturday, Ring
saw Carlisle play the University of Chicago (which had its own
legendary coach, Amos Alonzo Stagg) and win 17 to 0, with Jim
Thorpe in the starring role. In December and January, Ring covered the hot-stove league, making daily visits to the local baseball
people: Charles Murphy of the Cubs, Charlie Comiskey of the
White Sox, American League President Ban Johnson, and whatever ballplayers he could find in their "haunts"—for which read
"saloons." He would "pick up what news there was, and write
something, whether there was news or not."

His winter beat also included wrestling (which was "the same
old bowl of cherries" that it is now), indoor track, swimming and
boxing (which was outlawed in Chicago and therefore was held
in Wisconsin). He covered basketball once, "a ghastly affair between Yale and the Central Y.M.C.A. of Chicago," hated it with
a passion and later was "proud to state that never since that evening
have I consciously been within a block of an armory or gymnasium
where basket ball was scheduled."

Ring's writing was conventional and predictable. He was in
what amounted to a trial, and his principal concern was to do his
work accurately and thoroughly. That he did, writing straightforward news stories and giving them "life" with the overblown
language expected by his editor. For his professional future, what
he did at the *Inter-Ocean* was probably of less moment than the
journalistic friends he made, principal among them the three most
prominent Chicago baseball writers of the time: Hugh Fullerton,
I. E. (Sy) Sanborn and Charles Dryden. Though Fullerton's effect
on his rise to local prominence was most immediate, it was Dryden who had the greatest influence on his writing style. Dryden
was a witty, irreverent writer (as much, perhaps, as Ring he
deserves credit for founding the "aw nuts" school of sports writing)
who achieved a kind of immortality by describing Washington as
"first in war, first in peace, and last in the American League," and

Ed Walsh of the White Sox as the "only man in the world who can strut sitting down." It is easy to see why Ring admired Dryden's work and why he may have consciously imitated it. Here is Dryden at his best:

> TAMPA, FLA., March 9—Just as the golden orb of day burnished the pellucid waters of Tampa Bay (print this at top of column, next to pure reading matter) the Cubs departed on board a flat little steamboat to play a team of soldiers forty miles away. This sure was tough luck, for we had just arrived to do some regular experting, the first of the season, and were too late to grab the steamer. Our notion of nothing to expert is the tail end of a steamboat wiggling down a wine-colored creek. Charley Williams and the noble athletes in his charge offered to heave us a line from the deck to the dock, but when a fellow has his Sunday clothes on for the first time in five months he feels too dignified to take roughhouse chances. . . .
>
> We might have started experting on the boat this morning but for the difficulties of getting to this camp. From Ocean Springs, Miss., to Tampa, Fla., as the sea gull flies is 300 miles. To get here we traveled 900 miles by rail, making three complete circuits of 300 miles each over a nervous landscape that rose up and sifted through the coach windows and down a fellow's back for a period of two nights and one day. That certainly was going some, believe us. Having paid first-class fare all the way, it is proper to criticise the nervous landscape and flea-bitten aspect of things en route. . . .

Dryden, Fullerton, Sanborn and Ring's other journalistic friends frequented Stillson's saloon, which was where Ring often could be found after work. But drinking in the company of newspaper people was not his only nocturnal diversion. He went regularly to vaudeville and the theater, and in the fall of 1907 he saw the first of Flo Ziegfeld's *Follies*, which had gone on the road and was having a great success. Ring enjoyed it hugely: "Some of us had seen the show during its Chicago run—you could buy a balcony seat then for a dollar or so—and had adjudged it the best all-around entertainment ever given in a theater, which, at that time, it probably was. Flo was just as prodigal with girls, costumes and scenery . . . as he is today [1932], and his comedy was unbelievably better."

Ring did not brag to Ellis about his swift rise through Chicago journalism, but neither did he fail to provide information from which she could infer that he was doing well. In January, 1908, scarcely two months after he reported to work at the *Inter-Ocean*, he wrote: "I think the Chicago *American* is going to want me soon, strange as it may seem. And if the opportunity comes, I am going to take it, because the reasons why I should outnumber and outweigh the reasons why I should not. This latter class consists almost entirely of my innate aversion to the sheet." Why he disliked the *American* is not clear—it was a Hearst newspaper, published in the afternoon—but the reason he gave for leaning toward accepting the position was that "it will give me one or two journeys through the East during the coming Spring and Summer," journeys which he hoped would enable him to visit Northampton. Other reasons for looking favorably on the *American* were the unstable condition of the *Inter-Ocean* and the prospect that the rich Hearst organization would improve his pay.

When opportunity knocked, on February 1, Hearst was the knocker, but in the person of his six-year-old morning paper, the *Examiner*. Its sports editor was Harry Shroudenbach and its star reporter was Fullerton, who was "hibernating" prior to heading south with the world-champion Cubs for spring training. Shroudenbach offered Ring $25 a week, an increase of $6.50 over his *Inter-Ocean* salary, and just as important the security and prestige of working for a fiercely competitive newspaper that was giving the *Tribune* all it could handle in the brutal fight for morning domination.

Shroudenbach stuck Ring on the sports desk, where his most time-consuming task was to write "startling, pretty, perfectly fitting headlines of an intricacy which still makes me shiver in retrospect." They were in the shape of triangles with the base on top:

GOTCH BREAKS BEALL'S
FOOT WITH TOE HOLD
AS RECORD CROWD
AT COLISEUM
GOES STARK
MAD

Writing one of those a night, Ring felt, was manageable, but "when you had to tear off four or six, with a two-minute limit for each, you were ready to spend your off day seeking oblivion." That is what he was doing one day off, a Monday, in the saloons of the South Side, and the treatment he gave his numbed mind was so successful that before long he was told it was Tuesday afternoon and time to go to work. He got there to find a note informing him that the other members of the staff had gone en masse to Milwaukee for a boxing match. All three of the departed staffers were good boxing writers, and all three were going to send in their copy piece by piece: "I would have to figure out whose stuff was whose and keep it all straightened out." Ring did not save the results, though he later wished he had, but from memory he was able to reconstruct a whimsical facsimile:

> The boys were called to the center of the ring and received instructions from William Hale Thompson, Ernest Byfield, Percy Hammond, Charles Richter, the Spring Valley Thunderbolt tore in as if he had never heard another crowd made the trip as guests of William Lydon on his yatch the Lydonia Steve cut loose with a left uppercut that nearly this makes certain another meeting between the Battling Nelson and Packey McFarland were also introduced. Steve slipped as he was about to. Seven special trains but the majority thought the round was even it was Papke's round.

When the first edition reached the main copy desk "it was greeted with such hilarity that even I woke up and took the advice of a reporter friend who told me to get out of the office before the Milwaukee train bearing my boss and his colleagues arrived back in town." He sought out his friend Walter Eckersall, the erstwhile University of Chicago football star who had become a sports writer for the *Tribune*; Eckie consoled him and sent him home in a taxi. But Ring did not go to bed. Instead he got another taxi and went off on another tour of Chicago, an account of which "would be extremely dull, even if I were able to recall any of the details." Eventually he ended up at the *Examiner* building, crocked out of his mind, and, as he later recalled (probably hyperbolically), with a $132 reading on the meter—$130.20 more than he had. None other than Shroudenbach met him at the door, settled with the cabdriver, told Ring he was not fired, and sent him home with the promise that on Thursday "we'll start over." Much later Ring learned that Eckersall "had pleaded my cause for hours and had even gone to his own boss, Harvey Woodruff, of the *Tribune*, and persuaded him to make room for me in the event I got the air from the *Examiner*."

Shortly thereafter Ring was given the "James Clarkson" convenience by-line assignment to cover the White Sox, and he sent his private correspondents "The Route of Ringlets." The reply he presently received from Ellis must have given him a start, for she showed that she could play in his league when it came to versifying. Her letter of March 22 bore no salutation. Under the heading "Extract from the Chicago *Examiner*" it read:

It is rumored about that a poem written by the fair Ellis Abbott of Smith College is about to be published in book form. We consider ourselves very fortunate in being able to print it at this early date. We regret to say that the only adverse criticism we have heard concerning it is that it has a decided tang of the famous bard—namely Ringlets Lardner. The poem is given below . . .

———

The Run of the Rabbit

The Rabbit thanks the Ringlets kind
For thus enlightening her mind
And she would like to do the same
For one who's long been known to fame.
The twenty fifth of March, dear sir,
Northampton sees the last of her.
For she will leave the place at last
And to far Boston journey fast.
From there to Andover she'll go
And there remain 5 days or so.
From April "2" to April "4"
She'll visit West Newton once more.
On April 5th this girl will be
In Merrimac close by the sea
Where she will stay so says her fate
Until of April it is late.
In case you'd like to write, you know
Her addresses are here below.
In Andover of this same state
At 34 Essex till said date;
In Newton (West) at 221
Highland Avenu̱—till visit's done;
In care of Austin Sawyer, sir—

A letter surely would reach her,
While she is at Merri'mac, Mass.
And now it's time for her to pass.

E.A.

The little poem is of interest for considerably more than its sly cleverness. For one thing, in volunteering a detailed itinerary for her spring holiday, Ellis made clear to Ring that she did not want a prolonged interruption in their correspondence; his pursuit, in other words, was beginning to pay off. For another, it does not take much reading between the lines to realize that Ellis was flattered and pleased that she had the attention of a young man who was moving upward so rapidly in Chicago journalism. The newspaper business then had little of the respectability it has since acquired (some would have argued, in fact, that in traveling about in the company of a bunch of disreputable baseball players Ring had merely settled to the level of his own profession) but it did have a certain aura of swashbuckling romance. Too, she must have thought it rather exciting and daring to be writing to a man who was out there in the real world of work, of paychecks and trolleys and diners and saloons, while most of her schoolmates presumably were cultivating the affections of peach-fuzzed naïfs from Amherst and Harvard and Yale.

It is most unlikely, however, that Ring was as sophisticated or worldly as Ellis may have thought him to be. Years later Hugh Fullerton described Ring in that spring of 1908: "What a season for a young and vitally interested kid to break into the business! And Ring Lardner, despite his pretense of indifference and sophistication, was just a green country boy trying to pretend. An odd sort of youth he was then. Although he pretended to be hard-boiled and indifferent to criticism, he was one of the most sensitive fellows I have ever known and sometimes his feelings remained hurt for weeks at a time." The ballplayers seem to have sensed this in him too, for though his reticence puzzled them, they liked him greatly and were far more relaxed around him than they were around most reporters; they called him "Lard" or, this being a time when rough men often nicknamed each other in honor of their hometowns, "Niles." Ed Reulbach, the former Notre Dame pitcher who was a Cubs star in 1909, described him to Donald Elder:

We often tried to make Ring break into a full laugh, but all we developed was a faint smile. Sometimes he would sit at the window of the train and stare out for a long time, if you sat down beside him he would greet you but never say another word, unless you forced him to answer a question.

Ring was a kindly fellow, modest, intelligent on the fine points of the game, always careful about writing something that might hurt the feelings of a player, and we responded by tipping him off to some inside deal and he was always appreciative.

We were all fond of Ring, but we were all at a loss as to why he never laughed. . . . If he had any faults, we liked him too much to notice them, he was one of us.

This silence of Ring's is a mystery, doubly so since he was not shy or silent as a child. Its sources can be guessed at, but only that. His shyness and his aristocratic aloofness have already been mentioned. In the summer of 1908, pure insecurity may have had something to do with it; for years his "real and only ambition was to associate with big league ball players," and now he was doing that—so he may in some degree simply have been awed into silence. Yet dime-store psychologizing of this sort is far less fruitful than what appears to be the simple truth: he was laconic, a listener rather than a talker.

That quality, combined with his innate decency, served both a White Sox player and himself that season. He never told the player's name (and in fact the mystery has been unsuccessfully puzzled over by countless amateur sleuths), but gave him the alias of Jack Gibbs, disguising him as a "regular infielder" who "had been graduated from college—*cum laude*—at the age of four, and everybody on the club knew that he could neither read nor write." Gibbs attempted to disguise this deficiency, but it showed in countless ways; he would peruse a menu, for example, and "after a long and careful study, order steak and baked potato, or ham and eggs, or both." Ring, sensing both Gibbs's embarrassment and his boredom with such limited cuisine, began mumbling menus out loud as he looked them over, and soon Gibbs was making a point of sitting near him at meals.

Gibbs took the relationship one step further when he heard Ring typing and asked if, as "a kind of a joke," he would type up a reply to a letter he had received from his wife, Myrtle. He wheedled Ring into reading Myrt's letter out loud: "It said, in effect: 'How can you expect me to meet you in Chicago unless you send me some money? I don't intend to make the trip out there on a freight, and I don't want to get my feet all blisters walking.' " Ring asked him what he wanted to tell Myrt, and he replied:

> "Well, I guess you better tell her where we are first. No. Start out this way: 'Dear Myrt.' And then tell her she knows damn well I don't get no pay till the last of April, and nothing then because I already drawed ahead. Tell her to borrow off Edith von Driska, and she can pay her back the first of May. Tell her I never felt better in my life and looks like I will have a great year, if they's nothing to worry me like worrying about money. Tell her the weather's been great, just like summer, only them two days it rained in Birmingham. It rained a couple days in Montgomery and a week in New Orleans. My old souper feels great. Detroit is the club we got to beat—them and Cleveland and St. Louis, and maybe the New York club. Oh, you know what to tell her. You know what they like to hear."

He may not have known what the ballplayers' girls and wives liked to hear, but he certainly knew what the ballplayers liked to say—and how they said it. In recounting the story years later Ring may or may not have embellished it (how, for example, did Myrtle Gibbs learn that Jack wanted her to meet him in Chicago?) but the essential point is absolutely accurate: that Ring found, on that first trip with the White Sox, the ballplayer who would become Jack Keefe and the language that would become *You Know Me Al.*

The regular season turned out to be unexpectedly exciting, sometimes in peculiar ways: "The season opened with Detroit at the Sox park, the park at Thirty-ninth street, where every day was a thriller to the reporters, for if the game failed to prove exciting there was always the possibility that the press box would leave the grand stand and carry us to Kenwood or the Stockyards." The Sox, scorned by all in the spring, put on a mighty rush all season long. Ed Walsh, the big right-hander, had one of the great seasons in pitching history: forty victories and only fifteen losses, 454 innings pitched, 269 strikeouts and an astonishing earned-run average of 1.42. Doc White, the lefty, won nineteen games and Ring's enduring friendship; the two discovered a mutual love of music and began a songwriting collaboration, with Ring providing the lyrics and White the music. At the end of the season it came down to one game against the Indians, on October 2. Ed Walsh pitched magnificently, permitting only four hits and striking out fifteen. But Addie Joss of Cleveland was better: he pitched a perfect game. The White Sox lost, 1 to 0. Ring was crushed. He rarely said much in his letters to Ellis about baseball, but this time he wrote:

> My poor ball team lost out on the last day of the season, when most of us expected it to cop. I am almost over the shock, but have resolved to quit the national pastime, i.e. baseball, forever.

The only surviving copies of the *Examiner* for 1908 have disappeared; a file of the paper that was owned by the Los Angeles Public Library was sold to a private collector who has not been identified, and no other copies are known to exist. So nothing can be said about Ring's journalistic development during that exciting and generally happy year except that when it was over, he had done well enough for the *Examiner* as James Clarkson to be invited to join the *Tribune* as R. W. Lardner. Charlie Dryden was leaving the *Tribune*, and he recommended that Ring replace him. A substantial raise of $10 a week was offered, to $35, and Ring accepted it. He was still only twenty-three years old, and he was already at the top in Chicago sports journalism.

He was elated, and he hastened to tell Ellis the good news. He did so by writing a poem:

> *And what is it, pray, this Chicago Tribune?*
> *Which Ringlets is gone to work on so soon?*
> *This is a paper that's gen'rally rated the best*
> *In North, or in South, or in East, or in West.*
> *And better than best it is quite sure to be*
> *When it has the services of Bright Young Me.*
> *I can't just yet tell you what I am to write,*
> *Whether checkers, or football, or racing, or fight.*
> *The chances are, Rabbit, I'll write not a thing*
> *Till winter has yielded once more to the spring.*
> *There'll be headlines, of course, and I'll send you a sheet*
> *With each little task marked in pencil so neat;*
> *I know this will please you, my innocent dove,*

In return for which act, as proof of your love
Devoted and grand, you must send out to me
Whatever that day's lesson happens to be,
And thus I can judge which is working the harder,
Miss Ellis, the Rabbit, or Ringlets, the Larder.

The *Tribune* had not actually gotten around to proclaiming itself "The World's Greatest Newspaper" (that extravagant claim was first made in a promotional advertisement in 1910, and was put into the page-one masthead in 1911) but its institutional cockiness was in rapid ascent. The paper was in a period of steady growth, even though it was also in a period of transition; Joseph Medill, who controlled it for forty-four years, had died in 1899, and it was not until 1911 that Colonel Robert McCormick would take over. Its circulation had been a mere 80,000 at the turn of the century, but it was moving toward a half million, and despite the serious challenge of the *Examiner*, had established clear leadership in the morning competition. It had a building at Madison and Dearborn, a couple of blocks from Marshall Field's huge department store. The editor was James Keeley, a legendary figure in Chicago journalism whose hell-bent-for-leather style helped shape the *Front Page* aura of the newsroom. The managing editor, Edward S. Beck, on the other hand, was "courteous, cultured, intelligent, hard-working, unassuming, beloved by his staff." The "sporting editor" was Harvey Woodruff, the sports-page cartoonist was Clare Briggs, and Hugh E. Keough wrote a daily column of humor and commentary; it had been established in 1904 as "Sidelights on Sports," then as "Some Off Side Plays," and finally as "In the Wake of the News." The column was already a Chicago institution, in large measure due to the admirable qualities of its author. When Keough died in 1913, Fullerton paid him this tribute: "Broad, liberal and forgiving toward human frailties; understanding and giving quick sympathy, he was tolerant toward everything save sham and hypocrisy." The other notable *Tribune* columnist was Bert Leston Taylor, whose "A Line o' Type or Two" published uplifting poetry by readers—Lena Lardner was one of them—and folksy, sentimental commentary. B.L.T., as Taylor was generally known, was Midwestern corn through and through, but was held in high affection by his fellow journalists and was respected for his professional diligence. In its news pages the *Tribune* was brassy and sensationalistic, and it was known at times to place its rigid Republicanism ahead of the facts. Editorially it was isolationist, chauvinistic and simplistic.

That mattered not in the least to Ring, who could not have cared less about his employer's politics. He was happy to be on if not the best newspaper in Chicago, certainly the most prominent, and his private life had also taken a turn for the better. His sister Anne married Dick Tobin in October; when they set up housekeeping in Chicago, Ring and Rex joined them. That arrangement may seem excessively cozy now, but it needs to be kept in mind that the three youngest Lardners were unusually close and that Tobin quickly became "family" in the truest sense. There is not a scintilla of evidence that the presence of two bachelor boarders had any ill effects on the Tobins' marriage, which was long and happy.

For the first several months he was on the *Tribune*, Ring apparently did desk work; he did not get his first by-line until March, 1909. He had a daily routine, which he described to Ellis:

> And as for me, what have I done? Arisen daily at the noon hour, breakfasted, gone to town, wished for dinner, labored, come home at two of the clock, retired, dreamed of elusive Rabbits, awakened, arisen at the same hour, with only five pictures of said elusive R. and a map of Massachusetts nearby to comfort me. Infrequently, missives arrive from said E.R. as a ray of sunshine through the mist of winter clouds.

Then, in March, his routine changed sharply: he went on the road with the Cubs, the world champions, and with his own by-line. This, along with spring training the next year, was when he picked up much of the material that became "Pullman Pastimes." It was also the beginning of the real development of his journalistic style. He was to be with the *Tribune* for two years, and the evolution of that style would be very slow, yet in his first spring-training trip it was already emerging. The Cubs trained in West Baden, Indiana, a small mineral-springs resort near French Lick, then moved on to Arkansas. As early as March he found he could get away with some gentle fun at the players' expense, even a personage as formidable as Frank Chance:

Doc McKinlock came here for the purpose of taking care of Chance's wounded foot, but the pesky pedal extremity refused to get sore, and the Peerless Leader objects to having it examined until there is something the matter with it again. He played five innings on Little Rock's rock diamond, and the foot never knew it was in the game.

His style generally was leaner, less self-conscious, more inventive: "pesky pedal extremity" is a nice turn of phrase, not merely a sports-page cliché. Woodruff was a demanding but tolerant editor who recognized a lively talent when he saw one and then gave it maximum freedom to develop. He was also a sensible editor who knew that reporters can get too close to the teams they cover, so throughout the season he switched Ring and Sy Sanborn back and forth between the Cubs and the Sox. No matter which team he covered, Ring was expected to file a daily story of about 1,500 words. The story had to tell the reader what happened in the game, so to a degree it had to be both chronological and detailed, but Ring was free to be whimsical and frequently was. He was also free to be frank: "Sometimes ball games are played in which there is so little of interest that it is extremely difficult to tell the tale. Yesterday's combat on the south side was one of them." In addition to his stories he filed a gossipy sidebar called "Notes of the Cubs" or "Notes of the White Sox," in which he had a chance to be funny or irreverent or just pleasantly trivial:

A Chicago bug said to Evers after the game, "I'd have murdered you if we'd lost that one." "You wouldn't have had the chance," replied Johnny. "I would have done the job myself."

———

President Comiskey was not in attendance. He took his wife and son Louis to St. Joseph, Mich., for the baths.

———

Cap. Zeider had only two chances at second after he went in. He limped perceptibly, but tried not to.

In May, Ring's duties took him East, to Boston—and, at last, to Northampton. He reached the Smith campus on a Sunday, found his way to Washburn House, and met Ellis. They went for a walk, during which for some reason she took him around the grounds of the nearby Northampton Insane Hospital. They returned to the campus, where they chatted for an hour "till the tinkler tinked for supper"; Ring was not permitted to stay and spent "the longest hour of that shortest of all Sabbaths" at a downtown eatery frequented by Amherst students. After he returned they made a round trip along the Connecticut River to Hatfield, and when they got back to Smith, talked for the last half-hour available to them:

> I admit my chat was chatter,
> Less I knew of what I uttered
> Than a catnip knows 'bout tennis
> So engrossed was I in looking
> At the Rabbit seated near me.

They parted when the Washburn House curfew was rung, but they did not kiss. Their first kiss was still almost a year in the future.

In June, Ellis graduated from Smith. Ring treated the event lightly and with a suggestion of indifference, but Ellis knew it was a milestone and marked it with a letter to her father:

Well! Work is over and in another week college will be a thing of the past. It is after ten o'clock and time I was in bed but I wanted to write this letter to you while I had time. I may not show it, Father, but I want you to know that I do appreciate your sending me to college. I know it has meant giving up other things and I am very, very grateful to you for your thought for us all. I might have done better perhaps but at least I have got my A.B. degree which means four years of more or less hard work and if I never accomplish anything else, I have accomplished one thing at least in this world. That is a good feeling to start on.

Degree in hand, Ellis faced the dilemma of the turn-of-the-century educated woman: whether to attempt to make a career for herself, or at least to do something productive with what she had learned, or to take the accepted course and head with all deliberate speed for matrimony and motherhood. Ring had offered her a chance, making a proposal during his Northampton visit, but she had neither accepted nor rejected him. Instead, she chose what amounted to a middle course, a period of genteel delay spent at home in Goshen pondering her future and giving Ring more chances to improve his prospects. In August she made a visit to Chicago which, by the tone of the subsequent letters, was a great success; Ring took her to a baseball game and introduced her to Rex and the Tobins—all of whom approved her wholeheartedly, and she them. But the most important sign of the speed with which the romance was intensifying took place in October, when Ellis made her first visit to the Lardners in Niles. She wrote to her sister Florence: "Well the latest development is that I am to go over to Niles Monday afternoon, stay for dinner and Ring is to bring me home. Scared? Yes, *just a little.*" But the occasion turned into a triumph, as Ellis described it in a second letter to Florence:

> . . . Monday afternoon at 2:30 I took the car for Niles and expected to get there at 4:30 but missed my car at South Bend and didn't get there until 5:30. Ring and Anna met me at the car. Their house is a *great big* tumbled down old fashioned one. Mr. & Mrs. Lardner, Anna & Dick—that is Mr. Tobin—and Lena and Ring were the only ones there. We really had a *good* dinner. I'm crazy about the whole family. Mrs. Lardner is enormous and queer but very bright & a great talker. Mr. Lardner is an old *dear.*
>
> We spent the evening playing and singing. Ring plays awfully well and played an hour or more. We tried to play authors but he cheated so that we had to stop. I am *crazy* about Anna. She is *great* and was too nice to me for words.
>
> We left on the 9:30 car—we meaning Ring and I—and got home at 11:40. Ring stayed at the Hascall [hotel] and came down here about 9 in the morning and stayed till 12:30 when he took a trolley to Elkhart to go to Chicago. Father took us out in the car and we went for a walk.

Ellis was getting closer and closer to accepting Ring's proposal, but she continued to see other men, however innocently. During the morning of Ring's Goshen visit, she wrote Florence: ". . . you never would guess who called me up—*Hugh Newell!!!*" He asked her to a dance that night, she accepted, and "had an awfully good time." It seems, however, that Newell's call did not unduly discombobulate the ordinarily jealous Ring, who went off to Chicago in a state of euphoria. He wrote Ellis that he had thirty-three days of vacation coming, probably would get much of it after the football season, and hoped to be in Goshen and Niles much of that time—as, their luck on such matters being good for once, he in fact was.

Ring returned to the *Tribune* to spend the autumn covering football, principally games involving colleges in what is now known as the Big Ten. He could look back on a baseball season in which he had established himself as the journalistic equal of Sy Sanborn and in which he had refined his skills impressively. A few paragraphs from a couple of his stories demonstrate the levels he had reached. In one, he was merely having fun:

> DETROIT, MICH., Aug. 17 [Special.]—Jim Scott pitched one of the worst games of his big league career today and beat the Tigers 3 to 2. This may sound paradoxical, or some such word, but it is true nevertheless.
>
> Jim pulled off things that never were seen in polite circles before and we hope never will be again. That he got away with them was due probably to his guardian angel, who was enjoying a vacation while Jim was in the east.
>
> The contest was a funny one—funny to those who were not in it. To those who were it was terribly serious, and fits of rage were as thick as Scott's bases on balls. Those most angered were Eddie Summers and Ownie Bush of the Tigers and Jake Atz and Frank Isbell of the Sox.
>
> Mr. Summers was sore because he thought Umpires Kerin and Connolly were not treating him justly. Mr. Bush's grouch was against Connolly alone. Jakey was peeved at Davy Jones because Davy tried to cut off his legs, so Jake said, and Issy's "madness" was caused by the fact that his foot was bruised by a batted ball which he said hit him and which Umpire Kerin said missed him.

The White Sox were a fifth-place club, and in that story Ring was practicing what he had learned first in South Bend: making something interesting out of an essentially uninteresting situation. In October, on the other hand, he was assigned to the World Series between Pittsburgh and Detroit, and he showed that he could tell a straight story with punch and authority, as well as provide a touch of atmosphere:

> PITTSBURGH, PA., Oct. 8 [Special.]—In the presence of the biggest crowd that ever saw a world's championship ball game, the Pittsburgh National League champions this afternoon took first blood in their series with the Detroit Tigers. The score was 4 to 1.
>
> The Pirates won because they outfielded their western foes and

because they solved [Detroit pitcher] George Mullin just at the right time. . . .

The day was perfect for baseball. After the usual Pittsburgh morning fog the sun came into its own long before play time, and with it thousands of bugs made their appearance. There was a line over six blocks long on Forbes Street, and it was not until almost 2 o'clock that the general admission gates were closed. A scattered few reserved seats in the lowest story of the grand stand were unoccupied. These seats had been sold, so it made no difference in the receipts whether or not they were empty. The two upper decks, the third and first base stands, and the new bleachers stretching all around the field just inside the fences were jammed to their capacity.

In accordance with the national commission's new rule the people were kept off the field, and the players had plenty of room for once in their lives. It was perhaps just as well for the Pirates that this was the case, for it is a certainty at least two long Detroit drives which Leach negotiated would have counted as safeties if the crowd had been allowed to encroach on Tommy's rightful territory.

The throng was handled perfectly. Barring a little trouble in getting the lines of general admission fans out of the way of the reserved seat holders before the hour of starting there was no confusion. There wasn't even a fight to mar the great occasion.

Take away an outdated phrase or two, and that report would be entirely acceptable to any sports editor today—indeed, for overall literacy and perceptiveness, it would shame the efforts of many of those now making a living writing sports. At the end of his first year with the *Tribune*, Ring could lay firm claim to being recognized as a thoroughgoing professional.

When his duties as football correspondent were fulfilled, Ring went off for a round of holiday festivities in Niles and Goshen and an all-out effort to win Ellis's hand. He declined to escort her to Goshen's annual Christmas dance at the Knights of Pythias Hall—he hated dancing—but he managed to get her alone in a sleigh, away from the amiable chaos of the Abbott household, and ask her once again to marry him. This time Ellis said yes, and a few days later they sealed the bargain. Ellis was in Chicago, they were alone on a sofa in the Tobins' apartment, and as he told her in a subsequent letter, "I have something on the whole world, sweetheart, for you have kissed me and you can't deny it." The date was January 26, 1910.

IN FEBRUARY, RING RETURNED to West Baden with the Cubs, but with his mind a bit less on baseball than in previous springs. He did not stay in the clouds for long. On February 26 Ellis wrote him full of second thoughts:

> . . . honestly, Ring, you know there is something the matter with us. I wouldn't have the courage to say it at all but I know that you know it, too. You know that neither of us feels very much at ease when we are together and I know that I always have a feeling of restraint. I never can say anything I want to or be the least bit natural. I don't know whether it is because you don't really love me or because I don't love you. Sometimes I think it is one and sometimes the other. . . . But listen, dear, I'll never marry you until I am absolutely sure. I have wanted to say all this before but couldn't. . . . I have given you so much, Ring, I have let you kiss me so often and I have given myself to you so much that I have got to be sure that I am giving you my whole self. . . . It is all so new to me for, though, I have had more or less attention and people have said they cared for me—it was always in just a childish foolish sort of a way.

The sentiments Ellis expressed are entirely understandable: the momentousness of what she had agreed upon was suddenly sweeping over her, and she couldn't help asking herself if she had gone too far. She wondered, not surprisingly, how wise she was to commit herself to a life with this young man whom she really didn't know too well. But no matter how scrutable the emotions she was feeling, her letter came as a thunderbolt to Ring. Only the night before, as part of a general campaign to improve himself for her sake, he had made an agreement with Frank Schulte that the two be "decent," i.e., go on the wagon, and all of a sudden

Ellis from out of the blue was saying that she had serious doubts. The reply he wrote was long, confused and dolorous:

> . . . Ever since that night at Anne's I have felt that it was only a question of time before hell would follow heaven. I believe people get out of life just what they earn. I have not earned such happiness as life with you would be. I don't deserve you. I don't think you want to be bound to me now, and I know you don't want to say so, so I am saying it for you. You are to consider yourself free unless you are sure and until you are sure. And if, as I think, you realize it was a mistake and that you never can care, please tell me so. And never reproach yourself for anything, dear. There is no one to blame except me. And you have given me a taste of more happiness than I ever thought of. I'm not trying to pose as a martyr. This all seems natural, as if it couldn't have happened any other way.

Calculated or not, Ring's elaborate display of contrition and self-pity had the desired effect. Ellis hastily replied:

> Can't the judge reconsider the death sentence and make it a life sentence or make the punishment just to take me back and keep me forever. I do know now, dear, and I will tell you how I know— it is just because I can't give you up. If you want me you can have me and I will be just the best kind of wife I can to you my big boy —but you know I haven't had much experience and I may not succeed just at first because I can't cook anything but cake and salad dressing.

Her reply reached Ring in time to prevent him from doing anything genuinely foolish, but not soon enough to keep him from ending his period of "decency" with a vengeance. When he next wrote her, it was with elation and self-castigation:

> It's heaven again now and it makes up for the two long days of hell, which was hell in its worst form and all its branches. . . .
> Now I am going to tell you about hell, admitting that it is a play for your sympathy to do so. Sunday night, after I had mailed the letter to you, I went out on the porch and ran into Mr. Schulte. He said: "How do you feel by this time?" and when I asked him about what, he said "about our agreement." I told him I thought we had better call it off awhile and he acted as if the suggestion pleased him. He was lonesome and I was worse than that. I think

if he had proposed a duel, I would have done it. It wouldn't have been any more foolish than, or half as unpleasantly expensive as what we did do. I'm afraid he is one athlete who hasn't profited much by his "training trip" to West Baden. After your dear letter came this afternoon, I told him the agreement was on again. He said "all right" without a question.

Ellis replied with equanimity. There can be no question that Ring's drinking dismayed her, but at this stage she does not seem to have fully understood how serious the problem was. Her instinct was to smooth things over, and she was sensible enough to realize that a drinking lecture would do no good: ". . . do you know that no matter how much I cared for anyone I never, never would ask them to give up anything. I think the only way one can grow at all is by absolute freedom. An occasional fall won't do anybody any harm if it isn't breaking a promise. That is what does the harm." How much longer Ring and Schulte stayed on the wagon is not known, but it probably wasn't for long. There were not, however, any more serious quarrels to send him racing to the nearest saloon. He was unhappy about Ellis' deciding that "we both need at least a year to try to learn to know each other a little better" before getting married, but he accepted the delay in reasonably good spirits. Over the long run, the most pronounced effect of the "heaven and hell" episode was that it made Ring doubly edgy about the sureness of his hold on Ellis' affections, and for the rest of the courtship there was a pleading undertone to his letters, a constant quest for her loving reassurances.

The Cubs left for New Orleans, their main training center that year, early in March and, after a couple of weeks there, made a long northward swing that took them to Mobile, Montgomery, Birmingham, Memphis, Nashville, Louisville, Indianapolis, Dayton, Columbus, Toledo and, for the season's opening game, Cincinnati. In some towns they played a local all-star team, in others they met another major-league club; it was through these spring excursions that small-town America saw the heroes it worshiped from afar. It was also during this spring that an important development took place in Ring's work: Frank Schulte, poet, began his contributions.

They were not, needless to say, actually poems by Schulte, though he probably had a hand in or inspired some of them.

Schulte provided a persona for Ring, a voice through which the versifier in him could speak:

> *Why do they have left handers,*
> *Why do they let them live?*
> *Nobody likes lefthanders.*
> *Then why do they let them live?*
> *If ever I own a ball team*
> *My first great task will be*
> *To chase the southpaw murderers*
> *Right down to the Kankakee.*

That was the first of the Schulte poems. As Ring became more comfortable with them, a "Schulte" personality merged that presaged Jack Keefe in conceit, pigheadedness and naïveté—all the more reason to realize how little Schulte, whom Ring liked so much, had to do with the composition of the verses. Evidently the *Tribune* was puzzled by them when they first started appearing, for Ring complained to Ellis in mid-March that "they are making such awful mistakes with Mr. Schulte's poetry up in the *Tribune* office that I am almost discouraged by it, or with it, and will pass it up entirely unless they leave it alone."

With Ellis in Goshen and Ring in Chicago, a new element entered their correspondence: prayers for rain, rain that would permit Ring to hop a train and visit her for a few hours—

> This is our last day without a ball game until April 13th. That's the day before the regular season opens and we'll be in Cincinnati. If it would only rain early on the 12th so that they would call off our last game in Toledo about noon, I might steal away to Goshen for a few hours. But, of course, it won't and there's no use talking about it. But, honey, you can come over to Chicago about the 21st of April and stay awhile, can't you?

Again, Ring's prediction of a missed opportunity was correct. The Cubs went directly from Toledo to Cincinnati, where he saw a ball game and got a job offer: "I could have had a sporting editor job on one of the papers here, but I couldn't make up my mind to leave the old *Trib*." Ellis did make the Chicago visit he yearned for, and it seems to have been a happy one on all counts. It gave the two a chance to put the final patches over their February quarrel, and it gave Rex and the Tobins—Anne especially, since she had been the most enthusiastic backer of the match—their first chance to congratulate the couple. It also permitted Ring to take Ellis to a ball game and show her off to his friends in the press box. He later reported their comments with a burst of pride. Clare Briggs, the cartoonist, said, "I'll have to hand it to you; there certainly was some class to her." John DeLong, "yachting expert," told him, "She didn't look it, but there must have been something wrong with her mind or she never would have stood for you." And Hugh E. Keough said, "I don't know how you get away with it, but she surely was a peach."

As in 1909, Ring and Sanborn switched assignments throughout the season. The Cubs won the pennant and the White Sox finished in sixth place, but Ring found ways to keep busy and happy no matter which team he covered. With the Cubs, he had the satisfaction of writing about an outstanding team and the knowledge that *Tribune* readers were almost certain to be reading his stories. With the White Sox, he resumed the friendships that had been so important to him in 1908, and he picked up his musical collaboration with Doc White. This time there were real results, with the publication in August by Victor Kremer Company of "Little Puff of Smoke, Good Night," a Southern "croon" in the Bert Williams manner. The "Little Puff of Smoke" was a lullabye sung to a pickaninny by his mother; the intent of the song was scarcely racist or condescending, merely sentimental and imitative. A year later Ring and White collaborated on "Gee! It's a Wonderful Game," a salute to baseball that failed to supplant the hit 1908 collaboration by Jack Norworth and Albert von Tilzer, "Take Me Out to the Ball Game." Increasingly, Ring's free time on baseball trips to New York was spent trying to sell the songs he was working on and to persuade "some musical comedy actor or actress to say he or she will sing it or them." He never had any success worth serious mention, but he attempted to write songs for the rest of his life and there is absolutely no question that he would have thrown over his entire literary/ journalistic career in a split second had the chance arisen to make a living as a "songsmith."

Ring's stylistic development during the season was faster and more impressive than ever before. With the exception of the routine game stories, the copy he filed was increasingly inventive and unpredictable. When rain fell, as it did with much frequency that season (except, of course, when rain might have helped Ring and Ellis get together), he used the obligatory daily dispatch to amuse himself and his readers. More and more, the elements of his style were taking shape: colloquialisms, folk hyperbole, nonsense, doggerel, self-mockery. Here, in full, is a 1910 vintage rain story:

NEW YORK, June 16. [Special.]—No game, for some reason or another. It was wet grounds, or rain, or something just as effective, and it certainly made a hit in this Cub camp. Nobody is going to protest when he is deprived of an hour's ride over to Washington Park, on Long Island, two hours or more of baseball, and another hour's ride back to this same metropolis of these here United States.

Charley Williams took a lot of abuse around the noon hour simply because President Ebbetts was slow about getting to the ball grounds and slower yet about informing us that there was to be no pastime. It wasn't Charley's fault at all. He can't call off ball games on other people's grounds. Finally, about 1 o'clock, Mr. Ebbetts was heard from and it was good news. Probably that's the reason it didn't travel fast. In marked contrast to the party in charge at the Polo Grounds on Saturday, Mr. Ebbetts came right across with the information about when the game would be played. It will be part of a double header on Monday, Aug. 15.

The office of Mr. Colonial's hotel was crowded uncomfortably by ball players before the news came from Brooklyn. The minute it arrived there was a scattering, and two minutes afterward you couldn't find a Cub with a forty horse power microscope.

Some of the boys went over to the racetrack to do a little donating. In the bunch were Manager Chance, Harry McIntire, King Cole, and "Turkey" Richie. King didn't intend to donate, saying that he needed all his money to keep his kingdom going in Chicago. Of course, there was a poker game.

Messrs. Hofman and Sheckard passed the afternoon and evening writing letters and telling some more of their experiences in Africa and Asia Minor. It seems that Artie played ball under Manager Solomon in the Wise league. This was in 729 B.C.

The Bengal Tigers and the Solomons were battling for the Turkish cigaret championship. The Tigers came to Walla Kalie for the deciding series and the games stood eighty nine apiece.

On the night before the last game which was to decide the championship, Manager Solomon sent out all his wives and told them to flirt with the Bengal players. They did so and so captivated the Tigers that the latter divulged all their hit and run signs and the Bengal pitchers agreed to tell just what they were going to pitch the next day.

Well, the Solomons had some hard luck and the Tigers managed to score a few times. In fact the two clubs were tied at two million runs each when the last half of the nine hundredth inning started. There was no one on base and thirty-six men out when Hofman came to bat. Just then Myrrha, one of the wives, telephoned to Tabby, the Bengal pitcher, and asked him what he was going to give Hofman. He told her and she wrote a note to Artie which said: "Look out for the stripe ball."

Now this ball was a terror to batsmen, because it really did have stripes, orange and black, and the hitters usually thought it was a Princeton stocking rolled up, and let it go by. Of course, it was a simple matter to hit it if they knew when it was coming and what it really was. So Artie laid for it and kept his eye right on the orange stripe all the time it was coming up to the plate. Then he cut into it with a fruit knife and the juice scattered all around and into all the fielders' eyes.

While they were on their way to different oculists, Artie jumped into a gondola and paddled himself around the bases and crossed the cut glass dish with the run that beat the Tigers nine million to two thousand and eighty-seven. Sheckard had a better one than that, but it is to be saved for another rainy day.

Mr. Schulte heard both stories and made the following comment:

> The hawks have got poor Hofman
> > They've got poor Sheckard, too;
> How soon will they get Schulte,
> > Is what I'm asking you.
> If I stay in that outfield,
> > With that peculiar pair,
> Why, treat me kindly, keeper,
> > Give me the best of care.

Aside from entertaining his readers, Ring was also engaging in a bit of demythologizing. He was showing the ballplayer to be a fairly ordinary guy, with a taste for horse racing, poker and silly, thumb-spinning conversation. It is important to note that there is a big difference between demythologizing and debunking, for there is none of the latter here. Ring was not attempting to make straw men out of the public's heroes, as the gently affectionate tone of the story makes clear, and contrary to widespread belief, he never really did engage in such efforts later in his career. But he saw the ballplayers as human beings, each with his own full share of foibles and fallibilities, and he described them with mounting honesty in his reporting. He knew exactly how far he could go without antagonizing the players; he very rarely went all the way to the limit, but he often indulged himself in print in the kind of raillery and good-natured criticism theretofore restricted to the field and the clubhouse.

That Ring was able to keep his mind on baseball and his reporting assignments is rather remarkable when one considers that for much of the summer he was strangely thwarted in his quest for what was then an utterly essential part of the long process of successful courtship: the permission of F. P. Abbott to let Ring marry his daughter. Precisely why Mr. Abbott fiddled and dawdled is far from clear, but the campaign to win him over took from early July to late October and eventually involved Ring, Ellis and Mrs. Abbott as supplicants.

At some point that spring Ellis, who was out of town, wrote her parents to warn them that Ring was planning to visit Goshen for a chat with Mr. Abbott. The undated letter explained:

> You see Ring wants me to marry him and I have said I would —if you didn't object. . . . Father do be nice to him if he comes down to see you. I would have told you before but Ring wanted me to wait just a little while until he was a little bit ahead in the financial line. Some big New York publishing house is going to publish some of his songs now and wants more so I guess he thinks prospects are quite bright. . . .
>
> Please, please write to me right away and tell me that you think it is all great and wonderful. And do be nice to Ring.

Ring wanted to make the formal request on July 5, but the *Tribune* did not allow reporters to skip regular games, having "some rule about not taking the signature off a baseball story during the championship season." Instead he wrote to Mr. Abbott that evening:

> Of course you have guessed by this time that I care a great deal for Ellis. I can't help it, although I realize that no one is really worthy of such a girl and do not flatter myself that I am. That she

cares for me in return is my only excuse for this letter, which is a request for your consent to our marriage. I know the life she has been used to and know I am not "well off." But I do believe I can take care of her. She told me she would like to wait awhile, and, although I want her just as soon as possible, I know it will be better to wait until I have done some more saving.

My present work takes me from home too often to suit me and I intend to have another arrangement after this season ends. I can tell you more about it after this trip. . . .

Ring explained that he was going on the road and said that Mr. Abbott could send him a reply care of the Somerset Hotel in New York, but none was forthcoming. Ellis wrote him that her father was sick, news which he regretted "and I don't suppose my letter did him any good"—which probably was true. Ring Lardner, Jr., has noted that "Mr. Abbott just didn't want to relinquish Ellis or any of his daughters," but there must have been more to it than that; as an episode early the next year would make plain, he had a real distaste for the life of a "sporting man," and in addition, he must have been concerned about the financial reverses suffered by Ring's father—reverses which would deny Ring a cushion of wealth upon which to rest a marriage.

So, for whatever reason, he kept his silence. Early in August, Ellis acknowledged to Ring that "he has not said a word to me about *us* since I came home," and speculated about his motives: "I think he doesn't know what to say and so doesn't say anything." Later that month Mrs. Abbott wrote Ring to invite him to Goshen and to attempt to ease his tension. He replied gracefully, saying that "I know how a father or a mother must feel about giving up a daughter and especially one like Ellis," and explaining that "I have been trying all summer to get down to Goshen, but I had to wait for rain, and it never came at the right time." Finally it seems to have been decided, openly or not, to ignore Mr. Abbott and carry on with the next steps in the minuet. On October 22 Ellis had "an awfully pretty little tea this afternoon after Ruby's dancing class" and told "the girls"—her friends from Goshen, Niles and points nearby—the good news. Three days later Ring at last managed to make it to Goshen, and the long-delayed meeting was held. It was a success. As Ring described it to Ellis, he reached Goshen in late afternoon, drove downtown with Mr. Abbott and "conversed at great length" with him: "Beyond informing you that he gave his consent and shook hands, I won't tell you about our interview until I see you and perhaps not then"—an enigmatic evasion to which no clue has been provided. It was, however, a happy ending to a long summer of suspense, with Mr. Abbott offering Ring a drink and Ring gladly accepting, then staying the night in the Abbott house.

Ellis was not at home for the great confrontation because she had taken an out-of-town job, teaching elementary school students at Culver Military Academy, forty miles southwest of Goshen. It was not a lark. Though there were times when she felt the children were "little beasts" who drove her "to the verge of hysteria," overall she enjoyed the year and felt it gave her what she needed: an extended period on her own, proving to herself that she could manage her own affairs, before entering marriage and housewifery.

Whether or not in the course of their October 25 conversation Mr. Abbott mentioned his unhappiness over the transient life of a baseball correspondent, Ring began looking that fall for more settled work—this despite his obvious happiness with his job, his colleagues and his prestige at the *Tribune*. In November he found what he was looking for, or so he thought: the editorship of the *Sporting News*, the baseball weekly with offices in St. Louis. The *Tribune* let him go reluctantly, and in fact sent him off with assurances that it would hold his post for him until he decided whether the St. Louis position was satisfactory. He was also sent off with a big banquet at the Chicago Automobile Club, held in his honor by Charles Comiskey and the Chicago baseball writers. Ring, who hated speechmaking, was both moved and discomforted by the occasion, as he told Ellis:

> I'm glad you didn't hear my speech at the "banquet" last night. They gave me a traveling bag and I had to thank them for it. It was awful. But I was all swelled up on myself because their efforts failed to knock me off the water wagon. Mr. Eckersall had tears in his eyes when he said farewell to me—they were extra dry tears.

Ring's tenure with the *Sporting News* was singularly brief, a mere three months, but it is among the more interesting periods of his life. He was trying his hand at editing, for which he was probably constitutionally unsuited, and he was also making, in the

"Pullman Pastimes," his first effort at a column. He was battling with demon rum, and he and Ellis were engaging, by mail, in their final period of premarital teasing. The period is additionally fascinating because so many conflicting and ambiguous accounts of it exist.

Hugh Fullerton, for example, was credited in a 1942 *Saturday Evening Post* article with recommending Ring for the editorship— but Fullerton himself is quoted by Donald Elder as writing: "I tried to keep Lardner from going to the *Sporting News*, because I knew him so well and because I knew and loved Charley Spink so well. I was certain those two never would understand each other, and they didn't." Ring himself said that Ban Johnson recommended him. Spink was the owner of the *Sporting News*, which had been founded by his family in 1886. Both in appearance and editorial content the publication was quite different then from what it is now, but its essential purpose was the same: to satisfy the sports fan's ravenous appetite for statistics and gossip. Now it is a tabloid and covers all professional sports of national interest; then it was eight pages of full-sized newsprint, and baseball was its sole concern. It claimed the "Largest Circulation of Any Sporting Paper"; later it would become known as "The Bible of Baseball." It contained box scores, batting averages and every other imaginable statistic gleaned from every imaginable league from Class D to the majors. Players read it just as eagerly as fans, scouring it to see how the competition was doing and how that kid in the minors with his eye on one's job was coming along. There were fiercely outspoken editorials and, on the editorial page, four gossip columns called "Said by the Magnates," "Scribbled by Scribes," "Tips by the Managers" and "Gossip of the Players." There was also a "Question and Answer Bureau Limited to Base Ball Topics." Copy not written in the office came—as it still does—from part-time correspondents, and a *Sporting News* press card was treasured by "bugs" in the provinces, to the extent that the paper occasionally had to read them the riot act:

> In answer to the many demands for 1911 credentials, we want to inform our correspondents that this matter cannot be attended to until the old credentials are in, and many have been dilatory about sending them. The new credentials will be issued and sent out in due time. Also, we ask that discouragement will not follow

the "cutting" or "trimming" of your letters by us, as news is beginning to "pick up" and space is at a premium.

Ring arrived in St. Louis on December 2, and promptly found a room at 5087 Fairmount Avenue, in a boardinghouse run by a landlady who "called me 'dear' twice in the first five minutes of our acquaintance"; he told Ellis that "across from me there dwelleth a rather pretty young lady—and her husband." He also went to the office that day and met Spink and his son, Taylor. Ring was being paid $50 a week, but he was expected to put out a weekly paper pretty much by himself and he anticipated a six-and-a-half-day week. He was nervous, and into the bargain things got off on the wrong foot: "It's a lot heavier than I was led to believe and I started wrong today by heartily hating my employers at first sight."

That didn't make him unique. Charles Spink was a dynamo, but he was also a tightwad who squeezed every drop of blood from a dollar and an employee. Ring had been in St. Louis less than a month when he was complaining about Spink in almost every letter to Ellis. Here are four examples, written between December 28, 1910, and January 13, 1911:

> I fought all day to overcome a mad longing to spit in Mr. Spink's eye. He will drive me crazy, I know.

> Mr. Spink is going on a vacation soon. I'm glad of it, but I don't know what his son will do with no one around to quarrel with. If he picks me out I'll kill him. Quarreling seems to be the favorite sport here.

> Speaking of smoking reminds me of one on Mr. Spink. He doesn't smoke and neither does his son. The president of one of the St. Louis ball teams, it seems, always sends a box of cigars on New Year's to the editor of the *Sporting News*. This year the box came as usual, but the Spinks, knowing I was ignorant of the custom and wanting the cigars for their friends, waylaid it and took it home. I think that outclasses Shylock. I heard about it and am saving it up to tell him with other things the day I kill him.

> Mr. Spink's latest—He had a boy about 15 working in the office, acting as assistant proof reader, errand boy, addresser of envelopes, etc., and the boy really was a hustler and competent. Yesterday he worked although he was sick. Today his mother called up and said he was too sick to come down, so Mr. Spink fired him.

Notwithstanding his difficulties with the Spinks, Ring gave the job his full energies and took it seriously. On December 5 he wrote with obvious excitement to Ellis: "*My* first paper goes to press at ten tomorrow morning and I must get down extra early to fix it." He was determined to make good, and until the situation became unbearable he put the best light possible on it to everyone except Ellis, writing to Mrs. Abbott: "The first two weeks here, I was a little doubtful of my ability to hold the job. I always forget that a new job is lots easier than it looks at first. I guess I'm all right now, and I'm beginning to be glad I made the move."

Ellis, for her part, was not helping matters much by sending along news bulletins about the attentions being paid to her by one Captain Willhite, an officer at Culver with whom she took moonlight strolls:

> He came over again last night and stayed until 11:45. He brought me a beautiful little book as a "Christmas gift" and we had lots of fun until just before he went. I think he forgot for a few minutes and said things he didn't mean to say. I am awfully sorry about it because we have had good times. *But* don't you think for a minute that I can't manage my own affairs. You stay right where you are.

Ring responded in a jealous fit:

> Right now you must sit down and write me exactly what Captain Willhite said and did, and what you said and did. I've got to know. It isn't just common curiosity—but it's just because you are concerned and I want to, and must, know all about it.

Ellis declined to give him any information, but even in saying so, she gave him another tidbit to gnaw on:

> Ring, I can't tell you about Captain Willhite. I can't tell you what he *said* but he didn't *do* anything but hold my hand a minute when he left.

Ring was not utterly blameless, however, for he tweaked Ellis' curiosity with occasional glimpses of the high life in his boarding house: "A prettier sister of the pretty Southern girl and a young lady named Miss Marshmallow came to supper and I had to play accompaniments for three hours straight. . . . But, young lady, we were all in a bunch in the parlor and not alone, like you and Captain Willhite—for four hours." There was also the matter of the lady across the hall, who, notwithstanding her marital status, sent him a note: "She wanted to be friends." Her name was Mabel Johns; eventually he joined her—and her husband—for an evening which, he told Ellis, he enjoyed. Many years later, by then divorced, Mrs. Johns sought Ring's advice before making a trip to Europe and he sent her a letter of introduction to Scott Fitzgerald.

For all the teasing, neither Ring nor Ellis was happy at the separation; she spoke for both of them when she wrote: "Indeed it's very strange but not a bit funny that you are in St. Louis and I am in Culver—neither of us caring very much for what we are doing." Ring tried his best to get along with the Spinks, but even when they invited him for Christmas dinner, things went wrong: "It was a very good dinner and I was told how much everything in the house cost. Mrs. Spink asked me, in her daughters' presence, how I liked them, which was very embarrassing." His determination to succeed despite all these obstacles was so intense that on January 10 he "burned my bridges" and told the *Tribune* "that it might as well go ahead and get a successor."

He did this in spite of having been driven off the wagon only a couple of weeks before, which should have been indication enough that he had nothing but trouble ahead of him in St. Louis. On December 28 he proudly informed Ellis that "I've been riding the wagon two calendar months . . . the longest for five years," but on January 3 he acknowledged, with his customary chagrin, that the record had been broken: "A piece of the truth is that I had been a little too good and something had to break." Ellis' reply was a shade less tolerant than her letter a year before after the "heaven and hell" bender. She was sorry "but not surprised," she said, and she was worried that if a drinking bat "can keep you from writing to me for two days *now*—that there is a strong probability of similar events in the future." Ring's ardent reply was that a relapse would be impossible after their marriage because "when I have you I will have *everything I want*," but he was merely deceiving himself, as invariably he did about his power to quit his two chief vices, drinking and smoking.

It was on February 1 that Ring realized he could not hope to hang on with the *Sporting News*. In a letter to Ellis that he clearly hated to write, he explained why:

> . . . It didn't take me all this time to discover that Mr. Spink was dishonest. I knew it before I'd been here a month, but I decided to swallow it "for the good of the cause." He did everything about a month ago without my knowledge that was against all newspaper rules, but I explained my innocence to the offended person and was believed. Day before yesterday he tried to put over something else, but he told me about it and I kicked. . . . But we had some warm words and I told him I would just as soon work for Jesse James and that I was going to leave very shortly. Yesterday he tried to square things and I just listened to him and didn't say anything.

What did Spink do? Ring never said, at least not for the record, but the odds are, in light of Spink's well-known parsimony, that it had something to do with money: nonpayment of a correspondent, perhaps, or failure to pay for reprinted material, or backing out of a contract or some other deal—the list of offenses "against all newspaper rules" could go on forever. The offense may, in fact, have been less heinous than Ring felt it to be, for he had a highly developed personal and professional morality that on occasion lapsed into judgmentalism. Whatever the case, he quit. Whether he had been any good at the job remained a bone of contention for years. In 1912 Taylor Spink wrote a letter to *Baseball* magazine, a competitor, in which he said that Ring was responsible for unfavorable comments the magazine had run about the *Sporting News*; he also said that Ring was incompetent and was going to be fired just before he resigned. But many years later, when Ring had been dead for nearly three decades and his fame was still widespread, Spink remembered differently; he told Gerald Holland of *Sports Illustrated* that although Ring "was a miserable failure as a desk man," it "was young Taylor (as he now recalls it) who encouraged Lardner to write some of the stories about his travels with the Chicago ball clubs." Certainly it is true that the writing of "Pullman Pastimes" was Ring's principal professional accomplishment during his weeks on the *Sporting News*, but whether the columns were written at Taylor Spink's behest is another matter altogether.

There is an ironic footnote to the story of Ring and the *Sporting News*. In 1962 the Baseball Writers' Association of America decided to establish an annual award for meritorious service to baseball writing. The Awards Committee made its first selection in 1963, and Ring Lardner was chosen. The plaque now hangs, next to the 1964 award honoring Charlie Dryden, in the National Baseball Library, adjacent to the Baseball Hall of Fame in Cooperstown. The award is named for J. G. Taylor Spink.

A few days after his showdown with Spink, Ring was back in Chicago looking for work. He had, in point of fact, been offered a position he found appealing before he left the *Sporting News*: to run the front office of the Louisville club in the American Association. It was not the same as being in the majors, but the job had prospects: Louisville was one of the strongest cities in a strong minor league, and it had reasonable aspirations of joining the majors in the future. Ring told Billy Grayson, owner of the team, that he could not accept the offer because the job would require him to travel with the team; but after an hour and a half of talking over lunch, Grayson promised Ring he would have to make only one trip that summer after his wedding, and further sweetened the offer by agreeing to match his St. Louis salary and to pay him a bonus if the team did well at the box office. Ring accepted contingent upon Ellis' approval, which she promptly gave in a telegram. She followed it with a more detailed letter, which left little doubt that Mr. Abbott was making life difficult again:

> . . . I am very proud of you for having principles and sticking to them. . . . On the other hand dad thinks a "sporting man" is a "sporting man" and can't change his spots—and that his daughters are delicate and rare things and that they must not come in contact with that "damned sporting crowd." He is in fact quite strenuously opposed to the Louisville idea. . . .
>
> Father wants to know whether it would be in any way possible for you to come up here before you decide definitely. But if it isn't he says go ahead and do whatever you think best—that you know more about it than he does—which is very strange indeed.

Ellis' reading of her father's behavior was correct. He seems to have been torn between his obvious horror that his daughter might be surrounded by boozy, tobacco-chewing "sporting men" and his desire not to make her life more troubled by throwing up obstacles to her fiancé's prospects for employment. Ring, however, found it wisest to try to placate his future father-in-law, and wrote him an obsequious explanation of how he would be able to keep Ellis from evil influences. He explained that he would no longer have to "mingle" with ballplayers, as he did as a reporter, but would "keep away from everyone but the manager, who, in this case, is one of the most decent men I ever met." Ellis, he vowed, "won't ever have to see a ball player or a ball game." He told Mr. Abbott he had accepted Grayson's offer, it being the best available: "The *Tribune* held my old place open until the first of February, but I couldn't go back there, because that would mean travelling about five months of the year, night work when I wasn't travelling, and it also would look as if I had failed to make good down here."

All of which makes it doubly interesting, not to mention puzzling, that the job Ring finally did take was as baseball correspondent for the Boston *American*. About all that can be said is that there is evidence of a compromise: Ring agreed to renege on his acceptance of the Louisville position, and Mr. Abbott gave no ultimatum about finding a job that would permit him to avoid traveling. It is possible, even likely, that Mr. Abbott attempted to lure him into a position with his lumber business, but if he did, Ring cannot have weighed the offer seriously. All things considered, the Boston assignment turned out to be for the best. The *American* gave Ring great professional freedom, to which he responded with some of his best journalism, and living in Boston permitted Ring and Ellis to enjoy the first months of their marriage nine hundred miles from the nearest parent—which, after the past several months, was probably the minimum distance allowable.

The job in Boston was originally offered to Hugh Fullerton, but he suggested that it go to Ring. The salary was $45 a week, not bad for a sports reporter, and the conditions appeared pleasant to Ring. The *American* was a Hearst paper, founded in 1904 as an organ of the Democratic Party; the other major Boston newspers were the *Globe*, the *Herald*, the *Post* and the *Transcript*, the last being the fabled voice of the Old Yankee aristocracy. Ring arrived for work in late February and was surprised, he told Ellis, that "before I had the chance to show humility befitting a new employee, they began to exhibit gratitude at my condescending to take the job." It may have been that Ring, in his desperation to find a position that would enable him to get married and support his bride, simply did not have time to pause and consider that his stint with the *Sporting News* had given him national exposure and a growing reputation. The *American* was not getting a celebrity, but it certainly was getting a respected baseball expert.

Ring reacted with evident enthusiasm to the reception he received, and when a colleague expressed a skeptical attitude about the paper, his reaction was that the man was a fool: "I wish you could meet a fellow worker of mine, who is the pessimistic limit. He told me this morning that no one could be sure of a job on the *American* because the men higher up were constantly firing people for no apparent reason." When his new employer asked, rather deferentially, if he would be willing to go South for spring training with the Boston National League club, he agreed, and on March 7 joined the Rustlers, as they were known, for the train trip to Augusta, Georgia.

His first stories from spring training were straightforward and somewhat tentative; he was feeling his way in new territory. But it did not take him long to get back into the groove he had established in his last months with the *Tribune* and, in fact, bolstered by the success of "Pullman Pastimes," to widen and deepen that groove. In the Rustlers he had exactly the kind of team in which he delighted. They were terrible on the field—they had finished the 1910 season solidly in last place, with a record of 53–100, and in 1911 they would outdo themselves, landing in the cellar again at a clip of 44–107—but they had their full share of characters. After writing the obligatory "straight" pre-season stories, Ring went South and had fun. For one thing, he did well at the poker table, as he boasted to Ellis: "Talk about economy. I left Boston with a hundred dollars and now I have two dollars more than that and I've been gone over two weeks. The answer is the poker game. I intend to keep out of it from now on and profit by my luck." He was having even more fun watching spring-training antics and reporting them to his readers. He got special delight from a hefty rookie pitcher named Hub Perdue, whose 5-foot 10½-inch frame supported 192 pounds and who talked the way Jack Keefe would three years hence:

Mr. Taft is President of the United States and a very big man, but I don't believe he eats as much as I do and I know I am a better pitcher than he is, even if I never stayed in the big leagues long enough to get more than a cup of coffee.

The comment brings to mind the famous story, described by Robert Creamer, the biographer, as "apocryphal," that when Babe Ruth was asked twenty years later if he felt it was right to be making more money than President Hoover, he replied, "Why not? I had a better year than he did."

The ball park in Augusta was small and rustic, the local pace slow and easygoing, and Ring soon fell into the customs of the country. One paragraph has a certain evocative charm, even though Ring offhandedly employed a couple of irritating racial terms:

The Pastime was witnessed by two ladies, sixteen white men and three dozen of the "cullud" population. Notwithstanding the scarcity of spectators, an enterprising darkey was on hand selling or trying to sell cold drinks. If he rode to the park in a street car, he lost on the day.

Ring found a substitute for Frank Schulte in an outfielder named Bill Collins, but he didn't get to use "his" poetry for long because Collins was soon traded to the Cubs. When five Rustlers decided to show their determination in a novel way, Ring gave it appropriate publicity as "Society Notes—Collins, Burke, Perdue, Rariden and Clarke have had their heads shaved." The next day, March 15, he had some more fun with the five:

Poet Collins, being informed that President Russell was tired to death with the showing so far of his recruits, thought it proper to express William Hepburn's sentiments in verse. So he took his pencil in hand and dashed off the following masterpiece:

> "Hurrah, hurrah," the magnate said,
>   said he,
> "Hurrah, hurrah," they all look good
>   to me.
> "Right now I'd like to bet we will
>   finish one or two or three,
> "While we are marching through
>   Georgia."

Mr. Collins said the word "Marching" should be capitalized, explaining that it meant spending the month of March, just as Wintering means—"Oh, well, you know what it means."

The five athletes . . . who had their heads shaved, have been dubbed the "convicts," and they certainly do look the part. Mr. Burke is sorry he fell for it now, but his sorrow won't hasten the return of his hair, which was one of his chief beauties. Wilbur Goode desires to inform the public that his name is pronounced just plain "good," to rhyme with "would, if he could," "stood," "hood," etc. He has been called "Goodey," "Goods," and lots of other things and has stood for the mispronunciations long enough. He says he can't see why it is so hard to get it right, for no one ever thinks of saying "Josh Clarkee," or "Bill Burkey." The "e" in all those name is silent, as in hippopotamus. Speaking of the hippopotamus, Hub Perdue announces that he is good enough to pitch in the National League or the American, and that it will take some hard luck to keep him away from a regular berth on the staff.

Hub hasn't had a chance to exhibit any real pitching powers to date, but he surely possesses confidence, ginger and a sense of humor three times very valuable to a big league slabman.

That last sentence makes clear why Ring liked Perdue so much, and why there was so much affection in the ribbing he gave him. He had "confidence, ginger and a sense of humor"—all of them qualities that Ring especially admired.

In late March the Rustlers headed back to Boston by way of Columbia, Greensboro, Roanoke, Richmond, Norfolk, Lynchburg and Baltimore. One of the stops gave Ring a chance to provide an amusing look at the pitfalls of life on the road:

Sunday at Greensboro was necessarily quiet. It would have been quiet anyhow from choice, for the players were so weary from Saturday's chase around the bases that they had no pepper to do anything but just sit around.

Peaches Graham remained in his apartments and conversed with the rats. One of them, a big fellow, told Peaches that he was a catcher on the Rodent team that plays a bunch of field mice every Saturday for a pound of cheese. His name is Trap, probably because he is a rat catcher. The manager on the team is the Pied Piper of Hamelin and he and Trap are having a disagreement over salary. So Peaches and the rat had much in common to discuss.

Hub Perdue stood up all day because he had slept on what he

called a tombstone and his feet having extended several feet over the end of it, were not as badly bruised as the rest of his body. However, there was one nice thing about that hotel, it gave you plenty to eat and the plenty was good, too, but as Hub said, you couldn't sleep in the dining room. There must have been a private dining room for the rats, for they didn't disturb the athletes at their meals. . . .

What a joy it must have been for Ring's editors in Boston to stand by the telegraph machines and watch such copy roll in. Not merely is it funny throughout, but it is funny in unexpected ways and places. By this point Ring obviously understood that anything within the bounds of taste and libel (neither of which ever was a problem for him, anyway) was permissible in his new job, and he set about to explore every avenue he found inviting. He was still just writing daily sports journalism, and no cosmic claims should or will be made for the results. What was obvious, however, was that he had become a writer of impressive abilities, with a sense of life's zaniness that he managed to communicate in a wholly sane manner and with a feel for the nuances of ordinary speech that he was able to set down perfectly on paper. It can be argued, in fact, that for the next two years he would be merely marking time, honing his skills for the challenge offered by "In the Wake of the News"—and even then honing them for the stories, the weekly columns and the nonsense plays still to come.

Arriving back in Boston in early April, Ring faced a major decision: the wedding was little more than two months away, and he had not yet found a place for them to live. He also, in that connection, had to deal with a "delicate subject" raised by Ellis. It may seem incredible, but at this late date in their engagement she had no idea how much money they would have to live on, and she asked him about it in the most hesitant fashion. He replied with equal discomfort, in one of his most revealing letters:

Dear, I never feel practical and never confidential while I'm on the water wagon. We'll not wait for one of those moods, because you really have a right to know things. So I'll discuss the "delicate subject" briefly. I can't talk by months, for newspapers don't pay that way. The *Tribune* was giving me $35 a week and I went to St. Louis for $50 and came down again to $45 at Boston. It's $45 now and still it isn't and that's the delicate part. My family used to be "well off," but got over it. My father is kept busy paying for insurance and taxes, and he and my mother and Lena have to have something to live on. Lena makes something and there's no use arguing with her about it. My brother Billy helps when he can. Harry has a crowd for a family of his own, so you see it's up to Rex and me. Each of us ships home $10. Balance for me—$35. If you had been anyone but you, I would have felt obliged to say something before. But I know you. Lena would rather die than ask us (Rex and me) for anything and I guess she thinks I'm going to "stop" when I'm married. But I'm not. R. W. Lardner and Company, which is you, now possess about $800. About $200 of this will go for the Goshen furniture and probably $150 or $200 for the furniture we are still to get. Another $200 for my typewriter (which I must have) and for my trousseau etc., and we'll be lucky to have $200 left when June comes, because I won't be able to save from now on. And I used to swear I'd never get married before I had $1,000 laid away. I hadn't known you when I swore that.

There'll be a pay-day on "Little Puff of Smoke" in July and perhaps something from other things some time. These can be used in helping to pay for a piano. I guess you know as I do now, and it's awful to love you with all this. But you brought it on yourself. Perhaps I won't mail this letter, but I guess I will, for you'll have to know about things some time.

Ellis' reply was brief and sympathetic: "I am rich whatever your income is in just you and *of course* you *must* keep on sending money home. I think we will have *plenty*. You see I'll need almost nothing new for a year *at least* so perhaps we can get a little ahead in spite of my aversion to putting money in the bank." But she was "dreadfully sleepy" when she wrote that, and the reply may not have expressed her full reaction to what was, all things considered, an entirely remarkable letter.

Among the many things Ring's letter makes clear is that he had told his fiancée very little about either himself or his personal affairs. For Ring, who was loath to reveal his emotions and insecurities, to acknowledge that "I never feel practical and never confidential while I'm on the water wagon" was an astonishing admission of his dependence upon alcohol. His embarrassment over his family's circumstances is revealed as acute; he was not ashamed of his family but of the inevitable comparisons that would be drawn between its genteel poverty and the Abbotts'

wealthy ease. He seems to have been equally embarrassed to dis-
close the details of his quiet generosity and loyalty to his family,
though it was a matter of such central importance to him that he
kept up these beneficences for the rest of his life, even when his
own circumstances were unfavorable. Finally, the letter ends on
a note of what comes close to financial irresponsibility: Ring was
saying, in effect, that despite lean times they were not going to
deny themselves an apartment full of furniture, piano included,
and Ellis plainly agreed; this self-indulgence ultimately would
prove Ring's professional ruin, for the Lardners' big-spending style
eventually forced him to dissipate his talent and declining energy
on hack work in order to pay the bills.

That Ring should have been the one to take on the responsibility
for finding an apartment and making it ready was ironic, for he
had a firm sense of what he regarded as the natural divisions of
labor between male and female, and domestic matters clearly
belonged to "girls," as he called them. Yet he probably was pleased
that he was forced to take on the assignment, for he also had an
urgent desire to shield Ellis from work of any sort, notwithstanding
her own expressed desire to be an equal partner:

> I don't want anyone to cook and do other "foolish things" for
> me. I am going to learn to do it all by myself. I don't want anyone
> else living in our house—at least not just at first and more than
> that—do you think I am going to take everything from you and
> do nothing in return? No indeed!

She was, on the other hand, not exactly the easiest person to
find living quarters for. A year before, when she first permitted
herself to begin daydreaming about housekeeping, she had left
little doubt that she would not hesitate to be particular:

> . . . Won't we want a little four roomed apartment and have
> you any idea at all about rent? I haven't. You do want to go to
> housekeeping don't you? I guess you'll have to anyway because I *just*
> *won't board.*

Now, as Ring set out to explore the streets of Brookline in
search of housing, Ellis laid down her ground rules:

> Isn't Brookline out the same way West Newton is and how
> far is it from there? It sounds awfully attractive but be sure to tell
> me whether they have built in bookcases and how much the rent is.

Honestly, I get crazier about living in Boston all the time. Oh, and be to tell me what color the wall decorations are in any apartments you look at—in every room—and find out whether they would redecorate and let us decide on things. Of course they wouldn't in new apartments. I want a tan or brown living room and one pink and one blue bedroom if it's possible but of course it doesn't matter so much if we can find everything else we want.

Ring began the search in mid-April and, not surprisingly, found it "an awful job." One renter cheered him by suggesting, "You might pick out something that she wouldn't like at all." He decided that "I have good taste in locations, but that's about all," so he solicited her preferences on several points:

1. First floor or not.
2. Perfectly plain paper or modest designs.
3. Large rooms or small ones.
4. Your bedroom off the front room or farther back.
5. Old place with decorations to suit you or new one with its own selection.
Also, I want a lot of information about anything you happen to think of.
Very few places have book shelves. They all have fireplaces, mantels, etc. in the living room, two or three closets, sort of cupboards in the bathroom, side-boards in the dining room and gas ranges in the kitchen. Another question, Do you insist on a back porch?

The reference to "your bedroom" seems to have been a bow to propriety and the shyness that both Ring and Ellis felt about discussing such intimate matters as sleeping arrangements. In point of fact, they shared a double bed for the first years of their marriage, and it was not until 1917 that Ellis, for reasons having to do with Ring's drinking, established a separate-bedrooms policy. In any event, her reply to Ring's questions had a dizziness that must have confounded him:

I'll answer your questions about apartments first, and in order. (1) I don't care whether it's first floor or not, if it doesn't go above the third—that's as high as I'll go but I think the first or second is a little bit nicer. However if you find a third floor one, that meets the requirements, more easily or nearly it's *all right*. (2) I think I prefer perfectly plain paper but I wouldn't mind a modest design if you are very sure it's pretty. (3) I don't care anything about the size of the rooms—just so they are big enough for you to get into and (4) I don't care anything about the bedroom being far back—in fact I think it's nicer near the front—but don't you think they are nicer when the rooms open into the hall—of course they probably do anyway, but I mean not into the living room at all? (5) I can't tell you about old places or new because I don't know anything at all about it—you'll have to judge that for yourself but I should think that if you could get a new one for the same amount and have it decorated the way we want it, it would be nicer. And while I think of it I'd just as soon have either of the bedrooms gray. The living room almost has to be light brown or tan if we can find it—but I'd just as soon have the dining room, green, *blue*, brown or gray. I don't know about a back porch— I don't care, if there is any arrangement at all—or any place to put the things that go on a back porch.

Notwithstanding the confusion those instructions surely must have aroused, Ring intensified the search and in mid-May came up with a first-floor flat, at 16 Park Drive in Brookline, that he liked. Hoping that he had chosen well, he sent Ellis a highly detailed drawing of the floor plan and an explanation of it:

> . . . I like the place more the more I see it and it's ours if you approve. The "built-in thing" isn't in the dining room, but in a sort of vestibule that leads into the kitchen. The woodwork in the living-room, alcove and front bedroom is white and in the rest of the house oak, but a little darker than usual. The alcove is rather big—about seven feet by twelve and the people who live there now use it for a bedroom. It has a small, high window. The living-room windows are two in a row and the ones on the end of the dining-room are three—the middle one wider than the others. There are two clothes-closets opposite the bath-room, in the hall, and one in the front bedroom. The floors are to be done over and the living-room (including alcove), dining room and front bedroom re-papered.

To what must have been Ring's vast relief, Ellis quickly replied that "I am crazy about it, *really*," so he arranged to rent it and she had cards printed up:

Will be at home
˙ after August first
16 Park Drive
Brookline, Massachusetts

That settled, Ring turned to the last days of bachelorhood. He had, depending on one's point of view, the good fortune or the bad luck to be joined in this momentous hour by his old friends the Cubs, in town for a late-May series against the Rustlers. As he first portrayed it to Ellis, it was to be an innocent occasion: "I had a letter today from a Cub, informing me that there would be quartet rehearsal next Tuesday night. They are without a bass now and I'm just better than nothing." When the team arrived it had several of Ring's favorite journalists in tow, and he gave them a public tweaking in the *American*: "Four scribes are here with the champs. They are 'Huge' Fullerton, the well-known secretary of the Hillsboro W.C.T.U., Morning Sy Sanborn, of Springfield, Mass., H. DeKalb Johnson, Inspector of Penetentiaries, and Oscar Complete Reichow, the Boy Wonder." The formalities taken care of, the scribes and the ballplayers proceeded to see how much Massachusetts liquor they could consume. On May 26 an exhausted Ring wrote to Ellis: "The Cubs have gone and I'm glad of it even if I do like them. It will take me about a week to recover my right mind, but I'm pretty sure that they succeeded in permanently curing my thirst." Fat chance.

Ring's last courtship letters to Ellis are both businesslike and high-spirited. He was looking forward to "the 'Little Puff of Smoke' money, which comes on the fifteenth of July," and he was delighted to report that the Remick Company, publisher of "Gee! It's a Wonderful Game," got some publicity for the song by having a quartet sing it "at the ball park in Chicago the other day." He counted down the days to his departure from Boston on Friday, June 23, and in his last letter, dated June 21, he said a joyful farewell to four years of correspondence:

I'm really very tired of writing to Ellis Abbott, and I guess this is the last letter she'll ever get from me. Our correspondence has been a very pleasant diversion—really a necessity—but I don't think I can carry it on any longer, for paper and stamps cost money. I'll drop in and see her at Goshen Saturday night, on my way to South Bend and Niles, and see what she thinks about it.

I'm sure I've done my part toward keeping up our pleasant acquaintance. My letters have been as regular as the devil, and very interesting. Hers, I'm sorry to say, have been irregular as the devil, and sometimes they read as if they had been addressed to a stranger instead of a true and loving friend. But I suppose she was doing her best, and that is the most anybody can do. I always respect a man or woman who does his or her best. Nobody can do more, and one is prone to overlook faults in a person who is really trying. . . .

Good-bye till Saturday, my own sweetheart. I want to kiss you and tell you I love you more than anything else in the world.

RING

The train ride from South Station in Boston to Goshen took twenty-five hours; Ring probably was awake all the way. When he arrived on Saturday evening, he was confronted with a dazzling display of wedding presents, among them several from his friends in baseball: a silver vegetable dish from Doc White, a two-hundred-piece set of dishes from the Cubs, a cut-glass dish from Ban Johnson, a set of glassware from Jimmy Callahan, manager of the White Sox, and from the *Tribune*, an electric lamp.

The quest that had begun almost exactly four years earlier at a St. Joe marshmallow roast ended for Ring and Ellis at eight o'clock on the evening of Wednesday, June 28. The ceremony was performed at the Abbotts' house by the pastor of the local Presbyterian church. Ellis' sister Ruby was matron of honor, and Arthur Jacks best man. The wedding march, according to the Niles *Daily Star*, "was played by Noble Kryder, a young musical prodigy of Goshen, which was of his own composition." Ellis "was gowned in Japanese hand-embroidered silk, trimmed with real lace, with tulle veil caught with orange blossoms. She carried a bouquet of bride's roses and lilies of the valley, and wore a cameo in antique setting, the gift of the groom." One hundred and seventy-five guests attended the ceremony, which took place before a screen of elderberry blossoms. In the dining room afterward, a Toledo caterer served a three-course meal. All in all, the *Star* concluded, "the affair was one of the most elaborate ever given in Goshen."

Part Four

Married

*"It is such fun having Ring
home two whole days together. We
go out to meals Monday & to the
theater or Keiths or somewhere to
celebrate. . . . Next Friday Ring & I
are going to West Newton to
chaperone a week-end houseparty. . . .
Can't you just see it?"*

THAT ELLIS ABBOTT LARDNER CAME TO HER NUPTIAL BED A VIRGIN can be said with as much certainty as if documents existed to prove it; a young woman of good family in the years before the upheavals triggered by World War I simply kept herself "pure" for her husband, and that was that. But it can be said with just about as much certainty that Ring, too, experienced his sexual initiation on his wedding night. Again, no documentation exists, and Ring was scarcely one to swap bedtime stories with other men, but he came from a part of the world, and a class within that part, in which sexual inhibition was encouraged and prudery was the customary attitude. It is true that he had spent the past four years with a good many crude men, and much of that time on the road with all the temptations it offered, but it is most likely that the distance he was always careful to keep between himself and those men extended to a refusal to accompany any of them to girlie shows or whorehouses. There can be no question that he went through what Ring Lardner, Jr., has called "a prolonged period of acute sexual frustration," and he must have reached his wedding day aching with physical desire, but his own morality was even more rigid than Ellis' and from the moment he met her, he must have determined to save himself for her just as she was saving herself for him.

Though he kept his private life as private as possible, he was not reluctant to testify in public to his prudishness. People who mistakenly associated him with the writers who came to maturity during or immediately after the war, and who assumed that he shared that generation's preoccupation with sex, were puzzled when, in late 1932, he undertook a campaign in the pages of *The New Yorker* to clean up the lyrics of popular songs he found to be "pornographic." Both Scott Fitzgerald and Ernest Hemingway commented on the campaign after Ring's death, Fitzgerald calling it an "odd little crusade," and Hemingway "those pitiful dying radio censorship pieces." It was entirely within character, however, for Ring, who found sex a serious and mysterious business:

> *I smoke too many cigarettes,*
> *I'm much too fond of rye;*
> *My meals are followed by regrets*
> *I should have shunned that pie.*
> *These traits are common, I am well*
> *Aware; but listen, folks,*
> *I'm some one who can neither tell*
> *Nor laugh at dirty jokes.*

It is reasonable to guess that Ring and Ellis, given the inhibitions implanted in them from childhood as well as Ring's pervasive shyness, had a difficult time of it those first nights. It is also reasonable to guess that, for the early years of their marriage at least, they solved whatever problems may have existed. Ellis was pregnant within a few weeks of the wedding day, but more persuasive evidence of true marital happiness exists in letters she wrote Ring while he was covering the World Series in 1911 and 1912. Both letters throb with longing. In 1911 she wrote: "I want your arms around me and I want you to kiss me and tell me you love me—I want you, I want you, and I love you, my darling." In 1912: "I miss slipping into your arms when I get into bed and I miss waking you up in the morning." Certainly the word "want" had a less torrid connotation romantically then than it does now, but in those two sentences Ellis came as close as her sense of propriety—not to mention her husband's—would permit her to expressing what is clearly physical desire.

THE HAPPINESS THAT THE NEWLYWEDS enjoyed in Boston was increased shortly after their honeymoon. Ellis described the good news in a letter to her sister Florence:

> Have you heard about Ring's new job. He is sporting editor of the Boston *American* with a raise in salary and all day Sunday and Monday off. Isn't that great. They are crazy about him on that paper and let him do just as he pleases. He is going to get a whole new sporting department and has sent for Rex to come take his place. Rex is coming in about two weeks. . . .
> It is such fun having Ring home two whole days together. We

go out to meals Monday & to the theater or Keiths [vaudeville] or somewhere to celebrate. Last Monday we went down to Squantum to the Aeromeet but it was such a bad day they didn't do much flying.

Next Friday Ring & I are going to West Newton to chaperone a week-end houseparty. . . . Can't you just see it?

Coming as she did from a large and boisterous family, Ellis had difficulty adjusting to being alone in the daytime five days a week, and she admitted to being lonesome. At night, however, Ring read aloud to her, they spent much time uncrating their belongings, and when they got a piano they had music. They blew $250 of $300 that Mr. Abbott had given them as a wedding present on the piano, Ring solemnly promising that the bank account would be repaid from what was rapidly becoming the household financial chimera, "song money." One day a week Ellis had the company of a cleaning woman, Katherine, who for $1.05 did seven hours of hard work: "She stays from about nine to four and in that time sweeps & wipes up all the floors, cleans all the wood work, dusts, scrubs the kitchen floor, bath room floor, bath tub etc., cleans out my refrigerator and today washed some shirts & stockings and handkerchiefs." Ellis, her earlier protestations to the contrary, put up no discernible resistance to paying someone else to do the dirty work, and by late summer she had what was then considered a legitimate reason for taking it easy, as she wrote to her mother:

Mother, dear, I have the most wonderful news for you. What would you think about being a grandmother? Well I think there is a very great probability that it won't be very, very, long before that happens. We are so happy about it mother dear. Ring is just perfect. I wish you could know how nice he is. Just think of having a little baby all my own. I won't ever be lonesome any more—and it is lonesome all by myself in the day time. We had a doctor about a week ago and he said it was sure. I was sick last the tenth of July which makes it just eight weeks yesterday.

I am not a bit afraid, mother though I don't care much for this horrid feeling I have every morning. It's hard to sit down and plan dinner and order food when the very thought of it makes you ill.

A particular advantage of Ring's new position as sporting editor was that he did not have to go on the road with the Rustlers or

Red Sox; he covered whichever team was in town, and another staffer reported on the team that was traveling. He now had, as Ellis told Florence, total freedom, which he used judiciously. His best work in Boston had been done before his marriage; aside from the attention he was lavishing on Ellis, he was also diverted from writing by administrative duties. He did, however, write, under the title "Oddities of Bleacher Bugs," the critical piece about ignorant baseball fans which is quoted at length in Part One, and he ran a six-day series of verses that gave an alphabetical preview of the coming World Series between the Philadelphia Athletics and the New York Giants:

> F is for Fletcher, the Giant shortstop,
> Expected hard liners and grounders to cop;
> And Polo Grounds fans are all eager to betcher
> That very few things will get by Arthur Fletcher.

> J is for Josh, whose last name is Devore,
> He's never been in a world's series before.
> To call him a Giant is only a habit.
> He isn't as big as a two weeks' old rabbit.

> Q is for Quakertown, slang term for Philly,
> The inmates of which have gone hopelessly silly
> About the Athletics. You can't blame them much,
> Though the team has more Irish than Quakers or
>   Dutch.

> V is for verses; this thing here's a verse,
> Though you may not believe it. Still, it might be
>   worse.
> But you can believe one thing—we're telling you
>   right,
> We're glad that the alphabet's end is in sight.

Ring did, as the *American's* most prominent by-lined sports reporter, feel it necessary that he cover the Series, which began in New York on October 14. It turned out to be the Series that gave Frank Baker, the Philadelphia third baseman, his famous nickname. He hit two homers, one in the second game and another in the third, a remarkable feat for that time which shot him into American legend as "Home Run" Baker. But Ring quickly lost interest in what was happening on the field, and with good reason: the *American* management, seizing the opportunity offered by the sporting editor's absence, promptly fired both Rex and Frank Smith, another Chicagoan hired by Ring. Ellis reacted with total outrage:

> I am wondering what you are going to do about this business at the office. . . . I never *knew* anything so horrid as to wait until you got out of town and then make all this trouble. I don't think Rex cares very much as he has this job in Cleveland and I only hope Mr. Smith can get out of it as well. But it is the very devil for you and I'd like to kill people for making all this trouble for you—when you are working so hard any way.

Ring was itching to get back to Boston for a showdown with his employer, and Ellis passionately wanted him at home, but an old family enemy entered the picture: rain. All the rain that had failed to fall on all those occasions when they hoped for a few hours together in Goshen seemed to descend on Philadelphia. Each afternoon for six days Ellis picked up a copy of the *American*, and each afternoon the story was the same:

> My heart broke when I bought a paper on the way home and found that there was no game today. Is the world's series *ever* going to end? It looks *hopeless.* . . .
> I am very anxious to know whether Mr. Smith has anything and of course I am *interested* in us. Poor, dear, boy! Don't worry *please.* . . .

Her concern about their own situation was well founded. Ring, out of professional honor and loyalty to his brother and a colleague, had decided to quit the *American* when the Series ended. It was a rash decision, all things considered: he had a pregnant wife, no cash to speak of, and considerable debts. His only immediate hope was a songwriting career in New York, but his inquiries proved fruitless. In early November he tried to ease Mrs. Abbott's mind:

> You are hereby ordered not to worry about us, although I'm free to admit that it is natural you should. We are through with the Boston *American*, but are finding out that we get along nicely without its help. I am doing some work for magazines that are not particular what they print, and waiting for a call to Chicago, New

York, or some other city of size and importance. We have three meals daily, and some of your grand pickles and preserves are on every bill-of-fare.

It was a brave but unconvincing front. He actually had only one magazine piece in the works—"The Cost of Baseball," written for *Collier's* and also quoted extensively in Part One—which could not have paid him more than $100, if that, and it did not appear until 1912. Despite his reputation and accomplishments, few jobs beckoned to a baseball writer just at the end of a baseball season. A decision had to be made quickly, and one was: to return to Chicago. Ring borrowed enough money to make the move from John Taylor, owner of the Red Sox, and Fred Tenney, owner of the Rustlers, "and to their astonishment eventually I paid them back." Other creditors were less fortunate: a chagrined Ring sent back some bills with the notation "Address unknown" on the envelopes.

In Chicago they moved in with Dick and Anne Tobin and their one-year-old son, Richard L. Tobin. Ring managed to find a job on the copy desk of the Chicago *American*—any port in a storm, he was going from one Hearst *American* to another. The job had two advantages, which were better than none: it gave him and Ellis enough money to relieve congestion in the Tobin household by moving to an apartment nearby, and it kept him in Chicago, his real journalistic home. It could not have been a very happy winter, but he and Ellis made the most of it. Rex was back in town, with a new wife, Dora, and a job at the Associated Press, so with all three young Lardners living in the same neighborhood they had ample opportunity for inexpensive and congenial family amusements.

In February, 1912, Ring got a break—not a big one, but a break. He was invited to rejoin the *Examiner* as a baseball correspondent, this time under his own by-line; he and Charlie Dryden would be the star reporters the *Examiner* would put up against the *Tribune*. The chances are that Ring and Ellis talked the offer over carefully, for it would send him back on the road—and he might be out of town when their first child, expected in the spring, was born. Presumably there was more money involved, however, and Ellis must have argued that Ring needed to get back to his first professional love, baseball. He accepted the offer, and joined the White Sox for spring training in Waco, Texas.

As Ring and Sy Sanborn had switched back and forth between the Sox and Cubs when he was on the *Tribune,* so he and Dryden switched for the *Examiner.* The White Sox were, as usual, a fourth-place club and the Cubs were a dynasty in decline; for fans the most poignant evidence of the Cubs' ill fortunes was that Chance, as manager, had benched himself and "Tinker to Evers to Chance" was no more. The two clubs had similar records in 1912 and 1913, so throughout his second career with the *Examiner,* Ring was again faced with the responsibility of provoking readers' interest in an essentially uninteresting situation. He succeeded admirably. Although he could not have been terribly stimulated by being back in the role of correspondent after two stints as editor, his enthusiasm for his work stayed at a high level and was reflected in his writing. He gave ever more emphasis to the people he was covering and less to the details of games; he began writing stories in the first person singular; he wrote many stories in un-lined verse; and he made tentative explorations into the chatty epistolary style he would later use so often and well.

By April, Ring was back with the Cubs. He was plainly glad to see Frank Schulte again. Here, in full, is one of the first results of their reunion:

It didn't rain so awful hard, it didn't rain so much; there wasn't any blizzard that could really be called such; we asked most everybody that we met upon the street and couldn't find a single soul who'd swear that there was sleet; we asked some information from the man who gathers mail, and he said that nowhere on his route had he encountered hail; we ran across a pioneer who'd lived here since a boy, and he vowed he'd seen a stronger wind sometimes in Illinois; but the awful combination of the wind and rain and all, it rendered quite impossible the scheduled game of ball.

And so the Cubs, who play (at times) with so much skill and science, were forced to wait until to-day to get back at the Giants.

We called up Chance to find out whom, to-day, he'd pick to pitch; he said it might be Lavender; again it might be Richie. We put the same thing to McGraw, and, looking through his list, he averred it might be Mathewson, whose Christian name is Christy.

And then we rang up Mister Murf, the owner and the boss, expecting that the atmosphere would make him very cross. But lo! his voice was cheerful when he said: "There is no news, except what you already know—that's one we didn't lose."

We phoned to Charley Williams, who had hastened home to dine, and ascertained that they would play it off on July 9. Another battle with New York is scheduled for that date, and so prepare, good people, to come early and stay late.

Opining that, this phoning done, we had no other duty, we donned the five buck rubber coat and went to call on Schulte. We found him in his shirtsleeves, also in a tow'ring rage, the cause of which, he said, was on the Sunday sporting page.

"Why, look at that," he shouted, loud enough to wound our ear. "Just take a slant at the Chicago batting records here."

"Well, have they robbed you of some hits?" we asked him, with a grin, "or have the thieves neglected to put all your homers in?"

This sparkling bit of comedy, it didn't seem to please him, and so we soon decided 'twould no longer pay to tease him.

"What is your kick," we then inquired. "Pray tell us, if you can."

"Why, look-a here"—he pointed to the name of Zimmerman— "They've got him hitting four-five-one, and that's a gol-darn shame."

"But listen, Frank," was our retort, "we've seen most every game; we've watched the Zimmerman most every time he came to bat and we are satisfied that he is hitting fully that."

"What? Hitting fully that?" the Schulte person fairly thundered, "and do you think that I don't know he's clouting 'round eight hundred? And yet they give him four-five-one, and publish it at that: Why, that means less than one base knock for every twice at bat. To cut a fellow's average like this is sure a crime. I've kept close tab on Heine, yes, I've kept it all the time. Now, since this season opened, there's just twice that I recall when Zimmerman went up to bat and failed to sting the ball. There's only twice that Heine failed to get a clean base hit; and, if it had been oftener, why, I'd have noticed it."

We then produced our score book, but he roared an awful roar.

"And now I s'pose you're going to tell me you know how to score. I guess that's where the trouble lies, yes, there lies all the trouble—you don't give him no hit at all unless he hits a double. Yes, now I've got it figured out, it's really very simple—you never score him half a hit unless he hits a triple, and then, when he decided it's time to wallop a home run, why, that's a real live Heine hit, and so you score him one."

We argued and we argued over Heine's batting record, and

finally we told him he was crazier than Sheckard. Instead of making
Schulte mad, this seemed to tickle him. He said:
  "I wish that I was half as crazy as Old Jim."
  We battled and we battled until it was time to go.
  What Heine's really hitting, please don't ask us; we don't know.
  But if you leave it up to Frank he'll tell you, cheerfully, that Zim-
merman's real average is eleven-forty-three.

It must be kept in mind that Ring did not learn the game
would be canceled until late morning, at the earliest. He then
had to perform the conscientious reporter's duties, calling the
owner and the managers and making sure he had the facts right.
Only then—midafternoon, perhaps—could he begin to compose
his story. For Ring, that no longer meant simply writing what is
known in journalism textbooks as "the inverted triangle"—the
basic news story with the meatiest material at the top and matter
of thinner and thinner interest as the story progresses, a story
designed to be cut from the bottom in the composing room in
order to facilitate the make-up process. Ring, instead, by now was
writing stories that really were *stories*, tightly organized pieces that
required far greater creative effort, yet had to be produced in the
same amount of time and under the same deadline pressures.
  Given the circumstances, a story such as this is an uncommon
piece of work. To begin with, it is marvelously entertaining. Even
though it is written under the restrictions of rhyme and meter,
it catches the flavor of baseball talk. Some of the rhymes are remarkably clever: "science/Giants" is good, but "pitch; he/Richie"
and "list, he/Christy" are first rate. The story contains all the
information it needs to—game called on account of rain, to be
played on July 9—and it takes some carefully calculated digs at
Heine Zimmerman, a player who both impressed and irritated
Ring. Zimmerman was a superb natural hitter, off to a roaring
start in what would prove to be a dandy year at the plate. But he
was also one of those ballplayers who watch batting statistics and
little else—an indifferent fielder and base runner who did not
play up to his great potential because he did not care enough to
develop a rounded game. Ring chose precisely the right way to get
in the dig. To have said directly that Zimmerman thought about
nothing but his average would have been to cross the line between
permissible and forbidden criticism; but to put it in the form of

a teammate saying that Heine was being robbed made it both subtle and acceptable, and to have that teammate be Frank Schulte, speaking in the hyperbole with which *Examiner* readers were by now familiar, made abundantly clear what was going on.

Ring did not dislike Zimmerman, however, and he even permitted him to enter the poetic lists, offering himself as a versifying rival to Schulte:

Heine Zimmerman's exuberant spirits, resulting from his tremendous batting streak, have overflowed in the form of poetry. "If Schulte can write it, why can't I?" remarked Heine last night, and slipped us this child of his brain:

> *There is an outfielder named Frankie,*
> *He's homely and ugly and lanky.*
> > *A good hitter once,*
> > *But now he just bunts,*
> *And daily grows more and more cranky.*
>
> *There is a third baseman called Heine,*
> *A better third baseman than Steiny;*
> > *When he meets one square,*
> > *Each lady bug fair*
> *Says: "Golly, I wish he was meine."*

"Steiny" was Harry Steinfeldt, a former Cub third baseman, by now retired, with whom Zimmerman had carried out a long and not very friendly rivalry. Ring, who enjoyed any case involving confused identities, once introduced Zimmerman to a friend as Steinfeldt. The friend said, "I'm glad to meet you, Mr. Steinfeldt. I think you're the greatest third baseman in the world." Zimmerman responded by hitting the fellow with his Sunday punch.

There was a lot more rain during the 1912 and 1913 seasons, so Ring's ingenuity was constantly put to work to produce new ways of holding reader interest. Showing how the players killed their spare time was one way to do it:

There weren't any White Sox left on bases yesterday, because the rain fell down and made the ground unfit for play. The Browns and White Sox had a day of rest, and I suppose they spent a lot of money in the moving picture shows.

The picture shows are something new, but some of them I've

seen. They're pictures of real people and they move right on the screen. The picture shows are very fine and I have learned to love them. You think the folks are real, but it is only pictures of them.

A girl sits at the piano, playing ragtime merrily, and once or twice she hits the proper key. She acts as if she meant it, but the listeners all know it doesn't often happen at a moving picture show.

When she has played for hours and hours, there then appears before us a gent who sings and asks us all to come in on the chorus. Then Cicotte, Kuhn and Jack Fournier and other White Sox birds horn in and sing their own queer tune, also their own queer words. Now Cicotte's voice is quite unique, it's neither poor nor rich, but as a singer Eddie Cicotte certainly certainly can pitch. And as for Red Kuhn's baritone, I've never heard its match. Yes, as a songbird Walter Kuhn can surely throw and catch. Fournier's sweet tones are most enjoyed the moments he keeps still. Oh, as a vocal expert, Jack can surely hit that pill. When these three guys are warbling all they need is Harry Lord to help in digging up again the famous old lost chord. . . .

In August, 1912, Ring wrote two stories in which he adopted the guise of an unnamed fan who was taking in the Eastern sights with his eyes wide open. The stories were in the form of letters to a friend, and as much as anything he wrote during this second period on the *Examiner* they point the way to Ring's future. The first began:

> Dear Friend—I suppose you fellows in Chicago are all wrought up to a high pitch of excitement about the wonderful work of the Cubs. Well, they certainly are going some, and I'm glad to hear it, for I want to see a world's series game or two and of course there won't be a chance for me unless part of the big show is staged in dear old Chi. This is all the vacation I expect to get this year. I'm going to visit all the big Eastern towns except Brooklyn. I may even go over there some night if Frank Hogarty invites me.

That paragraph is the second step in a process that began in Boston when Ring wrote "Oddities of Bleacher Bugs"; the next step would be the short stories collected under the titles *Gullible's Travels, Etc.* and *Own Your Own Home.* Ring was discovering, in the baseball fan, an archetypal American: fast-talking, egocentric, semiliterate, innocent, gullible and ill-informed, a character later known as the "wisecracker" or the "wise boob." Here, in his journalism, Ring was merely employing the character as a convenient device for relieving the boredom, for himself and his readers, of covering an ordinary ball club. Later, as he refined and expanded upon this character in his fiction, he would become Ring's quintessential American, a man he viewed with some affection, some vexation and some condescension—but with no hatred or bitterness, many critics notwithstanding.

When the 1912 Series ended—the Red Sox beat the Giants, with Mathewson losing the seventh game in that burst of bad luck so sadly described by Ring—he turned to a winter diet of college football and hot-stove-league chatter. Though baseball was his principal interest, Ring enjoyed football, followed it throughout his life, and taught himself to know it as well as he did baseball. (In the fall of 1910 he had written to Ellis: "I'm going to study this afternoon. The football guide will be my text book and I want to learn the new rules so I'll know what I'm writing about later on.") In 1912 he chose the *Examiner*'s all-star team for the Western Conference, of which Wisconsin was champion and which included, among others, Michigan, Notre Dame, Purdue and Chicago.

Covering the hot-stove league was mainly a matter of routine, much of which, as he later recalled, took him to his favorite haunts: "With the closing of the saloon, one of the best means of getting news vanished. It was in the saloon opposite the *Tribune* in Chicago that all the 'beats' were picked up. So that was where the boys spent most of their time. The saloon was where you got color for your baseball stories, too. The players wouldn't stand for your not meeting them as their equal." The reporter assigned to the off-season beat was constantly scrambling for items to fill his space, and much of it was sheer trivia. Here—not as an example of great journalism, but to indicate what Ring spent a great deal of time hunting up—is a sample:

> President Tom Lynch of the National League left Chicago yesterday in a sad frame of mind. He had failed to sign Henry O'Day to an umpire's contract and had also failed to get Henry's promise to return to his old love.
> While Mr. Lynch came here to attend the meeting of the National Commission, he figured that he could make his visit more profitable by persuading Hank to take back the job that was his

before he became manager of the Reds. He had a long talk with the veteran umpire, but Hank would not give him any satisfaction.

It is thought that O'Day would prefer an American League berth to one in the National. It might be embarrassing for him to officiate once more in a league in which he had been a manager. President Johnson would give Hank a place in a moment if he had the consent of the National League chief. However, there is no strings to O'Day and he is at liberty to sign wherever he pleases.

"I won't make up my mind until the first of next month," said Hank yesterday. "I have several managerial positions in sight and I'm not at all sure I will umpire this year. I don't consider myself under obligations to the National League nor any other body."

The Cub catching staff, which was trimmed a while ago by the release of George Yantz to New Orleans, took weight again yesterday when this same Yantz was turned back under the rules of organized baseball. In disposing of Yantz President Murphy overlooked the new law which provides that waivers must be secured from all major league clubs on a drafted player. The Cub owner may now seek waivers, or he may decide to carry Yantz on his list for a time.

Mr. Murphy received the signed contract of Utility Man Wilbur Good, who is Wintering in Baltimore. In the magnate's mail was also a letter from Frank Farrell, thanking Mr. Murphy for his good wishes toward Chance and the Yankees.

Manager Callahan of the Sox announced that Morris Rath, second baseman, had signed. Rath lives at Absecon Heights, N.J. He was not a holdout. Morris seems to have a tight hold on his job with the Sox and will go about his work here confidently after a successful season with the South Siders.

President Mike Sexton of the National Association of Minor Leagues is soon going to Auburn, N.Y., to clean up the work that has been left undone because of the illness of Secretary John Farrell. No one envies Mike his job.

This is the nuts and bolts of baseball—and of journalism. There is no surer sign of Ring's professionalism than his ability and willingness to do the routine dirty work that fills up the larger part of each day's newspaper. He was a conscientious employee who had no illusions that his facility with the typewriter or his prominence as a by-lined writer entitled him to shirk the more mundane obligations of his beat. He was glad to have a job that paid him enough to support his small family, and he was perfectly content to take the less glamorous aspects of that job without complaint. He had no reason to see anything more glorious or challenging in his immediate future.

RING'S LUCK AND THE BASEBALL SCHEDULE were both favorable for a change; he was in Chicago on May 4, 1912, for the birth of his son, John Abbott Lardner. It had been a painful spring for Ellis, who did not enjoy Ring's long absences and who was deeply concerned about her father's failing health (he died later that year), but she had no difficulties in childbirth. Her sister Ruby, of whom Ring was especially fond, came to live with them and, as Ring told Mrs. Abbott, "She has become indispensible to the welfare of our small family and will not be allowed to go to Goshen except for small visits." Ring, who had once told Ellis that "I never did see [a baby] that wasn't a fright," proved to be a doting, attentive and rather nervous father.

That summer Ellis and John spent much of the time in Goshen and Lake Wawasee, both because of the more benevolent climate and her father's illness. A couple of her letters leave no doubt that she was torn by concern for her father and bursting pride in her infant son:

Don't you think that is a cunning picture of the baby? I am going to have a post card picture taken of him some day this week.

We are going to the lake tomorrow or Wednesday for two days. I think John needs a change. Honey, he is the dearest, sweetest baby that ever lived. It is perfectly wicked that you can't see him all the time.

Father is much weaker tonight. I feel so sorry for poor Florence. It is awful to live in such a state of uncertainty. She is going on with all her plans but I do wish it were this Tuesday instead of next because I don't see how he can live that long. Still we have thought that so many times and he has been better again.

. . . We took John for a walk . . . and had to stop at fifty-nine places to let people admire the baby. Honey, I think he must be an unusually beautiful baby, because *everyone* says he is the most beautiful baby he ever saw. I am so proud of him—and he looks just like you. Everyone also takes pains to add that he doesn't look like me.

By February, 1913, Ellis felt sufficiently confident that John could manage without her for a while to leave him in Goshen with her mother—still new to widowhood, and no doubt grateful for the company and distraction the baby would provide—and join Ring for a spring-training trip around the West with the White Sox. She did, to be sure, worry about him, as she told Ruby:

Mother said John's bowels were doing all right but she didn't say whether she was still giving him the medicine. I think he does pretty well to sleep till four of five o'clock. . . . Does he wake up in the evening after he is put to bed? No one has said whether he did or not. You will be sure to answer these questions won't you because I wonder about him all the time. *Do you think he will know me when I get home?*

For the most part, however, Ellis was able to relax and enjoy herself, and the reports she sent back to her family tell more about the trip than do Ring's dispatches. It seems to have been her first extended exposure to "sporting men," and she had some interesting reactions to them. She did not find many people, she confided to Ruby, "with what I call 'class,' " yet neither did she take a judgmental or superior attitude. At times, in fact, she was clearly impressed at being part of such an eminent crowd:

It was very exciting at the [San Francisco] station to see all the crowds and hear them cheering for "us." The pressmen and their wives have one whole car with a whole section for each person. Thursday night after we started Mr. Comiskey sent around a big bunch of violets for each of the ladies and about eleven o'clock he invited all our party (the press) in to his private car for a supper. There are some *awfully* queer people on and some nice ones. Mr. and Mrs. [James] Crusinberry are great and don't know what we would do without them. You would be surprised to find how much nicer—as a general thing—the men are than their wives. I still think Dr. White is one of the nicest men I ever met and Mr. McLane of the "Post" is another of "our kind."

We had a dance last night and I danced with Doc White, Ed Walsh, Rollie Zeider and all the celebrities. They are good dancers, too. I even made Ring dance two twosteps with me—he does very well and as soon as I can teach him to reverse he will be a good dancer.

The trip took Ring and Ellis to San Francisco, Oakland, Paso Robles, Ogden, Los Angeles, Yuma, El Paso, Amarillo and Oklahoma City—the first tour of the West for either of them. Ellis did not stay with Ring for the entire trip; she spent a few days with a friend in Redlands, where, she wrote him, "I've been busy but have found plenty of time to miss you." As for Ring, he was writing his usual copy, filling it with dialogue, nonsense, anecdotes and verse:

> There is a young catcher named Kuhn,
> Who always gets up before nuhn.
> The hair on his head
> Is decidedly red,
> And not black or blue or maruhn.

The Lardners returned to Chicago to learn that the city's sports press had suffered a large loss: Hugh E. Keough, the beloved "H.E.K." of the *Tribune*'s "In the Wake of the News," had died. As his replacement the *Tribune* turned, logically enough, to Hugh Fullerton, but he did not work out. He was sensible enough to know it and to ask that someone else be hired. As he had on occasion in the past, he recommended Ring, and the top editors of the newspaper agreed with the suggestion. The job was offered to him; though he had deep reservations about his ability to follow the enormously popular Keough, he decided to accept both the job and the challenge. He was put on a three-month trial at a salary of about $50 a week. James Keeley, the editor, wrote him: "I am very glad indeed to know that you are coming back to us and I hope the reunion will take place just as soon as possible." It did, on June 3, 1913.

AS IT TURNED OUT, Ring had no cause to fear comparison of his work and Keough's; his was so far superior that there simply was no real basis for comparison. Instead, it soon became obvious that he was no longer a sports writer, or sports columnist, but a humorist, and that his work deserved to be placed alongside that of two older Chicago newspapermen whose national reputation were already securely fixed and whose work was widely popular in 1913.

George Ade and Finley Peter Dunne were in superficial respects similar, but as humorists they were markedly different. Both were born in the mid-1860's, both began their careers as writers for Chicago newspapers, both did some sports coverage (Dunne is said to have originated "southpaw" as a synonym for "left-hander"), both rose to the position of featured columnist, and both made extensive use of the vernacular. That both influenced Ring is undeniable, but they taught him different things. Ade helped point him toward a biting but compassionate view of the "common man," while Dunne helped him discover the uses of disguising his satiric punches by delivering them through a persona.

Ade was an Indianan who, like the other popular Hoosier humorists of the day, had a deep affection for the hicks and rubes so scorned by the city slickers of the East. He hated pretension and made it the principal target of many of the satiric pieces published in 1899 as *Fables in Slang*. The device was Aesop updated, fables told in the language of the American countryside with morals uniquely American. One of the best is called "The Fable of the New York Person Who Gave the Stage Fright to Fostoria, Ohio":

A New York man went to visit a Cousin in the Far West.

The name of the Town was Fostoria, Ohio.

When he came into Town he had his Watch-Chain on the outside of his Coat, and his Pink Spats were the first ever seen in Fostoria.

"Have you a Manicure Parlor in this Beastly Hole?" asked the New York Man, as they walked up from the Train.

"What's that?" asked the Cousin, stepping on his own Feet.

"Great Heavens!" exclaimed the New York Man, and was silent for several Moments.

At Dinner he called for Artichokes, and when told that there were none, he said, "Oh, very well," in a Tone of Chastened Resignation.

After Dinner he took the Family into the Parlor, and told the Members how much they would Enjoy going to Weber and Fields'. Seeing a Book on the Table, he sauntered up to It and said, "Ah, one of Dick Davis' Things." Later in the Evening he visited the only Club House in Town. The Local Editor of the Evening Paper was playing Pin-Pool with the Superintendent of the Trolley Line. When the New York Man came into the Room, they began to Tremble and fell down on their Shots.

The Manager of the Hub and Spoke Factory then asked the

New York Man to have a Drink. The New York Man wondered if a Small Bottle was already cold. They said Yes, but it was a Lie. The Boy had to go out for it.

He found One that had been in the Window of the Turf Exchange since the Grand Opening, the Year after Natural Gas was discovered. The New York Man drank it, remarking that it was hardly as Dry as he usually got it at Martin's.

The Club Members looked at Him and said Nothing. They thought he meant Bradley-Martin's.

Next Day the New York Man was Interviewed by the Local Editor. He said the West had a Great Future. In the Evening he attended the Annual Dinner of the Bicycle Club, and went Home early because the Man sitting next to him put Ice in his Claret.

In due time, he returned to New York, and Fosteria took off its White Shirt.

Some Weeks after that, the Cousin of the New York Man had an Opportunity to visit the Metropolis. He rode on an Extra Ticket with a Stockman who was shipping three Car-Load of Horses and got a Free Ticket for every Car-Load.

When the Cousin arrived at New York he went to the address, and found the New York Man at Dinner.

There was a Sheaf of Celery on the Table.

Opposite the New York Man sat a Chiropodist who drank.

At his right was a Large Woman in a Flowered Wrapper—she had been Weeping.

At his left was a Snake-Charmer from Huber's Museum.

The New York Man asked the Cousin to wait Outside, and then explained that he was stopping there Temporarily. That evening they went to Proctor's, and stood during the Performance.

MORAL: *A New York Man never begins to Cut Ice until he is west of Rahway.*

Many of Ade's comic references are by now hopelessly dated, and his use of capitalization for laughs is a worn-out device, yet it is easy to see how he influenced Ring. Ade's country cousin and Ring's Tom Finch—the narrator of one of his best books, *The Big Town*—go through the same country-come-to-town experience: wide-eyed and gullible at first, they get taken for a ride, but in the end their solid folk wisdom triumphs, more or less, and the façade of urban superiority is stripped away. Where Ring parted company with Ade is that he went several steps further in exposing the venality of the rube as well as the slicker; if there are few true villains among Ring's naïfs, neither are there any real heroes. Ring genuinely liked Ade's work, and on numerous occasions he paid him the high compliment of teasing him in print:

> . . . he wrote a book called *Fables in Slang,* the slang consisting in every other wd. being spelt with a capital letter. The success of this work was instantaneous as the public was sick in tired of reading wd. after wd. that began with little bits of letters. The telephone company took the hint and went Geo. one better by getting out a book where practically every wd. in it commenced with a capital. It is hard to tell what will come next in these days of radio and one way streets. . . .
> As a writer Mr. Ade has been compared with Eddie Guest, Dr. Frank Crane and Upton Sinclair among his contemporaries, and Jane Austen, Marilyn Miller and Hughie Fullerton amongst his predecessors. It is almost uncanny.

Considering Ring's near-total lack of interest in politics it may seem surprising that he admired Dunne, whose trenchant commentary on the folks and folkways of politics is still pertinent; not only that, Ring was inherently conservative while Dunne disguised a passionate humanitarianism, which eventually allied him with the muckrakers, behind the thick Irish brogue and rambling talk of his saloonkeeper, Mr. Dooley, and his friend Hennessey. But it is in Mr. Dooley that the key to Ring's admiration for Dunne lies. In the first place, even though much of Mr. Dooley's speech now seems almost impenetrable, Dunne plainly had a keen ear for common talk and was able to set it plausibly on paper. More important, Mr. Dooley provided a persona through which Dunne, himself rather shy and unprepossessing, could express his vigorous ideas:

> . . . "Th' Dimmycrats have gr-reat confidence, th' Raypublicans ar-re sure, th' Popylists are hopeful, th' Prohybitionists look f'r a landslide or a flood, or whativer you may call a Prohybition victhry, an' th' Socylists think this may be their year. That's what makes pollytics th' gr-reat game an' th' on'y wan to dhrive dull care away. . . . If ye get a bad hand at poker ye lay it down. But if ye get a bad hand at pollytics ye bet ye'er pair iv' deuces as blithe as an Englishman who has jus' larned th' game out iv th' spoortin' columns iv' th' London Times. If ye don't win fair ye may win

foul. If ye don't win ye may tie an' get th' money in th' confusion. . . . Ivry year men crawl out iv th' hospitals, where they've been since last iliction day, to vote th' Raypublican ticket in Mississippi. . . .

"As a pilgrim father that missed th' first boats, I must raise me claryon voice again' th' invasion iv this fair land be th' paupers an' arnychists in effete Europe. Ye bet I must—because I'm here first."

Eventually Dunne's writing was done for magazines of relatively small and elite circulation, but he began his Mr. Dooley pieces as a columnist for a mass-circulation newspaper; he recognized that by using common speech he could reach ordinary readers as well as couch his opinions in humorous terms. Ring relied on a similar device throughout his career. His "Weekly Letter," a nationally syndicated newspaper column written from November, 1919, to March, 1927, was composed in the voice of a coarse but witty and knowing ordinary American, Ring himself in the guise of the "wise boob"; the comments above about George Ade are taken from one of those columns. Ring's curious lack of confidence in the authority of his own voice was so large that it was not until the last five years of his life, when he began writing for *The New Yorker*, that he spoke publicly in it with any regularity. In his fiction, which he began writing within a few months of taking over the "Wake," he was infinitely more successful using a first-person voice that was not his own than as a third-person omniscient author. In the mid-twenties, when he began to get ideas about being a "serious" writer in the way Scott Fitzgerald and Maxwell Perkins wanted him to be, he made a concerted effort to write in the third person; he saw that as harder to do and therefore, presumably, somehow more noble than the first-person pieces he wrote with such facility. Yet very little of this work is durable, and none of it compares well with "Some Like Them Cold" and "I Can't Breathe" and the other superb first-person stories.

George Ade and Finley Peter Dunne obviously were not the only humorists whose work Ring read and admired, but they seem to have been the ones with whom he felt most comfortable. They were newspapermen; throughout his life he was far more at ease with newspaper people and what they wrote than he was with more "literary" writers. Ade and Dunne were also logical models for a young man—Ring was only twenty-eight when he took command of the "Wake"—who was assuming what he regarded as heavy responsibilities in the tough arena of Chicago journalism. It was not long before he would leave both of them far behind, but they gave him a solid foundation on which to build, a foundation rooted in the Middle West and the speech of its people. Ring, who had the sharpest ear of all, heard that speech more accurately than anyone, and it was during the years of the "Wake" that he found the means of articulating it.

The six years of the "Wake" were to be splendid for Ring in every way, and for Ellis too. The family's financial problems were soon to end, and three more sons were to be born. June 3, 1913, was in many ways the beginning of a new life.

Part Five

In the Wake of the News

"I now say that if it is necessary
that the undersigned's name be
never out of the paper, why not print
merely the undersigned's name on
Monday mornings, adding perhaps some
phrase such as 'who did not work
yesterday.' "

T HIS IS HOW RING INTRODUCED HIMSELF AS AUTHOR, OR "EDITOR"
as he was generally known, of "In the Wake of the News":

> *Good-by, everybody; good-by, Jimmy Cal;*
> *Good-by, William Gleason; good-by, Doc, old pal;*
> *Sully, Matty, Harry, and Morris, good-by, good-by,*
> *Sure I hope you all will feel sorry the same as I.*
> *Good-by, old Edward; good-by, little Ray;*
> *Good-by, all you White Sox—I quit gadding today.*
> [Encore.]
> *Good-by, Johnny Evers; good-by, Lurid Lew;*
> *Good-by, Charlie Williams; good-by, Lower Two;*
> *Schulte, Heine, Jimmy, and Larry, good-by, good-by.*
> *Perhaps you'll look me up when you tarry awhile in Chi.*
> *Good-by, clams and swordfish; good-by, Gay White Way;*
> *Good-by, joys of Brooklyn—I quit gadding today.*

It was a tentative and emotionally ambiguous beginning, but
the uncertainty did not last long. Within a matter of weeks Ring
was confidently at the helm of the "Wake," filling it every day
with items covering a remarkable variety of subjects and writing
styles. There were bits of baseball gossip, poems about his son,
serials, nonsense plays, short stories, parodies, letters, nursery tales
and self-satires. As he recalled it years later, "Turning out a daily
column isn't really very difficult, because you get into the habit
of working. Probably you will write only one good column out of
seven issues, but people think that because one issue is good, the
other six must be equally amusing." He underestimated himself.
In six years of writing the "Wake" Ring did his share of inferior
work, but overall the quality was so high that the work of those
years must be counted among the extraordinary accomplishments
of American journalism. Virtually everything upon which Ring's

later fame was built originated in the "Wake," and in some instances the "Wake" version was actually superior to the more celebrated work. He built up a large and loyal audience, and he was read by young would-be writers who consciously imitated him —in one case, with great consequences for American fiction. He was probably happier in the years of the "Wake" than in any other period of his adult life, and his happiness showed in the writing he did.

During the first four years Ring wrote the column, he produced it seven times a week—in itself almost enough of an accomplishment to place him in a journalistic hall of fame. He did, however, offer a change of pace on Mondays, as he told his readers three weeks after he took over the job:

> *A friend of mine, who reads the Wake (a friend he*
> *sure must be)*
> *Had me to dine a week ago last Sunday,*
> *And after we had dined awhile, the friend inquired*
> *of me:*
> *"Why is the Wake so very short on Monday?"*
>
> *I told him, and I'll tell you, too—'twas thus*
> *my boss did speak:*
> *"Each week, to rest your brain, we'll give you*
> *one day.*
> *We really can't expect a man to keep a Wake all*
> *week,*
> *So just send in a verse or two for Monday."*
>
> *And, yielding to the boss, which is the proper*
> *thing to do,*
> *I set aside each Sunday as a fun day,*
> *And Tuesday, Wednesday, Thursday, Friday—all the*
> *whole week through—*
> *I wonder wotinel to write for Monday.*

He solved that problem by writing verses about John and, as his family grew, all of his sons. Though he can be charged with and found guilty of a considerable degree of sentimentality, not to mention bad verse, the best of the poems retain a definite charm and a pleasant aura of paternal affection. Writing about one's children is like showing off their pictures; you have to know when to stop, and at times Ring didn't. But on the whole he had a large reservoir of the sixth sense essential to a successful newspaper columnist: he knew how to discern what in his own life would be of interest to readers, and how to describe it to them. Several of the best "Wake" poems were collected in Ring's first book, *Bib Ballads*, published in 1915. One of them is called "Taste":

> *I can't understand why you pass up the toys*
> *That Santa considered just right for small boys;*
> *I can't understand why you turn up your nose*
> *At dogs, hobby-horses, and treasures like those,*
> *And play a whole hour, sometimes longer than that,*
> *With a thing as prosaic as Daddy's old hat.*
>
> *The tables and shelves have been loaded for you*
> *With volumes of pictures—they're pretty ones, too—*
> *Of birds, beasts, and fishes, and old Mother Goose*
> *Repines in a corner and feels like the deuce,*
> *While you, on the floor, quite contentedly look*
> *At page after page of the telephone book.*

Another is "The Grocery Man and the Bear":

> *He was weary of all of his usual joys;*
> *   His books and his blocks made him tired.*
> *And so did his games and mechanical toys,*
> *   And the songs he had always admired;*
> *So I told him a story, a story so new*
> *   It had never been heard anywhere;*
> *A tale disconnected, unlikely, untrue,*
> *   Called The Grocery Man and the Bear.*
>
> *I didn't think much of the story despite*
> *   The fact 'twas a child of my brain,*
> *And I never dreamt, when I told it that night,*
> *   That I'd have to tell it again;*
> *I never imagined 'twould make such a hit*
> *   With the audience of one that was there*
> *That for hours at a time he would quietly sit*
> *   Through The Grocery Man and the Bear.*
>
> *To all other stories, this one is preferred;*
> *   It's the season's best seller so far,*

> And out at our house it's as frequently heard
> As cuss-words in Mexico are.
> When choo-choos and horses and picture books fail,
> He'll remain, quite content, in his chair,
> While I tell o'er and o'er the incredible tale
> Of The Grocery Man and the Bear.

Notwithstanding all his vaunted cynicism, which can neither be dismissed nor discounted, Ring had a remarkable feeling for universal human experience. Those little poems, trivial though of course they are, nicely convey the pride of fatherhood and the unpredictability of childhood. Both poems are amusing, but readers laughed because their response was rooted in their own lives, because their immediate reaction was, "Yes, that's the way it is."

Ring had all manner of ways to make his readers laugh, and he began trying them out at once. Eight days after he started the column he began "The Pennant Pursuit," described as "A Novel (By the Copy Boy)," in which a young collegian named Verne Dalton yearns for athletic glory: "O said Verne I wonder if I'll ever have a posickion on that team and figth for the glory of my ama mather, but he did not have much hope because his parents had said he must devoat all his time to study." The misspellings and illiteracies were too elaborate to be persuasive, but Ring was trying his hand at the vernacular and testing his ability to reproduce it. As early as September, he was sure enough of what he was doing to produce a three-episode serial "By a Athlete*" (*"Unassisted") that so clearly anticipates *You Know Me Al* that no analysis is necessary. It began: "We ought to of trimmed 'em. When Egan, the big slob, said I was out at second he musta been full o' hops, the big boob. I like t'know where he was at las' night, the big bum. Some o' them umps oughta be on the chain gang, the big boobs."

Another athletic "contributor," need it be said, was Frank Schulte, who could always be relied upon to come to the rescue if the column fell short of copy. In July, Schulte was credited as author of several verses of "A Epick," which got so bad that Ring finally suspended him:

Frank Milton Schulte, considered by many the most reliable and consistent hitter on the Wake team, was last night severely reprimanded and then indefinitely suspended for alleged soldiering on the job. The suspension followed a war of words between Schulte and the manager of the Wake, during which Schulte sassed his boss. Manager Lardner gave out the following statement:

"Ever since the start of the Epick series, I have been convinced that Schulte was not trying. I have been in the game long enough to know that he is one of the greatest poets of modern times, but I must say that his work on the Epick has been awful. I knew he was capable and naturally reached the conclusion that he was loafing. I won't stand for anything like that among my men. Hence his suspension. He will be reinstated only when he apologizes to me and promises to try to give me his best services."

A few details of the quarrel between the manager and his star were gleaned from some of the other players. After Saturday's Epick, Schulte was called on the club house carpet. "You've been laying down on me," the boss is reported to have told him. "You've got to brace up or stand for a fine." "If you don't like my stuff," Schulte retorted, "get somebody else." This made the manager mad and he said: "That remark means a vacation for you."

It is said that Schulte has long been dissatisfied with his berth on the Wake and wants to be traded to Breakfast Food or Day Dreams. But the Wake manager has no intention of letting go a man who is capable of filling up so much space.

Once again, excessive analysis would overinflate what is, after all, merely a four-paragraph item written to amuse readers of a sports section. Yet the skill and subtlety of those paragraphs are singular. The Lardner "statement" is a deft satire, by faithful imitation, of the ponderous self-justifications issued to the press by sports executives after they do anything remotely controversial. The snippet of dialogue between Schulte and Lardner is absolutely true to sporting language of the time. The reference to "Breakfast Food or Day Dreams" takes a back-of-the-hand swipe at other newspaper features of the day, which also included Jane Eddington's "Economical Housekeeping," "Lillian Russell's Beauty Secrets," "Marion Harland's Helping Hand" and "Laura Jean Libbey's Advice." The final sentence closes the item on a note of self-mockery: Ring was admitting to his readers that every once in a while a columnist gets desperate for something to write about, and in making the admission he was making friends.

Schulte was not the only ballplayer to figure regularly in the "Wake." A favorite target of Ring's gentle teasing was a White

Sox player with the splendid name of Ping Bodie and the figure to go with it: he was 5 feet 8 inches and weighed 195 pounds. When Bodie signed to do a vaudeville turn talking to audiences about baseball, Ring observed that "the subject, baseball, is a broad one, as is the monologuist." Ring then offered his readers a preview of how the monologue might go, a preview that leaves little doubt that there is more than a bit of Ping Bodie in Jack Keefe:

"I can sure hit that old pill.

"Some of your smart guys say I'm solid ivory. Do I look like solid ivory? Or solid anything? . . .

"I guess I'm a bonehead. I don't know anything. But the guys that talk that way about me are sitting on the bench while I'm out there working and winning ball games. How many games would we have won from Philly if Bonehead Bodie had been on the bench?

"I don't have to play ball. I can go out there to San Fran any time I want to and get a job. But I'll be playing ball long after some of those smart guys have got the can.

"I can sure hit that old pill.

"If I'm so rotten why do they play me? They've got a lot of fellers sitting on the bench, doing nothing. They don't have to use me. Let 'em put me on the bench. Iskabibble.

"I can sure hit that old pill."

No one was safe from Ring's barbs, and as he moved the column further and further away from sports he took on all comers. He disposed of James Whitcomb Riley, for example, in four stanzas of Highlands gibberish. Here is one of them:

> When the frast is on the heather an' the ice is
>   on the stream,
> An' the puttin' greens be covered deep wi' snow,
> An' yer breath blows out afore ye like a railway
>   engine's steam,
> That's the time o' year aw ca' the best of a'.

In a more serious vein, if serious is the word for it, Ring was also moving in directions that would become clearer in the future. In December, for example, he wrote an unusually long column that consisted of a play, "The Follies of 1919," in which the antecedents of the nonsense plays of the 1920's are obvious. It includes improbable casting ("A Wonder" played by Heine Zimmerman, "Prof. Killjoy" by "Old Man Grump"), equally improbable settings ("A Jungle in California") and dialogue marked by hints of what eventually would become Ring's trademark, the comic nonsequitur:

> MAGNATE—Do you keep books here?
> THE LIBRARIAN—No; you'll find them at the delicatessen.
> MAGNATE—Have you got a history?
> THE LIBRARIAN—What kind of history?
> MAGNATE—A big, thick one.
> THE LIBRARIAN—We keep all the big books on this shelf. You can look and see for yourself.
> MAGNATE—Let me see; let me see. Here's one that's all right. Let me see. It says the Battle of Ischkebibble was fought on July 12. May I use your phone?
> THE LIBRARIAN—Go to it.
> MAGNATE—Hello, hello! Is this the Eagle office? Give me the sporting department. Hello! Is that you, Tom? Say, we're going to have a double header and a dedication on the 12th of July. That's the date of the Battle of Ischkebibble. Get me? All right, good-by.
> THE LIBRARIAN—Good night, nurse.

Ring welcomed the New Year with what amounted to a short story. The column, called "New Year's Eve," tells about three men who go out on the town and, after boasting of their ability to hold their liquor, proceed to get drunk and disorderly. The story is told completely in dialogue; though it arrives at a predictable conclusion, it is skillfully done.

In March, Ring tried another device he would use frequently in the future, the mock autobiography:

> The Wake's ed. was born twenty-three years ago today at Niles, Mich. He received his first baseball training as a member of the Spartans, an amateur team that was defeated every Saturday by the Dickereels, sometimes called Depots. The Dickereels used only six men in their games with the Spartans, and if a few members of the latter club had been barred from competition, the results might have been different. R.W. played on the H.S. teams, baseball, tennis, and football. His football reputation once caused a scout from a large middle western university to look him over. The outcome was that the young athlete got no college education.

The subject of this sketch has helped manage the South Bend Central leaguers, the White Sox, and Cubs and the two Boston clubs. He knows Ed Walsh, Ty Cobb, Charles A. Comiskey, and Walter Eckersall personally, and has received personal letters from Jimmy Sheckard and Frank Schulte. He is for cleanness in politics and on the ball field, and will back up his umpires to the limit. He writes his own stuff and has never made an offer for a controlling interest in the Cubs.

Ring kept his readers abreast of his personal life in other ways. By April, 1914, war with Mexico was a possibility and Ring's enthusiasm for taking up arms was minimal; he was neither a warrior nor a superpatriot, and he regarded the conflict that threatened with undisguised disdain. In a Monday poem called "My Alibi," he told his readers how he intended to avoid the fray:

> And now I prize my little kid
> More highly than I ever did.
>
> I've always liked him more or less,
> Admired his baby ways;
> I've bored you lots of times, I guess,
> With verses in his praise.
>
> I've liked him for his funny talk,
> His laugh, his charming smile,
> His cute but most peculiar walk,
> His ev'ry trick and wile.
>
> But now there's war with Mexico,
> And that's where I would be;
> O, yes, I'd dearly love to go
> And have them shoot at me.
>
> I'd love to have some greaser bust
> A bullet through my dome;
> But it can't be, because I must
> Remain with him, at home.
>
> And so I prize my little kid
> More highly than I ever did.

Despite the enthusiasm of the powerful Hearst papers for a saber-rattling adventure, Woodrow Wilson managed to blunder out of his Mexican exercise in gunboat diplomacy just as he had blundered into it, so the threat of military service vanished. But when it arose more seriously in the summer of 1916, with the United States edging closer and closer to joining the World War, Ring was just as adamant about nonparticipation, reminding his children in print that "You're my three excuses for/Not competing in this war." To many American young men of the next generation, as Geoffrey Wolff has trenchantly observed, "there would be only two classes of men after the war: those who went, and those who did not," but Ring shared none of this zeal for shedding blood, his own or anyone else's. Eventually he made a series of patriotic gestures—he wrote a Jack Keefe letter supporting the second Liberty Loan in 1917, he made a brief visit to the French battlefront, and he sent Keefe into battle as "Jack the Kaiser Killer"—but his heart was not in any of them.

The family news Ring reported to his readers a month later was the birth, on May 18, of his second son, James Phillips Lardner. He welcomed him with a warning:

> *You'll have to take some licking, too,*
> *For Brother John will pick on you.*
> *But p'rhaps you'll grow to look like dad,*
> *So cheer up, kid, life's not so bad.*

For the Lardners, in point of fact, life had never been better. After three years of marriage spent in rented apartments of varying degrees of roominess and attractiveness, they now had their own house. Ellis had received the promise of an inheritance upon the death of her father, and she and Ring bought a lot in Riverside. Though Ring made frequent jokes at his own expense in the "Wake" by depicting Riverside as a rather ordinary suburb, the truth is that they had chosen expensively and well. To give a sense of the kind of place in which the Lardners would live for the next three years, it is worth quoting at length the authoritative *Chicago: Growth of a Metropolis*, by Harold M. Mayer and Richard C. Wade:

> Just a little to the south of Oak Park was Chicago's most famous suburb, Riverside. Laid out by the nation's leading landscapist, Frederick Law Olmsted, on David A. Gage's farm at the crossing of the Des Plaines River by the Chicago, Burlington and Quincy

Railroad, it was the most ambitious and successful planned suburb of its time. Although its natural advantages would seem obvious to later generations, an early directory in 1869 noted that the site presented "a plentiful lack of improvements, and an overwhelming generosity of raw prairie wind and waste prairie land which were anything but inviting." Yet, when completed, Riverside gave western Chicago, in the words of the same observer, what it always lacked—"at once an elegant drive, a handsome park, and a delightful suburban city."

Olmsted's town differed markedly from most other Chicago suburbs. Instead of being simply subdivided by developers with few or no controls, it was carefully planned in great detail. Lots were generous, 100 feet by 225 feet, and houses had to be set back thirty feet from the street. Olmsted rejected the conventional grid pattern as "too stiff and formal for such adornment and rusticity as should be combined in a model suburb." Instead, the roadways were "formed to curve lines which make a graceful and harmonious whole." Park land straddled the meandering Des Plaines River, providing a natural focus for the design and a public pleasure ground in the center of town. And the original development included every kind of essential service—water, drainage, lighting, schools, and recreational facilities. In short, it met the expectations of its creator: to "combine the conveniences peculiar to the finest modern towns with the domestic advantages of a most charming country."

The house that Ring and Ellis built in this delightful setting was small and unpretentious, but it gave them as much trouble in the construction as if it were a castle. Work began in the fall of 1913, after extended negotiations with the architect to get everything as Ellis wanted it: ". . . we must have a closet in the other room—I don't care if it is a small one. And if there is any possible way to do it have him put the pantry between the dining room and kitchen—it could be a long narrow one and then he could put the sink or the gas range in the alcove or . . . where the pantry is now. Don't say anything about the long windows upstairs. I think they are better as they are or at least they are all right that way." But fixing matters with the architect was only the beginning of their problems. Ellis was borrowing against her inheritance, and costs kept going up, to a total of around $4,000 for the house, a sidewalk, the architect's fee and related incidentals. Then, as an embellishment of sorts, they had one of those experiences that no one who builds a house expects and everyone who builds a house encounters: as Ellis, who was visiting her family in Goshen and thus well away from the carnage, put it in a letter to Ring, "Wasn't it crazy about their excavating the wrong way?"

Somehow they struggled through, however; not merely did they have a new house in a good neighborhood, but Ring had the raw material for one of his early short stories, "Own Your Own Home." It eventually became the title story of a small book about Fred Gross, a fat middle-aged Chicago assistant chief of detectives who, with his wife, Grace, decides to flee the South Side and build a house in the fictional suburb of Allison. Ring did not write autobiographical fiction in the accepted sense of the term, but almost everything he wrote sprang from one autobiographical impulse or another. In this case it was the experience—"the agony" may be more accurate—of housebuilding. This letter from Fred Gross to his brother, Charley, merely transcribes the Lardners' own experience into a semiliterate's prose:

> The latest is the archateck told me we should ought to do some gradeing on the lot a round the house because the weather was so good & then we wouldent have to do no gradeing in the spring but could get busy right a way & fix up the lawn & plant the grass seeds. Well I told Grace a bout it & she says it was in the contrack that the contrackter had to do the gradeing with the dirt that was dug out of the ground where the foundashun is at & I told the archateck a bout that & he says on acct of there digging the foundashun the rong way at the start they wasent no dirt left over because they had to fill in where they dug out and shouldent of dug so I had to go & get a hold of a man to come & do some gradeing a round the house & he stuck me for $60 but thats all over now & out of the way.
>
> Then Grace found out that they was only 2 of the rms. up stares that theys a place for closets in them & I says 2 closets was enough but she says no they got to be closets in all 4 of the rms. up stares & I asked the archateck a bout it & he says it was foolish, but Grace kicked like a mule & the archateck says he could put in the closets but it would make them 2 rms. smaller. I asked him if it would cost more money & he says no he dident think so so we had him go a head & make plans for 2 more closets & yest. he come & told me it would cost $50 more & I says I thot you told me it wouldent cost nothing more & he says I thot so my self but I was miss taken. So what could a man do but pay the extra $50 only I aint payed it yet but will half to.

Riverside was a clearly identifiable community, enough so to be considered in effect a small town, with its own customs and rituals. The Fourth of July, for example, involved a baby parade, a grand parade and a grand pageant, the latter a re-enactment of the signing of the Declaration of Independence; the community gathered to sing "America," a picnic was held with various games thereafter, and in the evening there were fireworks, movies and music. On other holidays, Riverside people headed for resorts in the area, or for the race tracks, or for ball games in Chicago.

The Lardners seem to have taken part in, and enjoyed, everything. An occasional feature of the "Wake" was a column under the heading "Riverside Locals," in which Ring brought his readers up to date on what was going on in his neighborhood. A few excerpts give a sense of what life was like in those days for the Lardner family, both in and out of the household:

> The Abbott boys came out last week to get a square meal. They paid for it by playing the ukalele, the instrument imported at great expense from Honolulu, and hitting the lead and tenor, respectively, in some mighty fine close harmony.

> J. A. Lardner and P. Torrence got lost Friday evening before tea and their parents figuratively scoured the town for them. The boys finally returned to their respective homes and calmly announced that they had been in a pool, an announcement which was unnecessary.

> The Married Men will play a practice game with the Fuller-Morrison nine this afternoon. Those of the former nine who live through it will pastime next Tuesday vs. the Singletons.

> The orchestra at the Chateau Des Plaines are all wearing the same kinds of shirts and look darned handsome.

> J. A. Lardner is picking up some queer language round the neighborhood.

> The ten-forty towards town was nearly on time Tuesday.

> Many have had their American flags hung out the past 10 days or so, on acct. of Lincoln's and Washington's birthdays both occurring the same month, strangely enough.

Riverside was not an inexpensive place to live, and in any case the Lardners managed to spend money freely no matter where they were situated, so it was a matter of extraordinarily good luck that their arrival there coincided with the beginning of Ring's lucrative career as a free-lance writer. How that career got its start has been the subject of innumerable accounts, all of them different in one way or another. What virtually all agree on is that the Sunday editor of the *Tribune* offered Ring $50 for a base-ball story, to be printed in the feature section. Ring gave him one, told in the form of letters from a ballplayer named Jack Keefe to his friend Al; the language was the vernacular and the spelling was that of a semiliterate. The editor decided he could not accept the story for his section, but Ring clearly felt he had hit on something, for he sent it off to George Horace Lorimer, editor of the *Saturday Evening Post*. What happened next is where the various accounts differ; some have the story coming back from the *Post* with aston-ishing rapidity, some ascribe a large role to a sports writer and friend of Ring's named Charles Van Loan, some suggest that Ring's carefully illiterate prose was gussied up by a fastidious minor editor. One such account, written in 1926 by Burton Rascoe, was so riddled with inaccuracies that Ring wrote to him in exasperation:

> . . . The first "busher" story was never sent back by the *Post*; it was accepted promptly by Mr. Lorimer himself. I didn't show it to Hugh Fullerton or Charlie Van Loan first; I sent it to Mr. Lori-mer at the *Post*'s office, not to his residence; I didn't write "Per-sonal" on the envelope in even one place; I didn't write any pre-liminary, special delivery, warning letter to Mr. Lorimer; no sub-editor ever asked me to correct the spelling and grammar, and I never sent any sub-editor or anyone else a bundle of letters I had received from ball players. Otherwise—

The story was "A Busher's Letters Home," the first of the six that would be collected in 1916 as *You Know Me Al*. It appeared in the *Post*'s issue dated March 7, 1914. The reaction was im-mediate and staggering. The *Post* must have been inundated with favorable letters from readers, for Lorimer was quick to ask Ring for more Jack Keefe stories and to begin a process that would gradually increase Ring's fee per story from $250 to $1,500; all six of the *You Know Me Al* stories appeared in 1914. The mail at the Lardner house increased, too. John N. Wheeler, a newsman who had gotten in on the ground floor of the syndication busi-

ness, wrote in April to inquire if Ring would be interested in doing
a "series of humorous articles to be run once a week, for syndication purposes," with Ring getting 50 percent of the net profits;
Ring must have said no, for nothing came of the offer, but he
did not forget Wheeler and it was to him that he turned when he
decided to go free-lance in 1919. Franklin P. Adams asked if Ring
might be interested in taking a journalistic position in New York.
Ring's reply was revealing:

> . . . it's dough and the prospect of it that would tempt me to
> tackle the New York game. I think a gent in this business would
> be foolish not to go to New York if he had a good chance. From
> all I can learn, that's where the real money is. . . . I could be torn
> away from here—and Riverside—for $8,000, and that's probably
> more than I'm worth. But you see how things are. It's not that
> I'm swelled on myself as much as some of our well-known diamond
> heroes, but that I'd have to get something like that to make the
> change pay.

In May, George H. Doran of Doran and Company made "immediate application for the book publishing rights" to a series
of busher pieces. Then, in the summer, more letters came pouring
in. Ray Long of *Redbook* magazine wrote to solicit stories; Cam-
eron MacKenzie, vice president of *McClure's*, invited stories at
7½ cents a word, offering an increase to 10 cents "if those prove
a success"; C. B. DeCamp of *Metropolitan* was interested in stories.
Ring—who, according to Ellis, was in good health "except for a
slight attack of swell head"—accepted just about every offer that
came along. It was a wise course to follow, for the unknown writer
who turns down assignments is not likely to be offered them again,
but it was an exhausting course as well; Ellis told her family Ring
was "working his head off." By the end of the year he had published ten stories, nine in the *Saturday Evening Post* and one in
Redbook—an extraordinary accomplishment for a young writer
who had come almost totally out of the blue.

Eventually the saga of Jack Keefe encompassed three books
and a large handful of uncollected short stories. *You Know Me Al*
is unquestionably the best of the lot, written as it was when Ring's
enthusiasm for his subject was at its peak. *Treat 'Em Rough* is
trivial, of interest now only to Lardner scholars, and not of much
interest to them. *The Real Dope* contains enough good moments

to compensate for its overall flatness. Of the loose odds and ends, the two best—"Call for Mr. Keefe!" and "Along Came Ruth"— are now available in the 1976 collection, *Some Champions.*

You Know Me Al is not a novel but it comes close to having the form of one. In the letters Jack Keefe writes to "Friend Al" back home in Bedford, Indiana, Ring tells the loosely structured tale of an incredibly brash rookie who joins the White Sox, fails in his initial major-league test, is sold to the minors, returns and pitches well, marries a gold-digging shrew, and ends the season as a reasonably well established big-league performer. It was, at the time of its publication, the first book to treat baseball and the men who played it as the subjects of literate fiction, and ever since it has suffered under the handicap of being dismissed, or condescended to, as a "baseball novel." It is indeed that, but it is also much more: Jack Keefe is one of the great "originals" in American fiction, and the language with which he writes his friend is an expression of the vernacular that has had a lasting effect on the way American writers describe American talk.

Jack Keefe may be a bit larger than life, but not much. From his very first appearance, his character was firmly set; Ring allowed no significant deviations from it. Jack is pigheaded, cocky, gullible, selfish, sentimental, naïve, stubborn, self-deceiving—and talented. He is a fountain of alibis, mangled axioms and witless repartee. He is a terrible tightwad, but at the bargaining table Charles Comiskey routinely takes him to the cleaners. He fancies himself a great lover, and in the course of his rookie season manages to propose to three equally horrible women, finally landing the dreadful Florrie. He has a great natural talent but—and here we have what Ring hated most—he abuses it; he allows himself to get "hog fat" and he makes no effort to learn the refinements and subtleties of the pitcher's trade; as Christy Mathewson tells him, when he complains of having a sore arm, "I wisht I had a sore arm like yourn and a little sence with it."

Jack is often confused by readers with another famous Lardner creation, "Alibi Ike"; the confusion is pardonable, for Jack is no slouch when it comes to handing out excuses. In an early test with the White Sox, he gives up only one hit in three innings, "and that was a ground ball that the recrut shortstop Johnson ought to of ate up." When Ty Cobb challenges him with a bunt, "I would of threw him out a block but I stubbed my toe in a rough place and fell down." In the City Series against the Cubs, "That lucky stiff Zimmerman was the only guy that got a real hit off of me and he must of shut his eyes and throwed his bat because the ball he hit was a foot over his head." Finally, in August of his second season, he sums it all up:

> This should ought to of gave me a record of 16 wins and 0 defeats because the only games I lost was throwed away behind me but instead of that my record is 10 games win and 6 defeats and that don't include the games I finished up and helped the other boys win which is about 6 more alltogether but what do I care about my record Al? because I am not the kind of man that is allways thinking about there record and playing for there record while I am satisfied if I give the club the best I got and if I win all O.K. And if I lose who's fault is it. Not mine Al.

Jack fancies himself a man of wit and savvy, with the consequence that he is the classic American rube in whose hands a little knowledge is a dangerous thing. He has a cliché ready for every occasion, and invariably he gets it wrong. Florrie, he tells Al, "maybe ain't as pretty as Violet and Hazel but as they say beauty isn't only so deep." Later he wishes he had never seen the woman, but "it is too late now to cry in the sour milk." In *The Real Dope* he reports that asking Florrie for favors "is like rolling off a duck's back you might say and its first in one ear and then the other," and he warns fellow soldiers who have put over a practical joke on him that "they's plenty of time for the laugh to be on the other foot before this war is over."

Similarly, Jack regards himself as a lively fellow in any debate, and he reports his devastating squelches to Al with obvious pride: "And then he says I wish we had of sent you to Milwaukee and I come back at him. I says I wish you had of." On another occasion, he has it out with Ty Cobb:

> . . . Cobb came pranceing up like he always does and yells Give me that slow one Boy. So I says All right. But I fooled him. Instead of giveing him a slow one like I said I was going I handed him a spitter. He hit it all right but it was a line drive right in Chase's hands. He says Pretty lucky Boy but I will get you next time. I says Yes you will.

Much of the commotion and excitement that the busher stories provoked when they first appeared was because of the language Ring used. It was immediately recognized as an authentic American voice, a faithful rendition of the way a person of the time with only rudimentary education would be likely to write in his letters to his best friend. Ring did permit himself occasional exaggerations for comic effect, but the accuracy of his ear and the care he took in writing prohibited him from indulging in the facile humor later practiced by Edward Streeter (". . . author of the 'Dere Mable' letters, for which I received many congratulations") and other Lardner imitators whose humor consisted primarily of misspelled words. Ring was trying to be both funny and accurate; he was also trying to get down on paper the words of a man who wrote the same way he talked. The scheme he devised was, if not provably accurate, certainly plausible. Jack misspelled simple words because he assumed he knew how to spell them, and he spelled long or unfamiliar words correctly because he presumably looked them up in the dictionary. Hence "there" for "their," "to" for "too," "sence" for "sense." Ring also made Jack a pure phonetic speller, with such results as "nosion" for "notion" and "balling" for "bawling." All in all, he kept tight control over the misspellings—much tighter than he did in the 1915 baseball pieces for *American* magazine—because he knew that too much illiteracy would get in the reader's way; he made Jack a fool but not an idiot.

He further enhanced the immediacy of the busher stories by making Jack and his family almost the only fictional characters in them. The players, coaches, managers and owners were actual baseball figures, and in fact the spring-training trip Jack takes in his rookie season follows the same route that Ring and Ellis took with the White Sox in 1913. The close mixture of fiction and reality inevitably led to some degree of confusion and an even greater degree of curiosity about the inspiration for the character of Jack. Ring got mail about it, reviewers and sports writers wrote about it, but he kept his mouth shut. He got a certain pleasure out of all the gossip; he also knew better than anyone else that Jack was at heart a creation of the imagination, so when he finally got around to writing something about the question, he put it in proper perspective. He laughed at it:

The writer has been asked frequently, or perhaps not very often after all, two vital questions regarding the letters published in this book: (1) Are they actual letters or copies of actual letters? and (2) Who is the original Jack Keefe?

The first question seemed highly complimentary until you thought it over and realized that no one with good sense could have asked it. Some of the letters run as long as a thousand words and there is only one person in the world who writes letters of that length. She is a sister-in-law of mine living in Indianapolis, and when she sits down to write a letter, she holds nothing back. But she is a Phi Beta and incapable of the mistakes in spelling and grammar that unfortunately have crept into this volume.

As for the other question, I have heretofore declined to reply to it, as a reply would have stopped the boys and girls from guessing, and their guesses have given me many a thrill. But now there are no ball players left whom they haven't guessed, from Noah to Bucky Harris, and I may as well give the correct answer. The original of Jack Keefe is not a ball player at all, but Jane Addams of Hull House, a former Follies girl.

The baseball in *You Know Me Al* is notable for the accuracy and sensitivity with which Ring, through Jack, reported it. John Lardner, who in his very different way was almost as successful and influential a sports writer as his father, wrote in his introduction to a 1960 edition of the book: "Its broader values to one side, there has never been a sounder baseball book. . . . [I]f you stop to pick over the accounts of ball games, you see that each detail is correct in relation to place, weather, time of year, and the hitting, pitching, or fielding idiosyncracies of a hundred players. . . . I have never read a piece of baseball fiction, besides this one, in which there was no technical mistake." Even allowing for filial pride, that is an accurate assessment.

It was when Ring took Jack away from the baseball diamond that he ran into trouble. The stories in *Treat 'Em Rough* and *The Real Dope* were written not out of Ring's own experience and observations, but out of a desire to meet the demands of the market. In 1918 and 1919, when they were published, the market wanted war stories with a strong dose of patriotism; the trouble was that Ring hated war, had no real sense of what was going on in Europe, and agreed with Dr. Johnson about patriotism. In

Treat 'Em Rough Jack enlists and reports to Al from Camp Grant, in Illinois, that "I am out of baseball now and in the big game," but Ring was merely going through the motions in suggesting that Jack was doing something noble. Jack's adventures include barracks scrapes, an inexplicable promotion to corporal, a flirtation, and assignment to Camp Logan, Texas, where he awaits transfer to Europe.

He gets there in *The Real Dope*, which picks up a bit because Ring had at least seen the European front and had an idea, albeit a foggy one, of what was happening over there. Jack tells Al that his letters will contain "the real dope that I seen myself," but it is Jack himself, in the book's too obvious title, who is the real dope. He is determined to win the war single-handedly, but when he finally does see "action" the enemy turns out to be a member of his own company. The device of most of the episodes is a practical joke played on Jack by one soldier or another, with the consequence that the stories are formula work, but there are some fine Lardner touches, such as this paragraph boasting of Jack's prowess in what he thought was French learned en route to the Continent:

> Well Al that shows we been learning something when the Frenchmans themself know what we are talking about and I and Lee will have the laugh on the rest of the boys when we get there that is if we do get there but for some reason another I have got a hunch that we won't never see France and I can't explain why but once in a while a man gets a hunch and a lot of times they are generally always right.

The busher stories developed a huge popular following immediately upon publication, but the critics did not pay much attention to them until the mid-twenties, when Ring's emergence as a leading Scribner author forced people who had theretofore ignored him to take him seriously. The least patronizing and most valuable comment on Jack Keefe came from England, of all places, and Virginia Woolf, of all people. Writing in the *Dial* in 1925, she encountered Ring with a sense of genuine discovery, a clear amazement at what she had found. Her assessment of his work contains a certain element of intellectual slumming, but her understanding that he was writing a definably American language was exactly correct:

. . . Mr. Lardner is not merely unaware that we [English readers] differ; he is unaware that we exist. . . . Mr. Lardner does not waste a moment when he writes in thinking whether he is using American slang or Shakespeare's English . . . ; all his mind is on the story. Hence all our minds are on the story. Hence, incidentally, he writes the best prose that has come our way. Hence we feel at last freely admitted to the society of our fellows.

. . . To what does he owe his success? Besides his unconsciousness and the additional power which he is thus free to devote to his art, Mr. Lardner has talents of a remarkable order. With extraordinary ease and aptitude, with the quickest strokes, the surest touch, the sharpest insight, he lets Jack Keefe the baseball player cut out his own outline, fill in his own depths, until the figure of the foolish, boastful, innocent athlete lives before us. . . . It is no coincidence that the best of Mr. Lardner's stories are about games, for one may guess that Mr. Lardner's interest in games has solved one of the most difficult problems of the American writer; it has given him a clue, a centre, a meeting place for the divers activities of people whom a vast continent isolates, whom no tradition controls. Games give him what society gives his English brother. Whatever the precise reason, Mr. Lardner at any rate provides something unique in its kind, something indigenous to the soil, which the traveller may carry off as a trophy to prove to the incredulous that he has actually been to America and found it a foreign land.

There can be little question that for many Americans as for Virginia Woolf, Ring was to be admired and imitated simply because he was so "American." Like the game he wrote about, Ring's fiction became another item of admissible evidence in the case proving the existence of a uniquely American character, culture and society; H. L. Mencken, who celebrated Ring's use of the American language to the point of absolute extravagance, was perhaps chief among these unwitting offenders. But when the busher stories first came out, readers responded to them with the same openness with which they were written. As with the little poems about his boys, Ring had found the sensitive nerve in his readers, the one that tingled with the pleasurable shock of recognition. This, indeed, was how it was, how we talked and wrote and thought, and Americans by the hundreds of thousands seized upon these stories with delight and gratitude.

Jack Keefe changed Ring's life forever. He made Ring, before his thirtieth birthday, a writer of large and still growing national reputation, a writer whose name alone was enough to sell whatever he wrote, whatever its quality. He made Ring a true celebrity in Chicago, the most important "name" writer in the city's large and talented press corps. He did not make Ring rich, but he did give him a hearty shove in that direction.

OF ALL THE SIGNS AVAILABLE by which to measure Ring's new standing in his profession, the most meaningful may have been that provided by his employer. The *Tribune* was as conservative in personnel policies as it was in its editorials, but after the success of the busher stories it realized that it had in Ring a salable commodity. On June 6, 1914, it changed his by-line from R. W. Lardner to Ring W. Lardner—the signature he used on the busher pieces in the *Saturday Evening Post*.

The "Wake" churned right along, otherwise, as though nothing of moment had happened to its author. It simply got better and better all the time. From the summer of 1914 until the spring of 1917, Ring continued what he had begun in his first year as a columnist: he tried new territory, and he sharpened his knowledge of territory already his. He began to devote most columns to a single subject instead of a series of items. He wrote "Friend Harvey" letters to his editor, Harvey Woodruff, in many of which he argued his case for changes in working conditions. He did a "Bill to Steve" series of letters that gave *Tribune* readers their own version of the busher stories. He spoofed everything from Sherlock Holmes to grand opera, from love letters to war-song lyrics. He took his readers on guided tours of the newspaper business. And he became increasingly open about his waning interest in baseball.

In one of the earliest letters to Woodruff, in September, 1914, Ring told about the vacation he had just ended. As he often did in these epistles, he adopted a complaining tone of voice, noting that "I suppose you got a hole lot of complaints because some people thinks a man should ought not never to have no vacation but should keep right on giveing them a treat all the time with out never takeing no rest." That out of the way, he went on to tell about seeing old friends and ball games in Niles, and then going on to Lake Wawasee, where "I had a grate time playing cards and danceing and batheing and pitching horseshoes and they was not no kind of game that I played that I got beat at includeing auction bridge whist and rum and cribige and pitching horseshoes and I guess the people I played against thought they would make a sucker out of me in all them games but instead of that I showed them all up." He lamented that Ellis and the boys had not yet returned to Riverside, and issued a plea:

> Well Harvey I must clothes and dust off an other chair because a man gets tired setting in 1 chair all the time and when I have got 2 chairs cleaned up I am going down to the store and see have they got some dough nuts and if they dont want to much money for ½ a dozen of them I will buy ½ a dozen and may be by the time I get them eat up some body will of gave me a invatation to supper. What kind of cook have you got out to your house. Yours resp'y. R.

The success of the busher stories had given Ring the idea of adopting a folksy guise for himself, and he was trying it out for size in these Harvey letters. Here, however, he was portraying himself as a Jack Keefe character, full of swagger and bluster; he was using too many misspellings and illiteracies, and none of it was plausible; it was not really until he began the syndicated column five years later that he refined, and settled comfortably into, the character of the "wise boob."

Jack Keefe's influence was also evident in the "Bill to Steve" letters, which began in June and continued intermittently into 1915. Bill was a marginal outfielder on the Cubs; his letters to Steve consisted in large measure of gripes about the unjust treatment he felt he received, and negative comments about other ballplayers. Ring probably wrote the columns because he felt an obligation to let the *Tribune* share the popularity of the busher stories (for a while the paper ran a half-column picture of Ring with the "Wake," with the caption "You Know Me Al"), but they are a pale imitation of the real thing. About all of interest they contain is one of Ring's few comments upon the rare plumage affected by many country-boy ballplayers:

> Schulte says the reason O'Days got it in for me is that I dress to good and O'Day dresses good him self but he cant begin to

look as swell as me and thats why he is sore on me. Well Steve I guess if I want to get a fare deal I will have to throw a way my good shirts includeing the new 1 I just bought with the big pink and green stripes and throw a way my ice cream suit and all the rest of the swell stuff I got and run a round with a sweater or overalls or some thing but I guess it would not do no good to throw away my close because the close dont make a man and I would not be no rotten looker if I did not ware nothing.

The best "Wake" pieces during this period were the satires, which ranged far and wide. In December, 1915, he wrote Harvey that "a musical comedy name Carmen" had come to town and that he had gone to see it. As he would later in the *Gullible* stories, he produced a mangled version of the plot:

Well they played rummy and did this in that up in the mountains and finely they all went off the stage and Miss Alda come on and did a singing turn and I thot it was good but a guy shot at her from off stage and mist her but scarred her in to her dressing rm. and then the man that shot come out on the stage and he was a bull fighter but not Jess Willard. Some other name. Well Josephs forgot he wasent a dick no longer and tride to pinch the bull fighter for toteing a gun. They had it back and 4th. and they couldent nether of them get $10 for a prelim. up to Kenosha so the crowd stopped the bout.

A couple of columns later, confident that he could succeed at the opera-writing game, Ring produced the scenario for "Un Sans Trompino (One No Trump)," which is "laid in Wisconsin during the reign of King Sup." The cast of characters includes Sigismund, "foreman of a cheese orchard"; his wife, Berta; "three of the hired help: Egberto, Jacopo, and Simone"; Berta's favorite cow, Teresa; and Guglielma, "the head milkmaid." The plot plunges through high drama and low, most of it centering on Sigismund's effort to kill the cow as Berta's punishment for playing rummy with the hired hands, and it ends, as Ring believed all grand opera should, with bodies all over the stage.

Ring's grasp of the nonsensical and ridiculous was increasing; he found it an effective weapon against what he regarded as pretentiousness in any form. In a deft parody called "Cubist Baseball," he showed that he was by no means unaware of literary modernism:

A SELDOM

A White Sox base bit, a base hit with a man on third base is a seldom. Is strange to. Is a curiosity. Is sincerely fainting to fans. Why not once in a while? Or why? The time to make a base hit a White Sox base hit is too late or later. The whole thing is unconscious.

ROLLIE ZEIDER

A hook a hook a hook a Hoosier hook a prominent proboscis a promontory a pre-eminence a peninsula. But a good guy a funny fella a perfect poker player a bear base runner and a hook slider. A hook.

Baseball took its lumps in other ways. A 1915 column called "Sample Spring Stuff" satirized standard baseball clichés and the equally standard stories that reported them: "That no man has a cinch on a regular job with the Blues was the positive assertion of Manager Pepper today. . . . 'If any of the old men thinks he is going to have an easy time he is mistaken,' was Pepper's unique remark." By the time of the 1916 World Series, Ring was so weary of the day-in, day-out routine of baseball that he ended an advance story with a plea for relief: "And may the best team win four straight." The Series, between Brooklyn and Boston, was one of many special sports events Ring covered in addition to his "Wake" duties; he made no effort to disguise his boredom:

Fourth Inning.

BROOKLYN—Nothing.

BOSTON—Hobby walked. He certainly can walk. Lewis sacrificed. Lewis is the only man on the Boston club who can sacrifice outside of the rest of the Red Sox. Gardner and Scott went out, forgetting it was their turn to bat.

Fifth Inning.

BROOKLYN—With two out Meyers got to first base, so the game must have been crooked. Pfeffer done nothing.

BOSTON—With one out Wheat made a great catch of Shore's liner, showing he can do something. Hooper singled and Janvrin doubled, if you could call it that. As a matter of fact, Meyers played the ball like a drayman. Anyway, Hooper scored. So Pfeffer didn't see how Janny was going to get to third unless he made a wild pitch, so he made a wild pitch and Janny ran to third, but Shorten struck out.

Sixth Inning.

Everybody went to sleep.

Seventh Inning.

I bid.

Football, on the other hand, kept Ring's lively interest. He lobbied in the column to be assigned to cover the 1914 game in Boston between Michigan and Harvard, and was delighted when his campaign succeeded; he was less delighted with the game, a big intersectional contest won by Harvard, 7 to 0. In an exceedingly rare serious column, he made a defense that fall of the football reporter, listing "what he is up against" in his effort to provide Sunday-morning readers with an accurate account of Saturday's game. He described the problems created by a 6 P.M. deadline, the "necessary evil" of providing play-by-play detail, the confusion the reporter had to cope with if the players wore unnumbered jerseys. "A statement of some of the facts," he wrote, "may soften . . . outsiders' hearts and make their comments less caustic."

On another occasion, Ring used a bit of "inside" journalism in order to stretch a vacation. He and Ellis planned a trip to Florida in February, 1916, but he did not want to use up all his vacation time at once. So he wrote a week's worth of columns in advance so "the office will think we're still round working," while "in reality, we'll be miles and miles away, not working." He decided to do a serial: "Newspaper work has long been shrouded in mystery. It is time that the shroud was yanked off. The title of the serial will be 'Office Secrets,' and the work will be an enthralling exposition of the fascinating life that goes on among the high salaried contributors to a great daily—the romances, the Bohemianisms, the jealousies, everything that is a part of a journalistic career." There was scarcely a shred of truth in what followed, but Ring had grand fun at the expense of his friends in the local room, the "society studio," the art department, the telegraph room and, of course, the sporting department:

The decorative scheme of every desk also testifies to the line of sport in which its owner is expert. The baseball writer's desk is inlaid with bone and diamonds; the golf writer's desk has eighteen pigeon holes; the football writer's desk has the general appearance of a rough scrimmage; the basketball editor's desk is surrounded by waste baskets; the fight writer's desk is of bone, smeared with blood; the bowling editor's desk is littered with pins and is next to the alley, etc.

The sporting editor is a small but wiry bundle of nerves, quick tempered and of the driving type. His desk is a veritable gymnasium, equipped with every imaginable kind of athletic Paraphernalia. When there is a moment's pause in the day's labor he is out of his chair in an instant, swinging heavy Indian clubs, exercising with the pulley weights or boxing with one of his men. Since leaving the University of Chicago he has moved rapidly up and is now as far as North Evanston.

Ring also took a friendly poke at Bert Leston Taylor, editor of "A Line o' Type or Two," the only rival in popularity to the "Wake" among the paper's columns:

Next in order we come to the Line studio. The editor lies in a hammock all afternoon reading the *Little Review* and sipping cordials. Every thirty-six minutes the latest mail is brought up with a crane. The skilled laborers immediately get busy with it. One man opens it, another pastes it on sheets of copy paper, a third reads it, a fourth writes captions on it, a fifth pastes all the sheets together, and a sixth hangs it on the wall, to be perused by the editor at his leisure. Occasionally he is seen to cease reading for a moment and to write a bit of poetry on his cuff. At 6 o'clock his help leaves, and at 7 he has thought of a last line and is through for the day.

If Ring was short of material to fill his column, he could always turn to his readers for inspiration. He once, for example, announced that the column "will pay ten cents a dozen for the most natural love letters. No letters copied from a book or magazine will be considered. Letters may be written on lined paper or souvenir post cards; if the latter, the writing must be done where it says 'This Space for Correspondence.'" He didn't pay the least attention to the results; just announcing the contest was enough to keep the column going another day, and by the next time he wrote it, he would have come up with a new idea. Another contest was announced shortly after the birth, on August 19, 1915, of his third son. At first he introduced the new Lardner in a Monday poem:

> *I love you, New Arrival;*
> *I love you, No. 3.*
> *That's why I won't allow them*
> *To name you after me.*
>
> *Make you the butt of wheezes*
> *Such as I'm subjected to!*
> *No, kid, I won't allow them*
> *To wish my name on you.*

So he decided, four days later, to hold a contest. "There is a small boy in this county," he told readers sorrowfully, "who has no given name." He explained that fierce pressures were being mustered to name the youngster Ring, but he had decided "that the common people should be consulted." In what he called "the most important election since Berrien County went dry," he offered a ballot offering such choices as William (Ring's own preference), Wilhelm, August "(in honor of the month)," Ring W., Tyrus C., Woodrow W., William Jennings B., Charles Murphy and Harvey "(in honor of the boss)." On September 1 he reported that nineteen votes had been cast, twelve for Ring W. and one apiece for seven others. That made a majority for Ring W. and, the "Wake" announced, "THE CHILD WILL THEREFORE BE CALLED BILL." Which, in fact, he was: he was christened Ringgold Wilmer Lardner, Jr., and called Bill by everyone in the family. His father made public his regrets:

> *When you are christened Ringworm by the humorists*
> *and wits;*
> *When people pun about you till they drive you into*
> *fits;*
> *When funny folks say "Ring, ring off," until they*
> *make you ill,*
> *Remember that your poor old dad tried hard to name*
> *you Bill.*

Having three children in the house was a boon for Ring as a columnist constantly in search of material. In addition to the Monday poems, he ran occasional "Bright Sayings of the Children," a satire on a popular feature of the time; the "bright sayings" he came up with were even less funny than those in the feature itself. He often reported, at length, on mealtime conversations, some-

times under the heading "Small Talk at Breakfast." He had great
success with a series of fairy tales as allegedly retold by John
Lardner. In "Hansul and Grinnel," for example, the mean stepmother puts the children out in the woods, where eventually they
come upon the equally wicked witch:

> Presently a which came out and got them. She was going to
> eat them. She was going to fat them and eat them.
> So the next day she put Hansul in a cage, but she could not see
> very well. Every morning she asked Hansul for a finger through
> the cage to see how he was fat. But Hansul put a bone through
> the cage and the which thought it was a finger. She did this.
> Presently she was going to boil him for dinner. She asked Grin-
> nel and told her the oven was hot enough for bread. Grinnel
> didn't know how.
> "Show me how."
> So when the which stuck her head in the oven, Grinnel pushed
> her in and she burned her dead and shut her up. The which.
> Then Hansul got out of the cage and they found some jewels
> and pearls and rings and dimes and found some water and Grinnel
> said: "There's a boat."
> They couldn't get across the water.
> "There's a duck."
> It was a duck. It wasn't a boat. They got on the duck's back to
> take away home.
> They ran home. They found the which dead. The which was
> dead and the stepmother was both dead. Their father was all right.
> So they threw themselves.
> They showed him the rings and pearls and dimes and sold them
> instead of money. They got plenty to eat. They were never hungry
> again or lost. With their father. That's all of it.

The piece is funny, but it is not a parody. Rather, it is a remarkably faithful reproduction of a child's talk. Imagine a boy
or girl of four (John's age at the time) who has been read the
story of Hansel and Gretel over and over. Ask the child to tell
the story himself, and he will go off onto a solemnly delivered
spiel, rushing through it as quickly as possible in order not to
forget anything but, in the process, producing enough confusion
to deliver such puzzlers as "She asked Grinnel and told her the
oven was hot enough for bread" and "So they threw themselves."
In the first case, the child is trying to say that the witch asked

Grinnel if the oven was hot enough, but Grinnel didn't know enough about cooking to give the answer; in the second, that the children embraced their father in pleasure. But Ring, with that incredible ear of his, heard how a child would try to articulate the images in his mind—and in putting it on paper, need it be said, he once again touched that universal chord.

The fairy tales he ran in the "Wake" anticipated those he wrote later for his syndicated column and for *Hearst's International* under the overall title of "Bed-Time Stories." An even more notable case of anticipation occurred on January 6, 1916. The column was titled "Fifteen Cents' Worth," and it contained a monologue by a barber who, a captive audience in his chair, delivered himself of his opinions on politics, sports, automobiles, Christmas and liquor, all the while dropping in wheedling offers of a massage: "I think a man'd ought to be able to get a drink Sunday if he wants it. Still I guess they's enough time durin' the week to get all that's good for you. I don't touch it myself. You got a couple o' blackheads there. Nice massage'd clean that all up. All right, you know best. Wet or dry?" Nine years later that barber would reappear, mindless chatter and all, as the narrator of Ring's most famous story, "Haircut."

As Ring's confidence in his free-lance short-story writing increased, he turned more and more to fiction in the "Wake." He did "The Diary of a Siren," a portrait of the hypocritical gold-digger who was rapidly becoming the "Lardner woman"; she has just ditched her fiancé because he has lost his job, but as she sees it, "Diary I too am glad I found out in time and all men are alike. Sooner or later they all show themselves in their true colors, selfish, brutal and always thinking of themselves." There was also "Crazy Kennedy, Detective," the tale of a sleuth who employs an "abmentis," which "registers absentmindedness," to solve two mysteries at the same time: ". . . the North Shore drive burglaries and the theft of over four hundred towels from a loop hotel." And finally there was "The Journalist," a two-part story whose lead paragraph leaves no doubt as to its tone:

John Brown, of the *Daily Times* staff, finished his breakfast of bacon and eggs, toast, and coffee, which had been furnished him gratis by a large mail order house as a reward for having mentioned its name in one of his stories; finished reading his free copy of the morning paper, and rang for the car that the Whizz Motor company had sent him for his personal use as long as he wanted it.

The story, which went on to describe the life of a freeloading journalist in some detail, no doubt made Ring an enemy or two in the Chicago press corps. This was a half-century or so before the newspaper business got religion on the subject of conflicts of interest, and almost every reporter was on the take in one form or another. But just because it was accepted practice to take free food or whiskey—or money—did not make it commendable, and Ring was touching a sore spot.

It was during the middle period of the "Wake," in late 1916 and early 1917, that Ring's work made a lasting impression on young Ernest Hemingway, a student at Oak Park High School and a prolific contributor to its newspaper, the *Trapeze*. His sister, Marcelline, was editor of the paper, and he once wrote a "Dear Marce" letter that read in part:

> Say, Marcelline, did you know that there is 5 pairs of brothers and sisters in school and invariabsolutely it is a strange coincidence that the sister is good looking and the brother is not? Schwabs, Shepherds, Condrons, Krafts and Hemingways, is it not most peculair that except in one family the sister is awful lot better looking than the brother. But we are too modest to say which family is the exception. Huh? Marce?

The imitation was not without skillfulness, and it was not done deceitfully; Hemingway titled the piece "Ring Lardner Returns." According to John Gehlmann, faculty supervisor of the paper, he was called on the carpet by the school's conservative superintendent for permitting Hemingway to imitate a mere journalist—not to mention one who dealt in the vernacular as written and spoken by Americans of coarser origins than the comfortable suburbanites of Oak Park. Gehlmann is quoted by Charles A. Fenton, author of *The Apprenticeship of Ernest Hemingway*, as saying that "I was always having to fight criticism by the superintendent that Ernie was writing like Ring Lardner—and consequently a lost soul!"

Of all those prominent writers influenced by Ring to one degree or another (among whom can be counted James T. Farrell, Sherwood Anderson, Nathaniel West, John O'Hara and James

Thurber) it was Hemingway who felt the influence most deeply, who made the most original use of it, and who turned most harshly against Ring in the end. As a young member of the ambulance corps in Italy in 1918, he venerated Ring to the degree that he told a friend he ranked high "as Jupiter on tiptoes," and in 1924, after the publication of his story collection, *In Our Time*, he wrote to Edmund Wilson: "I think there's nothing more discouraging than unintelligent appreciation. Not really discouraging; but just driving something back inside of you. Some bright guy said *In Our Time* was a series of thumbnail sketches showing a great deal of talent but obviously under the influence of Ring Lardner. Yeah! That kind of stuff is fine. It doesn't bother." Ring, in turn, admired Hemingway's work early on (though he was not happy with the obscenities and sexual activities in it), and no doubt was amused by Hemingway's reference, in the story "Fifty Grand," to his selection of Jess Willard over Jack Dempsey in their 1919 fight: "This Lardner he's so wise now, ask him about when he picked Willard at Toledo." Apparently the two men met only once, in New York in the fall of 1928, but it seems to have gone well; Fitzgerald wrote Hemingway: "Ring thought you were fine. He was uncharacteristically enthusiastic."

But finally Hemingway turned against Ring, as he did against all his literary benefactors: Fitzgerald, Gertrude Stein, Ford Madox Ford. The insecurities that began to gnaw at him in the early thirties simply refused to permit him to acknowledge debts as large and complex as these, so he turned to derogatory remarks. It is quite true that he did, in 1932, send Ring a copy of *Death in the Afternoon*, signed "To Ring Lardner, from his early imitator and always admirer, Ernest Hemingway," but the implication he made later in "Defense of Dirty Words" that Ring had solicited the copy and the autograph is self-serving. The book came from Maxwell Perkins, who wrote to Ring: "I am sending you Hemingway's book and I believe you will like it a lot." What seems most likely is that Perkins thought such a gesture by Hemingway would brighten Ring's flagging spirits, and himself initiated it. What also seems likely is that Hemingway's attitude toward Ring at the time was most accurately expressed in a 1933 letter to Arnold Gingrich of *Esquire*, as paraphrased by Hemingway's biographer, Carlos Baker: "In his youth he had gone through a period of imitating Ring Lardner. This, said he, had taught him nothing, largely because Lardner was an ignorant man. All he really had was a certain amount of experience of the world, along with a good false ear for illiterate speech." A year later he closed his case, with equal measures of cruelty and inaccuracy: "Ring Lardner was a Prince . . . , who with never a dirty word wrote of those who make it with their hands in the nightly tragic somewhere of their combat, distorting the language that they speak into a very comic diction, so there's no tragedy ever, because there is no truth." Hemingway never again commented publicly on Ring or his work, as if those few cold words could discharge an apprentice's heavy obligation.

THE "WAKE" WAS BY 1914 enough of a success so that the editors of the *Tribune* raised Ring's salary to $100 a week. That was sufficient to permit the Lardners to live with considerable comfort, but Ring Lardner, Jr., notes that "they always spent a hundred and five." Ring, luckily, was in great demand as a free-lance writer. Between January, 1915, and February, 1917, he had twenty-nine magazine pieces published. Considering that the *Saturday Evening Post* was steadily increasing his fee and that *Metropolitan* paid $600 for "Tour Y-10," the last story of this period, one can assign an arbitrary average fee of $400 to this work and come up with nearly $12,000 in free-lance income over a little more than two years. Ring's salary, in other words, by a conservative estimate was more than doubled.

The quality of the work is mixed. Two stories that belong in any volume of first-class Lardner, "Alibi Ike" and "Gullible's Travels," appeared in 1915 and 1916. Some of the stories are highly professional but rather slick: "The Facts" and "Harmony." Some are merely tentative: "Tour Y-10" is a pale version of the far more successful "Travelogue," which Ring would write in 1926. In addition to "Alibi Ike" the period produced an equally famous story, "Champion," but it has not survived the years well. There is some work most charitably described as indifferent; it includes the four baseball pieces for *American* magazine and a number of fugitive short stories.

The period also covers the beginning of Ring's career as the author of books—or, more accurately, as the author of newspaper and magazine pieces that were collected in books. *Bib Ballads*, the collection of poems, was published in 1915, *You Know Me Al* in 1916 and *Gullible's Travels, Etc.* in 1917. All the stories collected as *Own Your Own Home* were published in these years, but the book itself did not appear until 1919.

Purely in terms of Ring's later work and his literary reputation, the most important work of the period after the busher stories is *Gullible's Travels* and, more specifically, the title story itself. It was here that Ring truly established himself as a satirist of middle-class suburban life. He had, to be sure, taken on the subject in 1915 with the four *Own Your Own Home* stories, but they are now rather difficult to read because of the proliferation of misspellings, abbreviations and colloquialisms. In the *Gullible* stories, Ring used the same themes but explored them with more subtlety, satiric skill and stylistic sureness. His subjects, as they would be for the rest of his career, were acquisitiveness, social pretentiousness, domestic discord, the frailty of human relationships.

The stories are more accessible than those in *Own Your Own Home* because the form is conversational rather than epistolary. Whereas Fred Gross told about his housebuilding misadventures and his wife's efforts to establish herself in suburban society in the form of letters to his brother, Charley, these are monologues by Joe Gullible, delivered to a friend named Edgar. The device freed Ring from the obstacles created by semiliterate writing; by using the spoken word, he was able to use the vernacular without misspellings and abbreviations, with the result that the stories move more swiftly.

Joe Gullible and his wife, "the Missus," live on the South Side of Chicago, but they have their eyes on moving in more exalted company; they have caught what Joe calls "the society bacillus." The first manifestation of it occurs when, in the company of their equally ambitious friends, the Hatches, they take on grand opera. Even as Joe willingly tags along with the Missus on this and other expeditions into the world of the Four Hundred, he does so with his eyes wide open. He is truly the "wise boob," eager to be accepted by the upper crust but knowing all the time precisely what is going on. His folk wit is fast and true:

> Well, even if the prices was awfully high, they didn't have nothin' on our seats. If I was in trainin' to be a steeple jack I'd

go to grand op'ra every night and leave Hatch buy my ticket. And where he took us I'd of been more at home in overalls and a sport shirt.

"How do you like Denver?" says I to the Missus, but she'd sank for the third time.

"We're safe here," I says to Hatch. "Them French guns can't never reach us. We'd ought to brought more bombs."

"What did the seats cost?" I says to Hatch.

"One-fifty," he says.

"Very reasonable," says I. "One o' them aviators wouldn't take you more than half this height for a five spot."

The Gullibles return to the opera in a second story, in the company of a fourflusher named Bishop who has his eyes on another quintessential Lardner character, the unmarried sister-in-law. Joe knows a cad when he sees one, but the Missus and Bessie are so eager to make a match that they surge ahead. It is not until the fourth story in the book, nicely titled "The Water Cure," that Joe devises a formula to solve his problem: "I had him spotted for a loafer that couldn't earn a livin', and I knowed what the maritile nuptials between Bess and he meant—it meant that I and the Missus would have all the pleasures o' conductin' a family hotel without the pain o' makin' out receipts." So he dragoons Bishop into joining the Gullible household on a weekend boat to St. Joseph, Michigan, his theory being, "Make 'em stick round with each other for a day, or for two days, without no chance to separate, and it was a cinch that the alarm clock would break in on Love's Young Dream." His hunch proves a winner; Bishop flees, and when the Missus wonders what happened, Joe in his wisdom observes, "They got acquainted!"

It is in the long title story, however, that Ring's talents as a social satirist bloomed. The society bug sneaks up on the Gullibles and their pretensions take control of them. "We ain't swelled on ourself," the Missus tells Joe; "but I know and you know that the friends we been associatin' with ain't in our class. They don't know how to dress and they can't talk about nothin' but their goldfish and their meat bills. They don't try to get nowheres, but all they do is play rummy and take in the Majestic. I and you like nice people and good music and things that's worth w'ile. It's a crime for us to be wastin' our time with riff and raff that'd run round barefooted if it wasn't for the police." The upshot of it is that they decide to take a trip to Palm Beach, a trip they cannot afford, with the notion that "we'd be stayin' under the same roof with the Vanderbilts and Goulds, and eatin' at the same table, and probably, before we was there a week, callin' 'em Steve and Gus." They have scarcely reached St. Augustine before Joe realizes what is happening:

> The Missus slept, but I didn't. Instead, I done a few problems in arithmetic. Outside o' what she'd gave up for postcards and stamps in Jacksonville, I'd spent two bucks for our lunch, about two more for my shave and my refreshments, one for a rough ride in a bus, one more for havin' the clo'es pressed, and about half a buck in tips to people that I wouldn't never see again. Somewheres near nine dollars a day, not countin' no hotel bill, and over two weeks of it yet to come!

When they arrive at the Poinciana, Joe immediately finds out "why they called it Palm Beach"—there is a hand stretched out for a tip everywhere he turns. There is not, however, the remotest chance of a meeting with the high and mighty, and finally Joe explodes: " 'Look here,' I says; 'this is our eighth day in Palm Beach society. You're on speakin' terms with a maid and I've got acquainted with half a dozen o' the male hired help. It's cost us about a hundred and sixty-five dollars. . . . You know a whole lot o' swell people by sight, but you can't talk to 'em. It'd be just as much satisfaction and hundreds o' dollars cheaper to look up their names in the telephone directory at home; then phone to 'em and, when you got 'em, tell 'em it was the wrong number. That way, you'd get 'em speak to you at least.' " But the Missus is adamant; she has come this far, and pleads for three more days. Joe agrees, but despite "some desperate flirtin' " the Missus has gotten nowhere. Then there occurs one of the funniest, saddest and most devastating passages in Ring's fiction:

> We'd went up in our room after lunch. I was tired out and she was discouraged. We'd set round for over an hour, not sayin' or doin' nothin'.
> I wanted to talk about the chance of us gettin' away the next mornin', but I didn't dast bring up the subject.
> The Missus complained of it bein' hot and opened the door to leave the breeze go through. She was settin' in a chair near the

doorway, pretendin' to read the Palm Beach *News*. All of a sudden she jumped up and kind o' hissed at me.

"What's the matter?" I says, springin' from the lounge.

"Come here!" she says, and went out the door into the hall.

I got there as fast as I could, thinkin' it was a rat or a fire. But the Missus just pointed to a lady walkin' away from us, six or seven doors down.

"It's Mrs. Potter," she says; "*the* Mrs. Potter from Chicago!"

"Oh!" I says, puttin' all the excitement I could into my voice.

And I was just startin' back into the room when I seen Mrs. Potter stop and turn round and come to'rd us. She stopped again maybe twenty feet from where the Missus was standin'.

"Are you on this floor?" she says.

The Missus shook like a leaf.

"Yes," says she, so low you couldn't hardly hear her.

"Please see that they's some towels put in 559," says *the* Mrs. Potter from Chicago.

At first the Missus is crushed ("About five o'clock the Wife quieted down and I thought it was safe to talk to her"), but when they get back to Chicago she cheerfully acknowledges that "I think we both of us learned a lesson." To which Joe replies, ". . . and the tuition wasn't only a matter o' close to seven hundred bucks!"

It is a superb short story. Joe and the Missus are lively characters, Joe with his snappy humor and sly self-awareness, the Missus with puppyish earnestness—and both of them with their halting yet abundant affection for each other. The Palm Beach scenes are expertly done—Ring had made plenty of mental notes during his vacation there earlier in 1916—and there are many fine incidental moments, such as a casual conversation between Joe and another traeveler on the southbound train. The dialogue is clipped, sharp and true. Most of all, however, there is a particular and unusual gentleness to the story. Ring clearly loved these two silly but good people, and there is not a trace of malice in his satire. He understood the normal human longings that made them want to advance in "society"; he also understood that what they thought was better was really not any good at all, and the point of the story is to try to teach them this lesson. They do not, of course, learn it quite well enough, and the last story in the book finds them once again trying to crash the gates of what they perceive to be the elite, but he does not condemn them for having trouble in giving up their little dreams.

Too many critics with too many political axes to grind have seized upon Ring's social satire as a manifestation of his so-called "bitterness," of his alleged "hatred" for ordinary mankind. There were indeed things in life that he hated, but mankind was not one of them. He understood that it is the fate of most of us to struggle toward insubstantial goals and to fail even in that, and he was amused in a sad and pensive way by what he saw from that Olympian peak he occupied, but he watched with compassion rather than contempt, dismay rather than distaste.

NOTHING ELSE IN THIS PERIOD quite matches *Gullible*, but for its light-hearted charm, "Alibi Ike" is memorable. It was written in 1915, and its opening paragraph shows how Ring's mastery of the journalistic "lead" aided him as a writer of fiction:

> His right name was Frank X. Farrell, and I guess the X stood for "Excuse me." Because he never pulled a play, good or bad, on or off the field, without apologizin' for it.

The story is neither complicated nor profound; it is genial and professional, and neither attribute should be underestimated. The ballplayer, quickly nicknamed "Alibi Ike" when he reports as a rookie, has an apology for everything, even for going to bed: "I ain't sleepy, but I got some gravel in my shoes and it's killin' my feet." He is a fine player and his teammates hold him in affectionate regard, but a couple of them cannot resist playing a disastrous practical joke on him when he falls madly in love; the joke leads to termination of marital plans and a terrible slump at the plate. The jokesters manage to repair the damage, and at the story's end Ike is off to see his Dolly:

> "And you better have a drink before you go," I say.
> "Well," says Ike, "they claim it helps a cold."

Leaving aside its other qualities—Ring's carefully reproduced baseball talk, his seemingly offhanded reporting of minute details of the game, his creation of a fine cast of characters—"Alibi

Ike" is notable simply as an example of his craftsmanship, his ability to write for the commercial short-story market without lowering his own standards. "Alibi Ike" was written as an entertainment, because that is what the *Saturday Evening Post* promised its readers. That magazine, like its less successful competitors, was the nation's evening amusement. It provided a diversion from the troubles of the day just ended, and it demanded a high degree of competence from its contributors; whether their stories offered romance, drama, escape or humor, they were expected to engage the reader's immediate interest and hold it throughout. What is remarkable about Ring is that he met this requirement and went it one better: in his most successful stories he transcended mere entertainment. In some he created a small, real world; "Alibi Ike" is one of these. In others he created larger-than-life characters; Elliot, the brutally violent ballplayer of "My Roomy," is one. In still others he satirized pretensions of one sort or another; "The Facts," slick though it is, makes some telling points about a family of overwhelming self-righteousness and the hypocritical young man who wants to marry into it.

There was a natural progression from Ring Lardner the journalist to Ring Lardner the short-story writer. For one thing, as has already been noted, he was practicing fictional and semifictional techniques in the "Wake." But this is of less importance than that the kind of fiction he wrote took an essentially journalistic stance. Certainly it required the quality of invention, which journalists are at least supposed to keep in abeyance, but it also required the ability to report—to observe. Ring in these first-person stories was the mouthpiece for his characters. The statement is not derisive, for it took extraordinary skill to be able to distinguish the subtleties of the way these people talked and thought, and then to turn them into effective fiction; it also required Ring's controlling intelligence to determine what went in and what stayed out, what was emphasized and what was underplayed. But Ring himself stayed in the background, performing what was essentially the role of a creative editor. When he moved more into the foreground, in the third-person stories, he was less sure of himself.

"Champion" is one of the earliest of these—it was published in October, 1916—and it proves the point. It caused quite a shock when it first appeared because it was a tough exercise in debunking, as opposed to demythologizing. The subject was a boxer named Midge Kelley, and once again the first paragraph set the stage with quick precision:

> Midge Kelly scored his first knockout when he was seventeen. The knockee was his brother Connie, three years his junior and a cripple. The purse was a half dollar given to the younger Kelly by a lady whose electric had just missed bumping his soul from his frail little body.

The immediate reaction of readers was that Ring was telling the blunt, brutal truth about boxing, and indeed that may have been what Ring thought he was doing. But a closer examination of that paragraph reveals the flimsiness of the devices on which he was hanging his tale. Only the first of the three sentences, in point of fact, can accurately be called "tough." The other two are larded with melodrama, with easy tugs at the heartstrings: the crippled boy in "his frail little body." Such images are employed throughout the story. The doctor who examines the brother says, "The lad's mouth is swollen and his poor, skinny little leg is bruised." When Midge gets married, "the gift of the groom, when once they were alone, was a crushing blow on the bride's pale cheek." When Midge becomes a celebrity, written up in the New York News, "neither mother nor wife could have bought it. For the News on Sunday is a nickel a copy."

There can be no doubt that Ring was genuinely angered by the moral corruption that pervaded boxing—he often wrote about the stark differences between appearance and reality in the ring and the seedy enterprises constructed around it—yet the self-righteous tone of "Champion" is wholly unlike Ring. So, too, is the simplistic melodrama. The explanation probably lies in the discomfort Ring felt with a structure that required him to describe things rather than to let them describe themselves. "Champion" could well have been a splendid story had Ring told it through the eyes of Wallie Adams, Midge's manager, whose cynical description of Midge provides the raw material for an equally cynical reporter:

> "Just a kid; that's all he is; a regular boy. Get what I mean? Don't know the meanin' o' bad habits. Never tasted liquor in his life and would prob'ly get sick if he smelled it. Clean livin' put him up

where he's at. Get what I mean? And modest and unassumin' as a school girl. He's so quiet you wouldn't never know he was round. And he'd go to jail before he'd talk about himself.

"No job at all to get him in shape, 'cause he's always that way. The only trouble we have with him is gettin' him to light into these poor bums they match him up with. He's scared he'll hurt somebody. Get what I mean? He's tickled to death over this match with Milton, 'cause everybody says Milton can stand the gaff. Midge'll maybe be able to cut loose a little this time. But the last two bouts he had, the guys hadn't no business in the ring with him, and he was holdin' back all the w'ile for the fear he'd kill somebody. Get what I mean?

Any writer as topical as Ring is going to produce some period pieces, and Ring wrote his share. But "Champion" is not one because of what its people wear or how they talk. It is one because of the curious naïveté that is the soft underbelly of its purportedly tough talk. Ring seemed to think that if his boxer punched out such embarrassingly obvious targets as a crippled kid brother and a trembling young wife, the story would be an effective portrait of callousness. "Champion" is actually so out of character for Ring that it is as if he had written "Abie's Irish Rose."

WITH RING'S CAREER CONTINUING to pick up speed, it was probable that he and the *Tribune* would come to loggerheads over salary. That nearly happened in the summer of 1916. James Keeley had left the *Tribune* and become editor of the *Record-Herald*, which, according to Donald Elder, was "financed by Illinois liquor interests which wanted an organ to counteract the rising propaganda of the Prohibitionists, who were gaining ground at an alarming rate." Keeley tried to hire Ring away, knowing his presence would be an enormous shot in the arm for a paper badly in need of readers. But the *Tribune* got word of his offer and made a counterproposal: a three-year contract, at $200 a week. Ring accepted it, and it took effect on June 20, 1916.

By that point he may well have been making a salary as good as that paid to any by-lined writer in Chicago, but he continued to explore other ways of making money. He published a couple of songs that year, one of them a most unlikely political tribute to Theodore Roosevelt with music by Lee S. Roberts and words by Ring:

Oh! Mister Theodore
Teddy whom we adore,
There's something we must say.
The time is coming when
You'll have to move again
From old Oyster Bay.
Southward you'll have to go
Not where strange rivers flow,
And unknown reptiles roam,
But where there's work to do,
You hear us calling you
Back to your real home.

Chorus

Teddy, you are a bear,
Teddy we want you where
Our one best bet should be.
Teddy, pack up your grip.
Get ready to take a trip
To Washington, D.C.
You'll make 'em treat us right,
You're not too proud to fight,
You'll see that we prepare.
We're tired of being goats
We'll give you all our votes
For Teddy, you're a bear.

These lilting lines did the old Bull Moose not a bit of good. He failed to win the Republican nomination, and he wasn't even able to have any influence on the selection of the party's candidate. Ring, in one of the few overtly political gestures of his life, had managed to commit himself to a candidate bound for retirement.

As for the other song, it was called "Old Billy Baker," and what made it notable was that the music was written by Jerome Kern, the most famous songwriter Ring ever worked with and one he always held in the highest esteem.

Peddling songs probably had something to do with a trip Ring made to New York in the summer of 1916. So, too, did the forthcoming publication by Doran of *You Know Me Al,* an occasion which failed to pay off as hoped for, at least according to the few records that exist. Only one printing of the Doran edition is known, and it was not until Scribner's issued a reprint in 1925 as part of a uniform Lardner set that the book was again widely available. Inasmuch as Ring never wrote a real best seller—that almost certainly being explained by longstanding buyer resistance to collections of any sort by any writer—there seems no reason to surmise that *You Know Me Al* initially found in book form anything remotely like the audience it had reached through the *Saturday Evening Post*.

Ring's association with Doran effectively ended with that one book (Doran has been quoted as saying that he regretted not paying more attention to Ring and keeping him with the firm), so in the spring of 1917 he took his next book to Bobbs-Merrill, the Indianapolis company that was the Midwest's most prominent publisher. It was never a particularly profitable arrangement for either party, with royalties to Ring mostly being measured in the tens and hundreds of dollars rather than thousands, but it got a great deal of very good Lardner between hard covers. From 1917 to 1921 Bobbs brought out *Gullible's Travels, Etc.*, *My Four Weeks in France*, *Treat 'Em Rough*, *The Real Dope*, *Own Your Own Home*, *The Young Immigrunts*, *Symptoms of Being 35* and *The Big Town*. Though it was Scribner's and Maxwell Perkins whose efforts brought true literary recognition to Ring, it was Bobbs that made him available to serious readers and collectors at a time when he was regarded in the East, if he was regarded at all, as a talented but limited Midwestern sports writer. Ring seems to have had a friendly working relationship with Hewitt H. Howland of Bobbs, and the feeling was obviously reciprocated. Howland wrote a little poem to introduce *Treat 'Em Rough* that is worth reprinting because it is one of the few genuinely amusing plays on Ring's name:

> There's the wedding ring,
> And the circus ring—
> So dear to the heart of youth.
> And the pug's prize-ring,
> Where it's biff, bang, bing!
> And the well-known ring of truth.
>
> There's the telephone ring,
> And the political ring—
> Which is often out of tune,
> And the fairy ring

Where they dance and sing,
And the ring around the moon.

There's the rubber ring,
And the teething ring,
And rings in endless styles,
But the Lardner Ring
Is the best, by jing!
For it's made of a thousand smiles.

In 1924 Ring wrote Howland to ask that his Bobbs titles be released to Scribner's for the purpose of a uniform edition. The affectionate tone of that poem helps explain why Howland replied with such obvious distress, disguised though it was with good humor:

> Your letter sent me to the hospital for repairs; hence the delay in replying. I am still running a temperature, clear up over the transom, as Riley used to say, and am dictating this letter while the doctor and the nurse have their backs turned—not on each other.
>
> As Brown says when Smith dies: Why, I can't believe it. I saw him only three days ago and he never looked better. If you were going to some—but are you really going. And why do you have to "stick with 'em" as you say, just because they happened to have an idea? This getting an author with the uniform edition bait is such an old wheeze. Listen—if I lose you I'll probably lose my job, and it's a long time since I worked. I'd starve and you'd have me on your conscience and be most uncomfortable.
>
> You ask if we'd set a price on the plates of your books. As for me, I'd as soon sell my fee simple in my brother-in-law. But Lawrence Chambers will be in New York next week. Get hold of him, and there may be another story, as the girl said to the soldier.
>
> The doctor and the nurse have come to and are saying that if there is any dictating to be done they'll do it. And if you could see the nurse!

The first of the Lardner-Howland productions, *Gullible's Travels, Etc.*, came out in February, 1917. Ring wrote Howland: "The book is, I think, very attractive and ought to be a go on its appearance alone. Our book department last Sunday said it had been one of the six best sellers in Chicago last week, but perhaps our book critic was using her imagination and merely wanted to help me out." Ring himself "reviewed" the book for the *Tribune,* describing himself as "the masterful young writer" and recapitulating an alleged office conversation in which the book reviewer refused to read it on grounds of health: "It makes us all sick to laugh."

By spring, matters should have looked good for Ring—his rising celebrity was marked by a long and flattering interview in the *New York Times*—but they were bad for the country. In rapid succession, the events that sucked it into world war took place: all-out German submarine war in January and February, the Zimmerman Telegram in late February, formal American declaration of war on April 6, and the adoption of conscription in May. Even for a family as seemingly secure as the Lardners, the beginning of American involvement in the terrible European conflict made the future uncertain. The nation's entry into the war took place at a time when the Lardners had outgrown their little Riverside house and, in the situation, they decided to sell it. Ellis and the boys went to St. Joseph for the summer, and Ring went to see the war. When he returned he rented a house in Evanston; in renting rather than buying he took the first clear step toward severing the many ties that bound him and his family to Chicago.

Ring doubtless felt about the war as he did by now about the World Series: he wanted it over as soon as possible. That was understandable, for he was thirty-two years old, he had a family and a secure professional position; the next generation was younger, was not tied down, and felt an ardent desire to prove its worth. There is, however, an irony here that should not pass unnoticed. The world that the war was destroying was Ring and Ellis' world, the one we have already seen of picnics with strawberries and courtships at arm's length. Far more than the young men off in Europe defending the nation, Ring was the child of America's Victorian and Edwardian years, and when the war irrevocably ended that era, the adjustment would be infinitely more difficult for him than for them. He would never truly be young again.

THE LAST TWO YEARS of Ring's authorship of the "Wake" began with a public plea from Ring to Harvey:

It is a known fact that one day off per week is allowed everybody on this floor except the comical cartoonists, who have five to six, and the undersigned who has none. . . .

I now say that if it is necessary that the undersigned's name be never out of the paper, why not print merely the undersigned's name on Monday mornings, adding perhaps some phrase such as "who did not work yesterday."

"A little verse or two" sounded very reasonable to the undersigned at the time you mentioned it, and he agreed, as he usually does to everything, being at heart a prince of agreers. But for some months past the little verse or two has palled; it has become a drain on the nervous system not only of the writer but also of many of the circulation. . . .

He got it, and there is no evidence that *Tribune* circulation, then around 600,000, suffered any severe damages. He was, in fact, quite right that the Monday poems had become tiresome for all involved, and he certainly was right in his implication that he was giving the *Tribune* full value for its dollar. He probably was beginning to become a trifle bored with the responsibility of being funny, or at least diverting, six days a week—his own boredom is often a newspaper columnist's worst enemy—but he did fine work right up to the end. He was an intense writer who rarely wrote a second draft; he concentrated fiercely on the first before he was ready to commit it to paper. Ring Lardner, Jr., has written: "One of the major sound effects I retain from my childhood is silence, prolonged to the point of acute tension, followed by a sustained burst of rapid two-finger typing. He would think out a page or two of a story in meticulous detail and then set it down at high speed, rarely returning to it except for a copyreading when he was all through." There is visible evidence of this writing style in the too few Lardner typescripts that survive; they are oddly spaced, sometimes with double and triple spacing between words, sometimes with no space at all between a punctuation mark and the next letter, indications that when he swung into the rhythm of composition, Ring was oblivious to the beauties of the physical product before him.

As much as anything else it was Ring's nonsense writing that developed noticeably in the last years of the "Wake." He had a finely developed appreciation of the nonsensical, one doubtless increased by its constant intrusion into his own life. In a letter written a decade later to his friend Kate Rice, he described an incident that could only have happened to him: ". . . I had to go way downtown to buy an algebra book for John, and I came uptown on a bus. I sat on the roof and a lady sat down beside me. Her costume looked as if it had been cut out of a wash cloth. She said: 'What time is it?' I said: 'It is half past three.' She said: 'Oh, I thought you were a Mexican.'" Ring simply filed away such incidents in his mind, storing them for future use, just as he did the most trivial domestic occurrences. He may have seen a child fail to hit its mouth with a spoon, or he may merely have looked at a spoon, but in July, 1917, he gave "Wake" readers this marvelous bit of nonsense in the form of a parody of a golf instruction manual. The title of the column was simply "The Spoon":

> The spoon has more loft than the knife, but less carry. It is seldom used for meat or potato shots, but is valuable when it comes to cereals, pudding, soup, and ice cream. Some players even prefer it for peas. It is also used for short coffee shots, but only by the most experienced players, as the club has a tendency to tip and wabble and a novice is likely to discolor shirt or vest, as well as suffer physical discomfort if the coffee be too hot or two wet.
>
> The table spoon has more carry than the regulation spoon and is sometimes resorted to in cereal shots when the player is particularly hungry.
>
> The soup spoon was formerly little used, soup players as a rule preferring to use a piece of bread as a sponge or to tip up the plate

itself. Recently the club has come into favor, especially in cafes, though it is mighty dangerous in the hands of a beginner, particularly one who is dressed up. The soup spoon should always be used sideways to avoid the peril of getting it caught in the mouth. The players should be careful not to get the spoon too far under the soup. Short, snappy soup shots will pay better in the long run, even though you be in a hurry.

The regulation spoon is frequently utilized by doctors when a throat infection is suspected, the average leech preferring not to take a chance of having his fingers bitten off.

A recent invention is the glass spoon, played almost exclusively in high ball and rickey shots, in the former as a stirrer and in the latter to overcome lime seed hazards. Other spoons are the iced tea spoon and the demitasse, played only by professionals. The spoon should never be used for chocolate shots and only most sparingly for gravy.

Ring's fascination with nonsense took a form most recognizable to his later readers in a couple of plays published in the "Wake" in December, 1918. One was "La Bovina," the other "La Maledizione di Pudelaggio," a "Yuletide Opera in Two Acts." The first was set partly in "A Courtyard in the Stockyards," with one scene involving some society people and a tour guide:

CHORUS OF SOCIETY PEOPLE
O odor enduring!
   O perfume divine!
Was e'er so alluring
   A fragrance as thine!
GUIDE
(*Pointing.*)
There is the place where we butcher the hogs,
And there is the place where we massacre dogs.
While this pretty building behind you of course is
The place we receive and matriculate horses.

The second of the plays takes place at the Christmas dinner table. Its cast includes celery, dinner plates, olives, "Il Turkey," "La Yam," nuts, raisins and "Il Pudding." A couple of choruses convey the sense, or nonsense, of the thing:

CHORUS OF NAPKINS

Oh, we are the napkins
To lay in the lapkins
 Or tuck in the V's of the vests.
Just now we seem dressed up
But ugh! we'll be messed up
 By Mr. and Mrs. and Guests.

CHORUS OF BIBS

Oh, we are the bibs
Supposed to catch dribs
 From the wavering spoons of the brats.
Just now we look white,
But we'll soon be a sight,
 What with sugar and starches and fats.

By comparison with Ring's truly superb nonsense plays of the twenties, "I Gaspiri" and "Cora, or Fun at a Spa," these are relatively amateurish efforts; the inspired zaniness of those future efforts was still taking shape in Ring's mind. But considered within the context of a six-days-a-week newspaper column, they are seen in a very different light. Other newspaper columnists may have been as consistently funny as Ring, though that is debatable; but none has ever been as consistently ingenious, as full of surprises and inventions.

In August, Ring headed off for his one and only taste of warfare. Exactly whose auspices he was traveling under is unclear, since he was engaged to write eight "Reporter's Diary" pieces for *Collier's* and was also expected to write "In the Wake of the War" pieces for the *Tribune*. Inasmuch as he only wrote six war pieces for the "Wake" during the nearly two months he was gone, it would appear that *Collier's* paid his way; yet he also showed up at the Army Edition offices of the *Tribune* in France and announced to George Seldes, the managing editor, that "the Colonel [McCormick] sent me to France to write the comic side of the war."

En route, he seemed considerably more interested in what he found in New York than what awaited him overseas. He attended the 1917 *Follies* and heard Bert Williams sing a song for which, he wrote his mother, "I wrote both words and music." Apparently this was something called "Home, Sweet Home (That's Where the Real War Is)," and it may be the song of which he much later wrote: "Bert sang a song of mine once and I had it published; it was put on phonograph records, too, and I think the total royalties from sheet music and records amounted to $47.50." Whatever the case, neither the published nor the recorded version has been located.

Ring also found time in New York to pal around with the big-name journalists with whom he was becoming more and more friendly. He told readers of the "Wake" about what seems to have been an arduous drinking session with Damon Runyon, John Wheeler and Grantland Rice, a session that ended with their purses pretty well depleted. All three of these men would end up playing different roles in Ring's life. Runyon, though actually a year older than Ring, was well on his way to becoming the most prominent and financially successful Lardner imitator in journalism, transposing Ring's use of Middle Western vernacular to the Broadway world of show-biz people and small-time punks he himself knew well. Wheeler would syndicate Ring's work for seven and a half years, and Rice would become Ring's closest friend in the newspaper business.

It was, on the surface of it, a thoroughly peculiar friendship. Rice was as ebullient as Ring was reticent, as sentimental as Ring was skeptical, as corny and obvious as Ring was subdued and subtle. Ring must have gagged when he read Rice at his most florid and hero-worshipful, as in his notorious 1923 lead for the New York *Tribune*:

> Outlined against a blue-gray October sky, the Four Horsemen rode again. In dramatic lore they are known as Famine, Pestilence, Destruction and Death. These are only aliases. Their real names are Stuhldreher, Miller, Cowley and Laydon. They formed the crest of the South Bend cyclone before which another fighting Army football team was swept over the precipice at the Polo Grounds yesterday as 55,000 spectators peered down on the bewildering panorama spread on the green plain below.

Rice was also the author of two lines of verse which, like that paragraph, belong in any anthology of journalistic kitsch:

> For when the One Great Scorer comes to mark against
>   your name,
> He writes—not that you won or lost—but how you
>   played the Game.

Yet Ring loved him, and there is no evidence that he conde-scended toward him professionally. Ring and Ellis were so fond of Grant and Kate Rice that eventually they settled in side-by-side houses in East Hampton, and throughout the twenties the two families traveled together regularly. The explanation for the friendship is probably that the two men had a lively mutual interest in sports, gambling and strong drink, and that Ring found Rice's effusiveness enjoyable because it was natural and open; he found much the same qualities in Scott Fitzgerald, his other close writing friend of the post-Chicago years.

Whatever boozing Ring did with his journalistic pals seems to have kept right up when he boarded a steamship for Europe. He made frequent visits to Auguste, the bartender, as he reported to *Collier's* readers with what must be hoped was hyperbole:

> Un Americain aboard is now boasting of the world's champion-ship as a load carrier. It was too much trouble for him to pay Au-guste for each beverage as it was served, so he ran a two day's charge account. His bill was one hundred and seventy-eight francs, or thirty-five dollars and sixty cents.
> "Who got all the drinks?" he asked Auguste.
> "You, monsieur," said Auguste.
> "And what do you charge for a highball?"
> "One franc, monsieur," said Auguste.
> Which means, if Auguste is to be believed, that one hundred and seventy-eight highballs went down one throat in two days. And the owner of the throat is still alive and well. Also, he says he will hereafter pay as you enter.

Ring did not identify himself as the consumer of all that whiskey, but the passage has the tone of after-the-fact regret that characterized his public and private writing when he had been on an extended binge. He also seems to have found being aboard ship an excellent excuse for drinking, since on a later trip to Europe he was blotto going over and back.

The *Collier's* articles were collected in 1918 as *My Four Weeks in France*. They are of interest now chiefly for biographical reasons, since they give what appears to be an accurate account of what Ring did and saw while he was abroad, but they have little merit otherwise, and the same is true of the "Wake of the War" pieces. Ring wrote about the trip purely for money and out of a sense of obligation—he felt that as a self-respecting newsman he had to see and report on the war—but the writing is mostly flat, as in this curiously *pro forma* bit of "travel writing":

> But the scenery and the people were more interesting. . . . Perfect automobile roads, lined with trees; fields, and truck gardens in which aged men and woman, young girls and little boys were at work; green hills and valleys; winding rivers and brooks, and an occasional chateau or a town of fascinating architecture—these helped us forget the heat and dust of the trip and the ear-splitting shrieks of our engines.

Ring landed in Bordeaux on August 20 and promptly ran into what seemed to be real trouble with a French passport officer who refused to let him leave town. It was actually a joke, fabricated by Ring's fellow travelers and participated in with evident glee by the local chief of police, who told the conspirators, according to Joseph Pierson of the *Tribune*: "I'm on. I remember this guy and I'm going to give him the shock of his life. Tomorrow I will have my secretary serve a bale of legal looking papers on him in the worst possible French and tell him to prepare to be deported to America. Now keep this under your hat and go to Paris. I'll see that Ring, old boy, will be in Paris in two or three days."

Ring does not seem to have been terribly amused, but he did get to Paris as promised. There he made immediate application to go to the front and ran into the first of the bureaucratic snags that bothered him throughout the trip: "Permission to go to the British front was requested over a week ago. No reply. Daily calls at our own press bureau produce nothing but promises of a trip somewhere, some time." When he finally did reach the front, in early September, he revealed a notable lack of enthusiasm for his duties: "The major has wished on me for to-morrow a trip through the reconquered territory. My companions are to be the captain with the monocle, the Harvard professor, the philanthropist, and the philanthropist's secretary. We are to start off at eight o'clock. Perhaps I can manage to oversleep." He did.

Despite his clear desire to be done with it and go home, Ring did see some American soldiers, and he did one of them a gracious favor. It was recalled thirty-five years later by Mrs. Fredrica Smith of Neenah, Wisconsin, who told the *Tribune* that her husband, a doctor, had been serving in a hospital that was reported to have been bombed. Wartime censorship made it difficult for her to learn whether he had been killed or injured, but a few days later she read a story in the *Tribune* under Ring's by-line that began as follows:

> PARIS, Sept. 10—They took us the other day to a certain place where certain hospitals were bombed on a certain night by certain Germans. We visited one of the hospitals and talked to a nurse from whom we learned that one of the doctors wounded by a bomb was Dr. Smith of Neenah, Wis.
> You must call a man something, so why not Smith. I had heard of Neenah and I asked the nurse if I might see its wounded citizen. She was a nice nurse and she said yes.

The story went on to describe Ring's conversation with Dr. Smith in terms that made clear to his wife that this was her husband and that his wounds were not serious. As she later found out, Ring had asked her husband if "there might be a special service he wished performed," and the answer had been that he would like to circumvent censorship in order to reassure his wife.

Ring left Paris for London on September 17 "with tear-dimmed eyes," purchasing before he left a toy that must have enthralled his children: "It's a complete but ridiculously impractical system of trenches. French soldiers of leaden composition are resisting a boche attack. Some are supposed to be throwing bombs. Others are fighting with bayonets. A few are busy with the trench guns. There are threads to represent barbed-wire entanglements and a few Huns enmeshed in them. Other Huns are prone, the victims of the sturdy poilu defense."

Ring's stay in London lasted four days and gave him a chance to see several shows; the one he liked best was *Chu Chin Chow*, the music of which he found "the best since *The Merry Widow*." He spent most of his time with two newspapermen, Hal O'Flaherty and Webb Miller, and "Lew Payne, the actor, and Gene Corri, racing man and box-fight referee." They did some night-clubbing as well as theater-going, and Ring was not, for once, inclined to disguise his feelings: "Murray's Club's orchestra is jazz and it gave Mr. O'Flaherty and me an acute attack of homesickness." The case really *was* severe, for Ring did not like jazz.

He reached New York on October 2, full of homecoming gratitude and ready to take on his next journalistic assignment—the 1917 World Series, between the New York Giants and the White Sox, who had suddenly emerged as a real power. He gave the Series what had become his routine "may the better team win—in four games" line, but he undoubtedly was pleased to see his old club "cop" the Series in six games. The White Sox had changed a great deal since he stopped covering them regularly, but the two Eddies, Collins and Cicotte, were still around; their triumph must have pleased him very much.

It was shortly after his return that Ring made his principal contribution to the home-front war effort, a letter from Jack Keefe to Friend Al urging support for the second Liberty Loan: "They isn't nothing I would like better then get right in to the trenches but as long as I can't do that I feel like it is up to me to leave them have some of my money especially when it aint really giveing it to them but just loneing it." It was inferior Lardner for the simple reason that he was going through the expected motions. The same was surely the case in the spring of 1919, when he wrote a skit called "A Soldier's Mother," which was performed in Chicago theaters on behalf of another Liberty Loan effort; no copy of this skit has survived, which may be just as well.

The Lardners were living now in Evanston; on the basis of an "Evanston Locals" edition of the "Wake," life seems to have been pretty much the same as it was in Riverside:

S. P. Gross of Riverside dropped in to play bridge the other night and went southwest with $1.90.

The Misses Marguerite Clark and Mary Pickford played to full houses over on Chicago avenue this week.

J. A. Lardner's hair is being trained a la pompadour, but so far has proved an inept pupil. The hair's owner is embarking upon the unpleasant era of toothless days, having already parted with two junior incisors.

Miss Patricia Crusinberry called on the Lardner boys Tuesday and attempted to destroy some of their favorite records. The grown-ups would have given her a card of thanks had she succeeded in demolishing "The Pineville School Board," which a hostile cat must have dragged in.

Having a house full of boys, Ring felt especially qualified to comment on same in the "Wake," and that December he gave his readers some sage shopping advice. He ran a series called "Christmas Suggestions," with the fourth installment being "For the Son." He pointed out that "boys are much harder to please than girls, as their tastes are more pronounced and more refined." These were some of his suggestions:

AGE 0 TO 4.

If the little fellow gives lots of dinner parties to his friends, there is hardly anything he will appreciate as much as a cocktail shaker. A satisfactory one can be fashioned at home by inserting a tea strainer in the neck of a gallon thermos bottle. . . .

Other suitable presents for an infant son are a motorcycle, a home shoe shining set and a rotary printing press.

AGED 5 TO 10.

A parasol of his favorite color is the ideal gift for a boy between 5 and 10. If he can be persuaded to carry it every time he goes out it will do wonders for his complexion, thus saving him time, money, and worry in later years when he enters the motion picture field. . . .

A manicure set and a dime's worth of eating tobacco are among the less expensive of suitable gifts.

AGED 11 TO 16.

As a boy usually becomes bald at this period of life, there is nothing that will spare him embarrassment like a skull cap, to be worn in school, at church, or at the opera. . . .

A quart of mellow old whisky is never unwelcome.

AGED 17 AND OVER.

When a boy gets to be 17 it is high time he had a good mouth organ. This will not only bring him unlimited pleasure, but will be a blessing to his friends, male and female.

If he is subject to smallpox, a prettily put up bottle of vaccine will make his Christmas a merry one.

He will be overjoyed with a doghouse, particularly if he has a dog.

The Lardners stayed in Evanston through the spring of 1918, when Ellis and the boys went back to St. Joseph; when they returned, it was to an apartment on Buena Avenue in Chicago, just a stone's throw west of Lake Shore Drive and the Gold Coast.

While they were gone Ring had offered to take over the presidency for a while so that Woodrow Wilson could take a vacation: "If the President wants to take, say, two weeks off, I will go down to Washington and work for him for just my bear expenses and I will even pretend to be a Democrat for that period. And I will play a round of golf every A.M. like he does, or maybe a little better. And if necessary, I will set up half the night autographing baseballs" —but instead he ended up in the hospital having his tonsils out. It was one of the earliest of the dozens of hospital visits he would make, and he got a funny column out of it:

> . . . I got my suitcase and went out to the hospital because they wanted me to spend the night there so as I wouldn't be scared of it when the time come.
>
> Well, one of the birds interned out there pinched my arm as hard as he could and stuck a needle in the end of my finger to see if I could stand punishment and I never batted an eye and I'll bet he was thinking to himself "Here is one game bird." Well, they finely left me to go to sleep and I woke up Thursday A.M. and nobody remembered about my breakfast and the Doc come and said he was ready and they lent me a kimona and stuck me in a freight elevator and carried me up to the floor where they carve. . . .
>
> Well, they put a shroud on me like they have in the barber shops in Paris and laid me on the ironing board and then another Doc rummaged around my chest with a telephone receiver and then he stuck the antiseptic under my nose and told me to drink up.
>
> Well, it seems one of my relatives in law had had their tonsils amputated a wile previous and it only took ten minutes, but it was a whole hour before they pruned mine because I kept getting up and starting a argument right in the middle of the service and I guess they thought I was one of the kind that just a snifter would put me under the table, but nothing doing.
>
> Well, the tonsils finely come out, but I stayed in a long wile afterwards, but when I did get about halfway back here to Chi I thought of a whole lot of funny things that I was going to remember and tell them to you, but I forgot them and it's a dam shame because most of them was a scream, or anyway I thought so at the time. . . .

By the fall of 1918 Ellis was pregnant again, for the fourth and last time, and there seems to have been a general sense in the household that major decisions lay ahead. Ring's contract with the *Tribune* would expire the next summer; the question was whether to renew or go elsewhere. If Ring and Ellis had any difficulty in deciding, and the odds are they did not, matters were settled for them that winter. In February, Ring met with Morris Gest, of the Century Theater, and signed an agreement giving Gest exclusive rights to Ring's plays and musical comedies for "a period of five years." Ring was paid $3,000 for the rights, of which $300 went to an agent, with royalties to come. It proved, for Gest, to be money down the drain. The problem was not that Ring was taking him for a ride—the mere thought is preposterous—but that hard as he worked on the plays and sketches for Gest, he never came up with anything Gest thought worth being produced. In later years Ring remembered Gest with gratitude and respect, as a man who had taken a gamble and lost on it but had remained a gentleman throughout.

Perhaps it was because he realized that he'd better have something more substantial than a dim hope of income from the theater that he sought a firm journalistic commitment. Doubtless remembering John Wheeler's offer to syndicate him in 1914, he sought out Wheeler to discuss an arrangement for a national column. By 1919 Wheeler was in a far stronger position to help; the Wheeler Syndicate had become the Bell Syndicate, with a healthy supply of both writers and clients. As Wheeler recalled it in *I've Got News for You*—and Wheeler's memory is suspect—he and Ring met at "the square bar of the old Waldorf," where this conversation took place:

RING: "When my contract runs out with the Chicago *Tribune*, I would like to go to work for you."

WHEELER: "Sure. We certainly want to make a deal. How about a contract?"

RING: "How about another drink."

One drink led, as one drink will do, to several others, and the subject was not raised again for a couple of months, when Wheeler picked up a rumor that a competitor was trying to get Ring signed up. Worried, he fired off a wire: "UNDERSTAND A COMPETITOR IS TRYING TO MAKE A DEAL WITH YOU. WOULD LIKE TO TAKE CENTURY TODAY TO TALK TERMS AND SIGN A CONTRACT." Ring's famous reply shot right back: "IF YOU KNEW ANYTHING ABOUT CONTRACTS, YOU WOULD REALIZE WE MADE ONE IN THE WALDORF BEFORE FIVE WITNESSES, THREE OF WHOM WERE SOBER." The precise terms of the "contract" are not known, but presumably they ran along the lines of the fifty-fifty deal proposed by Wheeler five years earlier; by the time a hundred and fifty-odd papers had signed up, Ring was making the remarkable sum of $30,000 a year from the weekly column alone.

On March 11 their fourth child, another boy, was born. Ring reported to readers of the "Wake" that "Young Anonymous Lardner yesterday took up his residence on Buena and was given a rousing welcome, but had nothing to say in response." The name chosen for him was David Ellis Lardner—the middle name proving to be as close as they could come to naming a Lardner child after its mother.

A month later Ring was able to celebrate the publication of a song that was as close as he ever came to a hit—though he cannot have rejoiced in the circumstances of its composition. It was called "Prohibition Blues," and it lamented the ratification on January 16 of the Eighteenth Amendment, which would go into effect a year later. Ring had the incredibly naïve idea that Prohibition really could work and that his drinking problem therefore would be solved, but he did not sound especially happy about the forthcoming cure:

> I've had news that's bad news about my best pal.
> His name is Old Man Alcohol but I call him Al.
> The doctors say he's dyin'
> As sure as can be,
> And if that is so
> Then oh oh oh,
> The difference to me.
> There won't be no sunshine
> No stars, no moon,
> No laughter, no music
> 'Cept this one sad tune.
> Goodbye forever to my old friend "Booze."
> Doggone, I've got the Prohibition Blues.

The refrain was sung by a "brown man," a strong indication that Ring was still under the songwriting influence of Bert Williams, but the song was "introduced" by the popular white musical-comedy singer Nora Bayes. She also got credit for writing the music, though Ring himself actually composed it; it is unlikely that he would have received $250 advance royalties for the song had not her well-known name been on the sheet music.

Ring's long, happy and incredibly productive career with the Chicago *Tribune* came to an end on June 20, 1919, the date of his last column. He said his farewells as modestly as he had greeted his new readers six years before, ending with a welcome to his successor, Jack Lait. "In the Wake of the News" has never been the same since, whether because Ring's reputation cowed all who tried to fill his shoes or, far more likely, because the shoes simply were too big.

It is unlikely that as he parted with the *Tribune*, Ring had any real regrets over his decision. He had no way of knowing that in leaving Chicago and the Middle West he was cutting himself off from the land and people that nourished his work. He knew only that he was heading East, where both Broadway and "the dough" awaited him. He must have felt just as he did three lears later, when he told an interviewer: "If the philosopher was right, it now becomes a question of whether I live long enough. I yearned for baseball, and got more than I wanted. I dreamed of a day when my name would appear over a story in the *Saturday Evening Post*, and I tired of magazine writing. Now I have a third big yearn. If I yearn hard enough, work hard enough, and live long enough, I yet will write a play that someone will accept, and having got that far, I'll write more."

BUT BEFORE HE MOVED EAST to pursue that dream, he had a couple of obligations to fulfill in the Middle West; each, in its different way, was to prove fateful. He had promised John Wheeler to do occasional special coverage in addition to his weekly column —which would not begin until later in the year—and two promising events were taking place in his part of the country. One was the July 4 heavyweight fight between Jess Willard, the champion, and Jack Dempsey, the challenger, in Toledo, Ohio. The other was the World Series, which was to be played by the Cincinnati Reds and Ring's old friends, the White Sox.

The Willard-Dempsey fight turned out to be a turning point in boxing history, though there could not have been much advance suspicion to that effect. Willard was not merely older and more experienced than Dempsey, he was fifty-eight pounds heavier. That, in Ring's mind as in most, was enough to give him the decisive edge over the twenty-four-year-old challenger from Colorado; Ring put $500 on Willard and made no bones about it, telling his readers that "I can point with a whole lot of pride to some of my pickings in the past." He was dead wrong. By the end of the third round Willard was so pulverized by Dempsey's machinelike punches that he did not come out for the fourth, thereby surrendering his title. Dempsey was to hold it for seven years and in the process become one of the principal heroes of the so-called Golden Age of American sports, a hero to rank with Babe Ruth, Red Grange, Bill Tilden and Bobby Jones. About all Ring could do was try to wiggle out of the corner into which he had backed himself, telling his readers: "Well, gents, it was just a kind of practical joke on my part and to make it all the stronger I went and bet a little money on him, so pretty nearly everybody thought I was really in earnest."

But the outcome of the fight actually had little to do with the importance of the episode in Ring's life. Rather, it was that in Toledo he got his first taste—the word is used advisedly—of what life would be like under Prohibition. Though the Eighteenth Amendment would not take effect until January 16, 1920, states were free to pass Volstead Acts enforcing it before then, and Ohio had done so; the sale and consumption of alcoholic beverages became illegal in Ohio on July 1, 1919.

Ring and his friends saw the days of legalized liquor out in a boisterous way. They gathered at the house of one Herman Saxon, a Toledo theater owner, on the night of June 30. Ring composed a song called "Toledo Blues" which, he later wrote, "was learned and sung by a chorus composed of Tad, Tiny Maxwell, Jimmy Isaminger, Harry Witwer, Rube Goldberg and all the rest of the stews." It went:

> *I guess I've got those there Toledo Blues,*
> *About this fight I simply can't enthuse.*
> *I do not care if Dempsey win or lose,*
> *Owing to the fact I've got Toledo Blues.*

But the next morning they all woke up and things seemed pretty much the way they'd always been. A day or two before the fight Ring took to the golf course with a bottle of whiskey in his bag, which may help explain Damon Runyon's report: "Rube Goldberg snatched Ring Lardner in a golf contest this morning with Grantland Rice seconding Goldberg, and Bob Edgren behind Lardner. They took advantage of Lardner in getting him up early, however."

Any thought that Prohibition would be an effective deterrent to alcoholism was mocked in those first few days. Whiskey would be just about as available as ever, but at a vastly higher price: in dollars, in moral corruption, in physical health. Ring, who was a conservative and law-abiding man, cannot have been untouched by guilt at joining everyone else in violating this brand-new law so systematically and self-indulgently; the spectacle of a nation rising up in self-righteousness to cure itself of the "evil" of alcohol, and then rising up to reject its own cure, cannot have done any-thing for his faith in governmental institutions or, since he was a participant in the second part of the process, for his self-respect. As for his health, it was always fragile and was done no good at all when, as he later put it in a penetrating phrase, "Mr. Volstead substituted the lively ball for Schlitz in brown bottles"—when, that is, by outlawing alcohol in any form, no matter how subdued, the law in effect sent drinkers into the arms of the makers of bathtub gin and similar gut-rotters. Ring could see from the very beginning that there was to be nothing noble about the Noble Experiment.

THE 1919 WORLD SERIES should have been just another assign-ment for Ring—a nuisance, if anything, since the responsibility of covering it delayed preparations for his move East, and into the bargain it had been stretched from best of seven games to nine to accommodate wide public interest in the contest between the good-pitch, no-hit Reds and the good-everything White Sox. Ring did, on the other hand, have a couple of personal reasons for fol-lowing the Series. One was that his old friend Kid Gleason, after years as a coach, finally had become a manager and, with the powerful White Sox team, had a chance to win a World Series. Ring's affection for Gleason, a baseball man of the rough-hewn, no pretensions school, was abundant. He had made Gleason a major character in the Jack Keefe stories, and one of the most delightful moments in them takes place when Gleason comes to inspect Jack's new son:

The baby was woke up when Gleason come in and I and him went right in the room where he was laying. Gleason takes a look at him and says Well that is a mighty fine baby and you must of boughten him. I says What do you mean? And he says I don't believe he is your own baby because he looks humaner than most babys. And I says Why should not he look human. And he says Why should he.

Then he goes to work and picks the baby right up and I was a-scared he would drop him because even I have not never picked him up though I am his father and would be a-scared of hurting him. I says Here, don't pick him up and he says Why not? He says Are you going to leave him on that there bed the rest of his life? I says No but you don't know how to handle him. He says I have handled a hole lot bigger babys than him or else Callahan would not keep me.

Then he starts patting the baby's head and I says Here, don't do that because he has got a soft spot in his head and you might hit it. He says I thought he was your baby and I says Well he is my baby and he says Well then they can't be no soft spot in his head. Then he lays little Al down because he seen I was in ernest and as soon as he lays him down the baby begins to cry. Then Gleason says See he don't want me to lay him down and I says Maybe he has got a pane in his stumach and he says I would not be supprised because he just took a good look at his father. . . .

Pretty soon he says What are you going to make out of him, a ball player? I says Yes I am going to make a hitter out of him so as he can join the White Sox and then maybe they will get a couple of runs once in a while. He says If I was you I would let him pitch and then you won't have to give him no educasion. Besides, he says, he looks now like he would divellop into a grate spitter.

Ring's other rooting interest in the White Sox was Eddie Cicotte, the dandy little pitcher whom he had put on his 1915 all-star squad because of his all-round ability and hustle. Cicotte was only 5 feet 9 inches, but he had developed his talents to the fullest and, in the process, won Ring's admiration. He also had won Ring's affection, as a good companion with a sense of humor. The two had known each other in Boston, where Cicotte played for the Red Sox while Ring was with the *American,* and when Cicotte was traded to the White Sox in July, 1912, Ring told *Examiner* readers about him:

NEW YORK, July 21.—We interviewed the latest addition to the pitching corps on the proper pronunciation of his name. Here is what he has to say:

> This pretty name of mine is not,
> As some folks claim, just plain Si-cot;
> Nor is it, as some have it, Sic-ot,
> Although I'm sure I don't know why not.
> And furthermore, take this from me,
> I don't pronounce it Sick-o-tee;
> And you can also make a note
> That it is surely not Si-cote.
> You stand to win some easy cash
> By betting it's not succotash,
> Nor is it sassafras so cute,
> Nor any other kind of fruit.
> I do not call it Kokomo,
> Though many folks pronounce it so.
> I guess you're wise enough to know
> That this sweet name's not Cicero.
> And now you've learned it's none of those
> Why I will just jump back to prose
> And tell you plainly, truthfully,
> The way you should refer to me.

Having muttered all this, he went on to inform us that the proper way is See-cot, with the accent on the first syllable, as in Fogarty, McIntyre, Lord or Rath.

Yes, Rath: Morris Rath, the White Sox shortstop whom Ring also admired for his grit and vinegar. Now, seven years later, by an incredible twist of fate, this same Morris Rath was the shortstop for Cincinnati and the first batter scheduled to face the Chicago pitcher, Eddie Cicotte, in the first game of the World Series.

There was, alas, more to it even than that. The fix was in. Seven White Sox ballplayers—Shoeless Joe Jackson, Lefty Williams, Happy Felsch, Chick Gandil, Swede Risberg, Fred McMullin and Eddie Cicotte—had agreed to throw the Series in exchange for $100,000 to be paid by a syndicate headed by the New York gambler Arnold Rothstein; an eighth player, Buck Weaver, took no money but knew of the plot and did not report it. To prove that the fix was in, a signal had been agreed upon: Cicotte was to hit the first Cincinnati batter. He hit Morris Rath squarely in the back.

One wonders what Ring thought as he saw Rath lope to first. He knew that Cicotte had superb control; in pitching a league-leading 307 innings during the regular season, and in winning a league-leading twenty-nine games, he had walked only forty-nine men—yet here he had not merely walked but actually *hit* the first batter in the World Series. But Ring also knew that there had been strange talk in the Cincinnati air, that the odds had fluctuated wildly before the opening game, that big money was pouring in.

The final score was Cincinnati 9, Chicago 1. Cicotte lasted only three and two-thirds innings and gave up six runs. Knowledgeable baseball men, from Charlie Comiskey and Kid Gleason on down, knew that something was wrong. So did Ring. According to Donald Elder, Ring later told Arthur Jacks that he had confronted Cicotte in his hotel room after the game and asked him: "What was wrong? I was betting on you today." Cicotte—did he, in this moment, at last and with shattering impact realize what he had done?—gave Ring a lie and skirted the issue. But by now Ring knew for sure. The next day the White Sox lost, 4 to 2, with Lefty Williams giving the Reds the runs they needed; Williams, who had a 23–11 regular season record with a 2.64 earned-run average, would outdo himself as a tyro crook, losing all three of his Series starts with a 6.61 E.R.A.

What happened that night is the subject of as many different versions as there are accounts of the 1919 Series. In the circumstances, it seems wisest to accept the story as Ring told it. He was at a roadhouse in Bellevue, Kentucky, near Cincinnati, with three fellow journalists, Tiny Maxwell, Nick Flatley and his old friend from the Chicago *Tribune*, James Crusinberry. Together they wrote a new lyric for "I'm Forever Blowing Bubbles":

> *I'm forever blowing ball games,*
> *Pretty ball games in the air.*
> *I come from Chi.,*
> *I hardly try,*
> *Just go to bat and fade and die.*
> *Fortune's coming my way,*
> *That's why I don't care.*
> *I'm forever blowing ball games,*
> *For the gamblers treat me fair.*

The Reds won the Series—or, to be more accurate if unkind to the Reds, the White Sox lost it—in eight games. Cicotte lost two games, but, in what may have been a belated gesture of honor and defiance, beat the Reds once, 4 to 1. It is a measure of Joe Jackson's greatness that, not trying, he still batted .375 for the Series; this innocent, ignorant boy—this Jack Keefe—was the true tragic figure, his great talent ruined by the flaw of greed.

It would be nearly a year before what most baseball people already knew was confirmed as fact. According to Eliot Asinof's *Eight Men Out*, Ring and Jimmy Crusinberry were talking in a New York hotel room in July, 1920, when Kid Gleason called to tell them that Abe Attell, one of the fixers, was spilling the beans at Dinty Moore's restaurant and speakeasy. After they had heard Attell out, Crusinberry filed a story that Harvey Woodruff declined to print for reasons of potential libel. But the scandal was bound to emerge in full and on September 28, 1920, the eight Black Sox were indicted on charges of fixing the 1919 World Series—one week before the first game of the 1920 World Series. Eventually the indictments were dismissed on procedural grounds, but all eight players were barred from professional baseball for life.

The scandal led directly to the appointment of Kenesaw Mountain Landis, a federal judge with a keen taste for publicity who cultivated an image of rectitude and austerity, as baseball's first commissioner. It also led to the introduction of the "Br'er Rabbit Ball," the purpose of which was to put home-run power into the game and reawaken the interest of a now skeptical public. As it happens, baseball got lucky, for Babe Ruth was on hand to hit that lively ball and create an American legend; the public poured into the ball parks during the twenties as never before.

Baseball got the fans back, but it lost the best and most influential writer it ever had. To be sure, Ring covered every World Series save two until 1927, he continued to bet on games and he kept up his friendships in the baseball press. But there are more meaningful ways to measure the depth of his disenchantment. He never again wrote a Jack Keefe story. He wrote no baseball fiction of any sort until 1925, by which time he was writing almost entirely for money and was willing to do just about whatever the market wanted. Even when he did cover baseball games, he left no doubt in the stories he wrote that he was doing so purely out of duty; much of the material he wrote had nothing to do with the games he saw. As he wrote four months before his death: "My interest in the national pastime died a sudden death in the fall of 1919, when Kid Gleason saw his power-house White Sox lose a world's series to a club that was surprised to win even one game."

The degree to which the Black Sox Series affected Ring's outlook on larger questions is the subject of sharply divergent opinions. Some critics have argued that this corruption of a game he loved by the forces of rank materialism made Ring a bitter misanthrope. Others, finding less evidence of venom in his writing and personality, contend that the 1919 Series was merely the last step in a process of disillusionment that had begun years ago, that Ring was relatively unaffected and unsurprised by what happened.

The elusive truth may lean toward the latter view, but not much. It is clear, as by now has been made plain, that early in his "Wake" years Ring moved away from baseball as a central preoccupation both professionally and emotionally. By the fall of 1919 he was indisputably the foremost figure in the "aw nuts" school of sports writing, and his short stories had much to do with the gradual reduction of ballplayers from demigods to human beings in the eyes of their public. He was mature and worldly wise enough not to be sent into a psychological spin by a selfish misdeed perpetrated by a handful of men making a living playing a game.

But to say that Ring was unhurt by Eddie Cicotte's betrayal—for surely that is how he saw it—is to deny the most basic human feelings of friendship and trust. To say that the scandal was not a profoundly disillusioning act is to ignore the intimate association in Ring's mind of baseball and his youth. It is also to deny that he saw baseball as a small universe with its own inviolable order, an order which would endure no matter how venal or petty some of those who lived under it.

The Black Sox Scandal threatened that order, and though it did not destroy it, it irrevocably altered it. That was bad enough. What was worse was that no one seemed to care. Something Ring had once seen as beautiful was spoiled beyond rescue, and people actually liked the result. This refusal of the public to share Ring's disgust over the corruption of baseball may, as much as anything else, explain an article he contributed to *Civilization in the United States*, a symposium of thirty pieces edited by Harold Stearns and published in 1922. Ring's piece is called "Sport and Play." It is perhaps the most totally uncharacteristic piece he ever wrote. Its argument is that America is a nation of watchers rather than doers, that though "sport" is a national obsession, it is pursued by spectators rather than players. Its author, of course, had raised the business of watching other men play games to an intelligent and perceptive art, but never mind: the tone of the piece is intemperate, humorless and self-righteous. This is the note on which it closes:

> We don't play because (1) we lack imagination, and because (2) we are a nation of hero-worshippers.
> When we were kids, the nurse and the minister taught us that, if we weren't good, our next stop would be hell. But, to us, there was no chance of the train's starting for seventy years. And we couldn't visualize an infernal excursion that far off. It was too vague to be scary. We kept right on swiping the old man's cigars and giggling in the choir. If they had said that misdemeanors such as those would spell death and eternal fire, not when we were old, but to-morrow, most of us would have respected father's property rights and sat through the service with a sour pan. If the family doctor were to tell us now that unless we got outdoors and exercised every afternoon this week, we should die next Tuesday before lunch, you can bet we should get outdoors and exercise every afternoon this week. But when he tells us that, without healthful outdoor sport, we shall die in 1945 instead of 1949, why, it doesn't mean anything. It's a chimera, a myth, like the next war.
> But hero-worship is the national disease that does most to keep the grandstands full and the playgrounds empty. To hell with those four extra years of life, if they are going to cut in on our afternoon at the Polo Grounds, where, in blissful asininity, we may feast our eyes on the swarthy Champion of Swat, shouting now and then in an excess of anile idolatry, "Come on, you Babe. Come on, you Baby Doll!" And if an hour of tennis is going to make us late at the Garden, perhaps keep us out of our ringside seats, so close to Dempsey's corner that (O bounteous God!) a drop of the divine perspiration may splash our undeserving snout—Hang up, liver! You're on a busy wire!

Those words sprang from some well of anger deep within Ring. Obviously there is no way to say for certain that it was the Black Sox Scandal, but much of the evidence points in that direction. Among that evidence is a famous passage in Scott Fitzgerald's novel *The Great Gatsby.* The raw material for that novel was acquired by Fitzgerald from the fall of 1922 to the spring of 1924, when he was renting a house in Great Neck and seeing Ring frequently. They talked sports, probably many times, for Ring was an authority and Scott, in that enthusiastic way of his, a fan. They also talked under the influence of liquor much of the time, and liquor brought Ring out; as he had said to Ellis a decade earlier, there were some things he just couldn't discuss when he was on the water wagon. That at some point or another they talked about the 1919 World Series and Ring's feelings about it seems not only probable but certain. That their conversation inspired Scott to use that Series as yet another symbol of corruption in a novel filled with such symbols certainly is within the realm of possibility:

Roaring noon. In a well-fanned Forty-second Street cellar I met Gatsby for lunch. Blinking away the brightness of the street outside, my eyes picked him out obscurely in the anteroom, talking to another man.

"Mr. Carraway, this is my friend Mr. Wolfsheim."

A small, flat-nosed Jew raised his large head and regarded me with two fine growths of hair which luxuriated in either nostril. After a moment I discovered his tiny eyes in the half-darkness. . . .

As he shook hands and turned away his tragic nose was trembling. I wondered if I had said anything to offend him.

"He becomes very sentimental sometimes," explained Gatsby. "This is one of his sentimental days. He's quite a character around New York—a denizen of Broadway."

"Who is he, anyhow, an actor?"

"No."

"A dentist?"

"Meyer Wolfsheim? No, he's a gambler." Gatsby hesitated, then added coolly: "He's the man who fixed the World Series back in 1919."

The idea staggered me. I remembered, of course, that the World's Series had been fixed in 1919, but if I had thought of it at all I would have thought of it as a thing that merely *happened*, the end of some inevitable chain. It never occurred to me that one man could start to play with the faith of fifty million people— with the single-mindedness of a burglar blowing a safe.

"How did he happen to do that?" I asked after a minute.

"He just saw the opportunity."

"Why isn't he in jail?"

"They can't get him, old sport. He's a smart man."

Part Six

Fame

"He had come a long way to this
blue lawn, and his dream must
have seemed so close that he could
hardly fail to grasp it. He did not
know that it was already behind him,
somewhere back in that vast
obscurity beyond the city, where the dark
fields of the republic rolled on under
the night."

RING AND ELLIS SOUGHT A NEW RESIDENCE BEFITTING THEIR NEW station in life, and after consultation with friends in the East, settled upon Greenwich, Connecticut. No house was available for lease until mid-fall, so they spent a quiet late summer and early autumn at the Abbott cottage on Lake Wawasee. The family had by then been joined by a formidable German trained nurse named Gusti Feldman who, as it turned out, would have the most direct daily influence over the four boys for the next decade. When at last the Lardners headed East, it was Miss Feldman who took Jim, Bill and David on the train while John motored with his parents. Typically, Ring made creative use of the journey, and the result was one of his most inspired and durably funny efforts: "The Young Immigrunts," published by the *Saturday Evening Post* in January, 1920, and by Bobbs-Merrill as a little book in May.

"The Young Immigrunts" was intended as a parody of *The Young Visiters*, which had caused quite a stir because it was purported to be the work of an obviously precocious nine-year-old English girl, Daisy Ashford. Ring did not believe the claim, notwithstanding an impressive amount of documentation to prove it, and he found the book a sitting duck for a spoof. To write it as he wished to, however, required a certain juggling of young Lardners, as described by Ring Lardner, Jr.: ". . . Ring, wanting to tell the story from a child's standpoint and still have the sales value of his own name on the book, transferred me to the car and John to the train so the work could be credited to 'Ring W. Lardner, Jr.—With a Preface by the Father.'" Ring wrote that preface with the appearance of a straight face, but any reader could see through the disguise, even though some apparently did not. Ring said that the boy's narrative "is substantially true," but pointed out these exceptions:

1. "My Father," the leading character in the work, is depicted as a man of short temper, whereas the person from whom the character was drawn is in reality as pleasant a fellow as one would care to meet and seldom has a cross word for any one, let alone women and children.

2. The witty speeches accredited to "My Father" have, possibly owing to the limitations of a child's memory, been so garbled and twisted that they do not look half so good in print as they sounded in the open air.

3. More stops for gas were made than are mentioned in the story.

Since *The Young Visiters* has vanished from whatever niche it once occupied in our literary consciousness, it is fortunate that "The Young Immigrunts" is so successful purely as humor that it can be read with utter ignorance of the original. As he had in the "Wake" column about John's version of "Hansel and Gretel," Ring showed his mastery of childish language while embellishing it with pure Lardner: "I may as well exclaim to the reader that John is 7 and Jimmie is 5 and I am 4 and David is almost nothing as yet you might say and tho I was named for my father they call me Bill thank God." The story is simply an account of the journey as seen by Bill, relying for its humor principally on his characterization of his father, his eccentric spellings and his child's-eye view:

What have you been doing ever since 3 o'clock arsked my mother as it was now nerly 5.

Haveing a high ball my father replid.

I thorght Detroit was dry said my mother shyly.

Did you said my father with a rye smile and as it was now nerly time for the boat to leave we said good by to my uncle and ant and went on the boat. A messenger took our costly baggage and put it away wilst myself and parents went out on the porch and set looking at the peaple on the worf. Suddenly they was a grate hub bub on the worf and a young man and lady started up the gangs plank wilst a big crowd throwed rice and old shoes at them and made a up roar.

Bride and glum going to Niagara Falls said my father who is well travelled and seams to know everything.

Later, while the Lardners are sitting on the deck exchanging witty repartee, the bride and groom take nearby seats:

Some night said the young glum are you warm enough.

I am perfectly comfertible replied the fare bride tho her looks belid her words what time do we arive in Buffalo.

9 o'clock said the lordly glum are you warm enough.

I am perfectly comfertible replied the fare bride what time do we arive in Buffalo.

9 o'clock said the lordly glum I am afrade it is too cold for you out here.

Well maybe it is replid the fare bride and without farther adieu they went in the spacius parlers.

I wander will he be arsking her 8 years from now is she warm enough said my mother with a faint grimace.

The weather may change before then replid my father.

Are you warm enough said my father after a slite pause.

No was my mothers catchy reply.

The travelers finally reach what Bill calls "The Bureau of Manhattan," having gone through various escapades and horrors en route. They drop Ellis at the 125th Street Station, to meet the rest of the family, and Ring and Bill head for "Grenitch," at which point occurs one of Ring's greatest lines:

The lease said about my and my fathers trip from the Bureau of Manhattan to our new home the soonest mended. In some way ether I or he got balled up on the grand concorpse and next thing you know we was thretning to swoop down on Pittsfield.

Are you lost daddy I arsked tenderly.

Shut up he explained.

During this period between the end of Ring's association with the *Tribune* and the beginning of his syndicated column, the Lardners lived off their savings—which, considering his prolific free-lance work in recent years, must have been substantial even for a couple as free-spending as they were—as well as his income from the Bell Syndicate special coverage and various odds and ends. Notable among these was *Regular Fellows I Have Met*, a so-called "mug book" published in December and purchased by subscription by a number of prominent Chicagoans. Ring wrote amiably satiric portraits of the subscribers to accompany caricatures of them. It was pure hack work, but it doubtless paid well because of the prominence of the Lardner by-line. It was similar in tone to a 1914 booklet called *The Home Coming of Charles A Comiskey*, published as a souvenir for those attending a banquet to greet the White Sox owner and his team upon their return from a world tour; Ring contributed a greeting and the lyrics for a song, both entirely forgettable.

Ring got back to regular work and pay with the Bell column, the first one for newspapers of November 2. It was datelined Goshen and it began, as did the first edition of the "Wake,' with some uncertainty:

To the Editor:

No doubt your subscribers is wondering what has become of me and the last time I was in your city the genial editor of this paper whom this letter is addressed made the remark that it was to bad that a man like I whose friends was legions (according to the editor) did not keep in touch with their old friends in the different citys and correspond with their friends in all the different citys. So I says maybe some people has enough spare time to write to all their friends but personally time means money to a man like myself and if I was to even take time to drop a card once in a while to all my old pals why they would not be time for me to do nothing else, wile the wife and kiddies went out in the forest and gathered Herbs and wild burtleberry for the evening meal.

The editor laughed heartily at the way I put it, but after he had recovered made the remark that this paper reached all my old friends as well as people that takes a interest in a man like I and feel like they know me tho we have never met and if I cared to keep my old friends posted on my movements and etc. why he would feel highly honored would I write in a letter once in a while that he could published it in this paper containing news of my family and I as well as items of interest occurring in the big world which I have the privilege of comeing in contact with them more so than you dear people of this old town beautiful though it is.

I have excepted the kindly editor's genial offer and wile I do not claim merits as a literary man the editor says that does not matter and if I will just write in my own breezy style (the way I talk as he expressed it) he and his readers will be more than satisfied. I will do my best which as I often say is as much as any man can do and I will half to crave your indulgents if a word or 2 of up to date slang drops into these cols. once in a wile as I am only trying to be natural which is where a man is at their best after all.

Ring quickly settled into a comfortable role as author of the column, which Bell sold as "Ring Lardner's Weekly Letter," though each subscribing newspaper presented it as it pleased. More than anything else he did, writing the "Weekly Letter" made Ring a genuinely national figure, a "celebrity" as we now use the term. His magazine articles and stories found a substantial audience, and his books made him a prominent figure in literary circles, but the column reached Americans of almost all regions, ages and classes. By the mid-twenties the Bell Syndicate was able to claim in a broadside mailed to newspaper editors that some 150 newspapers, with a total readership of 8 million, published the column; they ranged in size from the New York *World*, the Boston *Globe* and the Los Angeles *Examiner* to the Anaconda *Standard*, the Goshen *Democrat* and the Zanesville *Times Signal*. Many of them presented the column along with a Dick Dorgan cartoon supplied by the syndicate; Dorgan was a friend of Ring's with a clumsy but appealing drawing style. The columns were addressed "To the Editor of 'The ——,' " and were written in the colloquial style of the "wise boob" character that Ring quickly established to gain rapport with his readers. He was not being condescending in doing so; he was deliberately inviting readers to laugh at him as well as with him by setting himself up as a semieducated rube whose fumbling prose nonetheless managed to convey a rich fund of common sense and folk wisdom. He was the country cousin come to town and telling the home folks about it: "I rolled a cigarette in the dining room this A.M. and the waiter looked at me like he thought I was a hick so I left him a dime to learn him different." Later Ring grew tired of the guise and began to write in a more straightforward style, but in the seven years he wrote the column he never completely gave up the pose of the wiseacre, for it served him well.

The "Weekly Letter" was a natural extension of the "Wake." It was about the same length—a thousand words—and it covered many subjects familiar to Chicago readers as well as new ones occasioned by Ring's changed circumstances. He wrote about his family a great deal; he told people how to play such nonexistent parlor games as "musical bridge" and "parlor bridge"; he described his travels, particularly his vacations in Florida and the Bahamas; he spoofed the diaries of celebrities, writing courses and what he called "the manly art of killing"; he told about life among the high and mighty; and in the final months of the column, he wrote a mock autobiography. The one thing he almost never wrote about was sports, except when he was on special assignment. In that sense the Black Sox Scandal was clearly a liberating event, freeing him from any important emotional ties to baseball as it was by now played; he frequently used sports metaphors, often ironically, but he no longer wrote about games with anything even remotely approaching a fan's enthusiasm.

He did, on the other hand, find another arena in which to be a spectator: he began to write about politics. It was probably Wheeler's idea to send him on special assignment to various political gatherings, and it proved to be a good one. Unlike some sports writers who move into political reporting, Ring did not treat politics as another game to be watched and taken seriously. He simply laughed at it. He pretty well summed up his feelings when he wrote, at the 1920 Republican National Convention in Chicago: "The bishop started in by saying 'O, G-D,' wich to my mind is the keynote speech of the whole convention." Despite this undisguised cynicism, Ring did quite a bit of political writing, if that is the term for it, for his Bell clients; he covered the conventions of both parties in 1920 and 1924, the inauguration of Warren Harding in 1921 and the Disarmament Conference that November.

It probably was helpful for Ring as a political satirist that he was utterly unbiased, his nominal Republicanism notwithstanding; he simply didn't care. If there is much to be said for satire fired by partisanship, there is also a strong case for wry indifference, and that certainly was Ring's position. He was capable of getting quite angry over such manifestations of bigotry as the Ku Klux Klan, but when it came to the matter of one candidate running against another, he merely yawned. In 1924, for example, one hundred members of "the half world of the seven arts" were asked by Vanity Fair to state their political preferences. Thirty-six said they would vote for Calvin Coolidge, twenty-seven for John W. Davis and nine for Robert La Follette. Fifteen did not plan to vote, twelve were undecided and one—Ring—announced himself for James Buchanan. In 1932 he did write a letter to the New Leader announcing that he would vote for Norman Thomas, the Socialist candidate, but he did so as a favor to his fellow journalist, Heywood Broun, and with a palpable lack of enthusiasm; he probably didn't vote at all or perhaps he followed Ellis' example, as she explained it in a letter to her son Jim:

> I am going to stay here [East Hampton] until next Wednesday so I can vote here. I sent in an application for an absentee vote on the grounds that your father was ill & I had to go to town to take care of him but they sent back word that my reasons were insufficient and illegal and refused my application. I think Mr. Roosevelt was behind it so I am going to stay here & vote for Mr. Hoover to spite him.

Ring's coverage of the 1924 Democratic National Convention was typical of his political commentary. Much of his attention was focused on "Abel Woose, the neutral delegate from Gangrene, Texas." As the balloting dragged on interminably, Ring offered to run, "but only on the condition that I specified yesterday, namely that Mr. Coolidge withdraws." Next he proposed the nomination of his friend and fellow newspaper humorist, Bugs Baer, whose real name, Ring disclosed, was "Jovial Whee." By the time the Democrats were staggering toward the hundredth ballot, Ring was referring to the gathering as "what we are laughingly calling the convention."

The best political satire Ring wrote has never been collected, perhaps because the occasion that provoked it seems, in hindsight, too laughable to inspire further humor. But Ring got a great deal out of the Harding inauguration in the three pieces he wrote in March, 1921. The affair had been billed as one of "Jeffersonian simplicity," and when Ring got to Washington he found that "the old town is filling up with simps." His description of the actual swearing-in is filled with lovely insights. Here are some excerpts:

> WASHINGTON, March 4.—Well, it's all over and everybody was here but Judge Landis. Mrs. Harding is now the first lady of the land and Mrs. Denby will soon be the first lady of the sea, while Mr. and Mrs. Wilson are the last couple out. The idear of simplicity was carried out to the bitter end. Even when the new Congressmen were swore in they looked simple-minded.
> When I entered the press gallery at 11:20, one of the first brother simps I seen was Hughie Fullerton, the dean of baseball mathematicians. Hugh came here under the impression that it was a

sporting event. But in a auguration you generally always know how it's coming out, where as in a sporting event they's an element of uncertainty unlest it's a wrestling match or a White Sox world serious or a football game at Yale.

When Ring entered the ring, the retiring Senators was being treated to some sweet words of fare well by hang over Senators with their fingers crossed. The Democratic side of the chamber was vacant, which is as it should be. Senators of this party had given up their seats to cabinet members and the ambassadors from foreign lands.

When the foreign diplomats come in and I seen their costumes I thought we was at the funeral of a prominent lodge man. The different dips wore the grave-yard uniform of the royal arcanum, the knights of Pythias, the knight Templars and the Loyal Order of Moose. One of them had ten medals on his chest to show that he had broke the commandments at one time or another. And one dip had on a dinner coat on account of the difference in time between Washington and wherever he come from.

The next bunch to arrive after the dips was the justices of the Supreme Court. You can't keep the kiddies home on a circus day.

Mr. Marshall, the retiring vice president, responded to a toast and got some applause but nowheres near enough for an encore. Amongst other things, Mr. Marshall said, "Clothes do not make the gentleman" and Heywood Broun, that was standing next to me, said the remark was a direct insult to the foreign ambassadors. But the latter didn't act insulted and seemed to be having a good time, as though they couldn't understand the speeches.

Pretty soon Mr. Harding come in and throwed his eyes all over the joint like he was looking for somebody, but by this time Mr. Broun was standing right in front of me. The president-elect wore the suit he bought the time they had that noon wedding in Marion.

One by one the other celebrities was broughten in and introduced. Beside Gamaliel, they was Gen. Pershing and the head of naval operations, who ever he is, and the chief of staff of the army and the head of the marines and vice-president Coolidge. I was tickled to death every time they was a new celebrity, as all the people that had seats was obliged to stand up and find out how my feet must feel standing up all the while. Mrs. Coolidge wasn't going to stand when her husband was showed in but the two kids made her.

The two administrations is supposed to change hands at 12 o'clock, but it was way past that before they was ready, so what did they do but set the senate clock back to where they wanted it.

This idea ought to be looked up in civil life and maybe you could fool the baby with it. . . .

A couple of those observations succinctly state Ring's contempt for the pretensions of politicians: "You can't keep the kiddies home on a circus day" and ". . . the head of naval operations, who ever he is." Still, he seems to have liked Harding, and in April, 1921, he and Grant Rice made a trip to Washington to play golf with the President. At the dinner table in the White House Ring uncorked the laconic conversational style for which he was known. Mrs. Harding remarked that "I expected you would be a man thirty years older," to which Ring "just smiled and said banteringly: 'Did you?'" An undersecretary of state joined them as a fourth for golf at a course in Maryland (". . . if Washington is the city of magnificent distances they's no words left to describe Chevy Chase"), and when Rice took a ten-stroke lead over the President, Ring was moved to observe: "Well, I would rather be Rice than President"—or so, at least, Ring told his readers. At the end of the match Ring was given ten golf balls, which he was told he had won, and "you could of knocked me down with a girder."

The Lardners and Rices had by this point become almost constant companions. Ellis and Kate Rice liked each other greatly—Ring Lardner, Jr., recalls the two women as actually being closer than the two men—and all the Lardners were fond of the Rices' beautiful daughter, Florence, nicknamed Floncy. They led a lively social life, as excerpts from a couple of Ellis' letters to her famly indicate:

> We went to Princeton last Saturday to the Princeton, Harvard game. About 25 of us went together and took our lunch which we ate on the Dean's side veranda. The same crowd—the Grantland Rices, John Wheelers, Arthur William Brouns, Damon Runyon, and a lot of others are going to the Yale, Princeton game at New Haven this Saturday. The Rices are going to take their little girl and we are going to take John—who has gone football mad.

> Helen & Arthur [Jacks] . . . spent Sunday with us and we had some good bridge. Saturday Ring & John & I spent in New Haven and last night we had dinner with the Damon Runyons & went to see Ethel Barrymore afterwards.

Greenwich was fun, but it was basically a stopping-off place. Ring and Ellis wanted to settle down in a house of their own, and they decided to move to Great Neck. It was a logical decision: Rex and Dora, who had preceded them to New York, were living there, and so were Helen and Arthur Jacks. In the summer of 1920 Ring and Ellis found a large house on East Shore Road overlooking Manhasset Bay. A good deal of work needed to be done to it, and into the bargain Ellis loved decorating and redecorating, so they moved into the Garden City Hotel, a grand, sprawling structure a few miles away. Ring changed the dateline on his columns to "Long's Island, N.Y."

Ring made a couple of excursions that summer and fall to do special syndicate assignments, in addition to the political conventions. In July he covered the 1920 America's Cup race between the American defender, *Resolute*, and Sir Thomas Lipton's latest candidate for bringing the Cup back to England's shores, *Shamrock IV*. The result was some fine Lardner, even though Ring knew nothing about yachting. To begin with, Ring thought the sea existed primarily as an excuse for drinking. Then there was the schedule, which required the gentlemen of the press to show up in New York at 5 A.M. for a tug ride out to a destroyer, which took them a few miles down the New Jersey coast to the race site off Sandy Hook. In order to get from the tug to the destroyer they had to walk an eight-foot rope bridge and in Ring's case he was not walking it under the best of conditions: ". . . when it was necessary to stay up till five o'clock so I would be up at five o'clock and then start the day with an eight-foot stroll on a piece of wire, I was all primed to turn out a column of sidelights that would keep readers in gales of silence." His humor was not improved by the breeze, of which there was very little, reducing an already boring spectacle to the point of total ennui: "Somebody must of shot an albatross between Thursday and Saturday noon. Anyhow when it was time for the 2 fishing smacks to make their getaway, the sea and wind was both what they call a dead calm, which just about agrees with my sentiments in regards to this here race." Years later, looking back on the event with a distaste that time had failed to erase, Ring wrote: "I do not claim (except when I am all by myself in a room) that I was worth a damn to begin with, but I do know that the . . . 'race' of 1920 is what is the matter with my stomach today. I was assigned to sidelights and accepted the assignment with pleasure, as I really love dat ole davil sea and thought the job would cure me of the effects of the Democratic Convention in San Francisco, which was something of a strain on the abdomen."

Ring also covered the World Series in October. Had it not been for the stain of the Black Sox Scandal, he probably would have watched it with interest, since it was between the Brooklyn Dodgers, who had his old friend Rube Marquard on their pitching staff, and the Cleveland Indians, managed by their great outfielder, Tris Speaker. The evidence provided by his coverage, however, leaves no doubt that Ring's attention was scarcely engaged. One of the most famous plays in baseball history took place—an unassisted triple play by the Cleveland second baseman, Bill Wambsganss— but Ring reduced it to a joke (and a good one): "In the next inning Kilduff and Miller got base hits off Bagby's master mind and Mitchell cleared the bases with a line drive to Wwammbbsssgggaaannnsss. A expert cuckoo setting in the press box told me that it was the 1st time in world serious history that a man named Wambsganss had ever made a triple play assisted by Consonants only."

Otherwise, Ring amused his newspaper readers that fall by commenting on men's and women's fashions, motion-picture comedies, the high price of coal (the remedy, he said, was to be an Eskimo), how to have a happy marriage ("Remember that you swore at each other at the altar that each was taking the other from bad to worse and may the best man win"), and how to write short stories. On the last question, he explained that "the kind that the editors and their clients eats up is a love story that boarders on the risky, you might say, but not to raw." The essential ingredients, he said, were: "(1) a snappy title. (2) the readers int. is griped at the start. (3) the dialect is racey. (4) the scenes is layed in a unusual place and (5) the results is a big surprise." He then offered a sample, a story called "Shad Roe":

1.

He hadn't never expected to find her there. Au contraire he had left the City to get away from the likes of she. But there she was, by golly, hopping from branch to branch of the trees that was in the woods witch he had long called his own private forest.

"A Squirrel Woman" he husked to himself, and indeed her features was a ringer for the furry little reptile that lives off of nuts.

"Listen," he yodelled, and the girl seeing him for the 1st time showed her squirrel teeth in a leer.

Arnold Wisecracker was much amused, for that was our hero's name.

2.

For a wk. they lived in adjoining whiffle trees, the well groomed New Yorker and the Lady of the Squirrels. One day wile they was setting on a root eating their whiffle cones the girl noticed that Wisecracker was squawking.

"What is the idear, dear?" she flang at him. "Don't you like my trees?"

"Your limbs is pretty," came the reply.

"Leave," she barked, and he took a bough.

The evidence of that sample to the contrary, Ring himself was doing some uncommonly successful short-story writing at the time. Between March, 1920, and May, 1921, he published the five stories that were collected in October, 1921, under the title *The Big Town*. Excluding the comprehensive Lardner anthologies that have been published since his death, only *You Know Me Al* is as successful among his books. Like that earlier work, *The Big Town* is in effect a novel, and even more so since it has an identifiable structure: Tom Finch and his wife, Ella, move from Indiana to New York with Ella's sister, Kate, in tow; their objectives are to live the high life and to find a husband for Kate; they succeed in both regards, more or less, but in the end Tom and Ella return, with relief, to the less complicated and less expensive life of the Middle West.

In a later edition of *The Big Town*, Ring wrote a demurrer: "This book deals with the adventures of a man and his wife and his sister-in-law who move to New York from a small Middle Western city. Because the writer and she who jokingly married him moved to New York from the Middle West, and because the writer has almost as many sister-in-laws as Solomon, several Nordic blondes have inquired whether the hero and heroines of the book are not actually us. Fortunately most of the inquirers made the inquiry of me, the possessor of a notoriously sweet disposition. Two of them, however, asked the madam herself and were both shot down." In point of fact, the book is riddled with obvious autobiographical references, both factual and psychological. The

Finches are from South Bend, and Ella is a native of Niles; they frequently vacation at Lake Wawasee. After living in a hotel in New York, they move to a Long Island resort that is clearly the Garden City Hotel. But more important than these connections with Ring's and Ellis' past are the connections between Tom Finch's outlook and that of Joe Gullible; both are personifications of the "wise boob" guise that Ring took for himself. Tom is a country boy in the city, looking at it with the awe one would expect but also with a large amount of down-home skepticism.

Tom is a South Bend cigar salesman with all the prospects that position implies, but he and Ella get a windfall when her father dies and leaves her an inheritance of $75,000; Kate receives the same amount, so Tom does not object when she moves in with them, figuring that the interest on their combined inheritances— $8,000 a year—will make a sister-in-law bearable. They decide to move to New York because, as Ella puts it, "I just want to be where they's Life and fun; where we can meet real live people." Once arrived in the big city, "the gals" go crazy at several expensive stores, and when they bring their goodies back to the hotel, Tom is dazzled by the latest in skimpy fashions: "Well, to make a short story out of it, the gals finally got what they called dressed, and I wished Niles, Michigan, or South Bend could of seen them. If boxers wore bathing skirts I'd of thought I was in the ring with a couple of bantams"—an attitude toward flimsy female attire that precisely reflects Ring's own.

Eventually the city gets too expensive for them and they move to Long Island, where Kate promptly falls for a horseman named Herbert Daley: "A cold stare from Kate might have scared him off, but if they was ever a gal with 'Welcome' embroidered on her pan, she's it." Soon Daley is equally enraptured and becomes the subject of another fine Lardner line: ". . . he give her a look that you could pour on a waffle." The romance is dashed when Daley is given the fate he deserves by an ungrateful employee, but before long Kate has found—and married—another true lover, and Tom and Ella are back where they belong:

> Oh yes, we been back here quite a wile. And we're liable to be here quite a wile. This town's good enough for me and it suits the Mrs. too, though they didn't neither one of us appreciate it till we'd give New York a try. If I was running the South Bend

Boosters' club, I'd make everybody spend a year on the Gay White Way. They'd be so tickled when they got to South Bend that you'd never hear them razz the old burg again.

Tom Finch is the most thoroughly effective portrayal of the "wise boob" that Ring ever created. He is sharp, funny, worldly in an unpretentious way: "I don't suppose they's anybody in the world harder to meet than a member of the *Follies*," he says, "unless it's an Elk in a Pullman washroom." He talks in mangled English, and he reduces the conversation of anyone he quotes to his own level, so that one as ostensibly cultured as Daley ends up saying: "I have a few horses over to the Jamaica race track. . . . And they's very few afternoons when one of my nags ain't entered." He really has very little liking for what Ella is up to, and he winces at the thought of all the money that is being poured down every available drain, but he loves her in his undemonstrative way and puts up nothing more than token resistance. He is a perceptive observer of the scene around him, with a particularly keen eye for pretense, and he reports what he sees with devastating insight, as in this comment on the rich women taking their leisure at the resort hotel:

> When the women has prepared themselves for the long day's grind with a four-course breakfast, they set round on the front porch and discuss the big questions of the hour, like for instance the last trunk murder or whether an Airedale is more loving than a Golden Bantam. Once in a wile one of them cracks that it looks like they was bound to be a panic pretty soon and a big drop in prices, and so forth. This shows they're broad-minded and are giving a good deal of thought to up-to-date topics. Every so often one of them'll say: "The present situation can't keep up." The hell it can't!
> By one o'clock their appetites is whetted so keen from brain exercise that they make a bum out of a plate of soup and an order of Long Island duckling, which they figure is caught fresh every day, and they wind up with salad and apple pie a la mode and a stein of coffee. Then they totter up to their rooms to sleep it off before Dear gets home from Business.

No other book of Ring's, *You Know Me Al* included, has the coherence of vision *and* structure that *The Big Town* has. He did better writing elsewhere, and told funnier stories, and had more penetrating perceptions—but for overall quality and unity this has a strong claim to being his best book. Its characters are lively and memorable, not the caricatures that would become all too common in Ring's later fiction. The depiction of the lures awaiting unsuspecting country suckers in the big city is knowing, and the portrayal of the Finches' struggles to avoid utter capitulation to temptation is funny but sympathetic. Perhaps, however, what is most important for readers more than a half-century later is that the book still reads easily and well; there are, to be sure, some dated references, but they would be roadblocks only for the most insistently literal-minded. The city has changed and so has the country, but the clash between the one and the other still goes on; the story Ring tells here of how one couple conducts its own little struggle is an enduring delight, and for the reader coming to it for the first time, a welcome surprise.

RING HAD TURNED THIRTY-FIVE on March 6, 1920, but it took him more than a year to get around to celebrating the occasion as he was wont to do, in print. He did so with a magazine piece, published in the May, 1921, issue of *American* magazine, and printed as a book that August under the title *Symptoms of Being 35*. He marked the passage of the years with a touch of nostalgia, the usual amount of humor at his own expense, and nine "gen. symptoms of 35 and vicinity as I have found them." The nostalgia took the form of reminiscences about buying beer as a teenager in Niles, and the self-mockery had a familiar note: "When a guy is named Ring W. and is expected to split their sides when ever somebody asks if your middle name is Worm which is an average of 35 times per annum over a period of 35 annums, why it can't help from telling on you." The best part of the piece, however, remains the symptoms, which are a touch anachronistic but still easily recognizable. A couple of them:

The invalid goes to a ball game and along comes the last ½ of the 14th. innings and the score is 1 and 1 and the 1st. guy up makes a base hit. The patient happens to look at his watch and it says 11 minutes to 6 and if he leaves the park right away he can make the 6:27 home where as if he waits a few min. he will half to take the 6:54. Without no hesitation he leaves the park right away and makes the 6:27. . . .

He buys a magazine in April and reads the first instalment of a misery serial. The instalment winds up with the servants finding their master's body in bed and his head in the ash tray. Everything pts. to the young wife. Our patient forgets to buy the May number.

Another piece published that spring received far less attention but was of considerably more importance. It was a review, in *The Bookman*, of a book by J. V. A. Weaver called *In American*, a collection of verse written, as Ring put it, "in the language we, this means you, speak." On the whole Ring seemed to admire the writer's effort, but his praise was laced with "a few pokes to the ear." Ring went on: "For the most part this organ has served Mr. Weaver well. But I think that on occasion it consciously or unconsciously plays him false. It has told him, for example, that we say *everythin'* and *anythin'*. We don't. We say *somethin'* and *nothin'*, but we say *anything* and *everything*. . . . Mr. Weaver's ear has also give or gave (not gi'n) him a bum hunch on *thing* itself. It has told him to make it *thin'*. But it's a real effort to drop the g off this little word and, as a rule, our language is not looking for trouble. His ear has gone wrong on the American for *fellow, kind of* and *sort of*. Only on the stage or in 'comic strips' do we use *feller, kinder* and *sorter. Kinda* and *sorta* are what us common fellas say."

Ring went on in a similar vein for several more paragraphs, picking Weaver apart with friendly meticulousness. The review is one of the few instances in which he commented at any length on his theories of language, the truth actually being that he had no theories in the academic or even journalistic sense. Like a natural-born musician he trusted his ear, and his ear only rarely misled him. As a result his writings became valued source material for students of the American language, and they responded to him with enthusiasm. Carl Van Doren wrote of *You Know Me Al*: "In Jack's maundering confidences Mr. Lardner has assembled countless examples of murdered English caught by one of the most accurate ears now occupied with the vernacular. Malapropisms, misspellings and mispronunciations, paradigms simplified and distorted by ignorance, incredible triumphs over syntax—these appear in such numbers that a treatise could be based upon them." Henry L. Mencken sent Ring a copy of the second edition (1921) of *The*

American Language with this inscription: "To my esteemed colleague the eminent philologist Ring W. Lardner, Esq., with respectful salutations . . . ," and in the preface to that volume he and George Jean Nathan wrote: "In his grotesque tales of baseball players, so immediately and so deservedly successful, Lardner reports the common speech not only with humor but with the utmost accuracy. His writings are a mine of authentic American; his service to etymology incomparable."

All of which was true, and almost all of which Ring surely regarded with benign amusement. It must have seemed a trifle silly to him that something he heard and recorded so naturally should have been, in Mencken's case, the subject of such ponderously Teutonic explication. Language was a source of endless delight to Ring. He loved the sound of certain words—"spa" and "Nordic" were two of his favorites—and he loved to play with them. Here are a few examples:

• A couple of weeks before they were married, Ellis wrote Ring that among their wedding presents was "a silver deposit bon bon dish." Ring replied: "I'm curious to know what a *deposit* bon bon dish is. Are we supposed to save up bon bons? Better make it bon mots, of which I am full."

• In 1915 a friend in Niles sent him a book by a Hoosier writer whose work has long since been swallowed up by history. In thanking her, Ring wrote: "I am very grateful to you for introducing me to him. His life couldn't be called a failure if he had written no more than that one line—'Which for convenience inhabited the tree.'"

• While living in Greenwich, the Lardners were served by a mailman who was inflicted with the versifying itch. After they moved he sent Ring a couple of his poems, dreadfully sentimental things, one line of which Ring underlined, checked, and commented upon in the margin: "*Good!*" The line read: "That I, a gawk from Caughnewaugh. . . ."

• Ring once participated in a twenties "literary game" in which participants were asked to name the ten most beautiful words in the English language. His list: "Gangrene, flit, scram, mange, wretch, smoot, guzzle, McNaboe, blute and crene." "Blute," he explained, is "a smoker who doesn't inhale," and "crene" is "a man who inhales but doesn't smoke."

• In 1929 Ring made an exception to his general boredom with baseball. He found the Philadelphia A's of that year a colorful group, and declared that "Jimmy Foxx would appeal to the imagination if he had nothing but a mania for needless consonants."

• In that same year he told readers of *Collier's* how Judge Landis got his name:

> . . . There was another little boy in the family and the parents had christened him Fred in honor of Sousa's Band, so when the new one was born there was nothing left to call him and yet it would never do to blight his infancy by leaving him with no name save the Baby or K.M. or Judge or Your Honor.
>
> The senior Landises were planning a trip to Colorado and had to take the kiddies with them as it was the nurse's day out. When the news was sprung on Fred and his little brother, the former cried excitedly:
>
> "Ooh! Colorado! Kenesaw mountains?"
>
> "That ain't right!" objected the Judge in baby talk. " 'Saw' is the past tense. What you should say is 'Tennessee mountain.' "
>
> It struck both parents at once that here was a hunch and from the combination of Kenesaw and mountain and Tennessee they evolved the name Kenesaw Mountain Landis with the result that he is known from coast to coast as Judge.

Playing with words is a tricky business; playing with them as much as Ring did almost suggests a self-destructive urge. Yet it is remarkable how rarely he lapsed into sophomoric humor, how infrequently he was guilty of the clumsy and the obvious, how often an instant of inspiration led him to a usage that invested a word with new and wholly unlikely meanings. This incredible ear was his true genius; it may also, paradoxically, have been his greatest liability, for it made writing so natural to him that he rarely had to wrench anything from deep inside, and as a result was rarely moved to.

BY EARLY 1921 AN IMPORTANT CHANGE had taken place for the Lardners: work on the Great Neck house had been completed and they had moved in. Nearly four years of roaming were at an end. More important than that, they had come to that end in a community of spectacular wealth, fame and self-indulgence. It was to prove for Ring, as it did for Jay Gatsby, "the green light," and it was to assume in Ring's life much the role it did in Gatsby's:

"He had come a long way to this blue lawn, and his dream must have seemed so close that he could hardly fail to grasp it. He did not know that it was already behind him, somewhere back in that vast obscurity beyond the city, where the dark fields of the republic rolled on under the night." But how could Ring have known that in 1921? There were no clouds then on a horizon where beckoned stories to be told, songs to be sung, comedies to be played, friendships to be joined, occasions to be celebrated, glasses to be drained.

Great Neck was the place for all of that. For Ring and Ellis, star-struck as they both were, it must have seemed as though a magical door had opened and they had been ushered into never-never land. As a local publication of the day put it: "Nowhere in America, probably, are there so many widely known celebrities as are located here. *To live in Great Neck is synonymous to being a national success!*" There were tycoons of business who made the magnates of baseball mere pikers: Solomon Guggenheim, Vincent Astor, Walter P. Chrysler, O. H. P. Belmont, Alfred P. Sloan, Harry Sinclair. One of the first prominent settlers of the area had been Lillian Russell, who set a show-biz pattern that thrived. The Lardners' neighbors included Ed Wynn, George M. Cohan, Leslie Howard, Basil Rathbone, Groucho Marx, Oscar Hammerstein II, Clifton Webb, Marilyn Miller, Eddie Cantor and others whose names are forgotten now but glittered then: Gene Buck, songwriter and author of eleven Ziegfeld *Follies*; Tom Meighan, star of the silent screen in such features as *The Trail of the Lonesome Pine* and *Male and Female*; Tad Dorgan, cartoonist and brother of Ring's illustrator, Dick; and the famous producer of smash Broadway hits, Sam Harris. Next door to the Lardners lived the Herbert Bayard Swopes—he was the already legendary editor of the New York *World*—who gave parties of incredible lavishness. Ben Hecht, in his biography of Charles MacArthur and in his accustomed breathless style, described Great Neck in the mid-twenties:

And how the hurdy gurdies played that summer! "Everybody" came to Syosset, and Syosset went to Mamaroneck, where Neysa McMein and her dashing husband, Jack Baragwaneth, managed the revels. From Mamaroneck, everybody went to the Swope baronetcy. Games were played—croquet and ping pong attracting the more athletic. There were charades, the Murder Game and an intellectual exercise called the Word Game at which Woollcott was a bullying champion. There were pool splashing, and talk fests, and fountains of mint juleps and gin rickeys. Treasure hunts were also patronized by the city guests, who went panting through the shrubbery in search of sapphire cuff links and gold-fitted dressing cases—free to the finder.

The merry ones of the summer were Benchley, Woollcott, Alice Duer Miller and her son, Dennie, Pat Kerrigan and the Mohican-faced Ring Lardner, Cissie Schlesinger (née Patterson, formerly the Countess Gizycki), with a small-sized steamliner to take her back and forth to her city luncheon dates. Harpo was present tooting a a clarinet and winning sizable sums from his admirers at cards. Harpo was a card player feared by professional gamblers. But how expect the intelligentsia to know that side of their beamish boy?

For a long time, not surprisingly, Ring loved it. Plays bound for Broadway stopped en route at the Great Neck Playhouse, and he and Ellis were in constant attendance. Stars shone in every direction he looked; he was among them as an equal, a full participant in if not the life of the party: "On the Fourth of July, Ed Wynn gave a fireworks party at his new estate in the Grenwolde division. After the children had been sent home, everybody got pie-eyed and I never enjoyed a night so much. All the Great Neck professionals did their stuff, the former chorus girls danced, Blanche Ring kissed me and sang, etc. The party lasted through the next day and wound up next evening at Tom Meighan's, where the principal entertainment was provided by Lila Lee and another dame, who did some funny imitations (really funny) in the moonlight on the tennis court. We would ask them to imitate Houdini, or Leon Errol, or Will Rogers, or Elsie Janis; the imitations were all the same, consisting of an aesthetic dance which ended with an unaesthetic fall onto the tennis court." It was a place where anything could happen and usually did, as Maxwell Perkins reminded Scott Fitzgerald not long after Scott had fled it for Europe:

Great Neck is Great Neck even when the Fitzgeralds are elsewhere. [Ring] told me of a newcomer who'd made money in the drug business—not dope but the regular line. This gentleman had evidently taken to Ring. One morning he called early with another man and a girl and Ring was not dressed. But he hurried down, unshaven. He was introduced to the *girl only* and he said he was sorry to appear that way but didn't want to keep them waiting while he shaved.

At this the drug man signals the other, who goes to the car for a black bag and from it produces razors, strops, etc., etc., and publicly shaves Ring. *This* was the drug man's private barber; the girl was his private manicurist. But as he was lonely he had made them also his companions. Ring declares this is true!

The Lardner house, which Ring referred to as "The Mange," had three stories and sat atop a two-acre plot that dropped sharply down to the road below. There was a large garage, which Ring described as "the 3 family garage where adjoining stalls is shared by a unpaid for touring car, the first D——e sedan and a cow with a Jersey license." Behind the house were vegetable and flower gardens, and farther back, a play area large enough to include a tennis court, an outdoor gymnasium and a small baseball diamond; Ring, perhaps motivated by the fervor of his "Sport and Play" essay, played tennis himself and insisted that the boys, none of them notably athletic, exercise regularly and vigorously. The bedrooms were on the second floor, six of them, but the boys were required to sleep as follows, in Ring Lardner, Jr.'s, description: "Where we (the three older boys, and David when he graduated to a regular bed) spent our nights . . . was a screened porch with awnings that could be lowered against unanticipated precipitation. The unanticipated kind made its way with considerable freedom through the screens, and I can recall lying awake while an inch of snow accumulated on the floor and each of us waited in silence for another, more enterprising one to get out of bed and let down the awnings." Miss Feldman had a bedroom on the second floor, from which she could keep close watch on her charges, while less exalted members of the servant class slept on the third; these usually were a chauffeur and a couple who had command over those parts of the house not controlled by Miss Feldman.

The house quickly became the Eastern headquarters for an unending parade of Lardner and Abbott cousins and aunts and what not. In the summer of 1924 Ellis told her mother that "we have scarcely had time to get the beds changed between guests," but this was the kind of company they most enjoyed and they bore whatever hardships it entailed with little complaint. Though

Ring liked to describe the household in his columns in terms suitable for the aftermath of a small but quite messy hurricane, in actuality it had to be run efficiently in order to handle the many demands placed on it, and it was Miss Feldman who eventually took command of almost every aspect of domestic life, freeing Ellis to follow her own interests and obligations not immediately related to children, meals and upkeep.

This was better for the parents than the boys. It freed Ring and Ellis for whatever they wanted or needed to do: they could go, as they did, to Florida and/or the Bahamas with the Rices for a month or more each winter, they could attend parties and the theater, Ring could write in isolation and relative silence. But not merely did this leave the boys pretty much at Miss Feldman's not very tender mercies, which they seem to have endured without traumatic effect; it also made their parents, Ring especially, part-time presences in their lives. Since we are concerned here with Ring, and with the boys only as they affected his life and work, an exploration of the psychological impact this arrangement had on them is not really germane. Suffice it to say that all four of them seem to have been more distant from him as younger boys than they would have liked to be, but that by the same token all of them grew closer to him—and he grew easier, more relaxed, with them—as they became young men. They all inherited the Lardner reticence, and there was little in their upbringing to release them from it. As for Ring as a father, he was devoted to them but uneasy with open expression of affection, within the family as elsewhere; the well-being of the boys was a principal reason he worked so hard, slaving to maintain the family's often outrageous level of luxury, though it is worth making the point that for much of his life he found it easier to give the boys money, or what it bought, than to give them himself; he also forced himself to stay away from the boys for long periods, either because he was on a binge or feared he would give them tuberculosis, and this certainly contributed to the feelings of guilt from which he suffered in his last years.

It would be utterly misleading, however, to portray the Lardner household as a cauldron of repressed angst. To the contrary, as described in Ring Lardner, Jr.'s, family memoir and Ring's own writings, it was a place of much liveliness and humor. The boys put out off-again, on-again family newspapers, they staged shows and wrote songs, read books, magazines and newspapers constantly and discussed them among themselves and with their parents. If Ring found it easier to express the pleasure he derived from their doings on paper than orally, at least he did express it, as in this column written after a long absence from home in early 1926:

Well, it seems that 3 of the 4 has been amusing themselves by choosing mottos or slogans and the motto selected by John, age 13, is "Quanti est sapere" which he says means "It is great to be wise," but his brother Jim, aged 11, says the real translation is "It is great to be a sap." Jim himself has 2 mottos, "Brains before bravery" and "To he—ll with music lessons." The choice of Bill, aged 10, is "Die Rache ist suess," meaning revenge is sweet. Maybe it is just as well that his general silhouette is such that his nurse has ordered him to lay off sweets.

Another pastime in which John and Bill appears to of been engaged is selecting their favorite so and sos, like for example each of them has picked out their 3 favorite men who they consider the 3 greatest men of all time. John's 3 is H.L. Mencken, Geo. Washington and himself and Bill's is himself, Lincoln and Kipling. Jim tipped us off that John also had a list of the 5 greatest women and when asked to name them the big Nordic said they were Mrs. Percy Hammond, Marjorie Rambeau, Susanne Lenglen and Amy Bemak. He refused to name the 5th, saying he had forgotten whom she was. It may as well be exclaimed that Amy Bemak is 4 yrs. old. The ages of the other 3 is not necessary to the plot. . . .

Jim said he would announce his favorite men at some later date and when urged to choose his favorite women replied that he hated them all.

That is about all I could learn in regards to the little ones except that they had played considerable hockey with David, age 6, on John's side vs. Bill and Jim and reported that they only had 3 sticks so that David had to play without a stick but they didn't seem to think that affected his game. This little upstart may be a chip of the old block, the last named having played bridge without cards ever since the d—m game was invented.

The house and the Great Neck community were the twin centers of Ring's life during much of the twenties, yet he is frequently associated with the alleged "wits" who gathered during the period at the Round Table of the Algonquin, even though he was rarely a member of their company. Ring did know the people who gathered there to exchange brittle and generally self-serving verbal darts—Dorothy Parker, Alexander Woollcott, George S. Kaufman, Franklin P. Adams, Robert E. Sherwood, Harold Ross, Heywood Broun and Robert Benchley—and in some cases he knew them well. Items about Ring and Ellis often appeared in Adams' column of pretentious chitchat, "The Conning Tower," in the *World*. Ring and Ross liked each other greatly, and in the last years of Ring's life Ross published him often in *The New Yorker*. Sherwood adapted his story "The Love Nest" for the stage, and Ring and Kaufman collaborated on the play *June Moon*. There is not a particle of evidence that Ring and Dorothy Parker actually had the affair sometimes attributed to them—the mere notion of Ring being unfaithful to Ellis is frankly preposterous, given both his love for her and his sexual timidity—but they did do some partying together and she was once a houseguest at The Mange.

But Ring preferred to take these brilliant and self-conscious people one or two at a time. The kind of chatter and patter they indulged in at the Algonquin, each trying to top the other, was anathema to him. He kept a certain distance between himself and them, with the perhaps unexpected result that, as described at the time by Edmund Wilson in his diaries, they worshiped him: "I was struck by the enormous reverence that the Algonquinites felt for Ring Lardner. He never mingled with them. He lived at Great Neck, Long Island, and came into town only for business; I never saw him at the Algonquin. He was somehow aloof and inscrutable, by nature rather saturnine, but a master whom all admired, though he was never present in person. It may be that all any such circle demands is such a presiding but invisible deity, who is assumed to regard them with a certain scorn." The second part of Wilson's analysis is questionable, but the first is not; the intense admiration the Algonquinites felt for Ring is reflected in their writings, such as Dorothy Parker's extravagant comment upon the publication of *Round Up*: "It is difficult to review these spare and beautiful stories; it would be difficult to review the Gettysburg address."

WHETHER BECAUSE OF FINANCIAL PRESSURES or plain good luck, Ring's first year and a half in Great Neck was a period of intense creativity. The "Weekly Letter" rolled along comfortably, with Ring doing special coverage, in addition to the Harding inauguration and the Disarmament Conference, of the Dempsey-Carpentier fight in July, 1921, and the World Series in both 1921 and 1922. He published thirteen magazine pieces, including his finest short story and one not far below it in quality. He also took the first noteworthy step toward fulfillment of his dream of theatrical success.

The column touched just about every base Ring could think of, and he maintained a remarkably high level of performance in it. Among other things, he told his readers how to pick a husband, that he was running for mayor of New York, how to write love letters, that new rules for war needed to be written, that the weekend should be moved to the middle of the week, and how to bring a chain letter to a halt (it should be sent to Ring). One of his best pieces, and one of the most representative as well, was a parody of the name-dropping diaries then being ostentatiously published in the press by purported highbrows:

Aug. 8

Peggy Hopkins called up and wanted we should go for a sail but I had a date to play golf with Sarazen, Hagen and Barnes. I and Hagen played the other two best ball and added score for a $25.00 nassua but only beat them by about 7 pts. as Hagen wasn't putting good. I had 12 eagles but only managed to get a couple of ones. When I got home Sousa was there and we played some Brahms and Grieg with me at the piano and him at one end of a cornet. "How well you play Lardy" was Sousa's remark. Brahms called up in the evening and him and his wife come over and played rummy. . . .

Aug. 12

This was Saturday and the banks close at noon on Saturdays so I visited them all dureing the forenoon and found everything lovely. Everywhere I went it was hello Lardy how is everything Lardy. Played 4 or 5 rounds of Beethoven and had lunch with Gatti-Casazza and Gen. Pershing. Went home to practice on my harp and the phone rung and it was Madame Jeritska who wanted I should take her to dinner I pretended like I was busy. Scotti and Gerry Farrar called up in the evening and wanted a game of bridge but I and the Mrs. was invited over to Luccini's to try out their new piano. "Well Lardy we will half to make it some other time," said Gerry. "You said a mouthful Gerry" was my smileing reply.

Ring was at his absolute best, however, in his special coverage of the 1922 World Series. It was played between the Yankees and the Giants, who won in four straight games. Ring could not have cared less about it to begin with, and the games did not give him much to write about anyway, so he found a superb device to hold his readers' interest. Before the first game, he told them that this would be "the most important world serious in history as far as I and my family are conserned and even more important to us than the famous world serious of 1919 which was win by the Cincinnati Reds greatly to their surprise." The reason, he explained, was that in 1919 he had promised his wife a fur coat after the Series, but bet on the White Sox "and that is why we did not go out much in Greenwich that winter and not for lack of invitations as certain smart Alex has left fall." Without saying so directly, he let it be known that a similar promise had been made this time. But the Yankees, on whom he was betting, lost the first game and he wrote: "Well friends you can imagine my surprise and horror when I found out last night that the impression had got around some way another that as soon as this serious was over I was planning to buy a expensive fur coat for my Mrs. . . . I will see that my Mrs. is dressed in as warm a style as she has been accustomed to but neither her or I is the kind that likes to make a big show and go up and down 5th ave sweltering in a $700 hogskin garment in order so as people will turn around and gap at us. Live and let live is my slocum." Then the Yankees lost another game, and Ring lowered the boom:

> Amongst the inmates of our heavily mortgaged home in Great Neck is 3 members of what is sometimes referred to as the feline tribe born the 11th day of last April and christened respectfully Barney, Blackie and Ringer.
> These 3 little ones is motherless, as the lady cat who bore them, aptly named Robin Hood, took sick one June day and was give away by Fred to a friend to whom he kindly refrained from mentioning her illness.
> These 3 little members of the feline tribe is the cutest and best behaved kitties in all catdom, their conduct having always been above all reproaches outside of a tendency on the part of Ringer to bite strangers knuckles. Nowhere on Long Island is a more loveable trio of grimalkins and how it pierces my old heart to think that some day next week these 3 little fellows must be shot down like a dog so as their fur can be fashioned into a warm winter coat for she who their antics has so often caused to screek with laughter.

Yes boys the 3 little kittens is practically doomed you might say and all because today's game at the polo grounds was not called on account of darkness long before it started though they was no time during the afternoon when the Yanks could see.

He had been told by an expert in furs, Ring explained, that "no finer or more warmer garment can be fashioned than is made from the skin of a milk fed kitty," and when Ring objected that the furs of three small kittens would make a rather small coat, the man replied: "Small coats is the rage . . . and I personally seen some of the best dressed women in New York strolling up and down 10th avenue during the last cold snap with cat skin garments no bigger than a guest towl."

So the fate of the three little kittens hung on the Yankees—and the Yankees lost. But Ring waited until his final story was more than half over before adding, almost as an afterthought, that after a great domestic contretemps "the master of the house compromised and decided to not doom the little members of the finny tribe to death." Instead, he sent out a plea "to all our friends and readers asking them to look around the old homestead and find their family albums and take the plush off of the covers and send it to the undersigned and make a plush coat which everybody tells me is the most fashionable fur on the green footstool."

If the 1922 World Series coverage was a highlight of Ring's journalistic work during this period, the short story "Some Like Them Cold" was far and away the best of his fiction. Published by the *Saturday Evening Post* on October 1, 1921, it is told in the epistolary form, the letter writers being Charles F. Lewis, a would-be songwriter trying to cut a swath in New York, and Mabelle Gillespie, a young woman he has met at the LaSalle Street Station in Chicago, shortly before his departure. He is brash and cocky, she is coy and calculating. New York, he tells her in his first letter, "is the only spot and specially for a man that expects to make my liveing in the song writeing game as here is the Mecca for that line of work and no matter how good a man may be they don't get no recognition unless they live in N.Y."—a comment that, needless to say, reflected Ring's own feelings about his eastward move. He calls her "girlie" and she responds by calling him "Mr. Man." Her pose is a masterpiece of contrived bashfulness: she puts words and phrases in quotes ("Well, that certainly was a 'surprise party' getting your letter and you are certainly a 'wonder man'"), meanwhile insinuating as much information as possible into each letter about her prowess at the stove and her love of culture: "Personally there is nothing I love more than to just sit and read a good book or sit and listen to somebody play the piano, I mean if they can really play and I really believe I like popular music better than the classical though I suppose that is a terrible thing to confess, but I love all kinds of music but a specially the piano when it is played by somebody who can really play." His reply comes slowly, but contains news that he and the lyricist Paul Sears are collaborating on a song with these lyrics:

> Some like them hot, some like them cold.
> Some like them when they're not too darn old.
> Some like them fat, some like them lean.
> Some like them only at sweet sixteen.
> Some like them dark, some like them light.
> Some like them in the park, late at night.
> Some like them fickle, some like them true,
> But the time I like them is when they're you.

He adds that he has only met a couple of girls, one too fast for him and the other Sear's sister, but "Paul says she is the coldest proposition he ever seen."

Her next letter is full of more exploratory gold digging, and his is curt and evasive; he says "we have not had no luck with the song," but he has taken a job as pianist with an orchestra: "They pay good money $60 and it will keep me going." When she writes to ask why his letter sounded so strange, he replies that he and Sears's sister are engaged:

> Well girlie I may write to you again once in a wile as Betsy says she don't give a dam if I write to all the girls in the world just so I don't make her read the answers but that is all I can think of to say now except good bye and good luck and may the right man come along soon and he will be a lucky man getting a girl that is such a good cook and got all that furniture etc.

In Mabelle's last letter, all the pettiness and vindictiveness lurking in her tiny mind come rushing to the surface:

Thanks for your advice and also thank your fiance for her generosity in allowing you to continue your correspondence with her "rivals," but personly I have no desire to take advantage of that generosity as I have something better to do than read letters from a man like you, a specially as I have a man friend who is not so generous as Miss Sears and would strongly object to my continuing a correspondence with another man. It is at his request that I am writing this note to tell you not to expect to hear from me again.

Allow me to congratulate you on your engagement to Miss Sears and I am sure she is to be congratulated too, though if I met the lady I would be tempted to ask her to tell me her secret, namely how she is going to "run wild" on $60.

The self-portraits that Charles and Mabelle paint are absolutely devastating. Each letter adds a few more touches of oil to the canvas, so that eventually a young man who had seemed amiable and naïve turns out to be gullible and ignorant, and a young woman who had seemed hopeful and sympathetic is shown to be conniving and contemptible. Each of them, in the end, is living a lie: his is that he can make a success out of songwriting and his marriage to a venal shrew, hers that she has found a new suitor or, for that matter, that she has the charm, intelligence, personality and beauty to attract any suitor, any time.

Not much of the milk of human kindness dripped from Ring's pen in the composition of this story; still, it is not the work of a "hater," but of a writer looking at two particularly unappealing subjects with a cold, honest eye. Underlying the story, too, is the unrealized wish that if these two people were not so hopelessly vain and self-deluding, they might find each other and some measure of happiness; but it is precisely because they are merely human, with all the possibilities of failure that implies, that they cannot make what is probably the most promising connection available to either one of them.

Further proof of the humane if uncompromising vision that guided Ring's craft is another story published during this period. "The Golden Honeymoon" was written while Ring and Ellis were at the West Florida resort of Belleair in the spring of 1922. George Horace Lorimer turned it down at the *Post* because it struck him as so unlike Ring's previous work that Lardner fans might be jarred by it. Ray Long at *Cosmopolitan* jumped at the chance to get Ring onto his list of contributors, and in this case at least, he had a better eye for excellence than Lorimer. He wrote Ring: "I see what the *Post* meant. That story isn't the usual Ring Lardner story. All it is is a fine piece of sympathetic human interest writing. I should be glad to trade you a check for $1,500 for it and I shall be very proud to publish it. If those terms are satisfactory to you, give me the high-sign." Ring did and *Cosmopolitan*—this was when it was still a general-readership magazine—published the story in July, 1922. It was the beginning of a half-year association with the magazine, during which Ring would write eight pieces for it, most of them collections of miscellaneous humor.

"The Golden Honeymoon" is narrated by Charles, a garrulous old gentleman who is going to St. Petersburg with his wife, Lucy, to celebrate their fiftieth wedding anniversary. He is incapable of separating the trivial from the important; along the way he reports every moment of the timetable, and when they arrive he tells us what we already know: "St. Pete is what folks calls the town, though they also call it the Sunshine City, as they claim they's no other place in the country where they's fewer days when Old Sol don't smile down on Mother Earth." Once settled at their rooming house, they do all the predictable things elderly tourists do in St. Petersburg, such as their bit for New Jersey: "Well, one of the first things we done . . . was to go to the Chamber of Commerce and register our names and where we was from as they's great rivalry amongst the different States in regards to the number of their citizens visiting in town and of course our little State don't stand much of a show, but still every little bit helps, as the fella says." Soon they run into a former suitor of Lucy's and his wife, and the two couples begin a companionship that is one part mutual need and one part competitiveness. It finally ends in a confrontation over horseshoes and cards, and Charley and Lucy find more congenial companions before ending their journey and heading back North.

In 1933 the young Clifton Fadiman, a book reviewer still making his reputation, celebrated Ring in the *Nation* as the ultimate in literary hatred and pounced on "The Golden Honeymoon" as a case in point: ". . . it is one of the most smashing indictments of a 'happy marriage' ever written, composed with a fury so gelid as to hide completely the bitter passion seething beneath every line. Under the level of homey sentiment lies a terrific contempt for this quarrelsome, vain, literal old couple who for fifty years have disliked life and each other without ever having had the courage or the imagination to face the reality of their own meanness." Fadiman was indeed young, so his failure to comprehend the modus vivendi of a long and reasonably successful marriage was pardonable. Ring understood, doubtless from watching the old folks of St. Pete from his perch at nearby Belleair, the unwritten rules that permitted these people to have their minor spats and running arguments while maintaining a foundation of affection and mutual understanding. If the story is not, as Ray Long thought it was, purely "human interest writing," it is still much closer to that in its respect for two people who have managed to muddle through a half-century together than it is to the venomous vision that Fadiman discerned.

DURING THE EARLY GREAT NECK YEARS Ring poured much of his energy into the theater—with mixed success. He had little luck with the Century Theater of Morris Gest, to whom he was under contract. As he explained to an interviewer in the fall of 1922: "I joined the parade to New York because, in common with some hundred million Americans, I wanted to write plays, and there is only one market. . . . Mr. Gest likes to think of himself as a gambler. He certainly gambled on me. Hearing of my ambition, he gave me a five-year contract with an advance fee. Ever since I have been writing what I conceived to be plays, but which Mr. Gest does not recognize as such. He has been very nice about it, permitting me to offer them to anyone once he has refused them. The other managers, however, agree with Mr. Gest."

It was not that Ring was taking the contract lightly. To the contrary, he poured himself into theatrical work with wholehearted enthusiasm. Between 1919 and 1928 he wrote five musical comedies and one play—but only the play, *Elmer the Great*, was produced, and it lost money. Among these efforts was a collaboration with Gene Buck in the early twenties on a show for Fanny Brice; later the two wrote another equally unsuccessful musical called *Going South*. On his own, Ring did a modern adaptation of *Carmen*, set on Long Island in the Jazz Age and populated with bootleggers and flappers; it was an ingenious piece of work, but its only known production was at a private showing in 1976.

Ring's first small break in the line of resistance to his theatrical endeavors came in 1922, when he managed to sell two skits to Flo

Ziegfeld for his *Follies* of that year, a sale probably helped by Ring's friendship with Buck, his neighbor in Great Neck. The skits were "Rip Van Winkle, Jr." and "The Bull Pen," the latter featuring Will Rogers as one of three ballplayers; this association between Ring and Rogers was one of the early stages of a relationship in which neither man was comfortable, since an obvious rivalry existed. Like most vaudeville material, the skits are now thoroughly dated and warrant no discussion. That they were produced was an important psychological triumph for Ring, however, and there can be no question that he was proud to be associated with Ziegfeld, even if tenuously. Ziegfeld was a difficult, unpredictable man who exploited talent of every kind with no apparent thought for the consequences except as they affected the immediate prospects of his shows; but he was indisputably at the top of the popular theater, and that is where Ring so desperately wanted to be.

It is, however, the chief irony of Ring's career in the theater that his real accomplishment came in a form so completely different from the *Follies*—or, for that matter, from the kind of slick success Ring later enjoyed with *June Moon*—that comparisons are impossible. The first clear indication of what was to come occurred in the fall of 1922, with the presentation of a revue called *The Forty-Niners*, in which Ring's playlet "The Tridget of Greva" was included. The revue was put on by some members of the Algonquin Round Table crowd; this was a circumstance in which Ring was happy to be formally associated with them, since Benchley, Sherwood, Kaufman and others had brilliant theatrical careers.

"The Tridget of Greva" was the first of Ring's nonsense plays to be produced. It is not one of the best, but it shows continuing progress beyond the last such efforts Ring had done in the "Wake." Its cast consists of "Louis Barhooter, *the Tridget*, Desire Corby, *a Corn Vitter*, and Basil Laffler, *a Wham Salesman*." The three are "seated in three small flat-bottomed boats," fishing and talking:

> BARHOOTER (*to Corby*): Can you imitate birds?
> CORBY: No. Why?
> BARHOOTER: I'm always afraid I'll be near somebody that can imitate birds.

CORBY (*to Barhooter*): That reminds me, Louis—Do you shave yourself?

BARHOOTER: Who would I shave?

CORBY: Well, when you shave, what do you do with your old whiskers?

BARHOOTER: I don't do anything with them.

CORBY: Will you save them for me?

BARHOOTER: What do you do with them?

CORBY: I play with them. . . .

LAFFLER: Mr. Corby—

CORBY: Well?

LAFFLER: I often wonder how you spell your name.

CORBY: A great many people have asked me that. The answer is, I don't even try, I just let it go.

LAFFLER: I think that's kind of risky.

CORBY: I'm getting hungry. I wish we could catch some fish.

BARHOOTER: I'm hungry too, but not for fish.

LAFFLER: I can't eat fish either. I've got no teeth. (*Opens his mouth and shows his teeth*) About all I can eat is broth.

BARHOOTER: Well, let's go to a brothel.

For years Ring had listened to conversations in Pullmans and elsewhere in which people chattered on without listening to each other. Now, in the earliest of the twenties nonsense plays, he was beginning to experiment with what might happen if the phenomenon of noncommunication were taken to a perhaps logical extreme, in which not merely was no one listening to anyone else but nothing that anyone was saying made any sense. He envisioned a world in which the nonsequitur was king, in which the only connections that existed had a logic entirely too bizarre to explain —yet connections did, somehow, exist.

If "The Tridget of Greva" made any money for Ring it would be a surprise; the nonsense plays were written either for the enjoyment of friends or as contributions to revues that played to small audiences. But Ring was scarcely hurting for funds by late 1922, what with the "Weekly Letter" and frequent magazine contributions. That fall he opened up a significant new source of revenue by agreeing to do the continuity for a "You Know Me Al" comic strip syndicated by Bell; the drawing was at first done by Will B. Johnstone and, after March 26, 1923, by Dick Dorgan. The strip began on September 26, 1922, and was featured on the comics pages of subscribing newspapers along with such other strips of the day as "Pa's Son-in-Law," "Freckles and His Friends," "Out Our Way," "Petey," "Doings of the Duffs" and "Hairbreadth Harry."

It would be nice to say that the strip in some way enlarged upon what Ring had begun with the busher stories, but it really did not. His enthusiasm for doing it was never high to begin with, despite the approximately $17,000 a year it brought him. It was another drain on his energies offering only money with not a particle of professional, much less artistic, satisfaction, yet he was not able to wiggle out of it until January, 1925; he had stayed with it not merely to make money for himself but out of loyalty to Dorgan, as described by Max Perkins to Scott Fitzgerald in August, 1924: "He won't drop the strip:—the artist hasn't an idea in his head and counts upon Ring for his living;—is even building a house on the strength of the association."

No matter how facile Ring was capable of being, the strip took a great deal out of him. He wrote continuity through September, 1925; over three years he wrote 3,744 comic panels—four panels a day, six days a week, fifty-two weeks a year. He did not make things easier on himself by beginning or ending most strips with a miniature letter to Friend Al running as much as one hundred words. Beyond the sheer drain of work, the strip also imposed heavy demands on Ring's imagination; to keep things going he eventually traded Jack and his friend, Joe Whelan, to the Yankees, and then traded Jack back to the White Sox; he taught Jack how to play bridge; he spent a good deal of space on the rigors of train travel; he sent Jack to Europe. To give sports fans a sense of identification with the strip he regularly brought in well-known baseball people, among them Babe Ruth, Frank Chance, Ed Walsh, Kid Gleason and Charlie Comiskey, for supporting or starring roles.

He came to hate doing it, describing it to Perkins as "me bete noir as the Scotch have it," but the money was good. What with the income from the strip and the "Weekly Letter," Ring had a cushion of nearly $50,000 a year before he began piling short-story income on top of it—and within five years he was getting as much as $4,500 for a single story. He was well on his way to becoming, at least temporarily, a rich man. His income eventually would rise to the neighborhood of $100,000 from writing alone, a staggering figure for a writer who never had any particular success with the sale of his books; measured in the most meaningful terms, purchasing power, it was the approximate equivalent of a late-seventies income of $500,000.

That Ring committed himself to the comic strip in the fall of 1922 is perhaps the most persuasive evidence available that he had also committed himself to a writing career in which financial gain would be the principal pursuit. That same September, however, he made the most important "literary" connection of his life, and suddenly questions began to arise. Up to now he had been treated as a journalist and a popular entertainer; he was widely respected for his skill and for his honorable professionalism, but in most minds Jack Keefe pretty well summed him up. Yet in the months to come he began to hear, from a couple of men whose opinions had to be taken seriously, that he too had to be taken seriously. He came to understand that his work could have more than dollar value, and to be bothered more and more by a nagging worry: Can one write for the dollar *and* for "art," or does a choice have to be made? And beyond that, how much "art" did he have within him: How much further could he go than he already had?

SCOTT AND ZELDA FITZGERALD had come East in September, 1922, and were living in New York in the style to which they had become accustomed, at the Plaza. They had it in mind to rent a place in Great Neck; one day after lunch with Sherwood Anderson and John Dos Passos, they decided to do some house hunting. As Dos Passos described it to Zelda's biographer, Nancy Milford: "This was just before they moved into their house on Great Neck —so off we went. We wound up seeing Ring. Lardner was a very drunk and mournful man. Somehow, perhaps to cheer ourselves, we all decided to go to a carnival that was nearby." It was a meeting that set the stage for countless ones to follow, a mixture of gaiety and melancholy that typified this most peculiar, and most influential, literary friendship.

If Scott had not taken what Zelda called "our nifty little Babbitt-home" at 6 Gateway Drive, just a bit down toward the narrow end of Manhasset Bay from The Mange, he and Ring probably never would have been friends. It is less likely, but possible, that they would not have been the intimate friends they were had Scott not been married to Zelda, with whom Ring was entranced and to whom he was devoted, as were all the Lardners. But they did indeed became close, to the puzzlement of all who have studied them, for there were profound differences between them.

Both were Middle Westerners, but similarities of background largely ended there. Scott was more than eleven years younger than Ring; the disparity in years was less important than that in experience, Ring having been molded by the Victorian and Edwardian eras, Scott by the World War and the early Jazz Age. Notwithstanding Scott's later disparaging remark about "Frank Chance's diamond," Ring had far more acquaintance with the real world than this young man of often astonishing naïveté who still viewed his alma mater, Princeton, with the awe of the newly graduated. Ring was a seasoned professional who was capable of harsh self-discipline; Scott had an enormous natural talent and a casual inclination to fritter it away. Beyond all that, they were simply different people in virtually every way evident, so there is more than a little plausibility in the interpretation advanced by Andrew Turnbull in his *Scott Fitzgerald*: "There is a brotherhood of the intemperate which helps to explain the bond between Lardner and Fitzgerald, different as they were on the surface: the light and the dark, the short and the tall, the expansive and the reticent, the merry and the dismal."

They were, they found, mutually intemperate in several ways: in drink most of all, but also in their delight in foolery and, of all things, talk. Many nights were spent drinking and talking, Ring holding his liquor far better than Scott but apparently unconcerned about his friend's limited capacity. One such evening in April, 1924, they were joined by Edmund Wilson, who recorded in his notebooks a scene that must have occurred, with necessary variations, many times:

> *Great Neck, mid-April.* Fitz said he was going abroad because his reputation was diminishing in America, and he wanted to stay away till he had accomplished something important and then come back and have people give him dinners. There was great talk on Lardner's part of going to the Red Lion or some other roadhouse, but when we did leave—all the liquor now gone—we simply went on to Lardner's, where we drank Grand Marnier—he insisted on presenting us each with a little bottle—and more Scotch. . . . Loud laughter. Zelda had gone to sleep in an armchair and covered herself with a shawl—she was bored by Scott's chart of the Middle Ages and had made herself very disagreeable about it. Scott was sore. . . . "You pronounce too many words wrong," Lardner had said. Lardner read the golf rules aloud. (This was a little book put out by the local golf club. Lardner read these rules at length with a cold and somber scorn that was funny yet really conveyed his disgust with his successful suburban life.)—Then we went back to the Fitzgeralds'. Lardner and I started talking about the oil scandal, and Fitz fell asleep in his chair. Lardner and I went on talking about baseball, Heywood Broun, Lardner's writing, the Americanized *Carmen*, the Rascoes, etc. Deep blue patches appeared at the windows. I couldn't think at first what they were— then I realized it was the dawn. The birds tuned up one at a time. It grew light. It was seven o'clock. Scott asked what we had been

talking about. Lardner said we had been talking about him.—"I suppose you analyzed me ruthlessly." Zelda was sick and had to have the doctor and apologized profusely for her "rudeness."

When we were talking about his own work, Lardner said that the trouble was he couldn't write straight English. I asked him what he meant, and he said: "I can't write a sentence like 'We were sitting in the Fitzgeralds' house and the fire was burning brightly.' "

Still, the drink and the talk and the hell-raising do not fully explain a friendship that broadened and deepened despite the competitive note so perceptively described by Wilson. It is a matter of record why Scott liked Ring. He found him, as he wrote in the obituary essay "Ring," to be "proud, shy, solemn, shrewd, polite, brave, kind, merciful, honorable—with the affection these qualities aroused he created in addition a certain awe in people." Like the Algonquinites, Scott stood before him with deference and more than a touch of veneration.

Why Ring returned Scott's affection equally is less easily explained because he never wrote about it. His few published words about Scott are jocular. "Mr. Fitzgerald is a novelist," he wrote in the most memorable of them, "and Mrs. Fitzgerald a novelty" —and, in the same piece: "I made Mr. Fitzgerald a present of some rare perfume that said Johnny Walker on the outside of it which I had picked up at Marseilles. It was coals to Newcastle, so I took it back to the hotel." On another occasion: "Another prominent writer of the younger set is F. Scott Fitzgerald. Mr. Fitzgerald sprang into fame with his novel *This Side of Paradise* which he turned out when only three years old and wrote the entire book with one hand. Mr. Fitzgerald never shaves while at work on his novels and looks very funny along towards the last five or six chapters."

It does not seem unreasonable, nonetheless, to assume that Ring was much more than merely amused by Scott. No overt enthusiast himself, he was capable of responding to passion when he could perceive it was genuine. Fitzgerald's always was, and in all likelihood he made plain early in their friendship that he had a great enthusiasm for Ring's work; he probably also phrased that enthusiasm in terms new to Ring, terms of literary accomplishment rather than popular success as a journalist and humorist. Ring's own generosity must have recognized Scott's, which in its more open way was just as great. As Ring's letters to Scott and Zelda reveal, they both shared a taste for gossip of show biz and the literary world, a choice sample of which Ring sent to Scott in 1925: "Here is some more 'low down': Some of the Algonquin bunch was sort of riding Michael Arlen, I don't know why. Anyway, when Edna Ferber was introduced to him, she said: 'Why, Mr. Arlen, you look almost like a woman!' 'So do you, Miss Ferber,' was Michael's reply."

The real foundation of this friendship, however, was that Ring and Scott were both outsiders. They were drawn to Great Neck by the glamour, wealth and position concentrated there—they each knew that being in Great Neck was a firm sign that they had arrived—but in their different ways they were contemptuous of what they saw around them. Scott's infatuation with wealth, to the extent that he actually had an infatuation, was far more with the old and established money he had encountered at Princeton than with the vulgar new money that poured into Great Neck; for Ring, his own money was to be spent for the comfort and security of his family, and he took considerable, somewhat malicious, pleasure in observing the ostentatious ways his neighbors found to spend theirs. He and Scott would sit on the porch of The Mange and watch the goings on at the Swopes', commenting to each other as they drank Canadian ale or bootleg whiskey, recording in their minds little details that would reappear in Ring's journalism or Scott's fiction. They were writers and for all their folly they were serious men; that was enough to separate them from the rest of Great Neck, to forge a bond between them, to give them an increasingly urgent sense not only that they did not belong there but that being there was destructive for both of them. Still, before that awareness set in, there was the sheer pleasure of their laughter at what they saw. There was Ring, for example, immortalizing Gene Buck's cavernous living room as "the Yale Bowl—with lamps" or, as he put it in a "Weekly Letter":

. . . friends of the Gene Bucks reports that Gene made a big mistake not leasing his living rm. for the six-day bicycle race as the new Madison Square Garden could not begin to accommodate the devotees of this soul stirring pastime. Gene wired that he wanted to keep the rm. neat for the Olympic Games of 1932. Gene Jr. is entered in the Marathon that yr. and is all ready a top heavy favorite having circled the rm. twice in practice in 2 days, 4 hrs., 20 min., 3 2-5 sec. with two stops for engine trouble and milk.

Scott looked on Great Neck with humor too, though his was darker than Ring's:

I believe that on the first night I went to Gatsby's house I was one of the few guests who had actually been invited. People were not invited—they went there. They got into automobiles which bore them out to Long Island, and somehow they ended up at Gatsby's door. Once there they were introduced by somebody who knew Gatsby, and after that they conducted themselves according to the rules of behavior associated with an amusement park. Sometimes they came and went without having met Gatsby at all, came for the party with a simplicity of heart that was its own ticket of admission. . . .

There was dancing now on the canvas in the garden; old men pushing young girls backward in eternal graceless circles, superior couples holding each other tortuously, fashionably, and keeping in the corners—and a great number of single girls dancing individualistically or relieving the orchestra for a moment of the burden of the banjo or the traps. By midnight the hilarity had increased. A celebrated tenor had sung in Italian, and a notorious contralto had sung in jazz, and between the numbers people were doing "stunts" all over the garden, while happy, vacuous bursts of laughter rose toward the summer sky. . . .

The large room was full of people. One of the girls in yellow was playing the piano, and beside her stood a tall, red-haired young lady from a famous chorus, engaged in song. She had drunk a quantity of champagne, and during the course of her song she had decided, ineptly, that everything was very, very sad—she was not only singing, she was weeping too. . . . The tears coursed down her cheeks—not freely, however, for when they came into contact with her heavily beaded eyelashes they assumed an inky color, and pursued the rest of their way in slow black rivulets. A humorous suggestion was made that she sing the notes on her face, whereupon she threw up her hands, sank into a chair, and went off into a deep vinous sleep.

One had to be closer to the Swope mansion than the Lardners' porch to observe such details so closely: Ring and Scott, for all the aloofness they sometimes elaborately maintained, were fully capable of crashing parties and drinking someone else's liquor. Ring, in fact, was something of an expert at it; he probably felt Swope owed him a few drinks, since, as he once told an interviewer, he watered and amused more than a few Swope guests: "Mr. Swope of the *World* lives across the way and he conducts an almost continuous house-party. A number of other neighbors do the same; there are guests in large numbers roaming the woods all the time. Apparently they become confused occasionally and forget at whose house they are really stopping, for they wander in at all hours demanding refreshment and entertainment at the place that happens to be nearest at the moment. The telephone is going almost continuously." Ring, when he was in a partying mood—it took several drinks to get him there—would wander over to the Swopes', and if the piano were not in use, proceed to entertain. According to Donald Elder, he was wont to perform Lardneresque operas, one of them dominated by the line "Gretchen, I'm retchin' for you."

Ring and Scott were also prone to improvisations that had nothing to do with Great Neck but might not have been performed elsewhere without legal consequences. One of the more notable of these occurred when Joseph Conrad came to Great Neck to visit his publisher, Frank Nelson Doubleday. Ring and Scott sat around having several drinks, their determination to meet the master—not to mention their courage—increasing with each one. Ring later recalled the incident: "I wish I could have met [Conrad] when he was over here. Just to see him would have been enough; if I had had a chance to talk with him, I'm sure I would not have been able to say a word. Fitzgerald and I concocted a scheme to dress up as sailors and dance a hornpipe on Mr. Doubleday's front lawn. Mr. Conrad might have seen us from the window, we argued, and come out and let us have a look at him, at any rate." All their ingenuity got them was the bum's rush from the Doubleday caretaker.

Given the amount of boozing that went on, and Fitzgerald's tendency to get morose if the mood and the liquor did not mix properly, it should come as no surprise that there were bad moments as well as happy ones during Fitzgerald's year and a half in Great Neck. One of particularly unsettling dimensions is described by Anita Loos, as quoted by Aaron Latham in *Crazy Sundays*. Miss Loos was walking along Fifth Avenue when Scott pulled up beside her in his car and invited her for a ride; not knowing that he was drunk, she accepted. After a "wild ride," they reached Great Neck: ". . . Zelda was at home and we sat down to dinner. Scott was very moody, and not saying much. Zelda and I ignored him, and that seemed to make him angry. Finally he jumped up from the table and said, 'I'm going to kill you two.' And he tried. He jerked off the tablecloth with everything on it and then started throwing the candelabra and other big, heavy things at us. Scott had locked all the doors, but the butler—he will always be a hero to me—broke through a glass pane in one of the doors and came in and held Scott. Then Zelda and I ran across to Ring Lardner's house. Ring decided to go out looking for Scott. He looked for quite a while before he found him. When he did, Scott was kneeling on the road eating dirt. 'I'm a monster,' he was saying. 'I tried to kill those two darling girls and now I've got to eat dirt.' " On another occasion Ring and Ellis left a gathering at the Fitzgeralds' "on account of dullness." Later they learned that a half-hour after their departure, Scott had gotten into a fight with Gene Buck's brother-in-law: "Scott is nursing a broken hand as a result of hitting him in the head. This was the semi-final bout. The wind-up was won by Mrs. Buck, who hit Mr. Buck three times in the nose for not taking his brother-in-law's part."

Such events were the exception rather than the rule, however, during a friendship that in only a year and a half had a profound effect on both men. Before considering how Scott helped change Ring's career, it is worth noting the ways in which Ring altered, or influenced, Scott's—since the general assumption is that it was a one-way matter with Scott doing all the influencing. It is not possible, of course, to demonstrate any psychological impact Ring may have had, but there can be little doubt that Scott was flattered and encouraged by the attention and affection he was given by this tall, forbidding, imposing figure of a man—this man whose celebrity was at the time far greater than his own. The perceptions of Great Neck that Scott and Ring exchanged undoubtedly played a large part in helping him arrive at the clinical disdain for opulent vulgarity that is so central to *The Great Gatsby*.

The sources of the novel are obviously complex and can be quarreled over endlessly, but there is little reason to question that Scott saw himself in both Gatsby and Ring or that, twisting the equation, both he and Ring are present in the "good," or "lost," side of Gatsby. Scott could see in Ring, a decade older than himself, his own future: physical depletion by alcoholism, creative depletion by labors beneath his talents. It was his despair over this aching sense of loss from which Jay Gatsby was formed.

Or so it is argued here. But of the influence of Ring upon the shaping of another notable Fitzgerald character, Abe North in *Tender Is the Night,* there has been little significant dispute. Readers who think that a real person must be literally transcribed into fictional form for such an influence to be valid have pointed out that Abe North is a musician, not a writer, and that his death comes after he is beaten up in a speakeasy in New York. But a few of the passages in which Abe North appears make almost painfully clear that he is Ring thinly disguised:

His voice was slow and shy; he had one of the saddest faces Rosemary had ever seen, the high cheekbones of an Indian, a long upper lip, and enormous deep-set eyes. He had spoken out of the side of his mouth, as if he hoped his words would reach Mrs. McKisco by a circuitous and unobtrusive route.

. . .

He turned his noble head slowly so that his eyes rested with tenderness and affection on the two Divers.

. . .

Since reaching Paris Abe North had a thin vinous fur over him; his eyes were bloodshot from sun and wine. Rosemary realized for the first time that he was always stopping in places to get a drink, and she wondered how Mary North liked it.

. . .

Abe, who was desperate and witty . . .

. . .

They stood in an uncomfortable little group weighted down by Abe's gigantic presence: he lay athwart them like the wreck of a galleon, dominating with his presence his own weakness and self-indulgence, his narrowness and bitterness. All of them were conscious of the solemn dignity that flowed from him, of his achievement, fragmentary, suggestive and surpassed. But they were frightened at his survivant will, once a will to live, now become a will to die.

Some of it is transparently Ring: the "noble head" that looked like an Indian's (Ring had probably told Scott how, at a Carlisle football practice, he was mistaken by a spectator for one of the Indian players); the affection his gaze must have conveyed to Scott and Zelda; the drinking. With regard to the last, there is more than passing similarity between the third quotation above and this comment in a letter from Zelda to a friend during the Great Neck years: "Ring is drinking himself to an embalmed state so he'll be all ready for the grim reaper. I don't think he'll have long to wait, if he keeps on. His wife is worried sick." Mary North, Abe's wife, is described by Scott as having "a face so merry that it was impossible not to smile back into the white mirrors of her teeth—the whole area around her parted lips was a lovely little circle of delight." That, in the years Scott knew her, was Ellis, before the pain of Ring's alcoholism and illness began to weigh on her and suppress her gaiety.

The portrait of Abe North also contains aspects of Ring as Scott saw him rather than as, necessarily, he actually was. Scott cannot have seen "narrowness and bitterness" in Ring—here he must have been adding truly fictional embellishments—but he did believe that Ring's work was "fragmentary, suggestive and surpassed," and he had a profound conviction that Ring in his last years was willing his own death. The final version of *Tender Is the Night* was plotted in 1932, and Scott last visited Ring in 1931: "When my wife and I last saw him . . . he looked already like a man on his deathbed—it was terribly sad to see that six feet three inches of kindness stretched out ineffectual in the hospital room. His fingers trembled with a match, the tight skin on his handsome skull was marked as a mask of misery and nervous pain."

If there is any lingering doubt that Abe North was formed from Ring, it is dispelled in the novel's final reference to him. Dick Diver (for whom read "Scott") is grieving at Abe's murder: ". . . Dick's lungs burst for a moment with regret for Abe's death, and his own youth of ten years ago."

SCOTT'S INVETERATE ENTHUSIASM often led him into the role of self-appointed literary agent. He had an uncannily sharp eye—he really can be said to have discovered Ernest Hemingway, for which Hemingway never forgave him—and when that eye led him to a new discovery, invariably he reported the news to Maxwell Evarts

Perkins. That is what he did with Ring, when he decided that it was time to take Ring out of the popular press and into the literary salons.

Max Perkins helped bring three notable writers to fame—Fitzgerald, Hemingway and Thomas Wolfe—but he himself stayed, so far as he could, out of the limelight. He believed that it was his job to sit at his desk at Charles Scribner's Sons on Fifth Avenue and read the manuscripts that came to him—editing the work of writers already known, looking up occasionally to see if something unknown might come in, as it is said in publishing, over the transom. He was a Vermont Yankee of methodical habits—to work at ten, lunch at one, back at two-thirty, a pre-train drink at five—and subdued demeanor. John Hall Wheelock, the poet who was also his fellow editor and, ultimately, successor, remembered among his many virtues his capacity to listen: "A New Englander, and reserved, he was naturally inclined to silence. But his silence was attractive, perceptive, helpful to the talker, a positive kind of silence, charged with the awareness and judgments of a superior intelligence. . . . There were days when his entire time in the office was given over to this silent listening. That silence could, on occasion, be terrifying and, when driven to desperation by some long-winded speaker, Perkins would sometimes puncture it with an irritable, 'Well, what about it?' which usually served to bring things to a head. He was not by any means always amiable." For all his reticence, he had a strong romantic streak, and Wheelock found a conflict between "the Puritan and the Cavalier, the shrewd Yankee and the generous and disarming artist." John Kuehl and Jackson Bryer, editors of the Fitzgerald-Perkins correspondence, suggest that this romantic streak helps explain "his attachment to Lardner, Fitzgerald, Hemingway and Wolfe—all romantic figures—who, perhaps, depended on Perkins's steadiness more than Perkins needed their flare." It was, however, precisely this steadiness that Perkins needed in an occupation that Wheelock has described with a feeling born of experience:

> The job of editor in a publishing house is the dullest, hardest, most exciting, exasperating and rewarding of perhaps any job in the world. Most writers are in a state of gloom a good deal of the time; they need perpetual reassurance. When a writer has written his masterpiece he will often be certain that the whole thing is

266 / RING: A Biography of Ring Lardner

worthless. The perpetrator of the dimmest literary effort, on the other hand, is apt to be invincibly cocksure and combative about it. No book gets enough advertising (the old superstition regarding its magic power still persists), or it is the wrong kind. And, obviously, almost every writer needs money and needs it before, not after, delivery of the goods. There is the writer whose manuscript proves that Shakespeare's plays are merely an elaborate system of political code; another has written a book to demonstrate that the earth is round, but that we are living on the inside of it; still another has completed a novel in five volumes, entitled "God." Through it all Max kept his countenance. To the many aspects of an editor's work he brought a tremendous seriousness, masculine drive and energy, daring coupled with shrewd judgment, quiet strength, and a self-effacement and delicacy of feeling almost feminine in character. But he brought a sense of humor too.

It must have been among the great frustrations of Max Perkins' career that he was never permitted to bring these formidable editorial resources to bear on the work of Ring Lardner. For though Ring liked and respected Perkins, and trusted his literary judgment, he never did what Perkins wanted him to do: he never wrote a novel. Perkins ended up performing a clipping-and-pasting service for Ring, rounding up his stories and columns and plays and putting them into volumes, and a clerk could have done that. Perkins felt that Ring's literary possibilities were greater than most of his work indicated, and he badly wanted to develop them: ". . . I wish there were something I could do to compel you to write that 40,000 word story, or novel, or whatever it ought to be called. I do not know of any publishing news that would be more interesting than that such a book by you was to come out." Ring ignored, or evaded, all such suggestions.

Scott first began to press Perkins to consider Ring as a possible Scribner author in the spring of 1923, and by July, Perkins was ready to move. He wrote Ring a friendly if formal letter complimenting him on "The Golden Honeymoon" and noting that Scott had "suggested that you might have other material of the same sort, which, with this, could form a volume." The letter then turned markedly deferential: "I would hardly have ventured to do this if Scott had not spoken of the possibility, because your position in the literary world is such that you must be besieged by publishers, and to people in that situation their letters of interest are rather a nuisance. I am certainly mighty glad to have the chance of expressing our interest though, if, as Scott thought, you would not feel that we were merely bothering you." Apparently Ring responded by phone or through Scott, for no reply to this invitation exists, but apparently he did respond quickly, as that same month Scott brought Perkins to Great Neck for a meeting with Ring.

It turned out to be a memorable one. They went for dinner at a Manhasset restaurant called René Durand's; the discussion of a volume of stories got specific enough so that the table of contents was virtually decided upon. Scott drank a great deal, and when the evening ended he chauffeured Perkins into a pond on Durand's grounds. Max for a time remembered the incident as "that eventful night when Scott drove into the lake," so it came as a disappointment to him when, in the summer of 1924, Ring took him to Durand's in the cold light of day. "I had yesterday a disillusioning afternoon at Great Neck," he said in a letter to Scott, "not in respect to Ring Lardner, who gains on you whenever you see him, but in respect to Durand's where he took me for lunch. I thought that night a year ago that we ran down a steep place into a lake. There was no steep place and no lake. We sat on a balcony in front. It was dripping hot and Durand took his police dog down to the margin of that puddle of a lily pond,—the dog waded almost across it;—and I'd been calling it a lake all these months. But they've put up a fence to keep others from doing as we did."

Ring and Perkins agreed on the publication of a volume of stories, though there was a basic problem that Scott remembered a decade later with undiminished astonishment: "My God! he hadn't even saved them—the material of *How to Write Short Stories* was obtained by photographing old issues of magazines in the public library!" Finally, on December 7, Perkins was able to write Ring and thank him for a copy of "Champion" (where Ring had found it is a mystery), which rounded out the table of contents to ten stories: "The Facts," "Some Like Them Cold," "Alibi Ike," "The Golden Honeymoon," "Champion," "My Roomy," "A Caddy's Diary," "A Frame-Up," "Harmony" and "Horseshoes." Four days later Scott and Perkins met over lunch at the Hotel Chatham in New York, with Ring the principal subject of discussion. Whether it was here that Scott suggested the ironical and self-mocking *How to Write Short Stories* as the title for the collection is not certain, but he did outline, on the back of a menu, a program for a uniform edition of Ring's work. It showed how closely he knew everything Ring had written; not merely did he propose that the set include *You Know Me Al*, *Gullible's Travels* and *The Big Town*—all of them obvious choices —but he also remembered *The Young Immigrunts*, *Symptoms of Being 35* and a recently published autobiographical piece called "What I Ought to of Learnt in High School," which remained undeservedly uncollected until 1976, when it appeared in *Some Champions*.

That Scott maintained this high degree of interest in and advocacy of Ring's work was remarkable, but it was even more so considering that the fall of 1923 was a hard period in his own career. He was between books: his latest novel, *The Beautiful and the Damned*, had been published a year and a half before, and *The Great Gatsby* was a year and a half away. In addition, he had written a play entitled *The Vegetable*, a political satire, and the omens did not seem good when the Fitzgeralds and Lardners went to Atlantic City in late November for its opening. It turned out to be a disaster. The second act bombed, and members of the audience began departing noisily. Before the third act Ring and Scott sought out their Great Neck neighbor Ernest Truex, who was playing the lead, to ask if he was going to bother to do the third act. When he said yes, one of them told him, "Don't be silly. We've got a bartender down the street who's an old friend of ours"—and that, according to Andrew Turnbull, "was the last Truex saw of them."

Ring, too, had more on his mind during 1923 than the publication of a collection of stories. The column was rolling along smoothly, but it took time and so did several trips. In early 1923 he and Ellis went to Belleair, Palm Beach and Miami; a year later they visited Miami and Nassau with the Rices. Special assignments took him to two fights involving the Wild Bull of the Pampas, the Argentine heavyweight Luis Firpo: in July, 1923, against Jess Willard and in September against Jack Dempsey. The second bout was held in Jersey City and won by Dempsey. It was a brilliantly fought contest in which Firpo gave the champion as much as he could handle; this was the bout in which he knocked Dempsey out of the ring, a moment frozen on a great sporting canvas by the artist Edward Hopper. Ring's report on the bout showed that even though his interest in the outcome of sports events was by now minimal (unless he had a bet down), his admiration for skill and courage was undiminished:

They was a big question before the fight as to whether or no the Wild Bull could take it. He took it and took it plenty and come back for more, and got it. They aint nobody living that could take what he took before he finely took that left and right in succession and became the tame cow of the pampas. Anybody that said he quit ought to be writing jokes for the theater program. In fact Luis didn't know when the fight was over and was still groggy when he staggered down the steep stairs out of the ring, escorted by some of the same policemens that had tried to keep me from seeing the fight.

And they was another question settled to-night, namely can Dempsey take it. Jack was on the receiving end of four or five of the most murderous blows ever delivered in a prize ring, but he come back after each one and fought all the harder. Even when he fell into Mr. Rice's lap, he picked himself up without assistance and stepped right back to the place where all the shooting was going on. . . .

He never lost sight of the main idear, that he must get this guy and get him quick. He didn't get him none too quick and if the fight had went a round longer they would of been wholesale deaths from heart disease with maybe some of the victims in Dempsey's corner. All and all you won't hear no squawks to the effect that those who paid to get in didn't get their money's worth, even they paid a hundred smacks for a seat. It was a FIGHT.

Ring published no fiction during this period—there is a two-year gap between "The Golden Honeymoon" and "What of It?" —but he did a considerable amount of nonfiction for *Cosmopolitan* and then for *Hearst's International.* These included several parodies, among them a particularly funny one of "Cinderella" in which Ring paid tribute to a friend: "Well, the guy's own daughter was a pip, so both her stepmother and the two stepsisters hated her and made her sleep in the ashcan. Her name was Zelda, but they called her Cinderella on account of how the ashes and clinkers clang to her when she got up noons."

Ring's most important work in the months before the publication of *How to Write Short Stories* was published in what was, for him, a most unlikely place, the *Chicago Literary Times,* edited by Ben Hecht; it appeared there in February, 1924, and five months later it was also published in the *Transatlantic Review,* then under the acting editorship of Ernest Hemingway. In the latter it was introduced by Hemingway in an unsigned editorial as an antidote to the pretensions of Dada and its leading spokesman, Tristan Tzara: ". . . what profound admiration we have for Americans who really do know French and how tired we get of others who pretend to and how very much better dadas the American dadas, who do not know they are dadas . . . are than the French and the Roumanians who know it so well." The piece was a nonsense play called "I Gaspiri (The Upholsterers)"; it was brought to Hemingway's attention by Donald Ogden Stewart, a popular young parodist who had performed in it. As he recalled the occasion in his memoirs, "The impulse toward 'crazy humor' was encouraged by the success of a skit which Bob Benchley, Marc Connelly and I did for the annual dinner of the Authors' League, which had been written for us by Ring Lardner, and was called 'I Gaspiri (The Upholsterers)'. . . . Bob played a mandolin while we conversed deadpan in sentences which had no relation to each other or to anything else." It deserves to be quoted in full:

I GASPIRI
(The Upholsterers)
A Drama in Three Acts
By Ring Lardner
Adapted from the Bukovinian of
Casper Redmonda

CHARACTERS
Ian Obri—A Blotter Salesman
Johan Wasper—His wife
Greta—Their daughter
Herbert Swope—A nonentity
Ffena—Their daughter, later their wife
Egso—A Pencil Guster
Tono—A Typical Wastebasket

ACT I

A public street in a bathroom. A man named Tupper has evidently just taken a bath. A man named Brindle is now taking a bath. A man named Newburn comes out of the faucet which has been left running. He exits through the exhaust. Two strangers to each other meet on the bath mat.

FIRST STRANGER

Where was you born?

SECOND STRANGER

Out of wedlock.

FIRST STRANGER

That's a mighty pretty country around there.

SECOND STRANGER

Are you married?

FIRST STRANGER

I don't know. There's a woman living with me, but I can't place her.

(*Three outsiders named Klein go across the stage three times. They think they are in a public library. A woman's cough is heard offstage left.*)

A NEW CHARACTER

Who is that cough?

TWO MOORS

That is my mother. She died a little while ago in a haphazard way.

A GREEK

And what a woman she was!

(*The curtain is lowered for seven days to denote the lapse of a week.*)

ACT II

(*Deleted by the censor.*)

ACT III

(*The Lincoln Highway. Two bearded glue lifters are seated at one side of the road.*)

(TRANSLATOR'S NOTE: *The principle industry in Phlace is hoarding hay. Peasants sit alongside of a road on which hay wagons are likely to pass. When a hay wagon does pass, the hay hoarders leap from their points of vantage and help themselves to a wisp of hay. On an average a hay hoarder accumulates a ton of hay every four years. This is called Mah Jong.*)

FIRST GLUE LIFTER

Well, my man, how goes it?

SECOND GLUE LIFTER

(*Sings "My Man," to show how it goes.*)

(*Eight realtors cross the stage in a friendly way. They are out of place.*)

CURTAIN

Ring wrote many other nonsense plays in the years to come, the best of them being "Cora, or Fun at a Spa" and "Taxidea Americana," but "I Gaspiri" is eminently representative—which is to say that it is a dazzling collection of verbal and visual non-sequiturs, all of them wildly comical. The plays do not submit to rational analysis for the simple reason that they are antirational. Though they were often seized upon as Dada or surrealism, they were not consciously written to conform to any literary movement or passing fancy. They were simply the direct products of Ring's invention, the final summations of all the nonsense he had seen in the world around him. They stand firmly enough on their own unique merits; they do not need to be encumbered with the weight of any literary "school," for the only one they belong to is their own—Ring's.

WHILE RING GALLIVANTED AROUND in the spring of 1924, from Miami to Nassau, back to Great Neck, then to Washington, Perkins worked to get the story collection into shape for publication. He cajoled Ring into writing a preface, and then into adding brief introductory comments for each story. He explained that he had alternated the baseball and nonbaseball stories for the sake of variety. He sent galley proofs to Ring and urged their speedy return. A May 9 publication date was set, and even before it was reached Perkins was busily looking beyond it, persuading Ring to write to Bobbs-Merrill and Doran about releasing the rights to his earlier books so Scribner's could put together a uniform edition: "We ought now to consider the question of getting the other books released by their publishers. . . . It would be much better strategy if you approached them. Could you write them saying that since the books were no longer active (assuming that they are not) you would like to get control of them, and asking what the steps would be thereto? This would let us know where we stand and when we heard from them we could say whether we thought the suggestion they made was fair." Ring did as he was asked, with ultimate success, but as we have already seen, at the price of causing some pain to his old friend Hewitt H. Howland.

Scott, meantime, was making plans to leave Great Neck and move to the French Riviera; it was almost as if, having gotten Ring headed into the mainstream of American literature, he himself needed to set sail again. But there were more practical reasons.

He was worried about matters between him and Zelda, and he was even more concerned about his declining productivity. He had, to be sure, produced a heavy volume of slick fiction in recent months due to a sudden financial crisis, but he knew that he could work neither seriously nor well in Great Neck. He wrote Perkins: "It is only in the last four months that I've realized how much I've—well, almost *deteriorated* in the three years since I finished the Beautiful and Damned. The last four months of course I've worked but in the two years—over two years—before that, I produced exactly *one* play, *half a dozen* short stories and three or four articles—an average of about *one hundred* words a day. If I'd spent this time reading or travelling or doing anything—even staying healthy—it'd be different but I spent it uselessly neither in study nor in contemplation but only in drinking and raising hell generally." Scott, though he was vastly less self-disciplined than Ring, in this case knew what Ring would not finally realize for another four years: he had to get out of Great Neck. That it was corroding his liver was bad enough; that it was destroying his art was intolerable.

The departure of the Fitzgeralds by no means ended their friendship with Ring and Ellis. The four would see little of each other for the remainder of their lives—a visit by the Lardners in the fall of 1924 was to be their last time together of any significant duration—but they kept in close touch by mail. In fact, Ring's friendship for Scott provoked him to a correspondence that was, for him, voluminous and chatty, and much of what we now know about the rest of his life has been learned from those letters.

The Fitzgeralds sailed in early May. They took with them this token of Ring's affection:

To Z. S. F.

Zelda, fair queel of Alabam',
Across the waves I kiss you!
You think I am a stone, a clam;
You think that I don't care a damn,
But God! how I will miss you!

For months and months you've meant to me
What Mario meant to Tosca.
You've gone, and I am all at sea
Just like the Minnewaska.

I once respected him you call
Your spouse, and that is why, dear,
I held my tongue—and then, last Fall
He bared a flippancy and gall
Of which I'd had no idear.

When I with pulmonary pain
Was seized, he had the gumption
To send me lives of Wilde and Crane,
Two brother craftsmen who in vain
Had battled with consumption.

We wreak our vengeance as we can,
And I have no objection
To getting even with this "man"
By stealing your affection.

So, dearie, when your tender heart
Of all his coarseness tires,
Just cable me and I will start
Immediately for Hyeres.

To hell with Scott Fitzgerald then!
To hell with Scott, his daughter!
It's you and I back home again,
To Great Neck, where the men are men
And booze is ¾ water.

My heart goes with you as you sail,
God grant you won't be seasick!
The thought of you abaft the rail,
Diffusing meat and ginger ale,
Makes both my wife and me sick.

But Ring, too, knew that it was time to get back to work. To Thomas Boyd, another Scribner author, he wrote on May 18: "Great Neck is like a cemetery since Scott and Zelda went. And I might say that as far as I'm concerned, it would have been more like one if they'd staid."

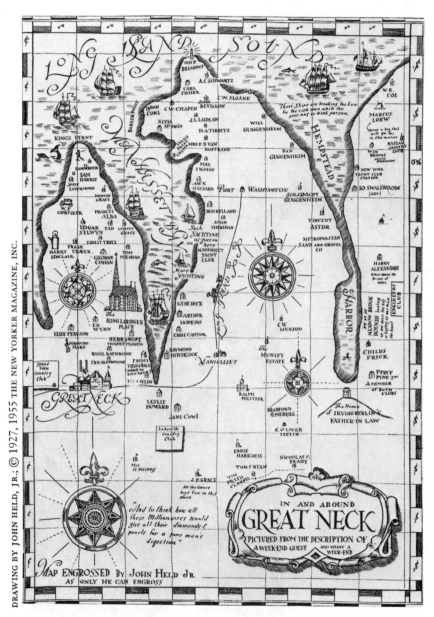

Great Neck in 1927, as seen by John Held of The New Yorker.

Maxwell Perkins, the editor who never got a real chance to edit Ring.

Scott and Zelda Fitzgerald with their daughter, Scotty; this is how they looked during the year and a half when Ring and Ellis knew them best.

1. My Life and Loves
   High School article   (American)
   How I built my house   Bill takes up the story
   On being Thirty five (American)
   ~~How I got my start in life~~
   My four weeks in France
2. Adventures in Idocy
3. The Art of The Short Story
4. You know me Al
5. Gullible's Travels
6. The Big Town <

Short Stories
—— Harmony (Mc Clures)
> The Facts (Metropolitan)
—— My Roomy (The Post)
—— Horseshoes (The Post)
   ~~The Young Immigrants~~
      ~~(The Post)~~
? ~~One story in Cosmopolitan~~
      ~~files~~

Good for the Soul
   Jan 26 - 1916

The Bib Ballads
Treat em Rough

On December 11, 1923, Fitzgerald and Perkins met over lunch and talked about Ring's future with Scribner's. On the back of a menu, Scott scribbled down the titles of Lardner's works that could be incorporated into a uniform edition; the notation in the lower right-hand corner is in Perkins' handwriting.

Ring and Ellis posing for a photographer from the window of a British train. They had just visited the Fitzgeralds on the Riviera, and were on their way home.

Ring had lost most of his interest in baseball by the twenties, but not all of it. This striking picture was taken during that period, possibly at a spring-training site.

Above: *Hollywood, 1926. From left: Ring, Floncy Rice, Ellis, Norman Kerry, and Kate and Grant Rice.* Below: *Ring with Gene Buck, owner of the living room that Ring called "the Yale Bowl—with lamps."*

Above: *The Lardners of Great Neck. Jim, Ellis, David, Bill, Ring—and John making an end run.* Left: *Ring on the golf course.*

Ring at the height of his fame: looking down at the world with compassion, not contempt, and dismay, not disgust.

Near the end. Ring and Ellis at East Hampton. "I think things are bad with Ring," Max Perkins wrote. "I hate to inquire. He is at Easthampton and nobody ever seems to see him."

RING'S RESPONSE TO PERKINS' REQUEST that he write a preface to *How to Write Short Stories* was characteristic: he refused to take the request, or himself, seriously. He wrote a seemingly offhand piece that doubtless looked familiar to readers of his January 13, 1924, "Weekly Letter," since it was in fact a refined and improved version of that same column. He pointed out that "whatever else this country may be shy of, there is certainly no lack of correspondence schools that learns you the art of short-story writing." He went on to observe that "you can't find no school in operation up to date, whether it be a general institution of learning or a school that specialized in story writing, which can make a great author out of a born druggist"—but as long as people insisted that writing skills could be taught, he would "give them a few hints in regards to the technic of the short story, how to go about planning it and writing it, when and where to plant the love interest and climax, and finally how to market the finished product without leaving no bad taste in the mouth."

It was a good idea to start with "a catchy title," he said, and suggested "Basil Hargrave's Vermiflage" or "Fun at the Incinerating Plant." From there he went on to offer some sample plots and some sound advice about getting a story to an editor's attention:

> . . . A good many young writers make the mistake of enclosing a stamped, self-addressed envelope, big enough for the manuscript to come back in. This is too much of a temptation to the editor.
>
> Personally I have found it a good scheme to not even sign my name to the story, and when I have got it sealed up in its envelope and stamped and addressed, I take it to some town where I don't live and mail it from there. The editor has no idea who wrote the story, so how can he send it back? He is in a quandary. . . .
>
> Stories ("yarns") of mine which have appeared in various pub-

lications—one of them having been accepted and published by the first editor that got it—are reprinted in the following pages and will illustrate in a half-hearted way what I am trying to get at.

If that did not make the point strongly enough, the little prefatory paragraphs with which he introduced each story certainly did. "Alibi Ike," for example, was preceded with this: "A typical tale of the backwoods of Indiana some seventy years ago, very interestingly depicted. The author acknowledges his indebtedness to Chief Justice Taft for some of the slang employed." This was his introduction to "Harmony": "When this story was first printed, the literary editor of the United Cigar Stores Premium Catalogue had the following to say: 'The love story, half earthly, half spiritual, of a beautiful snare drummer and a hospital interne; unique for its word pictures of the unpleasant after effects of anaesthesia. It explains what radio is and how it works.' "

The self-mockery puzzled Edmund Wilson, whose review was otherwise the most thoughtful the collection received and surely the one to which Ring paid closest heed. "Is all this an idea of the publishers," Wilson asked, "who do not want to forfeit the prestige of Mr. Lardner's reputation as a humorist, or is it due to Mr. Lardner, who is timid about coming forward in the role of serious writer?" But if Wilson was excessively solemn there, elsewhere he praised wisely. He found the stories "a series of studies of American types almost equal in importance to those of Sherwood Anderson and Sinclair Lewis," and then said Ring "is less likely than Lewis to caricature, and hence to falsify, because he is primarily interested in studying a kind of person rather than in drawing up an indictment"—a comment that effectively takes care of all the later business about Ring's cold-bloodedness. He noted Ring's "distinguished aloof intelligence," and then issued a challenge to him:

> Will Ring Lardner then, go on to his *Huckleberry Finn* or has he already told all he knows? It may be that the mechanical repitition of a trick that one finds in such a story as "Horseshoes" and the melodramatic exaggeration of "Champion" indicate limitations. But you never know: here is a man who has had the freedom of the modern West no less than Mark Twain did of the old one, who approaches it, as Mark Twain did, with a perceptive interest in human beings instead of with the naturalist's formula—a man who lives at a time when, if one be not sold irredeemably into bondage

to the *Saturday Evening Post*, it is far easier for a serious writer to get published and find a hearing than it was in Mark Twain's day. If Ring Lardner has anything more to give us, the time has now come to deliver it. He has not even popular glory to gain by pursuing any other course. . . . What bell might not Lardner ring if he set out to give us the works?

It was, of course, precisely the poppycock that people who spend too much time writing too many book reviews fall back on as a way of ending a piece with a crescendo: "And when, pray tell, will Mr. Jones step forward with the magnum opus his great talent has so long promised us, and so long denied." Into the bargain, Wilson refused to accept Ring's accomplishment for what it was, a problem Ring would, as of now, face for the rest of his career: Don't be what you are, the literati began to tell him in 1924, be what we want you to be—write a novel.

But the piece also came as confirmation, from a critic whom Ring surely respected, of what Scott and Perkins had been telling him. He *could* do serious work, they said, and it appears that now he began to believe them. Perkins came out to Great Neck in May, with a stack of books for Ring to autograph and, apparently, every intention of having serious words with him about his work; instead, as he confessed to Scott, "The reason I went down to Ring Lardner's—but I am ashamed to tell you about it. I meant to have a serious talk with him, but we arrived late and the drinks were already prepared. We did no business that night. He was very amusing." Still, Perkins persisted and Ring responded, writing a couple of months later that "I am trying to get up nerve enough to ask for release from the 'comic' strip" with the hope that "I will have a lot more time to spend on short stories." Then, in December, he wrote:

> I think I am going to be able to sever connections with the daily cartoon early next month. [He did.] This ought to leave me with plenty of time and it is my intention to write at least ten short stories a year. Whether I can do it or not, I don't know. I started one the other day and got through with about 700 words, which were so bad that I gave up. I seem to be out of the habit and it may take time to get back.

He was willing to make an effort, but on his terms rather than Perkins': he was going to write more short stories (and he did, in one of the most productive periods of his life), but nothing was said about a novel. Part of it was economic. Ring was giving up a great deal of money in abandoning the strip; the high life in Great Neck mandated that he somehow make up for the loss; with his short-story fee now $3,000 and up, he stood to make much more out of a year working within the familiar confines of short fiction than in the unknown territory of a novel. But it was, of course, much more than an economic problem. Ring was scared of the mere idea of writing a novel; he had the journalist's fear of taking on something so long and complex and structurally unclear. Beyond that, so many people had by now asked him so many times when he was going to write a "real" book that he must have felt that expectations had been raised past any point he could possibly hope to reach.

He had his excuses for not writing long fiction and they all sounded great. He told his son Bill, "Before I got a third of the way through I'd be even more bored than the reader would." He wrote once in *The New Yorker*: "It seems that the Scribner boys, who have been kind enough to publish collections of stories that I either wrote or that were ghost-written for me, have asked me time and again (that makes twice) to give them a full-length novel or book on one subject, but I kept refusing on the ground that I couldn't think of a subject that I could stretch into a novel or book." He also made a big thing out of pretentiousness. He was critical of George Gershwin after *Rhapsody in Blue* and other quasi-"classical" compositions, saying he preferred him "when he wasn't so Gershwinesque." He wrote a short story, "Rhythm," around the theme, the central character being a songwriter, Harry Hart, who gets big ideas after he scores a major hit: "When 'Upsy Daisy' had been running two months and its hit numbers were being sung, played, and whistled almost to cloyment, Hart was discovered by Spencer Deal. That he was the pioneer in a new American jazz, that his rhythms would revolutionize our music—these things and many more were set forth by Deal in a four-thousand word article called 'Harry Hart, Harbinger,' printed by the erudite Webster's Weekly. And Harry ate it up, though some of the words nearly choked him." Hart enters a collaboration with Spencer Deal himself: "The result of the collaboration was a score that required a new signature at the beginning of each bar, and a collection of six-syllable rhymes that has as much chance of being unriddled, let alone sung, by chorus girls as a pandect on biotaxy by Ernest Boyd." The further result is that Harry goes near-broke, and is not rescued until he resumes his old collaboration with Benny Kane, who proposes that they write "a rhythm song" around the theme, "I love you." Harry agrees, and his feet are quickly back on firm ground.

Those were Ring's excuses, and he used them enough to leave little doubt that the problem worried him. It is a mystery why he never simply said: Look, no one does what I do better than I do, so why not accept me for what I am? He could also have said, with utter legitimacy, that his mind functioned best over short, intense distances and that he did not think he was capable of writing a good novel—which in fact he probably was not. He was a master of the miniature, with a working method best suited to it. In one of his few revealing and, so far as it can be determined, accurate accounts of how he wrote, he described a story writer's discipline but most emphatically not a novelist's:

> I don't worry much about plots. I just start writing about something I think I know something about. I try to get him down cold. The other characters seem to walk into the story naturally enough. I seldom write a story of more than five thousand words—my mind seems to be geared to that length. I write three thousand words about nothing; that is a terrible struggle. Then I come to, and say to myself, "I must get a punch in this." I stop and figure out the punch, and then sail through to the finish.

There is obvious dissembling in that—the image of Ring wandering aimlessly through the first three fifths of a short story is something less than convincing—but the essential point is doubtless true. Ring's stories tend, especially the later ones, to fall into formulas, but few of them give much sense of being carefully plotted or organized, and many of them end with a loose-ends-tied-up sensation. It is just about impossible to imagine Ring sustaining such a performance over the length of a novel.

IN THE SUMMER OF 1924 Ring and Ellis decided to visit Scott and Zelda in France. Ring wrote Scott in San Raphael to discuss details of subletting their Great Neck house—Ring took on a number of financial responsibilities for the Fitzgeralds after they left—and closed with a warning: "She whom I married and I are going to leave for France on the *Paris*, September tenth; will stay in Paris a week or so, and then go to the south of France, where I have a first cousin, aged about 60, in Montpelier, and we may possibly drop in at San Raphael, but if we do, we're going to stop at a hotel, because we have agreed we don't like the service in private homes." He added a P.S.: "Could you go to Biarritz or Spain with us? I want to see a bullfight."

Ring and Ellis arrived in Paris on September 17 and checked in at the Crillon. From there they went on to Biarritz by themselves—Scott and Zelda couldn't or wouldn't go to the bullfights—and Ring prepared a disgusted dispatch for the readers of *Liberty* magazine, for which he was doing a diary of the trip:

> . . . in strode the matador, all dressed up like Escamillo and carrying a sword in one hand and in the other the little old red shawl that Maggie wore. The crowd cheered again, and the banderilleros supplied themselves with banderillas, which is a kind of barbed dart, which they stuck in the back of the bull's neck to take some of the fight out of him, and finally, when he couldn't even see no more, the bold matador shoved his sword through his bean and the first prelim was over.
>
> I kind of cast a sidelong glance at the madam and she was doing the same thing to me, and without no words passing between us we got up and staggered out of the grand stand, so I can't tell you the results of the last five bouts.

From Biarritz they went on to Toulouse and Marseilles, and met the Fitzgeralds as promised at San Raphael. The four went off for a tour of the Riviera, dropping in at Cannes, Nice and Monte Carlo: "We . . . went to the hotel to dress for dinner and while dressing I heard Mr. Fitzgerald in the next room mentioning prominent biblical characters. It developed that he had left the job of packing to the maid and instead of packing his new and fashionable dinner jacket she had put in a full dress coat that he had boughten seven years ago for the hops or proms or whatever you call the things they have at colleges. It took a lot of coaxing to get the guy to listen to reason, but finally we all had dinner and then went across the street to the Casino to buck the tiger." The "tiger" was the roulette wheel; Ring dropped $200 the first night, but came out ahead by winning $250 the second, "and we beat it, and I bet the boys that runs the Casino was glad to hear that we had left town." Ring's *Liberty* articles are the only significant record of the visit that remains, but on the basis of those it seems to have been a happy one for both the Lardners and their hosts.

They returned to Paris, where Ring, freed from the restraints of Prohibition, evidently was drinking everything he could get his hands on. How else is one to explain this delightful tidbit, as reported in the Chicago *Herald & Examiner* of September 29:

> PARIS, Sept. 28—A prank of Ring Lardner almost cost Jackie Coogan his curls. The humorist met the juvenile movie star here and took him to a barber shop. Ring got him into a chair and the clippers were about to be applied when the prodigy's mother dashed in and rescued him more or less in movie style.

In London the Lardners arranged a meeting with Sinclair Lewis, who introduced them to Rebecca West, and then "who should come to town but two ball clubs that called themself the Giants and White Sox, but they was several outsiders in the ranks of each." He obviously enjoyed visiting with the ballplayers, and he found John McGraw "in a reminiscent mood." Ring himself may have been put in a homesick mood by seeing the ballplayers, but his homesickness did not extend to Prohibition and on the trip home, aboard the *Mauretania*, he drank himself silly. Several years later he remarked in a letter that "I was in a dense fog all the way from England to New York," and upon his return to Great Neck he advised Scott and Zelda: "Instead of working on the ship coming home, as I intended, I did nothing but lap them up." He went on the wagon on Armistice Day.

This prolonged European binge came at a time when Ring's health was beginning to give warnings of serious difficulties ahead. The previous fall he had suffered the "pulmonary pain" referred to in his farewell poem to Zelda. In the spring of 1924 he had gone off to the Grove Park Inn in Asheville, North Carolina, for what was either a drying-out spell or a mountain-air cure for his sinuses; it may have been some of both, but in any event Burton Rascoe, when he interviewed Ring in June, 1924, made a point of noting that he "is looking very robust again after a period of ill-health and he told me he had put on twenty-four pounds by cutting out tobacco." Now, just back from Europe, he told the Fitzgeralds: "Speaking of noses . . . I was in the hospital having my antrum cut open. I'm nearly all right again now, I think, though if I get up suddenly or stoop over, a regular Niagara of blood pours from my shapely nostrils."

The note of humor did not disguise Ring's concern, but he did little to help himself. Despite frequent efforts to quit he kept right on smoking, and he persisted in his old pattern of alternating periods of total abstinence from alcohol and total immersion in it. It was a brutal combination for someone who was showing increasing signs of respiratory ailments, but Ring was by now totally hooked. His drinking habits were becoming New York legend, as during his bouts he often went into the city both for companionship and to keep the children from seeing him drunk. He would hop from speakeasy to speakeasy, joining old or new friends and then abandoning them, carrying on his sad one-man party into the morning and sometimes beyond because he had come under the grip of insomnia. He could be convivial or he could be profoundly distant. The most celebrated instance of the latter—it is a "Ring Lardner story" still told when times for such tales come around—took place at the Friars Club, where Ring showed up one evening in his dinner jacket and stayed, drinking steadily, for sixty hours—never showing any significant inebriation and never speaking. He recalled the occasion in a 1930 piece written for *The New Yorker*:

> I might state four uninteresting facts in connection with this Friars Club sitting: One was that five of the best music-writers in New York played their latest stuff and it all sounded good (at the time); another was that I and whoever happened to be with me at the moment ordered five meals and rejected them as fast as they were brought in; the third was that in this era they had kind of silly traffic laws in New York (not that that differentiates the era from any other era)—the code being that your car could face east for twelve hours and then must face west for twelve hours —and it was necessary to find a couple of bellmen capable of making the desired alterations at six A.M. and six P.M.; and the fourth was that though I was not even a neophyte when I entered the monastery, my long sojourn made me a regular member and I have been a Friar from those days and nights to this, probably because of some obscure squatters' law. Will say in conclusion of this interminable paragraph that the function occurred in June and I had no topcoat and the urge to get home and weed the bathtub

came at high noon, and it was kind of embarrassing passing all those policemen in dinner clothes instead of the conventional pajamas.

According to the story as it is usually told, Ring's "long sojourn" came to an end when someone walked up to him and asked: "Have you heard the one about . . .?" Ring, who detested jokes, stood up and left.

Strong drink consumed in theatrical surroundings brought a cutting edge to Ring's humor. At the Lambs Club one evening he was drinking with Paul Lannin, the composer, and spotted a particularly flamboyantly garbed and coiffed actor—presumably a Shakespearean, since actors of that specialty were notorious popinjays in the twenties. Ring studied the gentleman closely and finally asked him, "How do you look when I'm sober?"

Another much-told Lardner drinking story also took place at the Lambs Club. This, too, involved an actor, one who was steadily immobilizing conversation at the bar by delivering an interminable monologue from a play in which he was then featured. When at last he concluded, Ring applauded heartily and urged a second performance. The flattered actor gladly complied, and when he finished a second time, Ring urged him to go around one more time. "Do you really like it?" the actor asked him. Ring replied, "No, but I was a bad boy last night and this is my penance."

Ring had started drinking as a teenager because he liked liquor and the way it loosened him up; he kept on drinking as a young baseball correspondent because the atmosphere of life on the road was conducive to it; he did not shake the habit after marriage, all his good intentions notwithstanding, because it by then had become an integral part of his life. In Great Neck in the mid-twenties, however, he descended into true alcoholism. It is easier to state the fact than to attempt to explain it with any confidence. Certainly alcoholism is a disease, and Ring was thoroughly afflicted with it—but it is, by and large, a disease one catches for psychological reasons. If liquor brought out the light in Ring—if it made him gregarious and companionable and relaxed—it also gave comfort to the dark in him. Ring was not a bitter or hateful man, but he was indeed a troubled man. His sensibilities were too sharply exposed—as have been the sensibilities of so many other writers who became alcoholics—and liquor helped ease the pain of dealing with what he saw. Nor was he a man who despised himself; he was honest and unsparing with himself, and that was the trouble. As the twenties moved on and the thirties neared, as Ring's health declined and his work became more routine and repetitive, he must have looked at his life's work, and in doing so, he may well have reached a stern judgment. He was, it must be recalled, a man who despised profligacy and waste; he had no patience with ballplayers who did not play up to their abilities, and he used to warn Scott Fitzgerald that he frittered away his material—that he wasted good ideas on trivial stories, that he did not stretch his resources as far as they would go. Given that, this at least must be considered: what drove him to his final capitulation to alcohol may have been the realization that he had worked hard, exploited his talent to the fullest—and *this* was *all?*

BUT THAT CAPITULATION WAS, as he left the hospital near the end of 1924, still some time away. By early 1925 his prospects seemed to have revived encouragingly. He had finally managed to shake free of the comic strip, and he was writing short stories again. His first Scribner book had run up respectable if not spectacular sales— 16,325 copies by February—a second book was in the works, and rights for the uniform edition had been cleared.

Correspondence between Ring and Perkins was cordial and optimistic. Apparently Ring had talked with Scott about his next book while they visited in France, and Scott, as usual, had been full of advice. This was to be a collection of miscellaneous material, most of it humorous and/or nonsensical, though the final product turned out to be a curiously mixed bag. The inspired title, *What of It?*, was Grantland Rice's idea, and in his preface Ring explained its origins:

> It has been my favorite phrase since back in 1913 or '14, or whatever year it was that Hank O'Day managed the Cubs. A modern big league manager is supposed to observe the social amenities, but Mr. O'Day had been an umpire so long that the chip on his shoulder had become a permanent growth.
> The Cubs were making their first eastern trip of the season, and with them went their owner, Charles W. Murphy. Mr. Murphy and Mr. O'Day were standing by the desk in the Aldine Hotel in

Philadelphia one evening when the hotel's genial manager, whose name I have forgotten, joined them.

"Hello, there, Mr. ——!" said Mr. Murphy cordially. "Have you met my friend Mr. Henry O'Day?"

"Mr. ——," explained Mr. Murphy to Mr. O'Day, "is the manager of this hotel."

"What of it?" said Mr. O'Day.

The book was published in April, with a table of contents that listed "The Other Side," the articles Ring had written during his European journey the previous fall; three nonsense plays; "Bed-Time Stories," four fairy-tale satires; and "Obiter Dicta," a collection of odds and ends from the "Weekly Letter" and magazine pieces. (In the uniform edition, Scribner's added "The Young Immigrunts" and "Symptoms of Being 35" to it, and in so doing made it a far more satisfying book.) Unfortunately, *What of It?* provides pretty convincing proof of the validity of too many of the old saws about the perishability of journalism. The European pieces, save for the lovely line about Scott and Zelda as novelist and novelty, are, like the pieces he wrote from France in 1917, now only of biographical interest. The fairy-tale satires are pleasant but of peripheral interest, and much of the "Obiter Dicta" section is even more trivial; pieces such as "Lay Off the Thyroid" and "The Spulge Nine" undoubtedly were amusing when published in the "Weekly Letter" column, but whatever zip they had then has long since vanished. Were it not for the inclusion of the three plays—"I Gaspiri," "Taxidea Americana" and "Clemo Uti—'The Water Lilies'"—the book would be of interest now only to Lardner collectors.

What of It? was published at the same time as the first three volumes of the uniform set: *You Know Me Al, Gullible's Travels* and *The Big Town*; uniform editions of *What of It?* and *How to Write Short Stories* were added to these reprints, bringing the set to a total of five volumes. Perkins explained to Ring how it worked:

> I do not know how familiar you are with the way these sets are sold. It is almost altogether by canvassers, though sometimes in part by mail order advertising and it is largely in combination with a subscription to the magazine. In view of the expense of collections and of the general machinery of selling, the margin of profit is a very low one, and therefore the terms given to authors are low,

and may seem to you at first sight to be extremely so. We are ready to pay you the royalty of 20¢ per set; and this is to be paid according to the printing, and not according to the sale, and the first edition in this case would be 10,000 sets.

The only problem, he went on to say, was that Scribner's had paid $2,000 to Bobbs-Merrill and $500 to Doran for rights, "high prices in view of the fact that we virtually only purchased the rights in the plates, no stock to speak of that could be used." He proposed that Ring and Scribner's split this $2,500 cost, with the result that Ring stood to gain only $750 from the first edition of the uniform set. It must have puzzled Ring that his initial payment for a five-book set would be one-fourth what he was by then getting for a single short-story, but he accepted the conditions. Purely in terms of his literary reputation it is just as well that he did, for the joint publication of the uniform set and the trade edition of *What of It?* produced several major reviews. Gilbert Seldes, in *Vanity Fair*, observed: "The kind of reputation Ring Lardner enjoys today is exceptional in America. . . . He has become one of the most popular of our humorists, with a weekly syndicated article, a comic strip, and an inexhaustible market for 'pieces' of any description. But he is, at the same time, admired by the cognoscenti for whom, in his long life as a writer, he has apparently never cared a snap of his fingers." The *New York Times Book Review* devoted its April 19 front page to a Lardner retrospective by Henry Longan Stuart, who praised Ring's use of American idiom: "No humorist, not even Finley Peter Dunne, succeeds better in conveying the pith and pitch of the mind that is striving for expression." But the review that surely gave Ring the greatest pleasure—and perhaps a measure of bewilderment—was that by H. L. Mencken. Although he did not have kind words for *What of It?* ("The worst of it smacks of Bill Nye and the other journalistic humorists of the last generation. It is amusing, but it is hollow. One laughs at it, and then forgets it"), he went into rhapsodies over *You Know Me Al* and *How to Write Short Stories*. He piled compliment upon compliment: "They are simple and yet ingenious in construction; their characters are interesting and life-like; they are superb in detail. . . . they are filled with wholly fresh observation— that Lardner sought his materials, not in books, but in life itself"— and, at last spinning wildly out of control, "There is more of sheer reality in such a story as 'The Golden Honeymoon' than in the whole canon of Henry James, and there is also, I believe, more expert craftsmanship." In the end Mencken embraced Ring as an ally who in his fiction took the same view as Mencken in his journalism of "the Low Down American":

> Lardner sees into him, and clear through him. He is not senti-mentalized. One recognizes, at the start, mainly his racy and pre-posterous speech, but soon one recognizes, too, the shrunken and grotesque soul within him—his cheapness, his petty meanness and crookedness, his simian vanity, his cowardice, his shoddiness, his general low down orneriness.
>
> In brief, the portrait is penetrating and merciless. Please don't mistake it for a mere caricature, to be snickered at and then for-gotten. It is something far more than that. Study it hard enough, and you will begin to see the lineaments of Democratic Man.

Mencken, of course, was actually making a caricature out of the very Lardner character he said was *not* a caricature; if those on the left found Ring a mordant critic of American materialism, a "hater" of what they perceived as shoddy and false, Mencken and others to the right used Ring's ordinary people as proof posi-tive that "Democratic Man" was a foul creature incapable of self-government who needed the astute ministration of superior minds and consciences—to wit, their own. Ring may have been amused or irritated by it, more likely the former, but he did not let it affect his work; being beyond ideology himself, he was not about to bring it into his work.

By early 1925 that work was going remarkably well. In March, Ring made a great splash with the publication in *Liberty* (where Rex was fiction editor) of what remains his most famous story, "Haircut." Max Perkins, after reading it, wrote him that "I can't shake it out of my mind. . . . There's not a man alive who could have done better, that's certain," and readers around the country agreed. The story—is there a reader anywhere over the age of thirty who does not know?—consists of a monologue by a small-town barber who, as he tends to a customer, slowly unfolds the story of a local dolt, Jim Kendall, whose penchant for cruel practical jokes ultimately leads to the dissolution of a promising romance, and in an act of vengeance, his own death. The story's enormous impact at the time of its publication and its subsequent appearance in countless anthologies are explained by its conciseness, its tone and the skill with which it was constructed. Ring did not waste a word in telling it, and he told it exactly right: the barber's droning talk, his mindless laughter as he recalls Kendall's jokes, his unemotional reaction to a gruesome story—all create the mood of the tale while at the same time delivering a terse, harsh commentary on small-town mores. The last two paragraphs are small classics, containing as they do worlds of insight into both the barber and the small town's life-must-go-on indifference to what has happened:

> Personally I wouldn't never leave a person shoot a gun in the same boat I was in unless I was sure they knew somethin' about guns. Jim was a sucker to leave a new beginner have his gun, let alone a halfwit. It probably served Jim right, what he got. But still we miss him round here. He certainly was a card!
>
> Comb it wet or dry?

One of the more interesting reactions to the story came from Scott, who with a notable lack of generosity wrote to Max that "in strictest confidence I'll admit that I was disappointed in 'Haircut'—in fact I thought it was pretty lousy stuff—the crazy boy as the instrument of providence is many hundreds of years old." The immediate reason for his reaction was probably less literary than personal; Ring had recently read page proofs on *The Great Gatsby* and had reported a surprisingly subdued reaction. He sent Scott a brief list of errata that he admitted were trivial "but some of the critics pick on trivial errors for lack of anything else to pick on," but what galled Scott was that he called *Gatsby* "the best thing you've done" since *This Side of Paradise*—a novel that Scott knew perfectly well was a dated piece of apprentice work. Yet if there was an element of revenge in Scott's comment on "Haircut," there was also an element of truth. The use of the village idiot to take revenge on Jim Kendall is indeed a cliché, and the story as a whole is just a little bit too pat; it has been anthologized because of its quality and craftsmanship but also because, as is often the case with material that is anthologized, it is smooth enough to suit almost any taste. It may have seemed to readers of a popular magazine to have been a brutal portrait of small-town hypocrisy and callousness, but those readers probably were unfamiliar with Sherwood Anderson's *Winesburg, Ohio,* published six years earlier and far superior.

Any ill feelings Scott may have felt toward Ring vanished quickly, and, that summer he wrote to ask if he could dedicate a forthcoming volume of stories to Ring and Ellis; it was *All the Sad Young Men,* published in the spring of 1926. Ring accepted the honor with pleasure, and for his part lamented the poor sales *Gatsby* was having: "It certainly deserves a big sale. . . . Max Perkins said he thought the size of the book was against it (in the eyes of the buyers). That is a great commentary on American life and letters." He closed the letter on a thoughtful note: "We do miss you and Zelda a great deal. Write again and tell her to write, too. And I might add that I have a little money to lend at the proverbial six per cent, if worst comes to worst."

For Ring to offer financial help was characteristic; one reason he saved so little of the money he earned during the twenties was that he gave so much of it away or made loans that were never repaid. The charity he had been extending to the family in Niles continued long past his father's death in 1914 and his mother's in 1918; he sent regular subsidies to an unknown number of family members and more distant relatives, and he was a soft touch if an old friend from baseball days found himself in a pinch. It was indicative of Ring's continuing closeness to his family that when the uniform edition was published he sent Perkins a list of the names and addresses of his five brothers and sisters and asked that each be sent a full set.

The summer of 1925 was especially productive. In a story called "Zone of Quiet" Ring made use of a conversation he recalled from his hospital stay the previous winter. As he described it in a letter to the Fitzgeralds, "I took *Vanity Fair* (Thackeray's, not Crowningshield's) to the hospital with me and one day the nurse asked me what I was reading and I told her and she said, 'I haven't read it yet. I've been busy making Christmas presents.'" In the story a man is in the hospital recovering from surgery; he is supposed to be getting rest and quiet, but his ears are filled with the ceaseless chatter of the nurse, Miss Lyons:

"... I hate women! I mean sick ones. They treat a nurse like a dog, especially a pretty nurse. What's that you're reading?"

"Vanity Fair," replied the man in bed.

"Vanity Fair. I thought that was a magazine."

"Well, there's a magazine and a book. This is the book."

"Is it about a girl?"

"Yes."

"I haven't read it yet. I've been busy making this thing for my sister's birthday. She'll be twenty-nine. It's a bridge table cover. When you get that old, about all there is left is bridge or cross-word puzzles. . . ."

The nurse prattles on about her "G.F." (girl friend) and "B.F." (boyfriend) until, over the days, she has spun an incredibly tangled web in which she has stolen her G.F.'s B.F., but her G.F. gets her B.F. back and she has to find a new B.F. She is an empty-headed, self-satisfied thing who actually has nothing to be satisfied about but is too ignorant to sense her own limitations; she is also insensitive, selfish and opportunistic. She is, in sum, the "Lardner woman" as she was emerging more and more clearly in his fiction.

Because Ring wrote some utterly devastating portraits of women there has been a general misunderstanding of his attitude toward the opposite sex. He has been characterized as a misogynist, and the evidence of stories such as this and "The Love Nest" would seem to support the contention. In fact, however, he tended to divide women into two separate and absolutely hostile camps. One was composed of the harpies, gold diggers and two-timers typified by the women he had seen hanging around ballplayers; these were women who had somehow betrayed their sex because they were just as coarse as the men in their lives, and frequently more clever. In the other camp were those women who remained faithful to his pre–Jazz Age sense of femininity but who also had wit, humor, ebullience and style. This second group was large enough to embrace women as seemingly diverse as Zelda Fitzgerald, Kate Rice, Dorothy Parker, his sister Anne, and Ellis. He was willing to wink at peculiarities of behavior in some women he liked—Neysa McMein, a well-known artist of the time, was widely rumored to have had many prominent lovers—so long as they brought style, wit and class to the friendship. As a rule he seemed to prefer women of his own social level, but he hated the crassness of new money as it was often manifested in the wives of Great Neck. He once reported to the Fitzgeralds after a visit from the

Bucks: "Gene and Helen were over the other night and in the midst of one of Gene's stories, Helen said, 'Stop picking your nose, sweetheart.' That's all the dirt I know."

The Bucks, in fact, provided the raw material for another much-anthologized Lardner story from the summer of 1925, "The Love Nest." In it a reporter named Bartlett is assigned to interview "the great man," Lou Gregg, president of Modern Pictures, Inc. Gregg insists that he visit "the wife and family" in Ardsley-on-Hudson: "We've got plenty of room and extra pajamas, if you don't mind them silk." His wife is a former actress who, he says, has adapted beautifully to domestic life: "Celia's a great home girl. You'd never know she was the same girl now as the girl I married seven years ago. I mean she's different. I mean she's not the same. I mean her marriage and being a mother has developed her." The two men drive out to "a white house that might have been mistaken for the Yale Bowl," and Bartlett is taken into "a living-room that was five laps to the mile and suggestive of an Atlantic City auction sale." Bartlett is left alone with Celia, who begins to sneak sips of bourbon while feeding him the company line: ". . . Lou is so proud of our home! . . . It *is* wonderful! I call it our love nest. Quite a big nest, don't you think? . . . I always say a place is whatever one makes of it. A woman can be happy in a tent if they love each other. And miserable in a royal palace without love." Eventually the whiskey does its work and she explodes: "I could be a Swanson and get myself a marquis; maybe a prince! And look what I did get! A self-satisfied, self-centered ——! I thought he'd *make* me! . . . Well, he's made me all right; he's made me a chronic mother and it's a wonder I've got any looks left." What she does not know is that they richly deserve each other, with matching His and Hers tiny brains and elephantine egos. And Ring, after the story had appeared, reported to the Fitzgeralds with quiet amusement: "Gene didn't make any comment on 'The Love Nest,' but evidently had no suspicion. Anyway, we are still pals."

Both "Zone of Quiet" and "The Love Nest" were important departures for Ring because they marked a turn away from first-person narration to third-person. It does not seem coincidental that this change occurred at the same time that Ring was coming under favorable, yet tentative, scrutiny from respected reviewers and critics. Ring apparently took quite seriously the challenges issued by Wilson and others to do work somehow more "serious" and "big," but he seems to have decided that the way to do that was to enter his stories more directly as omniscient author. The trouble was that he only occasionally was able to avoid the problems he had encountered when he wrote "Champion"—basic among them a tendency to be too obvious in theme and exposition—even though the period from 1925 to 1930 was his most prolific as a writer of fiction. With the exception of "I Can't Breathe" and "Insomnia," all his most durable work was done by the time he had finished "Haircut"; it is scarcely mere happenstance that both of those stories are told in the first person.

This is not to say that the work of the prolific period was bad, rather that it was basically superior mass-circulation magazine fiction. The early and middle stories are notable for their freshness of style, outlook, subject matter and characters; in them Ring was bringing a whole new world into American fiction, the world of the ball park and the suburbs and the theater and the Pullman. The later stories have a surface ingenuity, but there is nothing in them to match the depth, complexity and sympathy of "Some Like Them Cold" or "The Golden Honeymoon" or the busher stories.

The early stories had a toughness of mind that, in these new ones, occasionally turned into something not much better than trickiness. One of the better-known, for example, is "A Day with Conrad Green," which certainly should have been written with vigor and bite. Its subject was Flo Ziegfeld, with whom Ring had been having continuing hassles in his effort to make a success on Broadway. Ring clearly felt the piece was tough; he wrote the Fitzgeralds: "I've got a story coming out in *Liberty* . . . of which Flo is the hero. When, and if, he reads it, he won't offer me any more contracts, even lousy ones"—and so did many readers at the time. Yet its portrait of the show-biz potentate as a blustering skinflint is etched not in acid but in sour milk; all the devices it uses to show him up as a cad—wiggling out of his faithful secretary's funeral, giving his wife a present intended for his mistress, buttering up a high-society hostess—are as embarrassingly obvious and melodramatic as the crippled kid brother whom Midge Kelly decks in "Champion." Ring was plainly uncomfortable manipulating plot and character with such heavy-handed puppetry, but he persisted in doing it probably because it seemed to him somehow more respectable and advanced than the natural, unaffected fiction he wrote at first.

Nine stories from this period were collected under the title *The Love Nest* and published by Scribner's in March, 1926; besides the title story, they were "Haircut," "Zone of Quiet," "Women," "A Day with Conrad Green," "Reunion," "Rhythm," "Mr. and Mrs. Fix-It" and "Who Dealt?" Of the ones not already discussed, the best is the last, and it is told in the first person. It is not so much a narration as one long gurgle by a brand-new bride who, playing bridge with her husband, Tom, and his friends Arthur and Helen (a friendly bow to the Jackses: Ring loved to drop the names of his friends into his stories), babbles her way into the kind of self-revelation that is Ring's fictional art at its finest. Try though she may, she just can't stop talking:

> I'll stop talking now and try and keep my mind on the game. You needn't look that way, Tommie. I *can* stop talking if I try. It's kind of hard to concentrate though, when you're, well, excited. It's not only meeting you people but I always get excited traveling. I was just terrible on our honeymoon, but then I guess a honeymoon's enough to make anybody nervous. I'll never forget when we went into the hotel in Chicago— All right, Tommie, I won't. But I can tell about meeting the Bakers.

The more she chatters the deeper she digs the hole into which she is bound to fall. One mindless outburst leads to another until she has managed to get Tom to think seriously about jumping off the wagon, where he has been perched for her benefit. As she dumbly presses on, she discloses, without understanding it herself, that Tom had once been in love with Helen and had been jilted by her. The story comes to a conclusion that may be predictable but is delicious all the same:

> I wish I could remember that poem of his I found. I memorized it once, but—wait! I believe I can still say it! Hush, Tommie! What hurt will it do anybody? Let me see; it goes:
>
> > *"I thought the sweetness of her song*
> > *Would ever, ever more belong*
> > *To me; I thought (O thought divine!)*
> > *My bird was really mine!*

"*But promises are made, it seems,*
Just to be broken. All my dreams
Fade out and leave me crushed, alone,
My bird, alas, has flown!"

Isn't that pretty. He wrote it four years ago. Why, Helen, you revoked! And, Tom, do you know that's Scotch you're drinking? You said—*Why, Tom!*

Once again Perkins asked Ring to write an introduction, and this time he outdid himself in self-mockery. (Whether Perkins ever hoped Ring would ever write a serious introduction is not clear in his letters, but he always responded gamely when Ring came through with his latest outrage.) The piece is cast in the form of a memorial tribute to Ring by one Sarah E. Spooldripper, identified as follows: "Miss Spooldripper lived with the Lardners for years and took care of their wolf. She knew all there was to know about Lardner, and her mind was virtually blank. It was part of her charm." Notwithstanding some dated references to Ring's friends and some celebrities of the day, it remains an uncommonly funny piece, Ring at his most charmingly nonsensical. After a preposterous introductory tour through several of the stories, it concludes as follows:

Those of the tales in this book which which have not already been mentioned were dashed off after the Master had contracted the cold that resulted in the fatal attack of conchoid, a disease which is superinduced by a rush of seashells to the auricle or outer ear. Present during the last hours were only myself and the wolf, [his wife] having chosen this time to get a shampoo and wave in preparation for the series of dinner dances that were bound to follow.

"Edna," whispered the Master as he lay there idly watching the doctor change a tire, "to-morrow I will be all right again and you and I will get in a taxi and be ourselves."

He called me Edna only when he was up to some devilment. It was his way.

The Master is gone* and the next question is who will succeed him? Perhaps some writer still unborn. Perhaps one who will never be born. That is what I hope.

* The joke is on Miss Spooldripper, for she is gone too. Two months ago she was found dead in the garage, her body covered with wolf bites left there by her former ward, who has probably forgotten where he left them.

Some people didn't quite know what to make of the introduction: the *New York Times Book Review* took it mock seriously, but some readers mistook its mock seriousness for genuine seriousness. "Reviews of *The Love Nest* have been perfectly elegant," Ring told the Fitzgeralds. "I don't know whether you've seen the book, but I had an introduction to it written as if I were dead. The Sunday *Times* ran a long review and played up the introduction strong, saying it was too bad I had died so young, etc., and the result was that Ellis was kept busy on the telephone all that Sunday assuring friends and reporters that I was alive and well. It just happened that I was at home and cold sober; if I had been out, she might have worried a little. Or maybe not."

Scott, though he apparently kept his opinion between himself and Perkins, did not much like the book. He doubted that it would "add to his reputation" and went on: "Several stories were fine, none were cheap but—God, I wish he'd write a more or less personal novel. Couldn't you persuade him? The real history of an American manager, say Ziegfeld or a theatrical girl. Think how far Anita Loos got with a mere imitation of him." Scott was incredibly naïve to think that Ring would ever be capable of bringing a "personal novel" out from under all the reticence within him, and he was a trifle presumptuous (as well as, in a way, condescending) in suggesting "Ziegfeld or a theatrical girl" as possible subjects, but the words "Several stories were fine, none were cheap but . . ." are an apt, and by no means unsympathetic, estimate of the contents of *The Love Nest*.

At the time of publication, however, his was a minority view. Burton Rascoe, whom Ring had known since both were on the *Tribune* in the 1910's (Rascoe as "literary editor"), weighed in with the theme of misanthropy: "A passionate hatred has animated nearly all of Lardner's stories; but I think this has never before been so evident as in his latest collection of short stories. . . . They are really superb tales; but in each he excoriates some shortcoming in human character. . . . These are all stories of modern life by one of the indubitable American masters of the short story form." Mencken simply rewrote himself: "I can recall no character in the Lardner gallery, early or late, male or female, old or young, who is not loathsome. . . . Lardner does not see situations; he sees people. And what people! They are all as revolting as so many Methodist evangelists, and they are all as thoroughly American. . . . He is trying to do something that no other current fictioneer has tried to do. Without wasting any wind upon statements of highfalutin aesthetic or ethical purpose, he is trying to get the low-down Americano between covers."

The publication of The Love Nest came as the literary if not popular climax to the period of Ring's greatest fame. The year and a half since he and Ellis returned from Europe had been productive for him in a number of areas outside the writing of fiction. He had done some fine columns, worked hard (if unsuccessfully) on a number of theatrical projects, had his first taste of what it was like to write for the movies, and made huge amounts of money —with even more in prospect as the direct result of his popularity.

The best of Ring's "Weekly Letter" pieces between the spring of 1924 and the summer of 1926 were about his family and his travels. "The home news" could always fill a column if nothing else sufficed, and Ring knew not to work the subject to death. In the summer of 1925, for example, he gave a gloomy report on "the curse or blight" that seemed to be descending on birthday shopping around the Lardner household: ". . . a yr. ago last xmas we invested in a radio as the kiddies had been squawking for one ever since they was put on the market and when we got it all set up and connected why we couldn't even hear static let alone Schenectady. The parrot we brought didn't say boo for a entire mo. Every bicycle we have ordered has been shy a couple pedals or wheels or something and the books has all had whole pages torn out of them and the games has been short 3 or 4 cards or men." That humorous tone characterized Ring's pieces of family news, but on rare occasions some genuine sentiment would slip through, as happened when Ring announced an unhappy domestic development:

> Now friends the paragraph I am now writing is supposed to ring tears from the reader, a specially those amongst you who is the male offspring. It ain't no secret by this time that I am the father of 4 boys and I have made it a rule that as soon as each of them got to be 7 yrs. old I would cease from kissing him good-night as boys of such advanced age don't relish being kissed by parents of their own sex. Well 3 of them has been over the age limit for some time and I only had one left on who to vent my osculatory affection namely David who was 6 yrs. old in May. Lately I noticed that he did not return my caress with any warmth and one night he held out his hand to shake like the other boys and then run upstairs and told his

brothers gloatingly that he had escaped daddy's good-night kiss. Naturally this remark was repeated to me and naturally it meant the end as far as I am conserned being a man of great pride and I suppose in time the wound will heal but mean while hardly a evening passes when I don't kind of wish down in my heart that one of them had been a daughter.

Ring tried to phrase his feelings as casually and unemotionally as he could in that paragraph, but the truth wiggled out anyway: He was hurt at losing one of the few means by which he could express his love for the boys physically. He was also going through what any parent of either sex experiences—the tangled emotional ordeal of watching one's children grow up.

He was, on the other hand, on the road enough to be spared that pain on a daily basis for long stretches at a time. In most cases his trips were made with Ellis and were principally for their amusement, but there were also Southern excursions made primarily for his health, such as the April, 1924, stay in Asheville. No matter how he was feeling, though, Ring had a marvelous ability to keep his writing fresh and funny, so that his report from the Grove Park Inn focused not on his health, but on an establishment that "shyly admits that it is the finest and most unique resort hotel in the world." He took particular delight in the iron "grab bars" bolted into the wall behind his bathtub, and explained why they were there: "One of the boys told me that the reason for this precaution was that one time a man had drove here from Seattle in a open Ford without never leaving his seat and on arriving in Asheville kind of felt he needed a bath so he climbed in and managed at first to keep his feet though his tub at home was lined with porcupine quills, but when he was pretty near through and had pulled the stopper, he slipped and fell and beaned himself on the porcelain and was washed out through the drain pipe without recovering consciousness." (It is, incidentally, a sad footnote to Ring's friendship with Scott Fitzgerald that a decade later, with Zelda by now institutionalized and the family financial situation desperate, Scott contracted a mild case of tuberculosis and came to the Grove Park Inn to recuperate.)

Spring a year later found the Lardners in the Deep South and the Caribbean. In April, 1925, they were in Hialeah, Florida, for the grand opening of that small boom city's beautiful new race track, and Ring used the occasion to tell his readers about the Florida gold rush:

> Surrounding the race track on all sides is outdoor real estate offices, refreshment stands, restaurants, cabarets and etc. and people that was out in Goldfield, Nevada, and them places during the gold rush say that Hialeah and the other suburbs of Miami reminds them of same. Two or three of the real estate boys tried to interest me in buying a lot and building a home in the neighborhood and they all pointed out how handy it would be living within walking distance from a big track, but I told them that where I live on Long Island is a short riding distance from 3 different race tracks and I have already found them so handy that I have wired the county poor farm to reserve me a permanent room without bath.

Precisely how tempted Ring was to invest in Florida real estate is not clear—he may well have found the idea appealing, considering that he and Ellis visited the state annually—but he was lucky that he did not; a year and a half later the "Gold Coast" was hit by a devastating hurricane and the boom was arrested for a quarter century. Ellis, in any event, did not like the turbulent social life of Miami: "It was too gay for me. I like Belleair better." Presumably she did like the quiet of Nassau, and doubtless she shared Ring's sentiments when he wrote: "After a person has went through a siege of the giddy whirl of a place like Miami Beach, Florida, it is genally always necessary to take a rest cure and on this occasion I and the Mrs. and party set sail on the board of a boat bound for Nassau which is the capital of the Bahama Islands and somebody had told us that when you got there they wasn't nothing to do only eat and sleep which has always been 2 of the great passions of my life." They customarily stayed in the New Colonial Hotel, and the other members of their party were the Rices.

Their regular party of four became five in the spring of 1926, when Floncy Rice joined them for a tour that went from Belleair to the West Coast, with the most significant stop en route being New Orleans. There, in February, they met Sherwood Anderson and were introduced by him to the local beau monde he occasionally frequented. The first evening the Lardners and Andersons and Rices went to a small upstairs restaurant in the French Quarter, where the chef was astonished at the news that he was serving the famous Ring Lardner; he gave them the most solicitous attention imaginable, constantly bringing in new bottles of wine and inquiring after the pleasure of his celebrated guest. Ring was in an expansive mood, and Anderson remembered the evening later with deep affection: "We loved him. I cannot help but think it was a rare, rich evening in his life. He laughed. He talked. He drank the wine. He told stories. If it was a good evening for him, it was something more than that for the rest of us." A couple of years later Anderson returned to the restaurant, and the fat little French chef brought a bottle of wine to his table: "He had come in from the kitchen and had on his white apron. He stood beside my table and poured wine for us both. 'To that man you brought here that time . . . to Ring,' he said, lifting his glass."

Anderson also joined Ring at a party "in a swell house in a swell part of town." The liquor was flowing, and so were Ring's good spirits. He commandeered a piano and an audience and began to sing the old-fashioned, innocent songs he loved the best: "Two Little Girls in Blue," "Just Tell Them That You Saw Me and That I Was Looking Well," "There'll Be a Hot Time in the Old Town Tonight." Finally he tired of the rich, empty people in the room and urged Anderson to swipe some of the contents of the butler's pantry preparatory to fleeing for less congested territory: "Get three or four bottles of good stuff, and get out." Their escape was complicated, however, when Ring was delivered to Anderson by the host. The scene, as recalled by Anderson, was memorable:

> His host had got out of his car. It was a Rolls-Royce. He was doing his own driving. "Your friend, your fellow-author—where is he?" he said to Ring, looking about. He seemed extraordinarily small and pale, standing there before Ring. It was like a big dog and a little dog, and the little dog was wagging his tail. He didn't care a hang about the liquor we had got. I guess he knew we were going somewhere to sit and drink and talk quietly, and I think he wanted to come along but he was too polite to ask and I think, also, that Ring was for a moment tempted to ask him to come.
>
> He was looking down at the man. I could see it all. There was an overhead light shining on them. I saw something happen to Ring. He had been wearing his mask all evening, but for a moment it dropped off. He started to ask the man to come along but was afraid

I wouldn't like it, so he said nothing but stood there, looking down at the man, his lips trembling. It was quite a different Ring Lardner from the one I had seen in the room with all those people.

This one was a shy man and so was the little banker. The two men just stood like that, looking hard at each other, and then, as by a common impulse, they both began to laugh. They laughed like two young boys, or for that matter like two girls, and then the banker ran quickly and got into his car and drove away, but as he did so he took a shot back at Ring. "I hope your friend got good stuff. I hope he got enough," he said, but Ring wasn't looking. He was a man whose habit it was to wear a mask and it had slipped off, and at the moment I was like a man standing in the dressing-room of a theater and watching an actor at work on his makeup. I saw him put the mask back on his face, and he wore it for the rest of the evening.

It would be interesting to know whether during the course of this visit Anderson introduced Ring to his young protégé, William Faulkner, who was then living in the French Quarter. But there is no record of a meeting, which, had it occurred, might have broken all records for reticence.

The Lardner-Rice caravan continued on to California, where they got the full treatment in Hollywood. They went to the Famous Players studio and watched the filming of scenes from *The Rainmaker, Beau Geste, Naughty Cinderella* and *Padlocked*. Ring was especially impressed "that everybody that is getting more than a beginner's salary, say $6,000.00 per wk., has their own chair to set in with their name painted on it." He decided as a result that "my first act when I get back home will be to have my name in full on the chair I generally always set in and if I catch one of the kiddies setting in that chair I will have one of the hired help give him a kind of a hint that he is de trop." From Famous Players they went to Charlie Chaplin's studio, where they sat "in nameless chairs" and watched Chaplin do several scenes for *The Circus,* which Ring predicted would be a "wow." They dined at the Chaplins' house later, and Chaplin entertained them by playing his pipe organ. On their last day in town they were introduced to Rudolph Valentino, Vilma Banky, Chaplin's elder brother Sydney, and Pola Negri. Ring was especially amused to meet the Polish star because he loved her name, and she gave him a royal reception. She was reading a magazine when he was introduced: "Miss Negri, this is Mr. Lardner, the writer." Without looking up she replied, "Oh."

Ring's entrée to Famous Players was gained because late in 1925 he had written the scenario for a film called *The New Klondike*. It starred his Great Neck drinking buddy Tom Meighan and was filmed in Florida in early 1926. Ring was paid $7,500 for spending four days dreaming up a plot about baseball players and Florida real-estate swindlers, and for writing the titles; he told the Fitzgeralds he had asked for such a high fee because "Tom gets that amount per week, work or no work, and I thought perhaps I could do it in a week and be as well paid as he is." He did not find the work, or the end result, enjoyable: "The picture, I believe, will be the worst ever seen on land or sea, and the titles are excruciatingly terrible."

The New Klondike was as close as Ring ever came to a serious involvement with the movies—and it obviously was far from serious. There does exist in his correspondence a mysterious letter to a "Mr. Griffen," written while Ring was living in Riverside, agreeing to write "the scenarios you desire (twelve in all, all delivered one per month) at $250 apiece and an advance of $250," but no clue has been found to solve the mystery. He is known to have written a couple of scenarios—one of them, a one-reeler called *The Fight*, was produced in 1930—and to have made a cameo appearance in something called *Glorifying the American Girl*, a Ziegfeld production of 1929, but other than that, the Lardner material that has been filmed was done by others: *June Moon* was filmed in 1931 and again in 1937 (as *Blonde Trouble*); Joe E. Brown did several baseball movies based on Ring's stories; *The Big Town* was adapted in 1948 by Stanley Kramer as *So This Is New York*; and in the best-known and most successful Lardner film, Kramer did *Champion* in 1949, with Kirk Douglas as Midge Kelly.

Ring just was not very interested in the movies. Not merely was he a conservative with an inherent distrust for what was then still a novelty, but he simply continued to regard the theater as the proper place for comedy and drama to be performed. Unfortunately, he was not having much luck in the mid-twenties at following up on the small success he had enjoyed in the *Follies of 1922*. But his lack of success was not for want of trying. He may well have put more energy into stillborn theatrical ventures during this period than into any other creative endeavor. Despite his clearly mixed feelings about Gene Buck, Ring entered into a long and singularly fruitless collaboration with him on a play called *Going South,* a loose adaptation of *Gullible's Travels.* Off and on they tinkered with the project for a couple of years, but Ziegfeld kept giving them the runaround. Finally he suggested that it be rewritten as a musical, but they couldn't agree on terms. Then, in August, 1925, he suddenly "had to have it" for September production. After the collaborators complained, he extended the deadline to October and gave them each $500, with another $500 to come when the show was completed. Ring described the climax of the fiasco to the Fitzgeralds:

> . . . I got busy and rewrote the play into a musical comedy book; also wrote some lyrics which I thought were not bad. On the first day of October, Ziegfeld had not yet signed a composer and as you know, it is impossible to turn in a complete book and lyrics these days unless you have a composer with whom to work on the numbers. On the second of October, Ziegfeld engaged Vincent Youmans to write the music. I showed him my lyrics and he didn't seem to care much for them. Neither did Gene. In fact, Gene wanted to write all the lyrics himself, though he didn't say so. Finally I said, "Well, I'm going to write the lyrics of three or four comedy songs and I want them to get a trial anyway." Then I went to the world's series and when I came back, not one tap of work had been done and Gene hadn't even turned over the book to Ziegfeld. Moreover, I think, though I'm not sure, that Youmans told Ziegfeld he had seen the book and didn't like it. Anyway, both Gene and I got telegrams saying we had broken the contract and I was sick and tired of the whole proceeding that I was glad of it, but Gene said he was going to give Ziegfeld a terrible bawling out. He saw him and Ziegfeld soft-soaped him and said that what he wanted to do was get rid of Youmans and when he did, he would produce the show, probably about the first of the year. So Gene thinks that is what is going to happen, but between you and me, dear Scott and darling Zelda, Ziegfeld is not going to produce the show at any time, whether he wants to or whether he doesn't. And I have written him a letter, to the effect that my stuff was probably known to more people than was that of any of the popular song writers of the day with the possible exception of Irving Berlin and that said stuff never would have got before the public if magazine and newspaper editors had jazz composers engaged to pass on manuscripts. I guess that will make him think, eh, girls?

Even before his showdown with Ziegfeld, Ring had gotten his public revenge: "A Day with Conrad Green" was published on October 3, right in the middle of the battle. Yet he was not, all his bold and angry words to the contrary, through with Ziegfeld; for Ziegfeld held what he most wanted, a passport to Broadway, and Ring would come back for more in hopes of getting it.

There were other theatrical projects in the middle and late twenties which had the same results. Inspired by heaven knows what flight of fancy, Ring undertook in 1925 an "Americanization" of Jacques Offenbach's operetta *Orpheus in the Underworld*; it was to be produced by the Actors' Theater, but it never came off. He tried a "modernization" of "Cinderella," to no avail, and he and Paul Lannin met a similar fate when they attempted to collaborate on a musical with the title *All at Sea*. But some of the lyrics Ring wrote show that he had not gone untouched by the witty and sophisticated work of Cole Porter and Lorenz Hart:

> *I feel just like poor Hamo-let*
> *Who said, "To be or not to?"*
> *To kill oneself is wrong, and yet*
> *I b'lieve I've almost got to.*
> *The girl I love is so unkind!*
> *When I am gone, she'll rue it.*
> *So I will die if I can find*
> *A pleasant way to do it.*
>
> *But cyanide, it gripes inside;*
> *Bichloride blights the liver;*
> *And I am told one catches cold*
> *When one jumps in the river.*
> *To cut my throat would stain my coat*
> *And make my valet furious.*
> *Death beckons me, but it must be*
> *A death that ain't injurious.*
>
> *A shot would make my eardrums ache*
> *And wake my niece, who's teething;*
> *A rope would wreck my classic neck*
> *And interfere with breathing;*
> *I can't take gas because, alas,*
> *The odor's unendurable.*
> *O Lord above, please tell me of*
> *A death that ain't incurable.*

Certainly, as those lines demonstrate, Ring had a flair for musical comedy, and in some of the dialogue he wrote for these various ventures there are snappy exchanges that probably would play well on the stage. By mid-1926, however, all he had to show for all this work was two forgettable skits in a 1922 vaudeville routine and a growing pile of rejected manuscripts. He had earned a negligible amount of money from the theater and an equal amount of critical praise. He was profoundly offended to have his work judged by "jazz composers" and impresarios of coarse tastes, yet it seems rarely to have occurred to him to stop subjecting himself to their offhand rejections and to concentrate on the newspaper and magazine work that was so eagerly accepted. For a man who usually saw the world clearly, he had in this regard a curious and inexplicable distortion of values. Many would not argue with whatever feeling he may have had that his magazine and newspaper work was inherently ephemeral; it is an old problem that nags at journalists who want to believe, but ultimately cannot, that their work has some manner of creative if not literary value. But why he thought he was devoting his energies to something more attractive in the Broadway stage is a puzzle. In his best journalism and fiction there glows a noble incorruptibility, a refusal to be anything except his own self; the work he did for the theater leaves no doubt that he was willing to do whatever was required, no matter how demeaning it was to his original conception of the material, in order to be successful, and his only notable theatrical accomplishment, *June Moon*, was achieved at the price of the thematic evisceration of his best short story.

It goes back, almost certainly, to the taste he acquired for fun as a child. It is the most puzzling contradiction of his life: that this man whose vision could be so acute and so dark should have poured so much of his energy into the most frivolous sort of theatrical endeavors. It does not seem to have been a question of his hoping that the fun on stage would somehow relieve his troubled awareness of what he saw elsewhere in life; he seems genuinely to have thought that success on Broadway was important, and he got more happiness out of the fleeting popularity of *June Moon* than he did out of any of his books or individual pieces.

Surely, if nowhere else, he could have read the message in his bank books and in the mail he was receiving from editors who by

1926 were lined up to receive his work. He was getting nothing to feed his family on from the theater, but the Lardners ate well indeed thanks to his magazine work and the column. His financial records are frustratingly incomplete, but a notebook he kept for a while shows income from various free-lance sources of $28,389.05 in 1926 and $48,305.74 in 1927, his best year. It was his best principally because of *Cosmopolitan*. In 1924 Ray Long of that magazine had offered him "for your next six short stories, $3,000 each, or, for your next twelve short stories, $3,500 each." Ring did not take him up on the offer at first because Rex was still fiction editor at *Liberty*, but in the fall of 1925, as he wrote the Fitzgeralds, his brother's fate there was uncertain: ". . . John Wheeler has been removed. . . . Harvey Deuel, a Chicago newspaper man, will succeed Jack as editor of *Liberty*. I guess my brother Rex is all right for a while, but if they do anything to him, I'm going to jump to *Cosmopolitan*." Rex's removal occurred soon after that letter was written, for Ring's last *Liberty* piece appeared in the issue of October 31, 1925; after that, both Rex and his stories were at what was now known as *Hearst's International-Cosmopolitan*. The magazine got much of Ring's most famous work, including "The Love Nest" and "I Can't Breathe," and the editors were grateful. By March, 1927, Ring was receiving a fee from *Cosmopolitan* of $4,500 per story, a rate that is inordinately high even by the standards of a half-century later. No writer of the time is known to have been paid more.

The increase in his fee at *Cosmopolitan* must have been a principal reason why Ring began, in 1926, to give serious thought to unburdening himself of the "Weekly Letter." He was at the absolute peak of his popularity, but of course he had no way of knowing that after 1927 he would be moving down rather than up; he seemed in 1926 to have every expectation of making a comfortable living without having to tie himself to any regular assignment. Journalism, even as practiced at the leisurely pace of one 1,000-word piece a week, was beginning to pall, and there were limits to his affection for the breezy, cocky Wheeler. Still, he was reluctant to break the association, and in the spring of 1926 he let himself be talked into writing a serialized "autobiography" in the column. He probably wrote it well in advance, but it began in the column on July 11, 1926, and ended twenty-seven installments later, on January 9, 1927. It was approximately as serious as his prefaces to his books and, in fact, when the pieces were collected and published in March, 1927, as *The Story of a Wonder Man*, Ring enlisted Sarah E. Spooldripper to provide a foreword:

> The publication of this autobiography is entirely without the late Master's sanction. He wrote it as a pastime and burnt up each chapter as soon as it was written; the salvaging was accomplished by ghouls who haunted the Lardners' ash bbl. during my whole tenure of office as night nurse to their dromedary.
> Some of the copy was so badly charred as to be illegible. The ghouls took the liberty of filling in these hiatuses with "stuff" of their own, which can be readily distinguished from the Master's as it is not nearly as good. Readers and critics are therefore asked to bear in mind that those portions of the book which they find entertaining are the work of the Master himself; those which bore them or sound forced are interpolations by milksops. . . .

It seems incredible, but some readers actually took the "autobiography" seriously; as recently as 1976, in fact, a reader of alleged critical eminence more or less fell for it. Yet there is scarcely a line of truth in it. It is nonsense throughout, some of it inspired nonsense and some of it merely silly, but all of it filled with jokes at the author's own expense. Consider the following:

> Alone in Seattle at the age of six, broke, and indebted to the hotel in the amount of $26.50 for board and room. How many kids would have faced a stiuation like this with equanimity! But I never lost confidence that I would find a way out. I forget just now what I did do; suffice it to say that inside of seven years I was in San Francisco playing a cornet, evenings, at Tait's on the beach, and in the daytime working in the park as a squirrel-tender. In those days there were no benches in the parks and a squirrel-tender's job was to keep the squirrels out of the trees so the people would have some place to sit. Inasmuch as there were 186 squirrels in this particular park and I had only one assistant, you may imagine that I was kept hustling; squirrels get mighty tired of staying on the ground and would employ every imaginable subterfuge in their efforts to climb the tempting trees with which the park was plentifully supplied. Outwitting them and keeping them on terra firma developed both my brains and speed and ten years later, when my three runs of the

length of the field won Yale a championship game, 4 to 2, an Associated Press commentator said, "Harvard was beaten in the parks of San Francisco."

The other *Wonder Man* episodes move along in a similar vein, ending at last with a description of that "literary and theatrical center," Great Neck, and a brief visit to some of its notable residents. That, needless to say, means the Swopeses ("He and his madam had Company every week-end, Company being used in the military sense, full strength") and the Bucks: "Up the hill was the home of Gene Buck boasting a living room of such dimensions that fifty or one hundred guests often visited the Bucks in a single evening, each thinking he was the only one that had come. Mr. Buck had formerly lived in a hovel of sixteen rooms, but when the first baby came, decided it was necessary to branch out. A second little Buck has since been added to the family and Gene is negotiating for the purchase or rental of the Paramount Building."

The "autobiography" is not among Ring's more important books, but it has a distinct zany charm and enough genuinely funny episodes to remain entertaining. A fair amount of Ring's work that has received more scholarly and/or critical attention is actually of less merit, but it is probable that the book's overall tone of deliberate silliness has scared some serious readers away from it.

Though Ring may have given himself a head start on the columns that make up *The Story of a Wonder Man*, he obviously was working on it as late as October, 1926, because one of the final installments contains a reference to the heavyweight championship fight of September 24 in which Gene Tunney took the title away from Jack Dempsey. The fight was one of the last major sports events Ring covered, and it left a bitter taste in his mouth. For one thing, he had come to admire Dempsey greatly, respecting his skill and courage. For another, he plainly thought Tunney, who spouted Shakespeare and ten-dollar words, was a P.R. man's creation. When Ring visited Tunney's training camp at a small town west of Saratoga, he and Grant Rice encountered the champion walking the countryside with a book under his arm. Ring asked him what it was. "*The Rubaiyat*," Tunney replied proudly, and then waxed rhapsodic on the beautiful scenery he had encountered during the day. To which Ring retorted: "Then why the book?" Ring was similarly disdainful in a letter to the Fitzgeralds: "You ought to meet this guy Tunney. We had lunch with him a few weeks before the fight and among a great many other things, he said he thought the New York State boxing commission was 'imbecilic' and that he hoped Dempsey would not think his (Tunney's) experience in pictures had 'cosmeticized' him."

Ring had no stated intention of attending the fight, much less covering it, but Heywood Broun declined at the last moment to report it; Herbert Swope and Jack Wheeler asked if he would fill in, and he reluctantly agreed. The fight was held in Philadelphia, and Tunney, at twenty-nine two years younger than Dempsey, won a shocking ten-round decision. Ring wrote just one story under his own by-line, and his assessment in that was concise: "It was only this morning that Dempsey told the papers he would fight like hell. He did. His favorite tune seemed to be 'Oh How I Miss You Tonight.'"

But that was not the only story he wrote. After the fight he repaired to his hotel with Rice and Benny Leonard, who had held the lightweight title for eight years and was widely respected for his knowledge of the game. The rain, a sore throat and a hangover had done Rice in, but he was under obligation to file a story to the *Herald-Tribune*. Ring told him, "Take a slug of bourbon and lie down. I'll file your overnight." He did, in a story that bore scarcely a syllable's resemblance to the florid Rice style:

> Gene Tunney, the fighting marine, is the new heavyweight champion of the world. In the presence of 135,000 persons, who sat through a driving rainstorm in Philadelphia's Sesquicentennial Stadium, Gene Tunney gave Dempsey one of the worst beatings any champion ever took. He not only outpointed Dempsey in every one of the ten rounds, but the challenger hammered the champion's face almost out of shape. It was like nothing human when the tenth round ended. . . .
>
> Tunney fought a great fight, but it was quite evident that when it came to a matter of pressure Dempsey had blown completely up. . . .
>
> Tunney took the best that Dempsey had to give without any sign of breaking down or leaving his feet. It might have been slightly different if Dempsey had been able to keep up his few head-long assaults, but after twenty or thirty seconds of hard rushing he tired quickly and was forced to slow down and take a lot of punishment.

The story portrayed a champion who was fighting listlessly and a challenger who could not finish him off, and it made neither fighter happy; since both thought Rice had written it, they refused to speak to him for some time. What presumably angered them was the story's between-the-lines implication that, at best, something was odd about a fight in which a fighter of Tunney's checkered pugilistic background could so completely dominate the champion, who was himself the most dominating fighter of his time. The implication was not accidental. Benny Leonard thought the fight was a fix; he said so, and Ring—who seems to have needed no persuading—agreed. He said so emphatically to Scott and Zelda: "I bet $500 on Dempsey, giving 2 to 1. The odds ought to have been 7 to 1. Tunney couldn't lick David [Lardner] if David was trying. The thing was a very well done fake, which lots of us would like to say in print, but you know what newspapers are where possible libel suits are concerned. As usual I did my heavy thinking too late; otherwise I would have bet the other way. The championship wasn't worth a dime to Jack; there was nobody else for him to fight and he had made all there was to be made (by him) out of vaudeville and pictures. The average odds were 3 to 1 and the money he made by losing was money that the income tax collectors will know nothing about." Ring added that he thought the entire chain of bouts leading to the championship fight was rigged "to give the public a popular war hero for champion." His comment on that was: "Well, he's about as popular as my plays." Whatever the actual facts in the case, Ring firmly believed his interpretation of the fight was correct; it was salt in whatever remained of the wound inflicted by the Black Sox seven years earlier.

A heavyweight championship fight in the pouring rain was the last place on earth Ring needed to be at this point in his life, for on a routine hospital visit early in the summer he had been given a checkup and tuberculosis had been diagnosed; the hospital visit may have come at the end of what he described as "a spree that broke a few records for longevity and dullness." In any case, the disease was serious and the cure involved rest, temperance and sensible diet. It was not in Ring's nature to pay much attention to any of the three.

The development of antibiotics since World War II has made tuberculosis far easier to treat now than it was when Ring contracted it, but it has never been as terrible or incurable a disease as its reputation would suggest. It is contagious but not highly so, and it can be kept under control by extended rest; that can mean a year or more in and out of bed, with work and exercise sharply reduced, but if followed, the regimen will usually lead to a cure. The disease is most likely to strike people whose general health and resistance are low, particularly in their respiratory system; for these people, building up their overall bodily strength is essential to dealing with the specific problem of tuberculosis.

Ring could have picked up tuberculosis in any number of places —a hospital would be the most likely possibility—and it is a cinch he was a fat target for the disease at a time when it was still comparatively common. He had been through heart trouble of some sort, he had persistent respiratory difficulties—and he smoked heavily. He had frequent digestive problems—and not merely was he an alcoholic, he was indifferent to food, and when he was on a bender, often went long periods without eating anything. He was increasingly an insomniac who rarely got enough sleep to rest a body that he punished in both work and play. Eventually he would get around to making a concerted effort to strengthen himself, but by 1930 it was too late; he needed to take care of himself in 1926, and at best he did so only sporadically.

The disease did, on the other hand, make him acutely sensitive to the possibility that he might communicate it to the children. No matter how the boys might feel, good-night kisses were now out of the question and so were virtually all other physical contacts. More and more he isolated himself in his new quarters, which he described in his "Weekly Letter" of June 6, 1926: ". . . we are in the throws of alterations and the main idear of same seems to be to provide a kind of private ward for the master which I don't never half to poke my head out of same even for meals and I can be kept a absolute secret from both friends and morbid curiosity seekers and will be living under practically the same conditions like Mrs. Haversham or the guy's wife in *Jane Eyre*." Since the date of the tuberculosis diagnosis is unknown, it is not clear whether the "private ward" was constructed for that purpose by accident or design, but it became the part of the house where he spent great amounts of time at work or otherwise in isolation.

The illness gave him the excuse he evidently was looking for to arrange termination of the column, yet under the circumstances it is rather strange that he chose to do so. The doctors had told him he needed rest; the column required very little work, and no travel or exertion except by his choice—he could write the entire piece, as he usually did, from within his own head. He clearly was going to be in need of money for doctors' and hospital bills and for as much life insurance as the companies would permit him to purchase; the "Weekly Letter," all things said and done, was probably the easiest money he ever made. About all that can be guessed is that he was misled by the huge *Cosmopolitan* payments into thinking his future with the magazine was much rosier than it was. He arranged, in any case, to stop writing the "Weekly Letter" in the spring of 1927.

Until then, life went on pretty much as normal in the Lardner house, Ring's isolation being the principal exception. John went off to Andover in September—eventually all four boys would attend that preparatory school—and that same month *Cosmopolitan* published one of his most durable and thoroughly delightful stories, "I Can't Breathe." It was one of the rare first-person stories he was writing by now, and the first person was a girl closely modeled after Floncy Rice, whose Byzantine romantic entanglements Ring had watched with affectionate amusement over the years.

The girl is at a resort with her uncle and aunt while her parents are abroad; she is eighteen years old, irritated at being in the stultifying charge of people "both at least 35 years old and maybe older," and rapturously contemplating her impending marriage to Walter, to whom she has been engaged for seventeen days: "There's the dance orchestra playing 'Always,'" she tells her diary, "what they played at the Biltmore the day I met Walter. 'Not for just an hour not for just a day.' I can't live. I can't breathe." It takes only one day for her life to liven up: she receives letters from Walter and another beau named Gordon Flint, and she meets a handsome young man named Frank Carswell who "has been out of Darthmouth a year and is 24 years old." Frank is a real winner: "He asked me if I knew the asthma song and I said I didn't and he said 'Oh, you must know that. It goes yes, sir, asthma baby.' Then he told me about the underwear song, 'I underwear my baby is tonight.' He keeps you in hysterics and yet he has his serious side, in fact he was awfully serious when he said good night to me and his eyes simply shown. I wish Walter were more like him in some ways, but I mustn't think about that." Frank has a

few drinks and proposes, and she, of course, accepts—and is astonished when he remembers it all the next morning:

> Sometimes I wish I were dead, maybe that is the only solution and
> it would be best for everyone concerned. I *will* die if things keep on
> the way they have been. But of course tomorrow it will be all over,
> with Frank I mean, for I must tell him the truth no matter how
> much it hurts us both. Though I don't care how much it hurts me.
> The thought of hurting him is what is driving me mad. I can't bear
> it.

Of course she can bear it; she is having the time of her life,
starring in her very own soap opera, and that is exactly Ring's
point. The story makes absolutely no attempt at profundity, and
only the most insistently ideological could find more than teenaged
giddiness in the girl's plunge into the social and matrimonial whirl.
What gives the story its genuine distinction—both as an entertainment and as a piece of social observation—is the skill with which
it is assembled and the brilliant rendering of the girl's prose.
Ring's chief source for the story was Floncy Rice's breathless conversation about her boyfriends rather than her diary (if indeed
she kept one), but he exactly caught the self-indulgence and self-
dramatization of a late adolescent who is getting too much attention for her own good and is too shallow to know how to handle
it. He sensed precisely how much to put into the diary and how
much to leave out, so that the story moves at a clip appropriate
to the speed of its narrator's misadventures. It is, like the rest of
Ring at his best, a near-perfect miniature.

Counting "I Can't Breathe," Ring published only six short stories
between September, 1926, and July, 1927—but all in *Hearst's International-Cosmopolitan*, which meant an income from them alone
of $27,000. During this same period Max Perkins made one
of his most concentrated efforts to get Ring to try his hand at
longer fiction. In December he wrote: "I just read with great delight, in the *Cosmo*, the story 'Sun Cure.' . . . I wish though, that
for the next book of stories, we could have one long one, and the
longer the better. I know that while you are writing for the *Cosmopolitan*, this is impossible for periodical use but couldn't you do
one long one just for a book? If it were twenty or twenty-five

thousand words, we would have something entirely new, and we could make ever so much of it, and we might be able to even get a financial return that would warrant the sacrifice of magazine publication." Perkins was undoubtedly right: a book containing wholly new material by Ring probably would have attracted great critical and popular attention at that time, and probably would have made a respectable, perhaps even generous, profit for the author and his publisher. But what Perkins was a long time in coming to understand was that not merely was Ring a professional who wrote fiction almost purely for money, he was also a professional trained in the journalistic school of writing for money he could see. Ray Long's $4,500 was right out there for him to get with five thousand words; Max Perkins' money seemed to him a chimera—he had no idea how much it would be or when, if at all, it would be forthcoming.

In the fall and winter of 1926 this was essentially a matter of Ring's preference: he could afford to do what he wanted. As it turned out, however, this would prove to be the last extended period when he had the luxury of choice. The *Cosmopolitan* arrangement would produce less and less income, and before long Ring would be scrambling to meet his large financial obligations. By late 1928 he no longer was in a position to do as he chose; he had to do what the market demanded. Given his failing health and his financial situation, it is clear in retrospect that in December, 1926, Perkins was making a last plea for long fiction under circumstances that might have permitted its composition. Whether Perkins ever embraced the notion that Ring had somehow shirked a "duty" in refusing to write a novel is not recorded, but Scott Fitzgerald and others made an elaborate point of it. So the rebuttal needs to be reiterated: Ring deserves to be judged, whether favorably or not, for what he did, not for what others expected him to do.

Ring's career as a journalist with regular employment ended to all intents and purposes on March 20, 1927, with the publication of the last "Weekly Letter." Since he did not believe in farewells, it is perhaps appropriate that the final column is one of his least successful, a rambling exercise in which the only hint of his departure was a vague comment about going into business: "My ambition had always been to run a brokerage business, but as seats on the regular Stock Exchange were then selling at $125,000 each and I had $1.80, I decided to try the Curb. I found it very uncomfortable. It was hard, and taxis kept crowding my feet back onto the sidewalk and finally, late one night, a policeman told me I could not sit there any longer."

That was it. Two decades of journalism were over. An era of astonishing productivity, growth and influence ended as quietly as it had begun. Ring was not inclined, however, to look back in sorrow. As he told the Fitzgeralds: "I am going to try to work half as hard and make the same amount of money, a feat which I believe can be done." For the last years of his life, that would be his dominant professional concern: to earn as much as possible at as little physical cost as possible.

Part Seven

The Last Years

"Do you think anything nice
will ever happen to the
Lardners again?"

IN THE SPRING OF 1927 ELLIS DECIDED TO INDULGE HER FLAIR FOR redecoration, engaging a Great Neck interior decorator named Elizabeth H. Peacock to overhaul the walls, woodwork and windows of the house on East Shore Drive. The bill added up to nearly $1,000 for wallpaper, damask, chintz, fittings and labor. But though Ellis proceeded more or less merrily about this work, her life was inexorably changing. She had little time left in which to be carefree. A process of steady familial transformation was under way in which Ring gradually moved into the role of invalid and Ellis into that of guardian. Ring continued until the end of his life to be the family provider, but more and more it was Ellis who ran the household, the bank books, the minutiae of daily life. She proved fully up to the task. Notwithstanding her sheltered upbringing and the ease in which she had lived for nearly a decade, she had the physical and psychological resources to respond to what was to be the greatest challenge of her life—to care for her husband, to keep the family as close as the situation permitted, and to help the boys remain emotionally stable despite the painful reality of their father's debilitating illness.

For a number of reasons, it is probable that there had been little if any physical relationship between Ring and Ellis for some time. They had occupied separate bedrooms for a decade. They had as many children as they wanted; whether either of them had overcome inhibitions to the degree of being able to enjoy sex for purely pleasurable reasons is, needless to say, unknown. Ring's alcoholism surely impaired his sexual prowess by this time, and his frail health further limited it. Still, the evidence indicates that in all other areas their marriage remained close and happy until the end. Ring's mounting sense of guilt certainly must have extended to a feeling that he was a burden to Ellis, but she accepted it as a necessary responsibility and bore it in good spirits. If anything, as Ring was forced to take to his bed for periods of greater frequency over the next six and a half years, as Ellis became the person around whom his "social" life increasingly revolved, they became closer and closer. Ring Lardner, Jr., remembers "how genuinely Ring and she seemed to enjoy being with each other, especially the way he continued to make her laugh."

The most significant professional development for Ring in early 1927 was the publication in March of "Hurry Kane." It led to an association, albeit an uneasy one, with George M. Cohan. The story, published in *Cosmopolitan*, established a pattern that soon would dominate Ring's fiction: it utilized a successful formula of the past. In this case, the formula involved a rookie named Elmer Kane of formidable talents and country-boy habits ("He had used up both the collars that he figured would see him through his first year in the big leagues") who is stuck on a girl back in Waco, where he pitched in the minors, and another in Yuma, his home-town; he wants to go back to one or the other. The White Sox need him on the team, so they concoct a scheme to work up a "romance" between him and a beautiful show girl by faking letters from her to him—a device Ring had used six years earlier in "A Frame-Up." The story is told in the first person by a White Sox catcher, but it has little of the easy humor of Ring's earlier base-ball efforts; it gives every sign of having been written because the market wanted a baseball story by Ring.

Still, the story attracted the attention of Cohan, who had met Ring while he was doing the "Wake" and had been impressed with a blunt question Ring had asked him: "Mr. Cohan, you've been in the theater twenty years. You write songs and sing them. You dance. You write plays and produce them. You know every-thing there is to know about the theater. You're the one man who can tell me what I want to know. Mr. Cohan, how the hell does a guy get on the water wagon?" The two kept in contact, and when Cohan read "Hurry Kane" he thought he saw the material for a Broadway show. In October, 1927, he and Ring signed a deal to adapt it, with Ring writing the dramatization; but it would be a year before the play was produced, under the title *Elmer the Great*.

Ring worked reasonably successfully during 1927, though his health got no better. That summer the Lardners took Victor Herbert's cottage at Lake Placid in hopes that the clean air would be beneficial for Ring's lungs; it was a pleasant interlude, but Ring was restless and it was not until late in the summer that he made much of an effort to cooperate with the rest cure. In December he wrote Scott and Zelda: "I have been on the wagon since August 22 and haven't smoked since October 31." Both resolves were nobly intended, both soon enough proved failures.

Ring said another farewell of sorts that October: he covered his last World Series. It was between the Pittsburgh Pirates and the New York Yankees, the latter being the team generally regarded as the greatest in the history of the game; Babe Ruth had hit sixty home runs and Lou Gehrig forty-seven, the team batting average was .307, the pitching staff was strong and deep. Ring, who had agreed to cover the Series for the Bell Syndicate perhaps because he missed being in the middle of the journalistic action more than he had anticipated, defined the basic situation in his first piece: ". . . the Yanks are entering the world's series as care free as a vegetable dinner. Whereas, on the other hand, the Pirates are nervous. If they ain't nervous, they ain't human." The Pittsburgh manager was Ring's old friend from Central League days, Donie Bush, and another old friend gave him a hot tip on the outcome: Jim Sheckard, "who played left field for Methuselah's club in the days when fly balls had to be caught in the beard," Allegedly told him, "It ought to be a short series. Both managers are short. If you took Bush and [Miller] Huggins and laid them end to end, the game warden would make you throw them back in the brook." It was Ring's idea that to help the Pirates "the game be played according to the etiquette observed in tennis or golf," and he made these suggestions to Commissioner Judge Landis:

1—The umpire shall request that while a Pittsburgh pitcher is pitching or a Pittsburgh fielder fielding or a Pittsburgh batter batting, the spectators maintain absolute silence.

2—There shall be no booing of any Pittsburgh player at any time.

3—The spectators shall not applaud Pittsburgh errors.

4—When a New York batter hits a ground ball or fly ball to any Pittsburgh infielder or outfielder, there shall be no demonstration of any kind until the play is completed.

5—If a Pittsburgh player is called out when a New York player thinks he is really safe, or when a safe hit by a Pittsburgh player is called foul and a New York player thinks it is fair the New York player shall purposely strike out the next time he comes to bat and then turn to the press box and smile as much as to say, "This is true sportmanship, typical of France."

6—No spectator shall be allowed to rise to his feet except between innings.

7—New York players, whether running bases or running after batted balls, shall stop and replace each divot made by their spikes before making another one.

8—In the game called golf it is annoying to most high-class players to have anyone stand close to them or directly behind them while they are making a stroke. Therefore, when Pittsburgh players are about to swing their bats, the New York catcher and the home plate umpire shall betake themselves to one or the other of the two benches and remain their quietly until the Pittsburgh player has swang.

An act of God probably would have done the Pirates no good; they succumbed in four straight games. But Ring doubtless cared not a bit; by now the World Series was a bore to him: ". . . a world series is a big thrill for a young baseball writer and for a baseball fan of any age, but for dotards like me it is just a golden opportunity to sit around and discuss the game as it was." That is exactly what he did one evening at the Hotel Schenley in Pittsburgh, and he obviously had a grand time. He ended up in a room with Bill Hinchman, a former Cleveland and Pittsburgh outfielder; Fred Clarke, an old-time Pirate outfielder who eventually made the Hall of Fame; Chick Fraser, who pitched for several teams between 1896 and 1909; Dan Howley, "my own personal hero of more than twenty years' standing"; and his old friends Jim Sheckard and Honus Wagner. They talked baseball and the old days, joshing each other while indulging in happy sentiment:

"We were wondering," explained Bill, "what Honus, here, would have done to that ball they played with today."

"He couldn't have hit it much farther than he hit the old one," I said, waving myself to a seat on the floor.

"You're right, boy," said the big Dutchman approvingly.

"Where do you get that 'boy'?" said Dan. "This guy was in the Central League with me in 1906, scoring an error against the third baseman if I hit the right-field fence on the fly."

"In South Bend?" said Chick. "I pitched an exhibition game there in 1906. They didn't have fences."

"Not after you got through pitching," said Dan.

"At that," put in Hinchman, "this ball wouldn't have made as much difference to Honus or big Larry as it would to the left-handed, fly-ball hitters like Crawford and Schulte and Lumley and Flick."

"How about me?" said Jim Sheckard.

"One ball will go as far as another if you miss it entirely," said Dan.

"I was looking over the final averages yesterday," said Clarke. "I didn't see the names of any of your men among the home-run hitters or the plain hitters, either one." He addressed this remark to Mr. Howley, who had just gone through a season as manager of the St. Louis Browns.

"You must have been looking at the big-league averages," said Dan. "I did have one fella that was way up around .210 the middle of July, but the boss sold him, for fear Boston would get him in the draft."

"Are you going back there again?"

"Not unless the fans demand it," said Dan. "You know those St. Louis fans. You think they're not paying any attention to you, and all of a sudden you find out you're the one big interest in their lives. Why, the last couple of series we played at home, the entire attendance sometimes running into double figures, they used to hang around after the game till I came out, and they'd follow me all the way home to my doorstep. What I really think I'll do is lay off a year to get even."

"Who with?"

"The fellas I was supposed to manage."

"You won't have no trouble landin' a job," said Honus soothingly.

"Thanks, Honus," said Dan. "And I believe you're right. If I can't teach them baseball I can at least teach them geography. My slogan is Join Grand Rapids and See the World. And speaking of Grand Rapids, I'll bet I could take the club we had there in 1906 and beat either club we saw out there today. . . ."

It was the quintessential nostalgic baseball conversation, with its full share of broad raillery, embroidered reminiscence and unprovable claims of past superiority, and Ring obviously enjoyed every moment of it. He was back, if only for an hour or two, in the world he had known as a young man.

In the real world of 1927, Ring was deep in the process of grinding out free-lance work. In the year beginning that September he published ten stories and seven articles, for a total income well over $50,000. He was also keeping his eye on a theatrical project: Robert E. Sherwood was adapting "The Love Nest," Ring's thinly veiled portrait of Gene and Helen Buck. Sherwood was still a relative newcomer to Broadway, and he was having difficulties with the central problem of stretching a short story into a three-act play. He never really solved it; the play ran only twenty-three performances after opening just before Christmas. Sherwood later remarked self-deprecatingly that "the Lardner part of it was good." Ring kept his own counsel publicly, but wrote candidly to the Fitzgeralds after they wired him good wishes: "Thanks for your telegram, which arrived this morning. This ain't my play, though of course I will share in the receipts (There won't be many). I saw a dress rehearsal last night. Bob has done some very clever writing and the second act is quite strong, with June Walker great as a drunk. But I'm afraid most of it will be over people's heads. This, of course, is under your hat (to use a slang expression)."

Ring's hopes were much higher for his collaboration with Cohan on *Elmer the Great*. In the same letter he told Scott and Zelda: "My thing with Cohan is supposed to go into rehearsal in February, but you never can tell. Walter Huston is to be our star." It actually was not until spring that rehearsals began, and it was then that the trouble started. Ring and Cohan had diametrically opposed ideas of what the play should be; Ring saw it as a satire, Cohan as a melodrama, and it was not long before they were after each other tooth and nail. An incident that seems to have been fairly typical occurred one evening when Ring telephoned his Great Neck neighbor George Holland, who was married to a sister-in-law of Cohan's, and issued the call: "Come on over here, George. We're going to fix this damn play and we're going to fix it right." The two worked on it feverishly, doing a scissors-and-paste job, and when they were through, Ring announced that at the next day's rehearsal "we'll beard the little bastard." In the morning Ring presented Cohan with the altered script: "Now this, George, is the way I want this comedy played." The Yankee Doodle Dandy scanned it, then laughed in Ring's face.

The quarrels were essentially theatrical and the "collaborators" remained cordial, but the play gave every sign of being an artistic disaster. Ring, however, was loyal to the people with whom he worked and spent a good part of the summer of 1928 traveling with the troupe during the pre-Broadway shakedown. In June, with the play opening at the Blackstone Theater in Chicago, he sent a letter to the *Tribune* urging his old friends to attend while at the same time leaving no doubt as to his true feelings:

Gents:—

I hope you won't stay away from the Blackstone . . . on my account as I have got a show opening there and will be on hand personally myself and when you see me please call me Fanny as this is my first play. When I say it is mine I am overstepping the bonds of reason a triffle because honest Fred the production which you will witness and the original version as I wrote it is as much alike as Edna Mae Oliver and Mae Tinee. I handed the script to Mr. Cohan and he said he would produce it if I would allow him to fix it up a little and that is the last I heard of it till I was invited to the first rehearsal which I listened all through it and then had to ask Sam Forrest the director if I hadn't fell into the wrong theater by mistake.

It is a double thrill collaborating on a play with Mr. Cohan because you can attend the performance and then go home and read your own script and that gives you two complete shows in one evening, but Mr. Cohan was absent from a couple of rehearsals during which I managed to slip in a line of my own and I am going to offer my dear little Chicago friends a prize of two tickets to the next White Sox world's series if they can tell me which line that is. . . .

Well, we ran half a week in Worcester Mass which is more than a plethora and now we are coming from a six weeks run (or walk) in Boston and I want to remind you at this junction that the Boston critics is far from dumb and from the notices they give us you would think that either Geo. or I or the both of us was having an affair with them.

His brave words notwithstanding, Ring prepared himself for the worst at the Chicago opening of *Elmer*. He got himself well pickled and finally arrived at the Blackstone midway through the first act. He reached his seat by climbing somewhat noisily past the others in his row, then sat down and listened for a while. At last he put his head in his hands, wailed an entirely audible "Oh, no!" and left the theater.

His reaction to the play's September 24, 1928, opening at the Lyceum Theater in New York is not recorded, but it doubtless was similar in spirit if not flamboyance. The reviewers bent over backwards to be kind to Ring, but they could not avoid the fundamental weakness of the play credited to his authorship. Brooks Atkinson in the *Times* credited him with "a tautly constructed first act" and "a great many lines of capital dialogue," but objected that "Mr. Lardner's craftsmanship does not join the various parts of his piece smoothly" and concluded: "Those who had come to *Elmer the Great* with the keenest expectations were no doubt disappointed. For all that, it yielded farce entertainment in an original vein." In the *Telegram*, Heywood Broun was blunt with his friend: "A great talent met a beautiful performance last night in a poor play. The familiar traffic court phrase, 'Guilty with an explanation,' must be used in regards to Ring Lardner's new comedy. . . . Lardner's peculiar ability does not move along well trodden lines. And he has compromised with theatrical tradition to the extent of endowing his play with a plot which is wholly conventional."

Elmer the Great ran for forty performances and then collapsed. It also ran Ring into debt, for his contract with Cohan provided that Ring assume 25 percent of losses should they be incurred, and they were: his first fling as the author of a Broadway play ended up costing him more than $6,000 out of pocket. Eventually he and Cohan sold the play to the movies and recouped some of their losses, but not enough to break even.

But *Elmer* did not totally preoccupy Ring. On March 17 he began what would be a two-year association with *Collier's*, during which he wrote twenty-four articles at $1,000 apiece. He was introduced to readers of the magazine by John Wheeler, in a discursive article noteworthy principally because he quoted a couple of the rhymed Christmas greetings that Ring and Ellis sent to their closer friends. One of them read:

> *We combed Fifth Avenue this last month*
> *A hundred times if we combed it onth,*
> *In search of something we thought would do*
> *To give to a person as nice as you.*

> *We had no trouble selecting gifts*
> *For the Ogden Armours and Louis Swifts,*
> *The Otto Kahns and the George F. Bakers,*
> *The Munns and the Rodman Wanamakers.*

It's a simple matter to pick things out
For people one isn't so wild about,
But you, you wonderful pal and friend, you!
We couldn't find anything fit to send you.

The money wasn't as good at *Collier's* as at *Cosmopolitan*, but the hours were better. Ring's monthly pieces ran only a couple of thousand words and could be about anything he wanted them to be. He wrote a rather uninspired Prohibition piece, conceding at the outset that he had leaped at the idea of such an article "as a starving dog goes after a deck of cards," but he went on anyway even though, as he knew perfectly well, there was nothing either serious or funny left to say. He told tall tales on Grant Rice and other golfing companions, he discussed politics in a predictably offhanded way, and he wrote a series of mock biographies of famous people. Not much of the writing in any of these was first-rank Lardner, but there were many good moments—and one that was absolutely superb, a piece of the most ingenious nonsense. It comes from "Pluck and Luck," his "biography" of Babe Ruth, and deserves extensive quotation:

One of Mr. Ruth's boyhood pals in Baltimore was Henry L. Mencken; they used to take long walks in the woods together, looking for odd Flora. It was an ideal companionship, for both loved to talk and as neither one could understand the other, no law of ethics was broken by their talking simultaneously. I would repeat some of their conversations, but Mencken's words can't be spelled and the Babe's can't be printed.

When the Babe was twelve years old and Mencken thirty-seven, their strolls together became infrequent; the Ruth boy would telephone Mencken and say "H.L., I won't be able to accompany you home this afternoon; I've got to stay home and mend the highboy." Or some other flimsy excuse.

Mencken was not deceived, but hardly hurt, and decided that some day when his little friend did not have to stay home and mend the highboy, he would ask him pointblank the real cause of the estrangement. Babe, however, confessed before H.L. had mustered courage to put the question.

They had been sitting in one of the lower branches of their favorite tree, a full-grown hickory, idly watching the antics of a couple of efts, MacDonald and Goldstein. It came time to go home and they dismounted.

"Wait a minute," said the Babe. "I think I'll take this along with me."

And before Mencken realized what he meant, he had picked up the tree, thrown it over his shoulder and started along the path toward town.

"You perhaps wonder," he said to his companion, "what I intend to do with it."

"No," replied Mencken. "But I do wonder whether you have noticed that [George Jean] Nathan has taken a fancy to the word 'presently,' using it to signify 'at the present time; now,' a definition called obsolete by Webster."

"I thought you would," said the Babe. "Well, I purpose biting off the roots, the branches and the bark and employing it as a bat."

It then dawned upon Mencken that the Babe had gone into baseball and his admiration for the youngster was so great that he, too, became a devotee of the game, and to this day, whenever the Yankees are playing in New York, you will find the famous editor and critic in the Algonquin Hotel, casting sheep's eyes at a blank page of copy paper.

The Lardners and the Fitzgeralds saw each other for one of the last times in the spring of 1928. The timing of the visit was appropriate: like the Fitzgeralds four years before, Ring and Ellis were now making plans to leave Great Neck. Their reason seems to have had less to do with the strains of the Great Neck social life than with increased congestion and urbanization there, and with Ring's need for the cleanest available air. They and the Rices decided to move far out on Long Island and to buy side-by-side oceanfront lots at East Hampton, then still a quiet, relatively isolated resort for the very wealthy. The Lardner house, which Ring named "Still Pond" because he planned "no more moving," was a shingled structure with thirteen rooms and a garage with a two-room apartment, and Ellis had a grand time setting it up. She and Ring sold much of their furniture at the same time they sold the house on East Shore Road, so she had a fine excuse for engaging the services of Elizabeth Peacock once again. The decorating and furnishing cost several thousand dollars, and no stone seems to have been left unturned; the Peacock bills include everything from a wicker settee ($165) to one yellow pitcher ($2). The furnishings were in the style favored at the time for the seaside "cottages" of the well-to-do: dark heavy wood, overstuffed chairs with colorful slipcovers, thick rugs. The house was spacious, pleasant, comfortable, and the entire family loved it.

In addition to the Rices, Ring and Ellis had other newspaper friends in East Hampton. The Wheelers bought a house there, and so did the Irvin S. Cobbs and Percy Hammonds. Cobb was a newspaper humorist, a Kentuckian known as the "Sage of Paducah" whose folksy style owed more than a little to Ring's influence, but whom Ring could take only in very small doses. Percy and Florence Hammond had been friends of the Lardners' since the 1910's, when Hammond was drama reviewer for the Chicago *Tribune*; he took the same position with the New York *Herald Tribune* in the early twenties, and was a powerful voice in the Broadway theater. He was a quiet, gentle man who enjoyed the birdwatching opportunities available in East Hampton. Ring and Grant Rice, by the same token, played the Maidstone golf links, and Grant liked fishing off Montauk. It was, all in all, a splendid place for rest and recuperation.

Neither of which Ring was in any particular mood for. He knew what was good for him but he did not necessarily want to do it, and when an opportunity came along to make what looked to be very, very good money, he jumped at it, rest be damned.

The offer came from a most unlikely source: the New York *Morning Telegraph*. Then as now it was principally a horse-racing newspaper, but it had been purchased by a group led by a gentleman named Joseph Moore who had grandiose notions of turning it into a leading journal of politics, sports and the arts. He was throwing money left and right for high-priced talent: Walter Winchell wrote a pseudonymous gossip column as "Beau Broadway," Ben Hecht covered boxing, Whitney Bolton was drama critic, and Westbrook Pegler was a featured sports columnist. In late 1928 Ring was offered the stunning sum of $50,000 a year to write a four-times-a-week column, and he accepted. He had, as he later explained, good reason for doing so:

> . . . I am a fourfather, i.e., the patriarchy of a male quartet of bambini, and three of them are senile enough to go away to school, so each year I have to
> Hand over
> Four grand over
> To Andover.

Ring's column was called "Ring's Side." It was announced on December 1 in a front-page announcement written by Pegler: "We are pleased to announce that Ring Lardner, a great writer who never went literary, has agreed to write for the *Morning Telegraph*, beginning next Tuesday. He is supposed to be writing around and about the news of the day, but he probably will write about anything. Sometimes he may write about nothing. We can imagine only one general topic more entertaining than Ring Lardner on ANYTHING; that is, Ring Lardner on NOTHING." On December 4, the *Morning Telegraph* trotted forth in a new make-up and with a new cast of stars, Ring foremost among them. The *New York Times* welcomed the change:

> In a gay new dress and leading Ring Lardner by the hand, the ninety-two-year-old *Morning Telegraph* appeared on the news stands yesterday. Mr. Moore and his associates, who bought the paper from the Thomas estate, have completely changed the format and the formula and the experiment they are making will be watched with interest and cordial good wishes by the remainder of the New York press.
>
> The *Morning Telegraph* has gone in strongly for names and columnists and for a generally more cultivated type of material. Its chief interest remains in sports and the drama, and the bulk of its type continues to be lavished on the performances of race horses. But throughout the new product there is sufficient evidence that "writing" is to be one of its large concerns and that the smart weeklies and monthlies, and the personal columnists, are going to have a pace set for them.
>
> Mr. Lardner's return to daily newspaper work will be hailed with pleasure on all sides; he used to do a column like this in the Chicago *Tribune* before the *Saturday Evening Post* found, to its delight, that a baseball writer out in Chicago was raising its circulation by the thousands with his stories of "You Know Me Al."

The move back to a regular newspaper column turned out to be more than Ring was physically or psychologically equipped for. He worked, as he always did, as hard as he could, but the inspiration just was not there for four pieces a week, and the lack showed in what Ring wrote. Only two of the thirty-eight pieces he did are worth mentioning. One was a nonsense play called "Abend di Anni Nouveau," which featured a cast of characters that included

Walter Winchell, "a nun"; Heywood Broun, "an usher at Roxy's"; Theodore Dreiser, "a former 'Follies' girl"; H. L. Mencken, "a kleagle in the Moose"; and Ben Hecht, "a taxi starter." The other was a Winchell parody called "Your Broadway, Beau, and You Can Have It." Ring was doing more and more parodies these days, and this was among the best of them:

> A. Lincoln and Gen. McClellan are on the verge. . . . Jimmy Madison and Dolly Payne Todd are THAT WAY. (ED: This is the absolute Choynskie.)
> Aleck Hamilton and Aaron Burr have phfft. . . . The Geo. Washingtons (she was Martha Lorber of the Follies) have moved into their Valley Forge snuggery for the Old Man Shiver Days. . . .
> What writer on what paper is taking whose golf clubs to what Bahamas? . . . Arthur Brisbane has signed up to do a daily column for William ("Randolph") Hearst.
> An Exchange Place investment firm is recommending stock in a company that will convert hootch from liquid to solid form and thus be able to peddle it legally, perhaps as sandwiches. . . . You can order me a Scotch on rye. . . .

If the strain of producing the column was too much for Ring, the financial burden was too much for the management of the *Morning Telegraph* and the paper began to strain at the seams. By what almost certainly was mutual consent, the last "Ring's Side" appeared on February 6, 1929. The separation came just in time, for a couple of major projects had begun to command Ring's attention. Scribner's was in the process of assembling what would come to be regarded as the "definitive" collection of his short stories, and he was in the early stages of a collaboration that held out genuine hope of producing the Broadway triumph he so sorely wanted.

It was nearly three years since the publication of *The Love Nest*, and if Max Perkins could not get the "long story" he pleaded with Ring to write, at least he wanted another collection. As far back as March, 1928, he had told Ring he wanted to put together a book with about fifteen stories in it, and by November of that year the project was well under way: "Here is a list of the stories for the book,—'And Other Stories' as we now call it. We have got a good jacket under way, but we have not put the title on because that may be changed. . . . Tell us anything you want us to do about these stories, but tell us soon." Then, the day after Christmas, an offer came in that changed the contents of the book completely:

> The Literary Guild wishes to take for their book of the month for either April, May, or June (probably April, and almost certainly not June) a book of your stories to embrace those in "How to Write Short Stories," "The Love Nest," and those we have already in type for the book we had planned to publish this spring. They agree to pay $13,500, which we propose should be divided equally between you and ourselves.
>
> The job is quite a big one, and we ought to get ahead immediately, and are even now making estimates on the printing so that we ought to know as soon as possible what stories you wish to omit. But as the book is to be about 250,000 words, it would be undesirable to omit more than two or three stories anyhow. . . .
>
> As to the general proposition we think it highly advantageous because it will put a very fine book by you in the hands of some 70,000 people, to say nothing of those to whom we can sell copies through the regular trade. . . . It will also lead, we think, to a re-estimation of you as a writer of stories, etc., in all the reviewing papers. . . .

The Literary Guild was a highly respected book club with an equally respected selection committee; Burton Rascoe was a member, and it can be assumed that he spoke strongly on behalf of his fellow Middle Westerner. The book that finally was published on April 5 was a 467-page collection of thirty-five stories—the nineteen that had first been collected in *How to Write Short Stories* and *The Love Nest,* and sixteen that had appeared in magazines since September, 1926. Perkins was sufficiently confident of the book's success to print 20,000 trade copies in addition to the Guild's 70,000.

The book did, as Perkins had predicted it would, receive major review attention—major, and favorable. Dorothy Parker, in *The New Yorker,* did not like the title, *Round Up* (". . . if there were ever a cup given for the most unfortunate title of the year, it would be resting at this very moment upon the Ring Lardner mantelpiece"), but loved the contents, emphasizing "Ring Lardner's unparalleled ear and eye, his strange, bitter pity, his utter sureness of characterization, his unceasing investigation, his beautiful economy." Lewis Mumford, in the *Herald Tribune*, perceptively noted that "proceeding from the inside, there is often a touch of human sympathy, even in the cruel strokes; the humor, far from being metallic, sometimes has the deepening quality of pathos," but then slipped partway into the by-now-familiar routine: "Mr. Lardner plainly hates the people he writes about, but he does not hate them to the exclusion of his own humanity. Their faults are yours and mine and Mr. Lardner's. He remembers that." In the *New York Times Book Review*, John Chamberlain called Ring "preeminently our best short-story writer," compared him with Marcel Proust in his understanding of the rituals of human society, and found his work more satisfactory than that of Sherwood Anderson, Morley Callaghan or Ernest Hemingway.

What is puzzling about these reviews is not their enthusiasm for Ring's work, but their failure to comprehend the degree to which he had begun repeating himself after *The Love Nest*. To an extent this can be explained by the lack of dates on the stories in *Round Up*, but presumably all of these reviewers were sufficiently familiar with Ring's work to have a fairly clear sense of where each story fell in his career. Of the sixteen new stories, only "I Can't Breathe" deserves to be ranked with Ring's best; the rest are professional, for Ring was always that, and entertaining, but they are the work of a writer who was working solely for money and consciously or unconsciously was reverting to material that had served him well in the past. "The Maysville Minstrel," for example, uses the device of the cruel practical joke, one dating back to his earliest fiction. "Mr. Frisbie" is a variation on one of the *How to Write Short Stories* pieces, "A Caddy's Diary"; both are about rich people who habitually cheat at trivial games, both are narrated by caddies. "Hurry Kane," as already noted, employs a trick of plot that was used better in "A Frame-Up." "Travelogue" is a refinement of an uncollected story, "Tour Y-10"—and, it certainly must be added, a great improvement on it.

In addition to repetition there is a strong element of obviousness in these later stories. That had been a problem with Ring's third-person fiction from the start, for he was never able to master the art of exposition when he assumed an omniscient stance, but in these stories the obviousness covers not just incidental moments of character development but plot itself. "There Are Smiles," a story of which Ring was inexplicably proud, tells of a jolly New

York policeman who smiles at all who pass by; he becomes harm-lessly infatuated with a beautiful girl who often zips by his corner in a bright-blue roadster; she is a carefree person and a careless driver, and she is killed in an accident; the cop's smile vanishes and he begins abusing motorists in New York's time-honored style. In "Now and Then," a woman named Irma writes letters to her friend Esther while on a delayed honeymoon in Nassau; Bob, her husband, is jealous and overprotective; three years later they return to Nassau, but now Bob is indifferent (". . . he was quite provoked at me being sick and threatened to leave me home the next time he was going anywhere on a boat") and clearly headed for unfaithfulness. In "Man Not Overboard," a young novelist dis-couraged over his prospects plans to commit suicide by leaping off an ocean liner; in the bar, drowning his sorrows, he begins a con-versation with an older gentleman, "a man of robust health"; as the conversation winds on, the man tells him a tale of woe that makes his own look trivial, and he decides not to do himself in; after he is put to bed, we learn that the conversation was a fraud collaborated in by a traveler and a friend who is purser of the ship.

A third new element, as that ending suggests, is sentimentality. All the reviewers who celebrated Ring's "hatred" conveniently managed to forget that there was a soft heart behind the surface toughness of many of these stories. In the fiction of the late twenties, the softness frequently pushed the toughness completely aside. In "Old Folks' Christmas," Tom and Grace Carter sit around on Christmas Eve waiting for their two children, aged nineteen and seventeen; but the children are too involved in their own busy social lives to pay attention to their parents, and when they do come home it is to accept their presents matter-of-factly and then zip right off again; Tom and Grace finally find consolation in each other, but it seems rather empty after what has gone before. In "The Maysville Minstrel" the poetizing young bookkeeper in the gas company is victimized by a heartless traveling salesman. In "Hurry Kane," the ballplayer triumphs over would-be fixers and returns to the girl in Yuma.

That having been said, however, the stories also demonstrate what an incredibly gifted observer he was of human character and the social situation. John Chamberlain was as silly in comparing him to Proust as Mencken had been earlier in ranking him ahead of Henry James, but he was absolutely correct in identifying him as a master of social ritual. Few writers, for instance, have ever made better use of tables than Ring—bridge tables, dinner tables, Pullman tables. How people reacted to each other across the tables fascinated him, and in an otherwise minor story like "Dinner" he could say worlds about the ways in which conversationalists reveal themselves at the semiformal ritual of a dinner party. We have already noted the bride who gives herself away while chattering over bridge in "Who Dealt?"; in "Contract" a man who is clearly speaking for Ring gets potted at a contract-bridge party and one by one exposes the pretentious, fatuous guests. Again through a character who plainly speaks for him, in "Liberty Hall" he describes a popular composer who is promised a rest if he visits the Thayers'; instead he finds himself trapped in a house with two pushy, nosy do-gooders who will not leave him alone.

Ring understood the rituals of the golf course, the tennis court, the bridge table, the baseball diamond; Virginia Woolf was absolutely right about his use of games as a meeting point for the diverse and scattered American populace. There is no evidence that he had made anything remotely approximating a systematic study of Americans at play, but his fiction in effect amounts to one. In much of what it depicts, it is harsh: the petty cheating, the mean practical joking, the self-aggrandizement, the one-upmanship, the trivial competitiveness. But there is also much innocence in his fiction, much joyfulness, much broad humor, much unsentimentalized human feeling. Ring as a writer of fiction was essentially a journalist, recording what he saw with a sharp and knowing eye, but also—and this is what too often is forgotten—a loving eye.

RING'S SHORT-STORY PRODUCTION decreased sharply during 1929 because he turned his most important energies to the theater; he did continue to write magazine pieces, but they were principally the easily ground-out *Collier's* articles. He did those for money; he did his work with George S. Kaufman on *June Moon* with enthusiasm, excitement and hope.

Kaufman was known as "the Great Collaborator," and with good reason. His Broadway career was still just beginning when he and Ring began work (though he was only four years younger than Ring), but he had already collaborated on eight shows with Marc Connelly, two with Edna Ferber, and one each with Herman J. Mankiewicz and Morrie Ryskind; still ahead were the eight famous shows written with Moss Hart, and others with Alexander Wooll-cott, Howard Dietz and John P. Marquand. "He had," Walter Kerr has said, "essentially an analytical mind. The person who collaborates tends to be a craftsman, constructionist, analyst, critic, what have you. It seems to me that he did extraordinarily well, that he was a beautiful craftsman, that his greatest strength as a playwright was his wit." He was tolerant of the eccentricities and occasional gaucheries of those with whom he collaborated, vir-tually all of whom have remembered him with affection and ad-miration; his private life was something less than spotless, but he was a thoroughgoing professional who brought diligence and craftsmanship to his work.

Ring and Kaufman had known each other throughout the twenties, but they were not close friends; they saw each other at the clubs to which they both belonged and at such occasions as the Dutch Treat shows where Ring's nonsense plays were per-formed. Evidently they had a mutual-admiration society, but Ring was skeptical all the same when Kaufman proposed in late 1928 that they do a stage version of "Some Like Them Cold." Since Ring had just been badly burned by his collaboration with Cohan on *Elmer the Great*, he was understandably reluctant to get singed again, and he begged off. But Ring must have been tempted, and he may have quizzed his friend Connelly about how Kaufman was to work with, for in the winter of 1929 he told Kaufman he would like to give the idea a try if they could work in a part for Floncy Rice, who was now twenty-one and had theatrical aspirations. Kaufman agreed and they set to work. Their method, according to Ring Lardner, Jr., was for Ring to write a draft, Kaufman to rewrite it, and Ring to rewrite the rewrite. The effect was a mixture of Ring's satire and Kaufman's structural sense; no small part of Kaufman's great success was his willingness to subordinate himself to a collaborator whose abilities and instincts he respected. The result was that Ring was happier than he had ever been in the theater; when they took the play to Atlantic City for tryouts in July, he had become appreciative enough of his collaborator to tweak him in the Atlantic City *Press*:

> One difference between Mr. Kaufman and me is that he selects
> his collaborators at random (and a mighty pretty place too), while
> I make it a rule never to work with anybody I can't call George. . . .

Readers are probably in a coma to be told the various working methods employed by me and my different Georges. . . . Mr. Cohan's and Mr. Kaufman's systems are quite a lot alike; you give them your script and they throw it in the ash bbl. after copying the names of the characters so they can change them. . . .

It is fascinating to watch Mr. Kaufman at work. He is a born housewife and keeps pacing your living room examining the floor for pieces of thread and unavoidable ravelings, which he picks up and puts in his pocket. After one of our sessions last March, I told Mrs. L. (Mrs. Lardner) about this and she said: "Maybe he is keeping Lint." She is a wow when you get to know her. Come out some time.

Returning to the subject of our play, *June Moon*, Mr. Kaufman, an extremist at heart, suggested that we emulate *Journey's End*, which has no woman characters, and *One Beautiful Evening*, which has no men . . . and write one in which all the parts are taken by leopards. Or else not write one at all. I don't know what we finally decided. You will have to judge for yourself. *June Moon* is Mr. Kaufman's title, and it's his play—unless it's good.

In Atlantic City, it wasn't. Only the first act was solid, which explains Ring's reply when a friend asked him what he was doing in Atlantic City: "I'm down here with an act." But play-doctoring was among Kaufman's many skills, and after several weeks of hard work they had a show that they could take to Washington with high hopes of success. Ring's arrival in the capital was greeted with warmth by John J. Daly in the *Post*, who recalled that Ring liked to hang out at the National Press Club during his visits there: "Many a good time the cubs of Washington journalism have had with that old bear, Ring Lardner. Generous of heart, he has dispensed of his time and talents in making for the boys nights never to be forgotten. Now, on the occasion of this visit, Mr. Lardner comes as a playwright. So, undoubtedly, there will be little time for the usual nocturnal gatherings, a playwright being a pretty busy man at the time of the play's opening. However, if all the newspapermen who count Ring Lardner their friend are present on the opening night . . . 'twill be a pretty sight."

Newspapermen or no, the show got an enthusiastic reception in Washington and headed for New York with a full head of steam. It opened at the Broadhurst Theater on West Forty-fourth Street on October 9. Sam Harris was the producer (he and Ring had been neighbors in Great Neck), Kaufman the director and Milano Tilden the stage manager. There was a cast of twelve, and in the program Ring supplied the "Facts About the Players." Some samples:

NORMAN FOSTER, who portrays the role of Fred Stevens, is well qualified to act the part of a song-writer as he is the stepfather of Stephen Foster. . . . Norman (as you begin to call him after a while) is married to Claudette ("Peaches") Colbert, who cannot be with us tonight, but sends regards.

. . .

JEAN DIXON is a great favorite with the producers and authors because she won't accept a salary. "It's just fun," is the way she puts it. She makes a good living betting on the whippet races at Grant's Tomb.

. . .

The writer of this exposé is not, at present, personally acquainted with MISS LEE PATRICK, MISS MARGARET LEE, MR. LEO KENNEDY or MR. EMIL HOCH and will have to postpone revelations concerning them until a later date. Perhaps our mutual shyness will wear off in time, but I nearly die when I first meet an actor, especially an actress.

. . .

A good pianist was required for the role of Maxie. Mr. Harris did not realize this and signed HARRY ROSENTHAL, who at once admitted that he knew nothing about the piano, but thought he could pick it up in two weeks. They say the country's hospitals are littered with people who thought they could pick up a piano in two weeks. Even two men, working in shifts, are likely to find it irksome. Mr. Rosenthal, however, took to it as a duck to golf and at the same time learned to say his lines with so many variations that the authors have to attend the theater every night to find out the name of the play.

. . .

FLORENCE D. RICE is the daughter of Grantland Rice, the taxidermist. Miss Rice's parents have no idea she is on the stage and every time she leaves the house to go to the theater, she tells them she has run down to the draper's to buy a stamp. On matinee days she writes two letters (that's what they think). She is very proud of her wire-haired fox terrier, Peter, because on the night the play opened in Atlantic City he sent her a wire.

The program notes got the opening night audience in a good mood for the play, and everything went smashingly. The reviews were excellent, setting off a chain reaction at the box office that kept the play running for 273 performances; a road company took it to audiences around the nation. Ring at last had the success he had yearned for, and he loved it.

He had a good deal to be proud of. The play was an absolutely professional job. One night young Moss Hart, all his success ahead of him but his own professionalism already formed, went to see it: "I sat in the balcony of the Broadhurst Theater and watched *June Moon* being performed on the stage below, much the way a young medical student might sit in a hospital amphitheater and watch a noted pair of surgeons perform a difficult operation. George Kaufman and Ring Lardner were at their satirical best in *June Moon,* and the experience of seeing two skilled men function at the top of their form is a very special pleasure." But it must be borne in mind that Hart's standards of excellence were those of the commercial theater, and the excellence of *June Moon* must be viewed within the limits of those standards. Viewed within the far more exacting limits of Ring's standards for his own writing, the play is something else again.

"Some Like Them Cold" is a story about two people, both of them vain and petty and foolish, but both of them viewed by Ring with sympathy and understanding. *June Moon* is a play about the songwriting business, a satire of Tin Pan Alley that has many funny moments but very little to do with the story upon which it is based. Compromise is of course a necessity in a collaborative effort, but Ring compromised his story almost out of existence. Some changes obviously were necessary in order to make the story workable on the stage; Edna, for example, now lives in New York, as correspondence with her would be difficult to handle dramatically. It can be argued, as well, that changing the emphasis to songwriting was a way to translate the story's satire into something that could "play" well before an audience.

The play is also a period piece. In 1974 a television adaptation by Burt Shevelove was staged on the Public Television program *Theater in America.* The adaptation was faithful and skillful, the cast excellent, the staging imaginative—and the production fell flat. What was funny in the twenties was merely a curiosity forty-five years later. Only Ring's takeoffs of song lyrics retained their freshness. In one, he satirized inspirational songs:

> *Life is a game; we are but players*
> *Playing the best we know how.*
> *If you are beat, don't let it wrangle;*
> *No one can win all the time.*
> *Sometimes the odds seem dead against you;*
> *What has to be, has to be,*
> *But smile just the same, for life is a game,*
> *And God is a fine referee.*

In another, he took on sentimental love songs set in unlikely surroundings:

> *Montana moonlight,*
> *As bright as noon light,*
> *Oh, may it soon light*
> > *My way to you!*
> *I know you're lonely,*
> *My one and only,*
> *For I am lonely,*
> > *Yes, lonely, too.*
>
> *My heart is yearning*
> *For kisses burning,*
> *For lips as sweet as a rose in June.*
> *I'm always dreaming*
> *Of your eyes gleaming,*
> *Beneath the beaming*
> > *Montana Moon.*

And in the show's big laugh number, he wrote one about "a fella here in New York that sees a pitcher of a Japanese princess and he's nuts about her, but he can't afford a trip to Japan just on a chance. So he calls her up—get it? 'Hello, Tokio' ":

> *Hello, hello, Tokio!*
> *Girlie, you'll excuse it, please,*
> *If I no spik Japanese.*
> *This little call will leave me broke-o,*
> *But I simply had to say, "I love you so."*
> *Believe me, dearie, it's no joke-o;*
> *I'd gladly fly through fire and smoke-o*
> *To share with you the marriage yok-o,*
> *Fairest flower of Tokio-oki-okio!*

Ring celebrated the end of the long grind involved in putting the play together and the success of the results by going on what seems to have been one of the worst, and longest, drunks of his life. In February, 1930, he told Scott that "when the New York opening was over, I went on a bat that lasted nearly three months and haven't been able to work since, so it's a good thing that the play paid dividends." In another letter, filled with contrition, he wrote: "I only hope I can stay well enough to work. If I can, I promise you and the world one thing: that never again will I take a vacation when I am through with a job. I think it is the biggest mistake a person can make—not to keep going. I never felt better in my life than when I was working twenty hours a day, trying to get *June Moon* into shape, and never felt worse than afterwards, when it was in shape and I treated myself to a 'layoff,' which was mostly spent in the lovely atmosphere of hospitals."

Ring must have sensed that trouble such as this was going to happen, because three weeks before the opening of *June Moon* he signed over to Ellis "all my right, title and interest in and to the profits to be derived from" the play. As his health failed he became more and more intensely concerned about her welfare and that of the boys, and he was increasingly concerned with taking precautions to assure their financial well-being, chief among them the life-insurance policies in which he so devoutly believed.

When Ring got out of the hospital that winter of 1929–30, he and Ellis began a seminomadic existence they would continue for the rest of his life. In the summers they lived at East Hampton, in the sharpest of winter they went South, and in between they lived at a succession of New York hotels: the Croyden, the Elysée, the Vanderbilt, the Carlyle. Hotel hopping got to be such a habit that by March, 1931, Ellis was sure they would touch base with every registration clerk in the city. "It will soon be," she wrote to Jim at Andover, "that there won't be a hotel in New York City in which I have not at some time taken up my residence." It was also during this period that Ring made frequent use of hotel rooms as refuges in which he could get work accomplished. He had fled to such sanctuaries from the hurly-burly of Great Neck, but now his need for money was far more urgent and he went into seclusion more often. In the spring of 1930 Ellis told John, who was by now at Harvard, of his father's new address: "Dad has been living at the Pennsylvania Hotel for a week. He has been in hiding from all the people who bother him—including me—and has done a tremendous lot of work—for him. He is spending the weekend with his family but is going back again for a few days this week to finish up the amount of work he had outlined."

Part of that work was a story for *Good Housekeeping* called "Mamma" and another for *Collier's* called "Second-Act Curtain." The stories are noteworthy as the first of the "dark" fiction he would try his hand at off and on for the rest of his writing career. "Mamma" is the story, told almost entirely in dialogue, of a woman whose husband and two children have died of the flu and who has been shocked into amnesia by the calamity; it borders on the sentimental, and the manner in which the cause of her strange behavior is disclosed is rather slick, but it is also moving and the dialogue is first rate. "Second-Act Curtain" is less dark and clearly autobiographical, drawing upon the problems Ring and Kaufman had faced in rewriting *June Moon* after the disaster in Atlantic City:

> "We'd be all set," said Mr. Rose, the manager, "if we just had a curtain for the second act."
> The authors, Mr. Chambers and Mr. Booth, walked away from him as fast as they could go. Neither of them wanted the blood, even of a manager, on his hands; and they had been told so often— by the manager, the company manager, various house managers, the entire office staff, every member of the cast and the citizens of New Jersey and the District of Columbia—that they lacked a second-act curtain (just as if it were news to them), that both had spent most of their prospective profits on scimitars, stiletti, grenades and sawed-off shotguns, and it was only a question of time before some of these trinkets would be brought into play.

The collaborator named Booth lives in "a hotel room in which he had spent nearly all of the summer working, because he found it impossible to work out on Long Island where everybody else was having a good time." There is, to put it mildly, a considerable similarity to a quasi-fictional piece Ring wrote shortly before the opening of *June Moon*. It was called "Large Coffee" and was an amusing account of his summer-long effort to get coffee as he wanted it from room service in the hotel where he had holed up to work: "At a conference of my wife and children, it was decided that I ought to contribute something to their support and they recommended that I do a little writing for the magazines or newspapers. I told them this would be impossible in our hut on Long Island unless they and the neighbors agreed to become hermits so that my mind would not be constantly distracted by the knowledge that other people were having fun. It is my plan to visit the family one day in the middle of each week, not at the weekend when there seems to be a tendency to drink cocktails and expect you to sit by, look on and like it."

That piece appeared in *The New Yorker;* it marked the beginning of what was to be one of Ring's happiest and most fruitful professional associations. *The New Yorker* was not the wealthy publication it has long since become, but a young weekly trying to establish itself with a sophisticated audience; it cared about writers and presented them well, and Ring was probably entirely sincere when he said that "I would rather write for *The New Yorker* at five cents a word than for *Cosmopolitan* at a dollar a word." He and Harold Ross, its editor, were friends and contemporaries; both had come East in 1919, both retained an affection for their roots in the West while thoroughly enjoying the life of New York. How big were the peanuts with which the magazine paid Ring is not known, but they were big enough to elicit much of the best writing of his last years. Ross was willing to take whatever Ring sent his way, and as a result Ring relaxed as he had not with any single publication since he left the *Tribune.* For the first time in his career he began to write large amounts of autobiographical material, and much of it was superb. "Jersey City Gendermerie, Je T'Aime" told of his unpleasant encounters with the police of that city while covering the Dempsey-Carpentier fight. "X-Ray" contained the account of his marathon drinking spree at the Friars Club. "Br'er Rabbit Ball" was both an attack on the jackrabbit ball and a reminiscence about his own early baseball days. "Asleep on the Deep" described his horrendous experience covering the 1920 America's Cup. In "A Reporter in Bed," he remembered "when my father used to take me from Niles, Mich. (Central Standard Time), to Chicago to see ball games." Eventually, in the last sixteen months of his life, Ring would enter an entirely new career in the pages of *The New Yorker,* as the author of radio criticism.

His health certainly would have been best served had he stuck to his desk writing pieces for *The New Yorker* and *Collier's,* but in October, 1930, the theater beckoned again and Ring answered the call. It came, specifically, from his old adversary Flo Ziegfeld, who was well past his glory days but was attempting to revive them with a musical called *Smiles.* The stars of the show were Marilyn Miller and Fred and Adele Astaire; Ziegfeld offered Ring "an unheard of advance royalty" if he would do the lyrics for a couple of numbers Vincent Youmans was writing for the Astaires. Ring said he would, and headed for Boston, where the show was trying out. There he set himself up at the Touraine Hotel and began work. But it seemed that every time he finished a song, he would get a phone call from Ziegfeld or Youmans or someone else, sending him off in an entirely different direction: "The song in the second act is out. Gotta have another one—same tune, but this time she's happy and cheerful, see? Light, romantic stuff." He fled the madness of the hotel for a restful weekend in South Byfield with Ellis' sister Jane and her husband, Francis Kitchell, and a visit with Jim and Bill at Andover—but when he returned to Boston, matters were even worse. Ziegfeld told him that the show needed a "light" duet for Marilyn Miller and Fred Astaire, and a "smart" number to open the first act, but Youmans was feuding with Ziegfeld and sulking, with the result that he refused to get out of bed. When at last Ring managed to get him to the piano, around ten o'clock Sunday night, their labors were promptly interrupted by a dyeing factory across the street, which chose that moment to erupt in flames. Youmans insisted on watching the spectacle to its conclusion, which did not arrive until after midnight—and at that point "several girls and the nutty dance director came in and made it a party." At two in the morning Ring gave up and went to bed.

The next afternoon—Ring finally got Youmans out of bed at noon—Ziegfeld said to forget the duet and get the opening number set. Ring wrote a lyric and then went to the show that evening; at the end of the first act "the curtain came down on confusion and I went back stage and found the three stars in hysterics." Back in his room he decided to knock himself out with paraldehyde and called room service for some orange juice to wash it down with. But when he answered the door he found the dance director "with a confidential, weeping jag." His visitor announced that "I'm going to tell you some tragic incidents in my life, and tomorrow I know

I'll be sorry I told them to you," to which Ring replied, "I know I will, too." At last the orange juice appeared; Ring mixed it with the paraldehyde, drank it, and "fell asleep with the dance director still telling me tragic incidents."

Ring escaped Boston the next night, but he did not escape Ziegfeld. He got back to his current residence, the Hotel Elysée, early Wednesday morning, and had been there only three hours when Ziegfeld called: he had changed his mind and wanted the Astaire-Miller duet. Ring managed to find "an old tune" in Youmans' New York office and to get to work on that, but then Ziegfeld called again—this time at one-thirty Thursday morning— with the news that Marilyn Miller refused to go on unless she had a song to replace something called "Carry On, Keep Smiling." Would Ring write a replacement? Yes, he said, but he had no tune. So Youmans, the point of total insanity drawing nearer and nearer, called Ring at noon on Saturday and sang him one, via long distance, "and while I respect him as a composer I would never recommend him to Gatti-Casazza as a thrush."

Somehow Ring managed to get the thing written—by now the original two lyrics he was supposed to write had multiplied to a dozen—but that was not the end of his problems. Astaire was unhappy with the opening ensemble "because it required the presence of some Park Avenue women on one side of the stage and he didn't want anybody to appear dressed up before his entrance." Then, too, there was the matter of the telegrams from Ziegfeld. Flo was infamous for the garrulity and internal confusion of his wires, and they were made even worse by the pixilated condition of *Smiles*. He sent this one to Ring on November 7:

MY DEAR RING I DO NOT WANT YOU TO FEEL THAT I AM IMPOSING ON YOU BECAUSE OUR AGREEMENT READS THAT YOU ARE TO WRITE THE NECESSARY LYRICS THE LYRIC I AM MOST ANXIOUS TO GET AND FIT TO THE TUNE OF THE SALVATION ARMY GIRL MARILYN MILLER THE LYRIC TO CONVEY AS NEAR AS POSSIBLE WHAT HUGH MORTON LYRIC IN THE BELLE OF NEW YORK DOES I HAVE JUST BEEN TALKING TO WAYBURN & WE WANT TO SPEND SUNDAY IN ROUTINE THE SHOW PUTTING IN THE NEW SALVATION ARMY NUMBER THE MILLER GREGORY DUET THE NEW FINALE MARILYN MILLER FRENCH PANTOMIME & THERE WILL BE NOT TIME TO GET TO THE OPENING OR THE BOWERY SCENE I DONT THINK WE WILL GET TO THAT BEFORE WEDNESDAY I WILL KEEP

YOU POSTED BUT PLEASE RUSH ME THE SALVATION ARMY GIRL LYRIC
FOR THAT IS VITAL TO THE SHOW IN THE MEANTIME I AM WORKING
OUT THE COSTUMES FOR THE OPENING OF THE BOWERY

ZIEGFELD

To what surely must have been the astonishment of everyone connected with it, *Smiles* staggered into the Ziegfeld Theater and opened there on November 16. Six of Ring's twelve lyrics, or parts thereof, were used.

The show ran sixty-three performances before dying a well-deserved death. It was the end of Ring's Broadway career and a peculiar way to go but, as he put it, "I wouldn't have missed it because it was so ludicrous."

RING WAS ABLE TO SMILE about *Smiles,* but daily it seemed there was less in life for him to laugh about. The exertions involved in catering to Ziegfeld's bizarre whims had done his health no good. Times were hard financially, too. The Depression was more than a year old, and at last it was beginning to penetrate the previously impervious bulwark of the Lardner bank account; the market for Ring's work was shrinking, and so were the fees for what he was able to sell. Ring and Ellis were able to keep John at the Sorbonne, where he had gone after becoming disenchanted with Harvard, and Bill and Jim at Andover, but they were scrimping to do so. Ellis' spirits were flagging, try though she might to keep them up, and a December 14, 1930, letter to John revealed her pain:

Dad is not very well. I get so discouraged about him. He is eating and trying to take care of himself but the results are not what they should be.

This seems to be a gloomy letter but I am not really gloomy. I could tell you several other bright and cheerful things—such as the fact that the Bank of United States failed with $3000.00 of Miss Feldman's in its clutches (there is hope of getting it back, see! I am cheerful); that the unemployed are still selling apples all over the place; that there isn't but one good show in town etc. But I won't. I'll just tell you one thing—that I love you and miss you and hope you get the box I sent you—though there isn't much in it.

Ring's condition continued to deteriorate. Before Christmas he and the doctor decided he would be best off in Doctors Hospital, on East End Avenue between Eighty-seventh and Eighty-eighth streets; he was assigned a room with a view of the river and, Ellis told John, "he gets fresh air and sunshine and can watch the boats, which he likes"—and suddenly there is a mental picture of this man, so alive with energy and feeling, lying in bed at the age of forty-five, idly watching boats.

The problem was that Ring seemed unable to stick to a sensible diet at home and that he could not sleep; he thought the stay in the hospital would force him to eat a regular, nutritious diet, and the doctor hoped experiments would reveal the source of the insomnia. Presumably at some point it occurred to the physician that years of heavy drink had made Ring rely on alcohol as a sedative—that it was something he used to help himself make it through the night—and that withdrawal from it for medical reasons was exacerbating the insomnia. But by this point it was a choice between the lesser of two evils, booze and insomnia, and for his overall health if not his peace of mind, the booze had to go.

Ring managed to get to the Elysée for Christmas with Ellis, Jim, Bill and David. He came in the morning and stayed for mid-day dinner and they had, Ellis told John, "quite a successful time—though times being hard with us, as with everybody, we were not as extravagant with presents as usual." Ellis, who had been used throughout her life to comfort and ease if not downright luxury, was being very brave about her straitened circumstances, but she found it hard, and when the chance arose to accept a free vacation she acquiesced to it with embarrassment. She wrote John in January from the Flamingo in Miami Beach:

> Here we all are at Miami Beach—three Lardners and two Rices, I mean the other way around. It is so cold I can't count. We have been here four days and it has been rainy and cold all six of them. None of us wanted to come here anyway but with a cottage and meals free for three weeks we couldn't afford to refuse. . . .
>
> We went over to Miami last night to the social event of the season—a movie opening of a picture called *Illicit*. We were guests of honor and what with flashlights and all the trimmings you would have thought it was a Ziegfeld opening. The hotels are all practically empty and all the hotel people are facing bankruptcy.

In all likelihood Ring and Ellis had visited Miami Beach and other resorts at the courtesy of the house for years; Ring was a celebrity, and hotelkeepers hoped that his presence would attract other guests in the heated competition of the Florida boom years. In those days the free ticket was just another by-product of Ring's success. Now they needed it, and that hurt.

In her letter to John, Ellis mentioned that "I think Dad is going to do the newspaper work I wrote you about in spite of my protests—but who ever did pay any attention to my protests." She was referring to an offer he had received from the combined forces of the Bell Syndicate and the Chicago Tribune-New York Daily News Syndicate to do a six-times-weekly newspaper column. After the failure of "Ring's Side" two years earlier one would think Ring would have had enough, but this offer had two attractive aspects: the syndicate wanted only about a hundred words a day, and it offered a minimum guarantee of $750 a week. That was a grand wage in the Depression and for what seemed very little work; Ring, notwithstanding Ellis' eminently sensible objections, accepted it.

The first column was dated February 1, 1931. As usual when he began a column, Ring got off to a nervous start. This is the first "Night Letter from Ring Lardner," in its inconsiderable entirety:

> Miami, Fla., Feb. 1.—My dear public: If I come out and see my shadow tomorrow noon you will probably get a message from me every day for the next six weeks or more and if I don't come out and see my shadow the same thing will happen. I will leave the government in the capable hands of Will Rogers and confine myself to things with which I am more familiar, such as what is going on in society and different hospitals. I trust Mr. Rogers will not think I am intruding. After all we are both Indians only he ain't been scalped.
>
> RING LARDNER

The "Night Letter" was a pathetic attempt to locate, much less recapture, a spark of the old Ring. Each of the little columns was a pale imitation of a single item in the "Wake" nearly two decades ago, and the subscribing newspapers knew it:

> East Hampton, L.I., Feb. 27—Subscribers to these dispatches have complained bitterly in the last few days that they were too short. Well, brothers, the editor of the magazines for which I used to write so erotically will tell you that I never crowded out any advertising matter and brevity was my slogan. Furthermore, the public is hard to please. I undestand that Mr. Coolidge has never been scolded for this fault.

That was the entire column.

Yet who could fairly criticize Ring for the paucity of these efforts? He was brutally ill, he had almost no energy; he was forced by financial obligations to work when he needed rest, to try to be funny when laughter hurt. On top of all that, he was ordered by his doctor to take refuge in the clear air of Tucson, at the Desert Sanatorium. He left in early March, and while he was en route there was yet another stroke of ill fortune. A heavy storm swept up the Atlantic coast and hit East Hampton full force. It was so strong, and the surf so fierce, that the one-hundred-foot lawn between the Lardner and Rice houses and the ocean was flushed away. Both residences were left hanging precariously over a newly formed cliff. The furniture was removed from both houses on March 4, but it was feared that another heavy sea would topple them into the ocean. That, at least, did not happen. Under Ellis' management, the Lardners were able to move their house back from the water—as the Rices did too—and save it. The cost was about $10,000.

Ring, in a March 6 letter to Jim and Bill thanking them for a wire "congratulating me on my twentieth birthday," managed to make light of the latest disaster, for their sake at least; he referred to "our houseboat in East Hampton." He also made the best he could of his new residence: "This joint is 2,500 feet up in the air and surrounded by mountains that are close to a mile high. It is is the middle of the desert and has queer flora and fauna. Among the latter are coyotes and the funniest looking rabbits I ever saw. The full grown ones are as big as ponies and have ears that are at least half a foot long. They say that one of the female patients saw one and thought it was a deer." He wrote to John in a similar spirit: "All my neighbors have radios (a recent invention) and just as I get ready for my sleeping potion at nine P.M. (Mountain Time) they turn on Amos and Andy, who, as you may not know, are now broadcasting twice per night. I can't hear them distinctly and wouldn't mind if I could, but what wrecks me is the kind of laughter with which one of said neighbors greets their gags. It is like the bleat of the coyotes in the surrounding mountains and keeps me awake long after it is hushed for the night." When his friend Millie Luthy, Kate Rice's sister, wrote from Georgia to offer her services as a nurse, he replied: "I would give a fabulous sum (if I had it) for one like you, even though I know you would try to force those funny drinks on me. The nurses here are a hard-boiled lot and evidently selected for their ugliness. There is only one pretty one and she, strange to say, is from Georgia. Stranger to say, she is incompetent." There can be no doubt that he was a long way down emotionally in this hard and lonely hour, that he was melancholy and depleted; yet he refused to take anyone else down with him, and to the very end he kept up his courage and his humor, giving the gift of laughter to those he loved.

He attempted also, though with less success, to keep his readers laughing. In the "Night Letter" he explained why he was in Tucson:

> Tucson, Ariz., March 19—I have just been informed of a report going the rounds in New York that I left home and sought shelter among these here hills because the Lambs Club was about to ask Gov. Roosevelt to institute a city-wide inquiry into my conduct of my office. The chief flaw in this story is that I have no office and my conduct has always been an open book, especially at the Lambs Club. The reason for my abrupt departure from Long Island and invasion of this cozy nook was to get out of the way of that Ole Davil Atlantic Ocean, which was chasing me all over the Eastern coast. If I were embarrassed by inquiries, this is the last place in the world I would visit. I have never been so thoroughly investigated in my life, and if any of my admirers want an autographed photograph of me turned inside out, I am ready to supply same.

A few days later he wrote in the column that "the reformatory in which I am serving a term" had a large sedan that made regular trips to Tucson and that he and other "trusties" had made the journey in hopes of killing time. The motto for the vehicle, he suggested, was "Nothing but coughs in a carload." On at least one occasion the ennui of the sanatorium got too great and he fled it, visiting an old friend from Chicago who now lived in Phoenix. He was shaky and ill at ease; but he had managed to find a bottle of whiskey, and after taking his first drinks in several months, relaxed and was good company. But that excursion was not sufficient to make the desert tolerable, and by early April he had quit it, heading back to New York with a stopover in Niles along the way.

He arrived in New York to find the "Night Letter" a dying proposition. The weekly guarantee had been cut to $500, and the column had become strictly a sports-page filler. Ring had descended to the desperate expedient of resurrecting Jack Keefe in the person of Willis Clough, a rookie pitcher from Tucson trying to catch on with the Pirates; his letters to a friend back home were hopelessly derivative, and they marked the demise of the column. The last Willis Clough letter, and the last "Night Letter," was dated April 24, 1931. Now, once and for all, Ring's career as a newspaper journalist was over.

He presided over its termination from a bed in Doctors Hospital, to which he had returned shortly after his arrival in New York; he was to be there throughout the summer. "Dad is here," Ellis told John in late April, "—not much better I am afraid—and I have been motoring up in Pennsylvania and other places trying to find the right place for him to spend the summer," but the search proved academic. As if Ring's illness were not difficulty enough for Ellis, Bill took a nasty tumble from a dormitory window at Andover, breaking his right arm; he was in Massachusetts General Hospital, flat on his back "with his arm stretched out at right angles to his body and weights attached." Small wonder that Ellis plaintively asked John: "Do you think anything nice will ever happen to the Lardners again?"

Now the burden was all on her, and it got heavier and heavier. More and more her letters to the boys were preoccupied with financial matters as she tried to keep the family above water. Here is a sampling of those letters, written between March, 1931, and May, 1932:

> The Lardners are pretty well broke nowadays what with Dad's expenses in Arizona and all we have to sink in East Hampton so try to make the money stretch as far as possible.
>
> . . .
>
> Make the money go as far as possible because we are under terrific expense in saving the house and money is very scarce.
>
> . . .
>
> I can probably send you another $10.00. . . . However money is tighter than it has ever been in the Lardner family just now.
>
> . . .
>
> Dad's checks come in every two weeks (from the *Sat. Eve. Post*) I have to make each one go as far as possible to get caught up.
>
> . . .

Have you enough money to last you a while longer? Dad is still in the hospital and has not been able yet to finish a story he expected to have finished ten days ago. I have to make a large payment on the East Hampton mortgage the first of May which will leave us broke till he gets a check for the yet unfinished story. If you can hold out I will make it up to you later.

Ring was indeed working, his physical condition notwithstanding, and all things considered he was working remarkably well. In February he had felt it necessary to give a self-deprecatory answer to a query from Max Perkins about the possibility of a new book of stories (". . . I'm not averaging more than four short stories a year. None of the recent ones has been anything to boast of and I'm afraid there won't be enough decent ones to print by fall. Maybe I'll get more energetic or inspired or something in the next few months"), but he actually had little to be ashamed of and much to be proud of. Perhaps it had something to do with his discomfort, but for the first time in his carrer he was writing regularly about himself; he was writing autobiographical pieces, and he was also making at least a small dent in the shell he put around himself when he faced the world outside.

The most significant step in the latter direction was a piece published in *Cosmopolitan* in May, 1931. Called "Insomnia," it was his penultimate article for this publication, and perhaps his best. It is difficult to categorize: it is part stream of consciousness, part nostalgic reminiscence, part short story. It opens with Ring lying in bed: "It's only ten o'clock, but I hardly slept at all last night and I ought to make up for it. I won't read. I'll turn off the light and not think about anything. Just go to sleep and stay asleep till breakfast-time." But he cannot sleep; his past, present and future whirl through his mind. He remembers a Bert Williams lyric:

> *Money is de root of evil, no matter where you happen*
> *to go,*
> *But nobody's got any objection to de root, now ain't*
> *dat so?*
> *You know how it is with money, how it makes you feel*
> *at ease;*
> *De world puts on a big broad smile, and your friends*
> *is as thick as bees.*

"The only way I can earn money," he thinks, "is by writing short stories. Short! By the time I'm half through with one, it's a serial to me." But obligations press in on him: ". . . I'll have to work tomorrow. There's the insurance and notes and interest on mortgages— But I won't get to sleep that way. I mustn't think about anything at all, or at least, I must think about something that doesn't make any difference." He tries counting sheep: "Sheckard, Evers, Schulte, Chance, Steinfeldt, Hofman, Tinker, Kling, Brown," but that just leads him more deeply into the past, into a memory of a girl named Lucy Faulkner with whom he was infatuated when he was sixteen:

> . . . One night in July, four of us young men about town drank a great many steins of Meusel's singing beer and, at half past two in the morning, decided to go serenading. Our first stop was in front of the Faulkners'. The night was hot and all the windows were open.
>
> Lucy, blessed with youth, slept through the horrible din. Not so her parents. From one of the windows came the sound of a voice that could talk even louder than we could sing and we decided to go somewhere else while a cloud still obscured the moon and kept our features secret.
>
> Well, they never knew who three of us were. But they knew who one of us was. And yet there is said to be a tendency on the part of medium-sized men to envy tall men their height.
>
> Lucy was given some orders at breakfast and obeyed them until she was safely engaged to a decent fella. There was no ban put on the other members of the quartet though I swear my bass had been barely audible against their deafening whoops.

The reminiscence leaves him more widely awake than ever: "It must be after midnight. I'll just turn the light on and look at my watch. Eight minutes after ten. Good Lord!" Reading might help, but it might also keep him awake, and he has to sleep so he can work the next day: "Ten or eleven high balls or a shot in the arm would be an effective lullaby. The trouble is, the more habits you have, the more you have to snap out of. At that, I guess too much coffee is as bad as too much Scotch. Too much of anything is bad; even too much sleep." He tries to make his mind "a perfect blank"; maybe at least he can think up a story idea while he drifts off to sleep. An idea does come to him—a story about a talented young man with a weakness for drink who marries a lovely heiress, falls off the wagon, and engages in risky financial manipulations that lead to a trick ending—but after developing it in his mind he loses interest in it:

> Now that's off my mind and I ought to be able to go to sleep. Maybe if I'd exercise every day— But golf is the only exercise I like and I can't make any money at it. I can't beat anybody. I might if I played three or four times a week.
>
> I'll turn on the light now and see what time it is. Eleven-eighteen. Well, at least it's after eleven. What I should do is get up and make a few notes for my story. And smoke one cigaret, just one. After that, I'll come right back to bed and turn off the light and not think of anything. That's the only way to go to sleep. Not thinking about anything at all.

Considering the author, it is an extraordinary piece of writing. For Ring to assert himself so directly in his work was, up to then, unheard of, yet in this piece he very deliberately bared the state of his own mind. He described in detail the night thoughts that kept him awake, the tangle of memory and worry and self-amusement and planning which is the insomniac's nocturnal diet. And that is why the piece is notable, apart from its autobiographical elements: it is a superb rendering of insomnia, which can be appreciatively read with no knowledge of Ring or his situation. It is a total mystery that the piece was not included in any of the three Lardner collections issued in the first four decades after his death; not until Matthew Bruccoli and Richard Layman put together *Some Champions* was it made available to today's readers.

The other autobiographical work in which Ring was engaged during this period was a series of six articles, later expanded to eight, for the *Saturday Evening Post*. They were his first work for that publication since March, 1922—he had stopped writing for the *Post* after it turned down "The Golden Honeymoon"—and the reunion was on all counts a happy one. These pieces, which are also included in *Some Champions*, amount to an autobiography of his early years. The titles of the first six are "Meet Mr. Howley," "Me, Boy Scout," "Caught in the Draft," "Heap Big Chief," "Chicago's Beau Monde" and "Alias James Clarkson"; the two that appeared later are "Eckie" and "Some Champions." They cover Ring's career from his joining the South Bend *Times* in 1906 to the Dempsey-Tunney fight in 1926. They leave some large gaps in the story and they raise some unanswered questions, but they are crucial source material for any study of Ring's life; they are quoted extensively in the sections here on baseball, Niles and Ring's journalistic apprenticeship. But they are much more than fertile territory for biographers. They are wonderful pieces of reminiscence, imbued with sunniness and gentle self-mockery and nostalgia of the most appealing sort; they are excursions into the past, not exploitations of it. They show, without embarrassment, the tenderness that Ring usually tried to disguise; they are pieces that must be called—again, without embarrassment—heart-warming.

They were written over a difficult summer and fall. In September, Ellis wrote to Max Perkins: "Ring is not much better and is still unable to do any work. I am rather discouraged about him because he worries so over not being able to work that the rest he is having does not do him the good it should." She also responded to the news that Zelda, after a breakdown, was in Perkins' words "well again": "I have been so sorry about Zelda and do hope they are still getting along all right. Do you suppose there is anyone left in the world who is well physically, mentally *and financially?*" Yet Ring rose above the circumstances and pressed on. In that same month, in fact, the *New York Times* reported that "the condition of Ring W. Lardner, author and playwright, was reported to have improved during the last three days" and the report was accurate. By early October, Ring was out of the hospital. He and Ellis took an apartment at 25 East End Avenue, at the corner of Eightieth Street, which they kept for nearly a year. He was glad to be out, as he told Jim: "The meals, nursing and beds here are much better than at the hospital. The day I left there, Dr. Erdman, who works about five days a year, performed three operations, while fifteen doctors stood around and watched. His total fees were $25,000. One was the removal, manicuring and replacement of the stomach of a seventy-year-old rake, who is now able to go out and get cock-eyed again." Ring did not say whether he envied the gentleman.

In that same letter Ring said that "I am awaiting a telephonic yes or no from Harold Lloyd as to whether I am to write the dialogue (not the scenario) for his new picture at an outrageous (not for Hollywood) price." The proposal never materialized, but the enthusiasm with which he wrote about it to Jim suggests that his frame of mind was remarkably good after the long hard year behind him. His mood certainly was improved by having John back from Paris and at work, soon to be joined by his nephew Dick Tobin, on the *Herald Tribune*. He followed John's work avidly and with enormous pride—with good reason, since at the age of nineteen John was already on the way to a career that would be the stuff of New York journalistic legend. "John has had five stories in the paper in the last three days," Ring told Jim, "and one of them each day carried a by-line. We are all swollen up like my ankles."

The reference was to swelling in his lower extremities, part of the price he was now paying for years of poor diet and alcoholism. There were other changes as well: ". . . I have a new habit; I grow very, very sleepy every evening at dinner, stay up after dinner, nodding and blinking, until your mother scolds me into bed, fall asleep at eleven, awake at 1:30, all through with sleep, and spend the balance of the night working or writing mash notes such as this. The habit has persisted ever since I left the hospital, where a kindly nurse gave me shots in the arm to insure a night's sleep (thereby also insuring herself one), but I have a hunch that during the coming week, I shall return to something near normalcy and then my correspondents (God help them!) will wonder why they aren't even receiving postcards from me any more."

Ring actually delighted in writing letters to the boys. Now that they were old enough to be treated in effect as equals—David, at twelve, being the obvious exception—he leaped at the chance to do so. His letters to Jim and Bill were often long, chatty and full of vigorous opinion. Jim, in particular, was the recipient of extensive epistles on college football, in which Ring's interest never lagged:

> In war or in football, the first lesson is that the attack is more wearisome than the defense. In football it is a cardinal principle that the team just scored against shall kick off and *not* receive the kick-off. If the man who kicks off is any good, the receiving team will have eighty yards to go for a touchdown. When it is finally forced to punt, your team will have the ball close to midfield. The blunder occurred only once at Harvard. At Notre Dame, it happened *three times*. And listen to this: when Notre Dame was leading 14 to 6, the broadcaster said, "Notre Dame *wisely* elected to receive the kick-off so it would be in possession of the ball," and on the first play after Notre Dame had received the kick-off, Schwartz threw a sixty-

yard pass from his own twenty-yard line, and the pass was knocked down. He proceeded to get himself into a hole and finally made a bad punt that gave U.S.C. its chance for a second touchdown. Even at that, Notre Dame could have kept its one-point advantage if it had slowed up its play. What is a five-yard delay penalty compared with defeat. Or three or four penalties?

Oh, well, let's not get mad. But I did get mad yesterday afternoon. Your mother, John and I were listening to both games over the radio (a new invention) and I am afraid your mother heard some "putrid" language.

Ring's loyalty to Notre Dame dated back to his boyhood and never lost its intensity. Grant Rice, writing in his memoirs about the first Dempsey-Tunney fight, said: "Ring Lardner . . . had two passions, Notre Dame and Dempsey. Both represented the West."

On one occasion that fall Ring's interest in football and his friendship with Rice paid a dividend for Dick Tobin, who was in his senior year at Ann Arbor and editor of the *Michigan Daily*. Rice's All-American team was published every December in *Collier's* and was awaited with breathless excitement at those schools —Michigan most emphatically among them—where football was taken seriously. Rice told Ring whom he had put on his 1931 team, and Ring relayed the information to Tobin by letter: ". . . may God have mercy on my soul and yours if you breathe a word even to your mother-in-law. There is nothing, however, to prevent you from digging up pictures for use at the proper time." Tobin got the message: he prepared a layout for the *Daily* and published it on December 18, the day *Collier's* went on sale.

Ring's strange sleeping habits were good for his correspondence but bad for his health in more ways than one. That winter Ellis told Jim about a disturbing episode: "Dad's room practically burned up—well anyway, springs, mattress, bedding, one pair of window curtains and one window frame—cause thought to be lighted cigarette either dropped or blown off the ash tray—as there was a hurricane blowing. I'll never know how Dad escaped being burned as he slept until the bedding was nearly gone." In light of Ring's past, the inference to be quickly drawn is that he had fallen into a drunken stupor, but Ring Lardner, Jr., believes not: ". . . I think he was unconscious from paraldehyde or chloroform, both of which he took for insomnia, rather than liquor, though the occurrence is a common one in alcoholism." He further believes that none of his father's hospital stays "in the last three years of his life was the result of a drinking bout," since by then the physical consequences of drinking were so dire that Ring had to all intents and purposes given it up.

Not, perhaps, totally. Alcohol or some other drug seems the only reasonable explanation for one of the more curious and amusing incidents of this stage of Ring's life. In the fall of 1931 he gave an interview to George Britt of the New York *World-Telegram* in which he made an emphatic literary pronouncement that was singularly uncharacteristic of his public statements: "You can say this for me, without any qualification or dread of a kickback. The prince of all bad writers is Dreiser. He takes a big subject. But so far as handling it and writing it—why, one of my children could do better. I should love to see him and Willa Cather take the same plot and handle it, each in his own way. Just for the demonstration."

An alert writer at *Time* magazine spotted the interview, pulled out the quote and made it the centerpiece of a "People" item that began: "Slowly recovering from pernicious anemia *Ring W. Lardner* was removed from hospital to home. In the course of a press interview, said he: . . ." Burton Rascoe, in turn, picked up the *Time* paragraph and criticized Ring in his column in the New York *Sun*. Ring clearly was upset, for he quickly wrote Rascoe a letter that was courteous but blunt:

> I believe that a great many football fatalities might be averted by the adoption of the following rule:
> "Before commenting on a statement attributed to an interviewee, the commentator must seek out the interviewee and ascertain what the latter did say. Penalty—Loss of two paragraphs."

What most concerned Ring, however, was Dreiser's feelings. On January 2, 1932, he wrote him a long letter attempting to "get the record straight." He explained that he and Britt had been talking about *An American Tragedy* "and, to the best of my recollection, I said that no one, not even one of my children, could fail to make a human story like that uninteresting [*sic*], and the more simply it was written, the better." He emphasized that "I am not in the habit of knocking writers (God help us all), and particularly novelists, whose patience and energy are far beyond any good traits I can claim." He noted that *Time* had said he was suffering from a disease that "aside from glanders, . . . is the only ailment I haven't had." And in a postscript he left no doubt as to how much distress the matter was causing him: "I seem to have made quite a fuss over what you doubtless consider nothing, but I do want you to know that I'm not a knocker."

Dreiser received the unsolicited apology with Olympian benevolence. "Courtesy and good will shine through your explanation," he wrote, and he even went so far as to credit Ring with the invention of a felicitous phrase: "None the less, the phrase 'the prince of bad writers' cheers me. It is glistering irony that ought to be said if for no more than the saying. I am grateful to you for having called my attention to it." The trouble was that Ring declined to accept authorship: ". . . whether or not 'The prince of bad writers' is glistering irony, it isn't my irony and I cannot accept the credit for somebody else's glistering."

That threatened to complicate matters still further, but Dreiser took Ring off the hook by stressing his full acceptance of "your assurance of innocence" and issuing a somewhat self-consciously good-fellowish invitation: "Anyhow you are a neighbor of mine. If you would trouble to walk so far we might drown this slight misunderstanding in hard likker. The mystic hour of five usually finds me turning from composition to speculation & drink." Ring felt duty-bound to decline, and not merely because Dreiser had gotten his New York geography confused:

> I want to ask for a rain check on that hard likker invitation. It is my misfortune that when I get started I seem to find it necessary to fight it out on those lines if it takes all winter, and having spent a whole year among the unemployed, I must now work until I am somewhere near even.
>
> We would be neighbors if I lived in West End Avenue, but as it is, the whole width of Manhattan divides us. I am within wading distance of Welfare Island and hope to finish there.
>
> Sincerely,
>
> Ring Lardner
> The Prince of Doltish Drinkers

That ended the correspondence between Ring and Dreiser, but it did not satisfy Ring's determination to get the facts straight. In a 1932 book called *Dreiser and the Land of the Free*, Dorothy Dudley Harvey claimed that "Ring Lardner, asked by a producer to serve with Dreiser and Robert Frost as one of three founders of an American theatre for only American plays, refused on the ground that Dreiser was both ridiculous and immoral." He wrote her that the explanation "must be that either some one was impersonating me or I was under an anaesthetic." He continued: "Never consciously did I speak of Mr. Dreiser's work as repellent to me in any way. I have never met him, but have had some very pleasant (to me) correspondence with him. I have undoubtedly expressed the opinion, in private conversation, that I thought his style awkward. Otherwise I admire him intensely for the drama of his writing and its wealth of detail."

What is of greatest interest in this elaborate wriggling that Ring engaged in is the very length he was willing to go to correct what he recognized as an injurious remark. His evaluation of Dreiser as a writer is of no special importance, but his determination not to hurt Dreiser's feelings is a sign of his essential decency and generosity of spirit. Whether his tongue was loosened by drink or drugs during the interview, the odds are that what he said was fairly close to what he was quoted as saying; his letters to Dreiser are not especially persuasive in their efforts to pass off "the prince of bad writers" as a misquotation. But he deeply regretted any hurt that he might have unwittingly done his fellow writer and fellow Chicagoan, and his letters convey nothing so much as this dogged insistence on healing the wounds.

There was certainly nothing contrived in Ring's begging off a drinking invitation on the grounds that he had to work. Times were hard and his medical bills were continuing to place heavy demands on the family treasury. Matters looked especially bleak by March: Ring was back in the hospital and Ellis had given up the East End Avenue apartment, returning to the Crowden. So it came as a windfall when the *Saturday Evening Post* offered Ring $4,000 apiece for short stories—the figure was extraordinary for the Depression, and presumably reflected a favorable reaction among the magazine's readers to the autobiographical pieces.

Sick though he was, much though his doctors wanted him to have complete rest, Ring pressed ahead in the hospital to give the *Post* its money's worth. He produced six stories, which were published between April 23 and September 5; in March, 1933, they were collected by Scribner's and published in book form as *Lose with a Smile*.

The stories consist of a correspondence between Danny Warner, a marginal Brooklyn outfielder, and Jessie Graham, his girl friend in Centralia, Illinois, They have much the same sunny nostalgia as the autobiographical pieces; they are amusing and diverting; they are written with Ring's customary professionalism and command of his material. They are derivative of much of his own work—notably *You Know Me Al*, "Some Like Them Cold" and *June Moon*—but not so much that they are incapable of standing on their own merits. Minor though it is, the book can be viewed as a summation of much of Ring's career, and in that respect it is much like William Faulkner's *The Reivers*—another exercise in amiable nostalgia which, though short of the writer's best work, somehow typifies it.

Ring probably decided to put Danny Warner with the Dodgers —then known as the Robins—because of the presence on that team of Casey Stengel as "a kind of asst mgr and coach of the club." He had followed Stengel's career with interest and amusement since its beginning with Brooklyn in 1912; Stengel was a hustling ballplayer who met Ring's prime requirement of playing to his full potential, and he had a quirky sense of humor in which Ring obviously delighted. In *Lose with a Smile* Stengel plays exactly the same role that Kid Gleason did in *You Know Me Al*: He is assigned to the rookie narrator *in loco parentis*: ". . . he kind of took me in toe the 1st day we beggin to work out and now mgr Carey has got him rooming with me so it looks like there taking a special interest in how I get a long as Stengel sets and talks to me by the hr about the fine points of the game that comes up durn practice."

Like Jack Keefe, Danny Warner is composed of equal amounts of ignorance and egocentricity; he is the butt of endless practical jokes and teasing, he fancies himself a Romeo and falls for every passing skirt, and he talks a better game than he plays. He also regards himself as a singer of no mean skills, and he shows off his skills so frequently that his teammates call him "Rudy" in honor of Rudy Vallée. In his letters to Jessie he is a paragon of romantic inconsistency, in one moment urging marriage and the next trying to wiggle out of it. He tells her about "Vivian the phone girl," and when Vivian sends him a couple of snapshots of herself in a bathing suit, he sends one along to Jessie "so as you can see what she looks like." Jessie's reply is worthy of Mabelle Gillespie in

"Some Like Them Cold": "Thanks for sending me Miss Duane's picture am sending it back though you did not say so but am afraid Mamma might see it. She is very pretty and I dont blame you, but cant understand why she wants to work for the phone company when she could surely obtain a position in some musical hall where the women come out bare."

Much of Danny's correspondence is taken up with his efforts to establish himself as a lyricist. That gave Ring a chance to continue the popular-song parodies he had begun in *June Moon*. This is one of Danny's more notable efforts:

> *Life is just a game of base ball*
> *If you get in it*
> *you want to win it*
> *But some times the mgr dont give you a chance*
> *But leave you setting there on the bench.*
> *Just give me a left handers fast ball*
> *and I will sock it a mile*
> *And if the empire calls it a foul*
> *laugh and dont say your blind as a owl*
> *Life is just a game of base ball*
> *so win or lose with a smile.*

Stengel takes Danny to a music publisher who suggests that he write "a torch song or a ballot like My Mom." He comes up with one he refers to as "the Dad Song":

> *My dad I love him.*
> *My mom she loves him.*
> *My sister Edna she loves him my dad.*
> *He is a wonder*
> *Will live to be a hundred*
> *And never made a blunder my dad.*
> *When I was a lad*
> *If I act it bad mom would scold me.*
> *Then I would go to him*
> *And on his lower limbs he would hold me.*
> *Theys no one greater*
> *Then my old pater.*
> *He is my alma mater my pop.*

Stengel, Danny explains to Jessie, "made me put Ednas name in and told me about alma mater but he says the line about never made a blunder dont ring true. Alma mater and pater are greek and means the same thing." His songwriting and baseball-playing efforts reach the same results: his lyrics are not published and he is sent down to Jersey City. But that is just fine with Jessie ("Well Danny it just happens that Jersey City has always been one of my favorite towns because papa has talked about it so much and what an interesting town it is there on the river seeing the big boats come in and go out") and she heads East with matrimony on her mind.

It is a predictable ending, but Ring by this point was scarcely interested in pulling surprises on his editors or readers. He knew exactly what the *Post* wanted from these stories, and he delivered it with unapologetic professionalism. Yet he managed to maintain a level of excellence that was high enough for him to keep his self-respect intact. He knew the stories were honorable work, and he was hurt when the *Post* seemed to feel otherwise. In August, writing to Max Perkins to inquire whether the stories might be made into a book, he described his feelings:

> Early in the summer, one of the *Post*'s associate editors wrote me such a tactless letter, suggesting that the new series of baseball letters be brought to a conclusion in two more installments that I, then in a low mental condition, thought the whole series must be pretty bad though I had felt quite proud of it when I had sent it in. His words were chosen with a view, I guess, to lessening the shock of the premature conclusion, whereas if he had written frankly, saying that the *Post* could no longer afford to pay the very liberal price it had set on the series, I would have understood perfectly and thought little of it. For a time I banished the idea of offering the series to you for a book, but later on I reread some of the acceptance letters from Lorimer and other *Post* editors, as well as a bunch of nice "fan mail," and got steamed up about it again. I honestly don't know how the present interest in baseball compares with the past, but I presume that Brooklyn's recent spurt . . . ought to be a help. Please read the whole thing when you feel strong and healthy and tell me what you think.

Perkins agreed to publish the stories "on the basis of a 10% royalty on the first five thousand." He wrote kindly about the book in his letters to Ring, but he was no longer trying to cajole him into writing something longer. Not merely did he know by now that he would get no novel from Ring; he also knew that Ring was sick and depressed, and that he needed cheering up. The last year of their correspondence would deal with his efforts to advance Ring as much money as possible—which was not much—and to brighten his spirits with chatter and free books.

Those spirits had indeed sunk. In May, Ring apologized to a correspondent for a delayed response, explaining that "I have not been able to write or even dictate"; evidently the effort of doing the initial Danny Warner stories had been so great that he was depleted by it, and depressed by his inability to work. Yet he had not lost his indomitable determination, and in June was at work on the last major writing project of his life, his assignment as radio critic for *The New Yorker*.

Only a few years before, it would have been preposterous to imagine Ring listening to a radio, much less writing a serious column about radio broadcasting. It was a newfangled invention that offended his fundamental conservatism, and when he finally bought one, it was as a present for the boys that he regarded as a noisy intruder in a household that presumably was already noisy enough. But illness changed all that. More and more of his time was spent in a hospital bed; frequently he was too tired to read; he no longer could attend shows or concerts. He could listen to the radio, however, and he soon came to delight in it at its best and despise it at its worst. He had sharp opinions about what he heard and he had the journalist's urge to write what he thought, so he suggested to Harold Ross that he do a radio column and Ross quickly accepted. The first of the pieces was published on June 18, 1932, and the last on August 26, 1933. There are twenty-five of them in all, an impressive number, and many of them are Ring at or near his best. They include his bizarre campaign against "pornography," but they also contain the best parody he ever wrote and a number of revealing disclosures about himself. Most of the names of performers and the call letters of stations are obviously now out of date—that is why Max Perkins thought a collection of the pieces would be impractical—but the quality of the writing and thinking is high. Overall, they show Ring as a person concerned with questions of taste, artistic quality and slick sentimentality. He was a close listener and a lively writer.

Ring's first piece was datelined, as most of its successors were, "NO VISITORS, N.Y.," and explained what he was up to:

To the Editor:

In this Home for Disabled World Series Experts they give you a *New Yorker* once a week as part of the treatment for insomnia, and in skimming over recent issues I have noticed that the publication always contains reviews of new productions on stage and screen, but hardly ever a mention of dat new davil radio which is largely responsible for the fact that there ain't more stage and screen productions to review. Now I am not a charity patient in this institution, and a man named Mr. Pest who works down in the front office claims I owe him three weeks' back rental for a concrete mattress, so I wonder how would it be if you took me on your staff as a radio critic and perhaps you would pay enough to keep Mr. Pest from running a temperature and I could do the work in my spare time which begins at seven o'clock in the morning and ends at eight the following forenoon.

You will want to know what are my qualifications. Well, for the last two months I have been a faithful listen-inner, leaving the thing run day and night with the exception of a few minutes during and after breakfast . . . , and am fortunate in having as special night nurse a hopeless radio addict who knows such inside details as that the Street Singer's real name ain't Arthur Tracy, that Bing Crosby resents Russ Columbo, or vice versa—in fact, everything save (and this is a universal feminine failing) who wrote what song and why.

In that first column Ring left no doubt that he would write forthrightly about the demigods and demigoddesses of the airwaves. He was especially offended by the singer Morton Downey, who was billed as a tenor but sounded to Ring like a soprano, and "his sweet-toned side-kick, Tony Wons, on whom I was developing such a crush that I started to write him a special cheer:

> " 'Tony Wons! Tony Twice!
> Holy, jumping—' "

Ring would have completed the cheer, he wrote, but "the flash came that he was temporarily through and at present reciting Edgar Guest's poetry to an audience of helpless Wisconsin pickerel."

To other singers Ring could be quite kind. Though he phrased his praise humorously, he liked Bing Crosby and Russ Columbo, and analyzed their styles with considerable perceptivity: "It is just about a toss-up between the lads in the matter of putting lyrics across. . . . Russ can outsyllable Bing over a distance; for example, Russ, without apparent effort, sings, 'Nahight shall be fa-fa-filled with mee-hew-hew-sic, na-hight shall be fa-fa-filled with luh-uh-uh-uhv,' or whatever it is. Bing, however, is unbeatable in a sprint, such as the word 'you,' which he nurses along till you would swear it was spelled yoohoohoohoohoohoo-oo. When Russ repeats a refrain whose lyric bores him, he usually substitutes dee-dee-dee-dum, whereas, in like circumstances, Bing uses da-dee-dee-do. Occasionally Bing even improves the song a lot by whistling eight or twelve or sixteen bars."

Ring's interest in lyrics led him to pay particular attention to those of Cole Porter's song "Night and Day," and to write a superb parody of them. ". . . it seems to me that in this number," he wrote, "Mr. Porter not only makes a monkey of his contemporaries but shows up [W. S.] Gilbert himself as a seventh-rate Gertrude Stein, and he does it all with one couplet, held back till late in the refrain and then delivered as a final, convincing sock in the ear, an ear already flopping from the sheer magnificence of the lines that have preceded." The couplet:

> *Night and day under the hide of me*
> *There's an Oh, such a hungry yearning, burning inside*
> *of me.*

Ring then modestly announced that he had undertaken "an attempt at improvement," though he confessed that he had had assistance: ". . . my own kiddies were left out of the conference, most of them being away at school, taking a course in cuts. A little niece of mine, Miss Ann (Jake the Barber) Tobin of Niles, Mich., was the only party consulted. We agreed that there must be no needless trifling with the impeccable five words—'There's an Oh, such a'—which begin the second line; they should stand as written except where our rhythm made changes imperative." He then offered what was allegedly Ann's effort, "with spelling corrected by uncle":

> *Night and day under the rind of me*
> *There's an Oh, such a zeal for spooning, ru'ning the*
> *mind of me.*

In Ann's second contribution, according to Ring, "she lapses into the patois":

> Night and day under the peel o' me
> There's a hert that will dree if ye think aucht but a'
>   weel o' me.

Then, at last, "a few by uncle himself":

> Night and day under the fleece of me
> There's an Oh, such a flaming furneth burneth the grease
>   of me.

> Night and day under the bark of me
> There's an Oh, such a mob of microbes making a park
>   of me.

> Night and day under my dermis, dear,
> There's a spot just as hot as coffee kept in a thermos,
>   dear.

> Night and day under my cuticle
> There's a love all for you so true it never would do
>   to kill.

> Night and day under my tegument
> There's a voice telling me I'm he, the good little egg
>   you meant.

This same interest in lyrics, however, also led Ring into his one-man campaign to rid the airwaves of what he considered smut. It began on July 30, 1932, in a piece called "Allie Bobs Oop Again." "I say these things," he acknowledged, "at the risk of being considered queasy and a prude. At the risk and in the hope." He then went to attack as "suggestive" and "immoral" the lyrics of a song called "As You Desire Me." Of Allie Wrubel's lyrics he observed: ". . . I doubt not but that it tempt many young girls and young men—particularly if it be true that Prohibition has started them drinking—to call up and find out whether their Destiny is home and if so, will he or she let come what may. I know that when I heard M. Downey blare it for the first time, I grabbed my hat and Mother Hubbard and told Nurse I was going out."

Having to listen to such "suggestive" lyrics in the presence of a nurse doubtless increased Ring's discomfort, but it was genuine and deep. On November 19 he was even more vigorous, in a piece called "Lyricists Strike Pay Dirt." By now his sense of humor had just about deserted him: "This department has been laughed at for prudishness, but has not been laughed out of it. This department has reached a stage where it almost doesn't mind a song whose only faults are inanity, terrible rhyming, and glaring infractions of simple grammatical rules. Unfortunately, the 'lyricists,' the singers, and the whimperers are not satisfied with that comparatively harmless kind. They are polluting the once-pure air of Golly's great out-of-doors with a gas barrage of the most suggestive songs ever conceived, published, and plugged in one year. . . . I don't like indecency in song or story, and sex appeal employed for financial gain in this manner makes me madder than anything except fruit salad." For the assistance of readers looking for "something educational to read aloud or sing to the baby," he listed several titles he found especially salacious. Here, in all their lurid squalor, are some of them: "I'll Never Have to Dream Again," "You're Telling Me," "Good Night, My Lady Love," "Let's Put Out the Lights and Go to Sleep," "Love Me Tonight," "I'm Yours Tonight," "And So to Bed," "Please," "Take Me in Your Arms," "Here Lies Love," "What Did I Get in Return?" "Ain'tcha Kinda Sorry Now?" and "Thrill Me!"

He never completely let go of the campaign, and he certainly never admitted defeat. He referred to himself whimsically as "this red-hot crusader against immorality," but to him the crusade itself was a serious business. He really did believe that the lyrics of popular songs had the power to corrupt, and he believed that the radio censors should be vigorously at work. He was both old-fashioned and Middle Western, and he held strongly to the conservatism and prudery he had learned as a boy. The postwar upheaval in sexual attitudes and behavior touched him only to the extent that he became all the more conservative, all the more priggish.

What Ring wanted from the radio, as from the theater, was good clean entertainment. It was absolutely appropriate that the last of his radio columns, titled "The Perfect Radio Program," was about the broadcast that would be "my own idea of perfection." Many of the names long ago vanished from memory, but a few selections from his program outline speak for themselves:

Ohman and Arden, on two pianos, without an orchestra, playing
early Gershwin or recent Schwartz or both. . . .

Jack Pearl and Cliff Hall, doing the kind of stuff they did before
they got to doing the kind of stuff they got to doing. . . .

Bing Crosby in a couple of his specials, with a good orchestra
such as Denny's or Goodman's or Lopez's to fight it out with. . . .

Ruth Etting, queen of the torchers, singing, perhaps, Irving Berlin's old "Remember." . . .

Eddie Cantor and James Wallington in dialogue written by
someone who knows how to write for Eddie Cantor. . . .

A fellow named Lawrence Tibbett, singing in English a song
called "Bendemeer's Stream," or in Italian, the aria in *Traviata*
which Daddy sings to the gal and which is virtually a complete
history of France up to the time the United States entered the
world war. . . .

Al Jolson in anything he wants to sing or say. . . .

And the remaining eight minutes to the best band in the land,
Marse Paul's [Whiteman's], who, I hope, will give me all the
"Music in the Air" and other recent Kern he can crowd into that
all too brief period.

Ring's tastes were still those of the boy who idolized Bert Williams. Though in many respect he was a skeptic and a cynic, he
could still be entertained only by that which was at heart innocent,
lyrical, unpretentious. He loved the comedy of vaudeville, the
harmonies of the barbershop, and the songs of the prewar years.
He saw no reason why the standards that prevailed in vaudeville
could not also apply in radio, and he viewed the march toward liber-
ation with profound distaste.

DOING THE COLUMN probably helped Ring stay alive, for in the
last year of his life it was his only source of real professional satisfaction. Outside of that work, and the continuing joy he found
in his family and friends, life by the fall of 1932 was bleak. He
was a dying man, and the likelihood is that he knew as much by
now. His financial obligations were becoming more and more
burdensome, yet at the same time he was finding it increasingly
difficult not merely to find work, but to do it when he could get
it.

Leaving aside such questions as the mortgage on the house at
East Hampton, tuition for his sons, and daily living expenses,

there was the continuing, and worsening, matter of Ring's medical expenses. There is on file at the Newberry Library in Chicago depressing evidence of what a dominant concern hospital and doctor's bills had by this point become. It is an envelope containing fifteen checks written by Ellis to Doctors Hospital and Dr. Cornelius John Tyson, Ring's personal physician; the checks were written between August 11, 1931, and December 16, 1932. The total expenditure was $5,947.22—in terms of late-seventies spending power, about $25,000. If Ring had not gotten the work for the *Saturday Evening Post* during the same period, there is simply no telling how desperate his financial position might have become.

Yet Ellis' letters to the boys from early 1932 until Ring's death a year and a half later show greater concern for his mental and physical condition than for the bank account. That may reflect her successful effort to manage family finances, but it clearly also reflects her own growing knowledge that her husband at best could work only sporadically and at worst might soon be dead. In March, 1932, she was almost casual in telling Jim: "Dad is at the hospital again but only for a week or so. I think the rest will do him good." In November she was less optimistic: "I am trying to economize as Dad has had a hard siege this time and I don't want him to work for some time. He is still at the hospital and is on a milk diet which seems to be the only thing he can keep down." By January she plainly knew the full dimensions of Ring's problems: "Dr. Tyson has been very dissatisfied because Dad did not improve and wants him to get away from New York. The chief obstacle to this has been financial but we have borrowed on his life insurance and have things arranged now. We are going to California by boat on the 4th of Feb." The trip meant she and Ring would have to miss seeing the boys over spring vacation, but life for the Lardners was full of such deprivations: "I do hate dreadfully to miss being with you all for vacation but Dad's health is the most important thing now and we will all have to make the best of it."

The trip was made possible, Ellis told John (who in turn told Dick Tobin), because an unidentified "rich man who admires Dad" had loaned them $10,000. Apparently Ellis believed the story for the rest of her life, but it was just that—a mere story. The $10,000 had been raised by Kate Rice, who was painfully aware of both the Lardners' severe financial circumstances and their refusal to accept anything that gave the appearance of charity. So she came to their aid by a circuitous route. First she approached the Wheelers and other friends of Ring and Ellis, and from them she got the money. Then she went to Ring and Ellis with an elaborate tale about the "rich man"—she seems to have identified him as someone who had made a fortune off Coca-Cola stock—whose admiration for Ring was such that he wanted to express it with the loan, knowing that times were hard for them. Kate had a genius for carrying off such tales, and she succeeded in persuading Ring and Ellis to accept the money. It was a "loan" in name only, and there is no record of its being repaid.

The day before he and Ellis sailed for California, Ring wrote a letter to Max Perkins. It was the last letter he was to write in a correspondence that had lasted nearly a decade, and it showed both how gruesome his professional circumstances had become and how he managed to hang on to his sense of humor:

> Some day I will probably realize that there is a depression. I wouldn't have asked you for any advance [on Lose with a Smile] if I hadn't got into a sudden jam. The doctor and I decided that my place was the desert for a while, and not having done any real work since June, I was obliged to borrow money. I borrowed less than I needed, figuring I would sell a story to the Post. Once I wrote a complete story, "Alibi Ike," between 2 P.M. and midnight, with an hour off for dinner. This last one was begun in July and finished ten days ago, and the Post turned it down just as promptly as it had accepted "Ike." Since then, Bill Lengel has said it was great (but he ain't the boss), Collier's has rejected it as too long and tenuous (it runs 7,500 words) and Mencken has told me it was too much of a domestica symphonica or something for the Mercury. Mr. Graeve (Delineator), suggested, perhaps sarcastically, by Mencken, now has it as a week-end guest and I have asked him to return it to my brother on the Times, who will give it to some poor author's agent to peddle. I have always scoffed at agents, but I am leaving tomorrow morning for La Quinta, California, to be gone till the money has disappeared. I have promised the doctor that I won't work on anything but a play which George Kaufman has been waiting for me to start for three years; of course I will have to cheat a little, but I can't cheat much.
>
> What I started to say is that the fiction story (really not bad, just as really not a Pulitzer Prize winner) has a great many local stops to make, and if I were to stay here and wait till the last possible purchaser has said no, I would die of jitters. Your loan has

made it possible for me to get out of here before I am committed to Bellevue, and I am truly grateful. I won't need the "other" two hundred, and if the sale of *Lose with a Smile* never totals the amount you have advanced me, I will see to it that you don't lose. The agent can make the rounds much quicker than I could from 3,500 miles away.

This letter doesn't seem to be properly constructed or quite clear. This is a symptom of my state of mind, but the fact that I can laugh at the succession of turn-downs of a story which everybody but the *Post* has had a kind word for but no inclination to buy, makes me hopeful for the future. Maybe some day I can write a piece about the story's Cook's Tour—it is the first one I ever wrote that wasn't accepted by the first or second publication to which it was offered, and that either means go West old man or quit writing fiction or both.

Thanks again, and honestly I want you to forget the "balance" because I can easily get along without it.

It is a harsh measure of how far Ring had fallen that the amount of money for which he was so profusely thanking Perkins was $300; his original request had been for $500. Perkins helped as best as his firm's own financial situation would permit. Even if he could no longer reasonably expect that Scribner's would make any immediate return on its investment in Ring, Max had too much respect for him to let him go unaided. As he put it soon after Ring's death, in answer to a suggestion from Scott Fitzgerald that a posthumous collection be published: "If we did it, I would want to get a really fine picture of Ring. I would almost rather have it after the Great Neck days because, although he did look terribly gaunt and ill, even before he went to the hospital, I do think that you could see what a remarkable creature he was then."

The short story whose travels so vexed and frustrated Ring was called "Poodle." To his considerable surprise it was accepted by *Delineator*, a women's magazine, for a fee of $750, which was a sharp comedown from his previous rates but good enough now. It is a story about a young man facing Depression job difficulties. It was not published until the following January, more than three months after his death; in fact, of the nine Lardner stories that eventually would be published, none appeared in his lifetime.

Ring and Ellis set sail for La Quinta on February 4, making

the passage through the Panama Canal. In a letter to the boys he told them "that boat-ride was okeh after a storm had laid Mrs. Lardner low the second day out, and would have been more okeh if my feet, unshod since last April, had not swole to elephantine proportions." The Canal left him singularly unmoved: "It is little more than a glorified Sault St. Marie, and when you have seen one lock, you have seen two locks, or my hair." The trip also gave him an opportunity to spring a couple of his better puns on the boys. The first involved the deck steward, who saw Ring reading *Van Loon's Geography* and remarked that it was "a great book": "Being a democratic fellow, I replied to him and observed that one of my sons had given it to me for Christmas. 'Isn't that queer, Mr. Lardner?' he said. 'Because I was planning to give it to one of my sons for his birthday. That's a paradox.' So now you know what a paradox is. Personally I had always thought it meant two physicians in consultation, or just two physicians." The other involved Warner Baxter, a movie star of particularly distinguished good looks: "Baxter was a shipmate and walked twelve or fourteen laps around the deck each evening before dinner. This is called the Baxter Mile. Mrs. L. pretended she didn't know who he was, but she followed him with her eyes every time we turned our Baxter."

They reached San Diego at midday on the 17th, and "stayed there long enough to permit the madam and myself to go to the races at Agua Caliente." A half-mile walk uphill was not precisely what Ring's feet needed, and he didn't do much at the track, either; he made a hunch bet on a horse named June Moon—he bet it across the board, ignoring Ellis' suggestion that he should only bet it to show because *June Moon* had been a show—"and the show money barely paid for itself."

From there they went to La Quinta, a desert resort not far from Palm Springs. If Ring had expected peace and rest, instead he got the lively company that doubtless was what he really wanted. Norman Foster, the erstwhile *June Moon* star, arrived with his wife, Claudette Colbert, and so did other friends and new acquaintances. In another letter to the boys, he described the general state of turmoil:

Vincent Lawrence, former playwright, now Hollywood scenarist, and Dorothy Speare, novelist, entered our hut uninvited and wanted to know whether I had an idea for Harold Lloyd. Mr. Lawrence wrote his last picture, *Movie Crazy* or something; it was a flop, so Harold came back to him for more. I said I had no idea, but would try to think of one. I did think of one and it was a good one; so I thought and so Mr. Lawrence thought. However, it is well-known (to me, at least) that I can't tell things in synopsis form, or any other form—I have to write them out at length.

Well, a week ago Sunday came. The Rices were visiting us, I think. So was Phillips Holmes. So, suddenly, were Mr. Lawrence, Miss Speare, Harold Lloyd, Sam Harris, some anonymous girl, and Louella O. Parsons and her latest husband, one Dr. Martin, who says he knew me in Chicago, which he did not if I am any judge. Louella also said that when she was working on the Chicago *Tribune*, she and I used to go on lots of parties together, which we did not if I am any judge.

Harold was all steamed up over my having an idea, and I was all steamed up over the same miracle, but when he and I managed to get a moment alone, it developed that all he wanted was the bare idea, told in two paragraphs (as he phrased it) and his scenarists and gag men would attend to the rest. Well, to be modest, this was like sending Babe Ruth to bat and letting him stand there till the umpire had called one ball, then taking him out and substituting a good hitter. Harold and I both steamed down as quickly as he had up—and I had wasted two or three days of thinking and writing. Unless, as Mr. Lawrence suggests, Buster Keaton can be caught sober and interested in the same idea, which remains, yours sincerely, a good idea, reeking with gags that Harold and his gag men wouldn't think of in a month of Sundays, and if there were a month of Sundays, you could all call yourselves Little Orphan Annie.

Early in his stay at La Quinta, Ring got in a great deal of rest and sleep, but the combination of frequent visitors and his urge to work soon had him stirring again. He wrote Jean Dixon: "I pass my sitting-up hours at the typewriter, working on the first act of a future Pulitzer winner. George [Kaufman] has promised that if I can complete an act and a half that are worth tearing to bits, he will come out here and do the tearing. I have a secret hunch that he wants to anyway, so perhaps the act and ½ need not be as good as normally."

The play, on which he worked sporadically for the rest of his

life, was to be an interlocking study of alcoholism and family relationships. He wrote a total of one act plus one scene, too little
to tell whether a collaboration with Kaufman could have whipped
the material into a presentable play. It is evident from what he
managed to get done that the play, like the stories of the last years,
was intended to be serious. The central and most sympathetic
character is twenty-five-year-old John Haskell, an ex-alcoholic who
has married into a wealthy and strait-laced family. He works for the
family business and is soon deliberately put to a test of his business acumen. He recognizes it as nothing but a test, and responds
to it by falling off the wagon and making a dramatic exit.

The plot, as Donald Elder has pointed out, owes something to
one of Ring's early third-person short stories, "The Facts." It
even more closely follows the outline of the unwritten story
dreamed up in "Insomnia," and in its preoccupation with alcohol it
is similar to a 1931 story called "Cured!," which comes closer than
anything else Ring wrote to confronting the sources of his own
drinking habits. In the twenties, when he was still consuming large
amounts of alcohol on extended binges, Ring tended to refer to
alcohol in his writing jokingly, if at all. Now that he was effectively through with it and paying the physical consequences of
years of intemperance, he tended to look at alcoholism ruefully
but sympathetically. John Haskell is far and away the most agree-
able person in the unfinished play, and Ring is not disapproving
in the least when he is driven back to drink by his self-righteous
in-laws. Similarly, in "Cured!," Ring is clearly on the side of Dick
Streeter, the cartoonist with "a great thirst for all kinds of in-
toxicating beverages excepting light wines and beer." There are
obvious memories of Ring's periods on the wagon in the story:
"Undoubtedly the host and hostess and the other guests found him
pretty tedious when he had had a few too many. Just as undoubtedly it was no great fun to sit around, cold sober, from half-past
seven to midnight, and listen to anecdotes, jokes and stories which
he had heard a score of times before, and watch the normal husbands and wives toy with one highball for an hour, enough time
for him to have got rid of nearly a dozen." By contrast, there is
the pleasure Streeter finds in the company of his buddies at Mike
Clayton's speakeasy "who, queerly enough, found him bright and
amusing when he was drinking, and a bore when he wasn't." It
didn't matter that the whiskey was rotgut:

To Dick it didn't taste any worse than what he had been wont to consume at private houses, and the advantages of Clayton's over them were several: You didn't have to be polite to anybody; you could stop or interrupt an anecdote or story any time you felt like it without causing resentment; you could order all the refreshments you wanted and no one would suggest by word or look that you were taking too many; you could play bridge (though he seldom cared to), and the penalty for a revoke was general laughter instead of points against you above the line, a fishy look from your partner and uncouth expressions of triumph from your opponents; you could sing with singers who didn't think bass was the melody pitched an octave below, or that tenor was alto.

Ring knew in his last years that alcohol was killing him, and he looked back on it with obvious mixed feelings. Dick Streeter in "Cured!" ends up returning to his wife and making an effort to go on the wagon; given the choice, he would rather have her than booze. But the writing in the paragraph above is affectionately reminiscent, and both passages are transparently autobiographical. A psychiatrist asks Streeter why he drinks, and the reply is: "Because I like to, and because it gives me a kind of mental release." Ring missed both the pleasure and the relaxation of drinking, not to mention the escape it provided from the various pains offered by life.

After a few weeks in La Quinta the physical pain had at least receded significantly, and Ring began to look eastward restlessly. He was getting more sleep, his general appearance was improved, and though his strength was limited, he felt he had to get back to work in a concentrated way; as Ellis wrote John, "he thinks he has to be back in New York to earn a living." He may, too, have gotten some of his old feistiness back after reading an article in a local paper about Clifton Fadiman's March 22 analysis of his work in the *Nation*. The story ran under the headline: "Hate Is Back of Ring Lardner's Fun; He Hates His Characters, Says Writer." The piece quoted Fadiman as saying: "Lardner . . . is the police dog of American fiction, except that his hatred is not the product of mere crabbedness but of an eye that sees too deep." Ring sent the clipping off to a friend to whom he had also sent a five-dollar bill: "The other enclosure (the one without Lincoln's picture) will tell you the latest news of me—and *to* me. The writer is evidently a fellow from whom you simply can't keep a secret.

But I do resent being called police dog, or dog of any kind." He signed the letter "A Born Hater." He regarded that as comment enough on an interpretation of his work that he plainly thought was preposterous, but the piece was the first serious consideration he had had in some time and it probably helped stir up his creative energies.

Ring and Ellis headed homeward by train in mid-April, stopping en route for various family reunions in Niles and Detroit; now Ring was beginning his farewells. Back in New York they stayed at the Biltmore until early May, when Ellis went out to open the East Hampton house and Ring moved to the Hotel Edison, at Broadway and Forty-seventh Street; he was in Room 1935, Ellis advised Jim, "where no one can reach him through any means of communications unless he knows the room number." He had gone incommunicado with just about everyone except the family and George Kaufman, with whom he conferred about the play in progress.

Ellis, meanwhile, was beginning the process of adjusting to a new life at East Hampton. The "help" consisted of Albert Mayer, a chauffeur-gardener of intense loyalty to her and Ring, and two Scandinavian women. Otherwise she was on her own, and she pitched in to help keep the household in good working order. She made new curtains for the dining room, started a garden and helped Albert put up the summer screens. Her principal difficulty was loneliness: Ring and John were in New York, Jim was at Harvard, Bill at Princeton and David at Andover. The Rices came out occasionally on weekends, but the rest of the time "I have a hard time keeping busy and out of mischief all by myself."

She got all the company she needed in June, when the three younger sons began their summer vacations and Ring came home. He was chauffeured by Albert, and accompanied by John and by Dick Tobin, who had graduated from Michigan and joined the *Herald Tribune*. Tobin tried to keep a conversation going, but Ring was obviously restless and distracted; he tried to be polite company but finally said, "My God, this a long ride." Tobin later recalled it as the day "when Ring went out to East Hampton to die."

His moods, like his strength, came and went. He had a room and a sleeping porch upstairs, and some days he simply stayed there; other times he would join the rest of the family for dinner, such of it as he could eat. Grant and Kate Rice, and any of Kate's sisters who might be visiting, were the only company he would see; he was reluctant to leave the house even to visit them, for "I am terrified while I am there because . . . they are never safe from invasion by people I used to like, but who, in my old age, make me jittery." He preferred to play bridge with the boys and Ellis and Kate, to amuse two kittens (whom he named "The Wedding Guest" and "The Loud Bassoon"), to listen to the radio, to read (mostly nonfiction, with an emphasis on history) and to work as his health allowed.

For a time it looked as if he indeed might be making a recovery, and when John's vacation came along in July "all the Lardners excepting the old man" piled into the family's gargantuan sixteen-cylinder Cadillac and headed to Chicago for the "Century of Progress" World's Fair. "They intend to see how cheaply they can make the trip," Ring told Kate's sister Millie Luthy, "for two reasons—the 'fun' of the experiment and the fact that they won't have anything to spend." Ring's health was regarded as good enough for him to be left in care of the servants, and he had the added bonus of visits from Millie's daughter. He had an abiding love for all the Hollises of Americus, Georgia, as he told Millie: "Your child is really beautiful and has the Hollis charm, which means that hundreds of members of my poor sex will suffer. If I didn't know how bored and uncomfortable it would make her, I would insist on her visiting me at least once a day, just so I could hear her talk and see her close up. I have refrained from demanding her presence (except once) because I don't want her to think of me as an old pest, but lots of times I watch and admire her from my cell without interfering with her normal activities."

The radio pieces continued to appear—there were two in June, one in July, two in August—but Ring's total absence from his former social life and his generally dilatory correspondence worried his friends. On August 4 Max Perkins wrote Scott Fitzgerald: "I think things are bad with Ring. I hate to inquire. He is at Easthampton and nobody ever seems to see him." Scott's reaction seems to have been that something needed to be done to perk up both his spirits and his self-confidence. Sometime in late August or early September he called John at the *Herald Tribune* to ask if a new collection of Ring's work might be assembled: Scott, with his own author's vanity, apparently thought that the publication of a new book would be a tonic for Ring. He seems to have had something in mind that would include the autobiographical pieces from the *Saturday Evening Post* as well as a variety of other uncollected material relating to his life. Whatever it was he suggested by phone, John followed up the conversation with an enthusiastic letter:

> Maybe you couldn't gather over the trans-Atlantic Baltimore–N.Y. phone what a swell idea I think it is to have the stuff published. I'm a sucker for the guy's work and always have been, although I can't talk about it very well over the phone or any other way. I don't want to let my part in this thing stop at getting the pieces together and sending them to you, which I'll do as soon as I can. If there's anything else I can do, to coin a phrase, I want to do it.

Scott, acting for the first time since the fall of 1924 in his self-created role of Ring's editor and advocate, pressed right on. The next question was who should edit the volume. "I can't do it myself because I am engrossed in work of my own," he told John, "and it seems to me the next best person would be Gilbert Seldes, consequently I called Gilbert Seldes and he said he would like to do the work. . . . Gilbert is one of the very first journalists in America and if anyone can make an interesting and consecutive narrative of it he can do it, and, to repeat, he is interested in the idea." Scott closed the letter, which was dated September 20, with an affectionate insult for Ring: "With regards to (Scarface) (Half-Wit) (Red Nose) (Pure Insult) Lardner. . . ."

Seldes did indeed take on the project, which was published by Scribner's as *First and Last* in June, 1934. That was too late to accomplish the bolstering mission Scott had in mind for Ring's morale, but it was very good for his reputation. *First and Last* is a volume of Ring's miscellaneous work, edited under a guiding principle Seldes described in his preface:

> This collection of Ring Lardner's non-fiction was begun before his death, so it is not, in any sense, a "memorial volume." The original intention, which has been followed, was to select from his early and later writings, those pieces which were not entirely transient and to group them in such a way as to give them the cohesion which, in the case of a writer of daily and weekly articles, is sometimes lost because of the variety of subjects and changes of treatment. In Lardner's case the central thing was the temper of

his mind. Except for a few pieces written under pressure, everything he wrote expressed that temper perfectly. The guiding principle in this selection was that every item should be "good Lardner." The flexibility of his newspaper writing, compared with his fiction, gave room for some minor excursions, and some of these have been included.

The book does not follow the sharply autobiographical directions that Scott seems to have had in mind, but it admirably fulfills Seldes' program. The table of contents includes "Symptoms of Being 35" and "The Young Immigrunts," and a dozen headings under which shorter pieces are assembled; among these are "Men and Women," "A Variety of Sports," "On Politics," "Children and Dogs," "A Few Parodies" and "Short Plays." The selection shows that Seldes had gone deeply into Ring's work, resurrected such splendid examples of it as the "three little kittens" coverage of the 1922 World Series, the Dempsey-Firpo pieces, the 1921 Disarmament Conference series, several of the radio pieces, the "Weekly Letter" that spoofed name-dropping diarists, the Winchell parody from the *Morning Telegraph*, and a fine selection of nonsense plays. Much of Ring's best journalism might have gone unresurrected for years had Seldes not applied such diligence to this assignment; and much of the Lardner material that later found its way into various collections and anthologies was first collected between hard covers in this book.

One of the pieces in *First and Last* is a parody called "Odds Bodkins." It appeared in *The New Yorker* of October 7, 1933, and it is the last piece of nonfiction Ring wrote. It almost certainly was composed in the last month of his life. The subject of the parody was a New York columnist named O. O. McIntyre, long since deservedly forgotten, who came from Gallipolis, Ohio, but had acquired and embellished all the affectations of the urban sophisticate. To readers in the more than five hundred newspapers that took the column, McIntyre described his life in breathlessly self-serving terms, painting a portrait of New York that bore no resemblance to reality but that made him seem, to small-town rubes from coast to coast, the very epitome of big-city wit and fashion. It is not in the least bit necessary to have read a single one of his columns in order to appreciate how devastating and funny Ring's parody was—and still is:

Diary of a Modern New Yorker: Up and out five hours before dawn, and by scooter to the Hermitage Hotel, where the big Seminole Indian Chef, Gwladys, cooked me a flagon of my favorite breakfast dish, beet root and wrestler's knees. Hallooed to Lily Langtry and we fell to arguing over the origin of the word "breakfast," she contending that it was a combination of "break" and "fast," derived from a horse's instructions to a starter in a six-furlong race, and I maintaining that it was five furlongs. . . .

Home for a moment to slit my mail and found invitations from Mussolini, Joan Blondell, Joan Crawford, Joan of Arc, President Buchanan, Joe Walcott, and Louisa M. Alcott. Then answered a pleasant long-distance call from Gwladys, the little French chef in the Café des Trois Outfielders in Sydney, her voice as plain as if she were in Melbourne. She had heard I had a cold, she said, and was worried. It was gratifying to hear her whimpers of relief when I assured her the crisis was past. . . .

Thingumabobs: I once motored around Vienna for two weeks thinking it was Vienna. When I chided the native jehu, Gwladys, he chirped: "Why, Massa, Ah done thought you knowed it was Vienna all de time." . . . If they did not wear identical hats, Jack Dempsey and Connie Bennett could easily pass for sisters. . . . One-word description of Franklin Delano Roosevelt—President. . . . There is something about the name Babe Ruth that suggests rare old Dresden filigree work. . . .

Thoughts while strolling: Damon Runyon's feet. Kate Smith, a small-town girl who became nationwide in a big city. Rosemond Pinchot and Theodore Dreiser could pass for twins. . . .

Mention of the name Rex Cole invariably reminds me of the Mother Goose rhyme, "Old King Cole," etc., and I never can figure out why. . . . Damon Runyon's feet. . . . If you saw only the left side of Theodore Dreiser's face you would swear it was the right side of Ruth Etting's. . . . One-word description of the Vice-President—Garner.

Insomniacs: While writing a novel "Red" (Socker) Lewis never eats anything but alphabet soup. . . . Theodore Dreiser always dresses according to the time of day he happens to be writing about. Thus, if an incident in one of his novels takes place in the morning, he puts on a morning coat; if at noon, a noon coat, etc. . . . There is a striking resemblance between Damon Runyon's feet and Ethel Merman. . . . Theodore Dreiser often arises at 2 A.M. and walks for two hours steadily. I once knew a fellow in Gallipolis who often arose at 6 P.M., and at 2 A.M. walked for two hours unsteadily. No dog as cunning as the Cubanola Glide.

That Ring could have written a piece as clever and amusing as this in the physical condition he by now was in is a tribute to his courageous determination to keep his spirits, and those of others, as high as possible. Certainly he had his times of depression; they were more frequent and of greater duration as his illness worsened and his physical pain intensified; sometimes he sat by himself, sobbing, his face in his hands. Yet the very existence of "Odds Bodkins," and the radio pieces, and the stories that were published posthumously, is the most striking evidence available to rebut the widespread assumption that he was willing himself toward death in the final years, that his alleged disgust with mankind and himself had produced in him a suicidal urge. All these pieces—not to mention all the letters he wrote to cheer people up, and the love he gave his family and friends—are proof positive that to the very end his dominant urge was to survive and to create, even if he knew that the pain of survival was great and that most of the writing that he did was but a pale reflection of what he had once been able to do.

By the time Ellis and the boys returned from Chicago, the end was near. Miss Feldman, who had left the family's service in 1930 and gone to work in New York as a registered nurse, came for a visit and, alarmed by Ring's condition, insisted upon staying on to nurse him. His weakness was such that one night he passed out on the toilet seat; Ellis had to summon Jim and Bill to carry him back to bed.

On the evening of September 24 Ring played bridge with Ellis, Kate Rice and Bill, who was the only one of the children still at home; John was at work in New York, and Jim and David were back at their respective schools. It was a quiet game, with Kate and Bill teamed against Ellis and Ring; he was by now very thin and had to sit in a heavily padded chair for such comfort as he could find. The next morning the family awoke to find that Ring had suffered a heart attack and was unconscious. Dr. Tyson was on the way out for a regular checkup; when he arrived he examined Ring and explained that there was nothing he could do. Ring remained unconscious and died later that day.

It was September 25, 1933. Ring was forty-eight years old.

Epilogue

R ING WAS CREMATED, WITHOUT CEREMONY, ON SEPTEMBER 28 at the Fresh Pond Crematory in Middle Village, Queens; he had many years before abandoned the religion of his boyhood, and it would have been squarely within character for him to have insisted that any religious service after his death would be both hypocritical and irrelevant. No friends were present, but they had already been heard from. An avalanche of condolences had descended on East Hampton. There were wires from Jerome Kern, George Kaufman, Nan and Walter Huston, William Harridge, Eddie Collins, George M. Cohan, Ben Bernie, Ellen and Irving Berlin, Bugs Baer, Will Rogers, Damon Runyon, Frank Sullivan, Herbert Swope, William L. Veeck and Fielding Yost. At the World Series, in Washington, a Western Union Press Message sheet was tacked onto the press-box bulletin board. A clumsily typed message at the top read: "Dear Mrs. Lardner: All of us in the press box at the world series newspapermen and old players some who were friends of Ring and others who knew him only by his fine work and reputation would like you to know that we sympathize deeply with you and your boys in your great loss which is our loss too." The signatures below included those of Walter Johnson, J. Honus Wagner, Frank Frisch, Westbrook Pegler, Tom Meany and Ford Frick. Pegler sent the sheet to Ellis with an explanatory note:

> During the world series in Washington some of the men who knew Ring, started a round-robin along the press rows, meaning to get the signatures of all the newspaper and baseball people who were present. But the press-box was peopled to a large extent by lawyers, bootleggers, advertisers and all such extraneous types and it was difficult to restrict our testimonial to those who belonged. It got lost once when some autograph hunter would have swiped it for the signatures of Walter Johnson, Hans Wagner, Casey

Stengel and some others and even so, on the last day, some one did make off with a second page of names from the bulletin board when it was too late to gather them again. So many friends of Ring are missing from the roll who signed the other sheet.

We were going to wire it to you but I thought you might prefer to have it as it is.

Ring's long illness had prepared Ellis for his death, and she handled it with grace, though hardly without visible evidence of grief. She was kept busy at first replying to messages of condolence, and then in early October went to New York to find a place to live; she did not want to stay on in the house where Ring had died, and in any event the East Hampton place was simply too big for her. She took a small furnished apartment at the Carlyle, 35 East Seventy-sixth Street: living room, bedroom and serving pantry. She moved there in the middle of the month.

Ellis was tired. She was tired of the emotional strain of seven years of Ring's illness and almost as many years of steadily declining financial security; she was also tired of parties and excitement and glamour and all the accouterments of life at the top. Almost immediately she settled into a semireclusive existence, seeing only the boys, other relatives, and such close friends as Kate and Grant Rice. She read, did puzzles and kept to herself. One of her sisters, Dorothy Kitchell, visited her in the Carlyle and reported to another sister, Ruby Hendry, that she was "certainly lonely" but that she was bearing up well:

> Ellis doesn't seem to me to be brooding unduly and she has Ring's picture on her dresser and talks of him and of the last week with him as though it were a treasure. I think it will always be the same grief to her but she may be able to find some comfort outside. John is simply adorable to her. I believe I shall always love him, no matter what comes up or if I shouldn't know him better than I do now, I'd love him for the sweet way he has with Ellis and the care he takes of her and the thought he gives her. . . .
> Ellis was talking about the boys, what fine boys they were and how happy she was in them. She had read an article where the women in like circumstances said My children are fine but they are another generation from me and my husband and there isn't any intimacy. As Ellis repeated it she said, "You see, that is what you miss, that intimacy which you can't have with anyone else and which nothing ever replaces."

Ellis did not have to worry about money. Ring's passion for insurance made certain a comfortable, though scarcely extravagant, future. He left an estate with a net value of $192,927.63. Of that, life-insurance policies with a total worth of $169,159.28 were payable to Ellis and the estate; smaller policies were payable to Ring's two sisters and three brothers. The East Hampton house was valued for tax purposes at $40,000.

Ellis did not sell the house, because it could produce a good income from summer rentals, but she moved her favorite furniture out of it and settled down in a Revolutionary farmhouse near New Milford, Connecticut, which she bought in 1934 for $17,000 and modernized for roughly the same amount. It is a small but roomy and comfortable dwelling that sits in a two-hundred-acre valley near a river. Once settled there, with plenty of room for the boys—and, later, their wives and children—she entered into near-total seclusion not because she was antisocial, but because she had had enough of that and was ready to enjoy her garden, her house and land, and her family, without unwelcome intrusions from the rest of the world.

She could not keep the world out of her life completely, however, and twice in the next decade it entered cruelly. In September, 1938, Jim was killed in Spain while fighting for the Republican cause; he was one of the last American volunteers to be killed in that cause; he was twenty-four years old. Six years later, David was also killed in warfare; he was in Germany as a correspondent when a jeep in which he was riding hit a pile of mines; he was twenty-five years old. For Ellis, in the recollection of Ring Lardner, Jr., "the cumulative effect of this third blow on top of the others was devastating." It was quite a while before she was able to resume a normal life.

In 1952 the New Milford house acquired long-term boarders. Ring Lardner, Jr.—he was by now called Bill only within the family—had finished serving nine and a half months at the Federal Correctional Institution in Danbury, Connecticut, after being convicted of contempt of Congress; he had, as one of the "Hollywood Ten," refused to answer the House Un-American Activities Committee's questions about Communist associations he had had. Now he was on the blacklist, and he and his wife, Francis (she was David's widow), had settled in New Milford with their children for what turned out to be a two-year stay.

Ellis died in the New Milford house on February 15, 1960; the immediate cause was pneumonia, but several strokes had rendered her too weak to fight it. She had been vigorous until her last days, and lived to be seventy-two years old. Within a month of her death, John—who was suffering from tuberculosis, multiple sclerosis and heart disease—was put in the hospital by a heart attack. A couple of weeks later, back at home, he had another attack and died. He was forty-seven years old.

BY THE TIME OF HIS DEATH Ring's books had to all intents and purposes stopped selling; in the last three years of his life Scribner's was able to pay him the sorry total of $1,019.83 in royalties. But in the years that followed, his popularity and reputation grew rather than shrank. He has never had a revival such as that Scott Fitzgerald began to enjoy after the publication in 1951 of Arthur Mizener's biography, *The Far Side of Paradise*; it is most unlikely that as a writer of short fiction, nonsense and satire, he ever will. But he has never vanished, either, as have many other popular writers of his period, and in large measure that is because of four posthumous collections of his work.

The first of these, *The Portable Ring Lardner*, was published by Viking in 1946. Edited by Gilbert Seldes, who wrote a sensitive and sympathetic introduction, the book contained much of what Seldes had included in *First and Last* as well as the full texts of *You Know Me Al* and *The Big Town*, and a discriminating selection of eleven short stories.

The second, *Shut Up, He Explained* (the comma, it should be noted, is a gratuitous intrusion on Ring's carefully unpunctuated original), was published by Scribner's in 1962. It was edited by Babette Rosmond and Henry Morgan, and concentrated on nonsense and parody. Its greatest value was that it contained a dozen first-book appearances, most of them *New Yorker* radio columns.

Scribner's published the third, *The Ring Lardner Reader*, a year later. This is the principal Lardner collection still in print, containing as it does six dozen separate pieces. Edited by Maxwell Geismar, it is clearly arranged to enhance the credibility of its editor's essentially political interpretation of Ring's work as a damnation of American middle-class society. The collection does not contain any new material and reprints a good deal of decidedly inferior fiction, but its encyclopedic quality makes it useful.

The fourth of these books has already been mentioned several times: *Some Champions,* edited by Matthew J. Bruccoli and Richard Layman, published by Scribner's in 1976. All twenty-six of these pieces are collected for the first time; the most valuable are the autobiographical articles from the *Saturday Evening Post,* "Insomnia," and several of the "dark" stories from Ring's last years.

Interest in Ring's work has remained high in large measure because of the American English teacher. In junior high schools, senior high schools and colleges, stories such as "Haircut," "Some Like Them Cold" and "The Love Nest" have been required reading for decades. Because of their smoothness of construction and high entertainment quotient, they have been regarded as excellent both as introductory material and as subjects for analysis of structure, plot, characterization and dialogue. Some of them, in fact, are now viewed at the college and university level as so carefully constructed as to be formulaic, with the unfortunate result that Ring's work is being phased out of some courses in American literature.

That probably also reflects Ring's current critical reputation, which is far less a matter of rejection than of inattention. Considering how widely admired he was during his lifetime and how greatly he influenced other, more definably "literary" writers, it is astonishing how little serious critical study his work has received —and how little of *that* has been of any particular quality. There are only eight titles listed as "Principal Works About Ring W. Lardner" in the Bruccoli-Layman bibliography, and three of those are unpublished dissertations; three of the rest are works of criticism, the best being Walton R. Patrick's undoctrinaire *Ring Lardner,* a volume in the Twayne series of critical studies. Of miscellaneous pieces of criticism and commentary, aside from the Virginia Woolf analysis published in 1925, there is not much beyond a first-rate review in the *New Statesman* by V. S. Pritchett of a 1959 British collection of Ring's stories, and a 1972 article in the *Journal of Popular Culture* by Leverett T. Smith, Jr., called " 'The Diameter of Frank Chance's Diamond': Ring Lardner and Professional Sports."

The very title of that second article suggests one reason why Ring's work has yet to receive the searching critical examination that it deserves: much of it is directly or tangentially about sport, and even though sport has caught the fancy of some intellectuals for its metaphoric possibilities, it continues to remain somehow disreputable as a subject of serious scrutiny. Even that, however, does not get to the heart of the puzzlement and occasional disdain with which Ring is generally viewed in scholarly circles. The real explanation lies in three interrelated considerations: Ring was basically a journalist, he declined to take his work with undue seriousness, and he refused to do what literary people thought he should do.

Ring knew that "serious" people held journalism and popular fiction in contempt, and—quite apart from a natural tendency to shrug his shoulders and say, "What of it?"—his awareness of this almost certainly was one reason why he offered his work to readers in such a self-deprecatory way. Particularly after he moved over to Scribner's and into the limelight of critical attention, he developed a defensiveness about his work that helps explain the prefaces so vexing to Edmund Wilson and other reviewers. The prefaces were basically self-mocking in intent, but they also gave Ring a form of protection against critical rejection; he could always let them stand as proof enough that he, too, didn't take his work seriously. He was scarcely as ignorant as Hemingway represented him to be—as if Hemingway were any intellectual—but he did have the understandable reticence of a person of limited formal education whose work was being presented to readers who were, in his eyes, his intellectual superiors.

In point of fact he knew full well that what he had written was honorable and in its own way serious. This workmanlike attitude and indifference to high artistic accomplishment infuriated many of his admirers, none more than Scott Fitzgerald. In his obituary piece he said that "Ring's achievement . . . fell short of the achievement he was capable of, and this because of a cynical attitude toward his work." A year after Ring's death he was far harsher. In November, 1934, Max Perkins wrote him that "you are profligate with your material as Ring told you." Scott replied with an explosion of anger and self-justification:

> . . . [Ring] never knew anything about composition, except as it concerned the shorter forms; that is why he always needed advice from us as to how to organize his material; it was his greatest fault the fault of many men brought up in the school of journalism—

while a novelist with his sempiternal sigh can cut a few breaths. It is a hell of a lot more difficult to build up a long groan than to develop a couple of short coughs!

It was a brutal assessment and, though not without its element of truth, an unfair one. Ring got an enormous amount of work done in his lifetime, enough of it of such quality that eventually he will be duly recognized. Basically he knew that. Basically he respected the work he had done.

Yet two things nagged at him, compounded the guilt and self-doubt into which he, too, often lapsed late in his life. One was that he had worked as hard as he could to fulfill his potential, and when he saw what he had created he felt cheated: his talent was too limited and so was what it produced. If he thought of himself in terms of the athletes whose accomplishments he measured, perhaps he saw himself as a Morris Rath or a Nap Rucker rather than a Ty Cobb or a Christy Mathewson—good enough, to be sure, and worthy of high respect, but when stretched to the limit, still not great.

The other was that although he did not want to write a novel and did not think it necessary to do so in order to prove himself, there nonetheless nagged in his mind the sense that he had shirked the ultimate challenge of the field into which he had somewhat accidentally fallen. Americans equate bigness with greatness, and all around him people were saying that he had to do something big if he wanted to be great. In truth, he probably did not care all that much about being great, but neither did he want to disappoint. He was a miniaturist to whom the world seemed to be shouting "Inflate! Inflate!" and he could not handle it.

Which is a great pity, because what he did do should command our respect and gratitude. To begin with, he told us how to write the way we talk. V. S. Pritchett has pointed out that the "specifically American contribution to literature" is "talk" and that it began with Ring: "Now," he wrote in his 1959 review, "mainly under the double influence of Joyce and Lardner's American successors—the stream of consciousness being married to the stream of garrulity—we begin to have a talking prose and are likely to have more." If Ring's ear was so keen that it permitted him to be facile, to avoid the struggles most writers must face, it was also the chief instrument of a revolution in American fiction.

Ring made people laugh, and he still does. Jack Keefe, that true American original, is a great comic character; so is the "wise boob," whether he takes the name of Joe Gullible or Tom Finch or Fred Gross—or Ring Lardner. The nonsense plays have lost none of their wild humor and never will, for they are timeless. Ring's humor is as American as his language: wisecracking, sardonic, earthy, self-mocking. He helped teach us not only to laugh at ourselves but to laugh at that which is unique in us, to delight in our very American-ness.

In doing that, he helped us to see ourselves. He was a writer of manners, and the manners he described were those of a society markedly different from that in the novels of Edith Wharton and Henry James. He wrote about the manners of the bleachers and the clubhouse, the mezzanine and the dressing room, the barbershop and the beauty parlor, the Pullman car and the touring car, the kitchen and the diner, the bridge table and the bowling alley. He watched us get rich, and he showed us how foolish we often looked as we threw our new money after idle and inane pleasures and possessions; if he had been truly bitter or misanthropic or hateful, he never would have succeeded in making us laugh at ourselves so heartily.

He wrote so perceptively and accurately about what he saw because he was a great journalist. This, in the end, is the singular accomplishment of his life. Ring came into the profession when it was held in far too much disdain even to be considered a "profession"; it was a line of work pursued by coarse people who had a coarse talent for putting words together in a speedy way. He was one of the very first people to bring creativity and felicity of style to the press. He set an example that was eagerly followed by younger writers. His aristocratic manner and confident bearing gave the lie to the argument that journalists were by their very nature guttersnipes. The quality of his writing and the doggedness with which he kept it so high proved that good prose and journalism were not mutually exclusive. So, too, he showed that in newspapers one could do serious work and be respected for it.

In assessing him, moreover, the work of his life must not be stressed at the expense of his life itself. Marc Connelly, in a letter to Ellis, got somewhere close to the point when he wrote ". . . behind all his fun, his bitter satire, his criticism and his pity, was a great dignity, the dignity of humanity. Everything Ring started to write had somewhere behind it a point of view essentially noble. His humor was the humor of protest, a demand, by implication, that mankind be something more than the idiocy he was exposing." He had a great heart, as Max Perkins knew:

> . . . Ring was not, strictly speaking, a great writer. The truth is he never regarded himself seriously as a writer. He always thought of himself as a newspaperman, anyhow. He had a sort of provincial scorn of literary people. If he had written much more, he would have been a great writer perhaps, but whatever it was that prevented him from writing more was the thing that prevented him from being a great writer. But he was a great man, and one of immense latent talent which got itself partly expressed. I guess Scott would think much the same way about it.

Scott did:

> . . . At no time did I feel that I had known him enough, or that anyone knew him—it was not the feeling that there was more stuff in him and that it should come out, it was rather a qualitative difference, it was rather as though, due to some inadequacy in one's self, one had not penetrated to something unsolved, new and unsaid. That is why one wishes that Ring had written down a larger proportion of what was in his mind and heart. It would have saved him longer for us, and that in itself would be something. But I would like to know what it was, and now I will go on wishing— what did Ring want, how did he want things to be, how did he think things were?
>
> A great and good American is dead. Let us not obscure him by the flowers, but walk up and look at that fine medallion, all torn by sorrows that perhaps we are not equipped to understand. Ring made no enemies, because he was kind, and to millions he gave release and delight.

Acknowledgments

My large debt to Richard Layman has already been described, to some extent at least, in the "Special Acknowledgment" at the front of this book. He is not the only person, however, whose assistance, cooperation, kindness and enthusiasm made important contributions to various aspects of my work. Sometimes an author's words of thanks seem pro forma and empty; I hope readers will understand that this book quite simply could not have been written without the help of the men and women whose names follow.

First among them is Ring Lardner, Jr. At times his courtesies astonished me; he permitted me, for example, to walk away from the house at New Milford with a large cardboard box filled with irreplaceable letters, clippings and papers that his mother had scrupulously saved. (All of this material is now at the Newberry Library in Chicago.) He read my manuscript with great care, and corrected me on a number of errors or misinterpretations of fact. But he never once challenged my interpretations of his father's life and work, though I feel sure he disagrees with a number of them, and for this more than anything else I am grateful to him: not merely did he give me much of the material for this book, but he further gave me the freedom to write it, for better or worse, as I felt it should be written.

When I first began to give serious thought to the notion of writing a biography of Ring Lardner, I almost automatically turned for initial advice and counsel to Matthew J. Bruccoli at the University of South Carolina. We had never met, but I knew that if anyone could give me a quick and accurate assessment of the state of Lardner scholarship, Matt Bruccoli would be that person. I was right. But his assistance went much further than mere counsel. He invited me to come up to his offices at Columbia, South Carolina, and gave me free run through the huge stacks of Lardner Xeroxes and photocopies that he and Rick Layman had assembled in connection with their work on the Lardner bibliography. The two weeks I spent there were as productive a period of research as any I enjoyed.

The kindness that Matt Bruccoli extended to me was repeated over and over by others as I traveled through the Middle West and Northeast in search of Lardner material. Of all the people who helped me so generously, I am especially grateful to Diana Haskell of the Newberry Library. Most of the important Lardner material is deposited there; when I arrived one September Monday it was with the expectation of plowing through Ring's courtship letters to Ellis but not hers to him, since Ring, Jr., had written in March, 1972, that "my mother's letters to my father were lost at some point, I suspect by her own hand." I spent the morning making an attack on a fat box labeled "Lardner Outgoing Letters" and was hard at work when my curiosity was piqued by another box, labeled "Lardner Incoming Letters." I opened it, and my heart stopped: there, inside, were all of Ellis' letters to Ring. I rushed back to my hotel and called Ring, Jr.—it was our first conversation—to tell him that I had chanced upon material that would greatly alter the books on which both of us were working.

Enter Diana Haskell. She had been out with a nasty cold that Monday, and when she came to work on Tuesday it was to be confronted with a would-be author fairly rattling with urgency: Xerox copies of the Ellis letters, all four hundred-plus of them, just *had* to be made, the sooner the better, one set for me and one for Ring. Diana, a true curator with a full understanding of the value of the material under her control, refused to let me or any of her subordinates take on the onerous assignment. She did it herself. For an entire workday she stood at the Xerox machine, performing with unflagging good spirits one of the most hopelessly boring—and fatiguing—tasks created by the new technology. In the months that followed she did many other kind and useful things for me, but it is that long, hard day at the Xerox machine I remember with the greatest gratitude.

Also in Chicago, I was granted access to the Lardner material in the files of the *Tribune* by Harold Hutchings, archivist of the paper; he further allowed me to read and make notes on *The Colonel and the Captain Take Command: The Chicago Tribune—1900 to 1920*, an unpublished manuscript by an old-time Chicago newspaperman that provided some nice nuggets of information. Robert V. Twilling, assistant marketing director of the *Tribune*, graciously granted me permission to quote Lardner writings published by the paper, and helped me get copies of several rare photographs in its files—among them the lovely picture that appears on the dust jacket. Lloyd Wendt interrupted work on his history of the *Tribune* to give me some helpful tips—as did his friendly competitor and frequent collaborator, Herman Kogan, book editor of the Chicago *Sun-Times*, one of the grand people in the book-reviewing business. Another grand book person is Kathleen Moloney, who introduced me to her colleagues on the *Tribune*, arranged a guest membership for me at the Chicago Press Club and—with her husband, Dominick Abel—made me feel welcome in a city I had not previously visited. It is a shame that she has abandoned book-reviewing, at which she did so well, to return to publishing.

Three other people performed acts of generosity almost as spectacular as Diana Haskell's. I arrived unannounced at the National Baseball Library in Cooperstown, New York, on a Saturday, only to find its files closed until Monday; so Clifford Kachline, the chief librarian, interrupted his weekend's rest to open the files on Sunday morning and thus permit me to examine the *Sporting News* during Ring's editorship. At Princeton's Firestone Library, Agnes Sherman made me welcome the moment I appeared, cut through red tape in order to grant me speedy access to the Fitzgerald and Perkins collections, and arranged large amounts of copying for me. In Miami my friend Taffy Beber of WPBT, the excellent Public Television station, responded with alacrity when I learned about the PBS production of *June Moon* and called to ask if I could see a tape; she ordered it from New York, fought near-mortal combat with the Postal Service to get it delivered at a reasonable rate, and showed it to me at a private screening.

Richard L. Tobin, one of Ring, Jr.'s, cousins, took an afternoon off from his duties at the *Saturday Review* to talk with me about his memories of his uncle and aunt. Although I only quote him by name a couple of times, many more of his perceptive insights are silently reflected in the book.

Of the others who helped me during my travels, I want in particular to thank Anne Frese of the Niles Community Library, Fran Reeves of the Fort St. Joseph Museum, and Arlene Warshaw of the Great Neck Public Library.

Authors don't often thank their agents. I don't know why; maybe theirs aren't as good as mine, Liz Darhansoff. A Lardner biography was her idea, and she managed to sell it to a publisher whom I respected. Her phone calls of encouragement during the long time of research and writing kept my spirits up, and once she began receiving the manuscript chapter by chapter, her kind words helped me muster the courage to face the typewriter another day.

Bob Loomis took over editorial responsibility for this book midway through its composition, and from the hour of our first conversation I realized that he was the perfect editor for it. That was confirmed when we sat down for several days of tinkering with the finished text; I resisted few of his suggestions because almost all were irresistible, and the book is far better because of them.

My friends and, at the time of the writing of this book, my colleagues at the Miami *Herald*, Larry Jinks and Ron Martin, were inordinately generous in granting me extended periods of leave and semi-leave; they put up with my infrequent appearances at the office for a year and a half, though I had best admit that neither of them was seen dancing in the streets when at last I returned full-time. Edwin Pope, the *Herald's* sports editor, allowed me a couple of important loans from his excellent sports library, and had good words to say about the baseball chapter at a time when good words were badly needed.

I remain deeply grateful to Sue Hartt, to whom I was married when this book was written, for her encouragement and support as I undertook a task about which I had grave apprehensions and misgivings.

Jonathan Yardley

A Note on Sources

To a degree that I frankly did not anticipate as I began my researches, the most important source materials for this book are the letters and published writings of Ring Lardner. He was by no stretch of the imagination an autobiographical writer in the sense that Thomas Wolfe was, yet I believe this book satisfactorily demonstrates that an understanding of who he was can in large measure be reached through what he wrote. It does not, however, seem to me to serve any purpose to footnote my many quotations from his work, and I have refrained from doing so. In the bibliography that follows, readers will find, purely for their information, a list of Ring's books, but I have not supplied one of his uncollected fiction and journalism; again, such a list seems to me to serve no purpose in this context save that of fine-print clutter, since scholars and the scholarly inclined can find everything they need in the Bruccoli-Layman bibliography. The source of most quotes is clearly indicated in the text; almost all the Lardner material quoted without attribution can be located in the autobiographical pieces collected by Bruccoli and Layman in *Some Champions*.

The bibliography—its title is *Ring Lardner: A Descriptive Bibliography*—was my single most valuable working tool. Its clear, categorical organization and its careful index allowed me to cut through many confusing thickets. Every biographer should have the luxury of such a thorough bibliography to fall back on, but the truth is that I am unlikely in any future project to be so well served.

The only other Lardner biography is Donald Elder's *Ring Lardner*, published in 1956. Elder was a competent, witty writer, but he had the misfortune to lose interest in his subject, and the book shows it. On the other hand, it is an absolutely indispensable source of Lardner material. Elder was able to talk with Ellis, Anna Tobin, John Lardner, Grant and Kate Rice, and a number of ballplayers who knew Ring well. All these people are long since dead, and thus their recollections as reported by Elder are invaluable. For the most part, my policy has been to identify Elder as the source of material that cannot be found elsewhere, but not to credit him when my own researches produced material that happens also to appear in his book.

Ring Lardner, Jr.'s, *The Lardners: My Family Remembered* is a wise and lovely book that I admire as much for its grace of style and thought as for the original Lardner anecdotes and insights it contains. There is some inevitable overlapping of his book and mine, though I have made a considerable effort to avoid poaching on territory that is uniquely his. Readers who find my portrait of Ellis interesting should be advised that there is more about her in Ring's book, and there is vastly more about the boys.

Four collections of letters were of special value to me in depicting Ring's friendship with Scott Fitzgerald and his business relationship with Maxwell Perkins. *Dear Scott, Dear Max*, edited by John Kuehl and Jackson Bryer, is a comprehensive record of the Fitzgerald-Perkins correspondence; it sheds new and revealing light on Scott's occasionally ambivalent feelings about Ring—the old competitive urge from time to time stirring in his breast. It is necessarily augmented by *The Letters of F. Scott Fitzgerald*, edited by Andrew Turnbull, since for some reason Kuehl and Bryer chose not to reprint several letters that had already appeared in Turnbull's book. *Ring Around Max*, edited by Clifford Caruthers, was a great convenience to me, since it spared me from squinting at the microfilm of the Lardner-Perkins correspondence. *Editor to Author*, a fine, highly selective collection of Perkins letters well edited by John Hall Wheelock, contains the letter about Ring's abilities and character quoted in the final pages; it was written, incidentally, to Ernest Hemingway, chiding him about his depiction of Ring in "Defense of Dirty Words."

For my account of baseball in the years Ring covered it, I relied heavily on two books that are essential to an understanding of the game, its history, and its place in the American consciousness. Harold Seymour's *Baseball: The Golden Age* is the second of what is to be a three-volume history, and it simply has no rivals; Seymour leaves no doubt, if any doubt remained, that baseball is a legitimate and fruitful study for the serious historian. Lawrence's Ritter's *The Glory of Their Times* is history of another sort—oral history, the recorded recollections of men who played the game when it was young; I am especially grateful to Ritter for having talked to Davy Jones, whose delightful anecdote about Germany Schaeffer is a particular favorite of mine.

The list of sources that follows is divided into three sections: Lardner books, other books, and magazine articles. Where moved to do so, I have provided brief comments on individual entries. Since I have done no footnoting, scholars are advised that my files and working materials, as well as my manuscript, will be placed at the Newberry Library for their inspection and, I hope, will answer any questions they may have.

Ring Lardner's Books

Bib Ballads. Chicago: P. F. Volland & Co., 1915.

You Know Me Al. New York: George H. Doran Company, 1916.

Gullible's Travels, Etc. Indianapolis: Bobbs-Merrill, 1917.

My Four Weeks in France. Indianapolis: Bobbs-Merrill, 1918.

Treat 'Em Rough. Indianapolis: Bobbs-Merrill, 1918.

The Real Dope. Indianapolis: Bobbs-Merrill, 1919.

Own Your Own Home. Indianapolis: Bobbs-Merrill, 1919.

Regular Fellows I Have Met. Chicago: B. A. Wilmot, 1919.

The Young Immigrunts. Indianapolis: Bobbs-Merrill, 1920.

Symptoms of Being 35. Indianapolis: Bobbs-Merrill, 1921.

The Big Town. Indianapolis: Bobbs-Merrill, 1921.

Say It with Oil. New York: George H. Doran Company, 1923.

How to Write Short Stories. New York: Scribner's, 1924.

What of It? New York: Scribner's, 1925.

The Love Nest and Other Stories. New York: Scribner's, 1926.

The Story of a Wonder Man. New York: Scribner's, 1927.

Round Up. New York: Scribner's, 1929.

June Moon, with George S. Kaufman. New York: Scribner's, 1930.

Lose with a Smile. New York: Scribner's, 1933.

First and Last. New York: Scribner's, 1934.

The Portable Lardner, edited by Gilbert Seldes. New York: Viking, 1946.

Shut Up, He Explained, edited by Babette Rosmond and Henry Morgan. New York: Scribner's, 1962.

The Ring Lardner Reader, edited by Maxwell Geismar. New York: Scribner's, 1963.

Some Champions, edited by Matthew J. Bruccoli and Richard Layman. New York: Scribner's, 1976.

Other Books

Ade, George, *Fables in Slang*. New York: Grosset & Dunlap, 1899.

Asinof, Eliot, *Eight Men Out*. New York: Holt, Rinehart and Winston, 1963. A thorough examination of the Black Sox Scandal.

Baker, Carlos, *Ernest Hemingway: A Life Story*. New York: Scribner's, 1969.

A Baseball Century. New York: Macmillan, 1976.

The Baseball Encyclopedia. New York: Macmillan, 1969.

Brown, John Mason, *The Worlds of Robert E. Sherwood: Mirror to His Times*. New York: Harper & Row, 1965.

Bruccoli, Matthew J., and Layman, Richard, *Ring Lardner: A Descriptive Bibliography*. Pittsburgh: University of Pittsburgh Press, 1976.

Bruccoli, Matthew J.; Smith, Scottie Fitzgerald; and Kerr, Joan P., *The Romantic Egotists*. New York: Scribner's, 1974. A coffee-table book filled with wonderful material about the Fitzgeralds, including the full text of Ring's farewell poem to Zelda.

Caruthers, Clifford, ed., *Ring Around Max: The Correspondence of Ring Lardner & Maxwell Perkins.* Dekalb, Ill.: Northern Illinois University Press, 1973.

Cleary, James M., *The Colonel and the Captain Take Command: The Chicago Tribune—1900 to 1920.* Unpublished manuscript on file in the archives of the Chicago *Tribune.*

Cohen, Richard M.; Neft, David S.; Johnson Roland T.; and Deutsch, Jordan A., *The World Series.* New York: Dial, 1976.

Creamer, Robert W., *Babe: The Legend Comes to Life.* New York: Simon & Schuster, 1974.

Drake, William A., *American Criticism 1926.* New York: Harcourt Brace, 1926. Contains an important early assessment of Lardner by Gilbert Seldes.

Dunne, Finley Peter, *The World of Mr. Dooley,* ed. by Louis Filler. New York: Collier Books, 1962.

Elder, Donald, *Ring Lardner.* New York: Doubleday, 1956.

Ewen, David, *American Popular Songs: From the Revolutionary War to the Present.* New York: Random House, 1966.

Farnsworth, Marjorie, *The Ziegfeld Follies.* New York: Putnam's, 1956.

Farr, Finis, *Chicago.* New Rochelle, N.Y.: Arlington House, 1973. A fine example of what can be done seriously and readably with local history.

Fenton, Charles A., *The Apprenticeship of Ernest Hemingway: The Early Years.* New York: Viking, 1958.

Fitzgerald, F. Scott, *The Crack-Up,* ed. by Edmund Wilson. New York: New Directions, 1945. This posthumous collection contains the full text of Scott's eulogy, "Ring."

———, *The Great Gatsby.* New York, Scribner's, 1925.

———, *Tender Is the Night,* New York: Schibner's, 1934.

———, *The Vegetable,* Scribner's, 1923.

Frakes, James R., *Ring Lardner: A Critical Survey.* Unpublished dissertation, University of Pennsylvania, 1953.

Friedrich, Otto, *Ring Lardner.* Minneapolis: University of Minnesota Press, 1965. A volume in the series "University of Minnesota Pamphlets on American Writers."

Geismar, Maxwell, *Ring Lardner and the Portrait of Folly.* New York: Crowell, 1972.

———, *Writers in Crisis.* Boston: Houghton Mifflin, 1942.

Graham, Sheilah, *The Real F. Scott Fitzgerald.* New York: Grosset & Dunlap, 1976.

Green, Abel, and Laurie, Joe, *Show Biz: From Vaude to Video.* Garden City: Garden City Books, 1952.

Hart, Moss. *Act One.* New York, Random House, 1959.

Hecht, Ben, *Charlie.* New York: Harper, 1957.

———, *A Child of the Century.* New York: Simon & Schuster, 1954.

Hemingway, Ernest, *Men Without Women.* New York: Scribner's, 1927.

Contains the short story "Fifty Grand," in which friendly reference to Lardner is made.

Joost, Nicholas, *Ernest Hemingway and the Little Magazines: The Paris Years*. Barre, Mass.: Barre Publishers, 1968.

Kahn, E. J., *The World of Swope*. New York: Simon & Schuster, 1965.

Kuehl, John, and Bryer, Jackson, ed., *Dear Scott, Dear Max: The Fitzgerald-Perkins Correspondence*. New York: Scribner's, 1971.

Kogan, Herman, and Kogan, Rick, *Yesterday's Chicago*. Miami: E. A. Seeman, 1976.

Kogan, Herman, and Wendt, Lloyd, *Chicago: A Pictorial History*. New York: E. P. Dutton, 1973.

Lardner, Ring, Jr., *The Lardners: My Family Remembered*. New York: Harper & Row, 1976.

Latham, Aaron, *Crazy Sundays: F. Scott Fitzgerald in Hollywood*. New York: Viking, 1971.

Layman, Richard, *Bibliographical Information for a Life of Ring Lardner*. Unpublished dissertation, University of South Carolina, 1975. An enormously useful, dispassionate account of Lardner's journalistic career; I relied on it often.

Loos, Anita, *A Girl Like I*. New York: Viking, 1966.

Mayer, Harold M., and Wade, Richard C., *Chicago: Growth of a Metropolis*. Chicago: University of Chicago Press, 1969. An absolutely remarkable book, in which the city's changing physical shape is revealed in photographs, maps and text.

McPhaul, John J., *Deadlines & Monkeyshines: The Fabled World of Chicago Journalism*. Englewood Cliffs, N.J.: Prentice-Hall, 1962.

Mencken, Henry L., *The American Language, Second Edition*. New York: Alfred A. Knopf, 1921.

———, *Prejudices: Fifth Series*. New York: Knopf, 1926.

Milford, Nancy, *Zelda: A Biography*. New York: Harper & Row, 1970.

Mizener, Arthur, *The Far Side of Paradise: A Biography of F. Scott Fitzgerald*. Boston: Houghton Mifflin, 1951.

Neft, David S.; Johnson, Roland T.; Cohen, Richard M.; and Deutsch, Jordan A., *The Sports Encyclopedia: Baseball*. New York: Grosset & Dunlap, 1974.

Parker, Dorothy, *The Portable Dorothy Parker*. New York: Viking, 1973.

Patrick, Walton R., *Ring Lardner*. New York: Twayne, 1963. An excellent volume in Twayne's series of critical studies.

Peterson, Harold, *The Man Who Invented Baseball*. New York: Scribner's, 1973.

Peterson, Robert W., *Only the Ball Was White*. Englewood Cliffs, N.J.: Prentice-Hall, 1970.

Phillips, David R., and Kart, Lawrence, *That Old Ball Game*. Chicago: Regnery, 1975.

Reichler, Joe, ed., *The Game and the Glory*. Englewood Cliffs, N.J.: Prentice-Hall, 1976.

Rice, Grantland, *The Tumult and the Shouting: My Life in Sport*. New

York: A. S. Barnes, 1954. Considering how close Rice was to Ring, it is astonishing (not to mention disappointing) how little Rice's memoirs tell us about their friendship.

Ritter, Lawrence, *The Glory of Their Times*. New York: Macmillian, 1966.

Seldes, Gilbert, *The Seven Lively Arts*. New York: Sagamore Press, 1957.

Seymour, Harold, *Baseball: The Golden Age*. New York: Oxford University Press, 1971.

Shannon, Bill, and Kalinsky, George, *The Ballparks*. New York: Hawthorn, 1975.

Stewart, Donald Ogden, *By a Stroke of Luck!* New York: Paddington Press/ Two Continents, 1975.

———, *Mr. and Mrs. Haddock Abroad*, reprint edition with an afterword by the author. Carbondale and Edwardsville, Ill.: Southern Illinois University Press, 1975.

Teichman, Howard, *George S. Kaufman: An Intimate Portrait*. New York: Atheneum, 1972.

This Great Game. Englewood Cliffs, N.J.: Prentice-Hall, 1971.

Thurber, James, *The Years with Ross*. Boston: Atlantic-Little, Brown, 1959.

Turnbull, Andrew, *The Letters of F. Scott Fitzgerald*. New York: Scribner's, 1963.

———, *Scott Fitzgerald: A Biography*. New York: Scribner's, 1962.

Webb, Howard W., *Ring Lardner's Conflict and Reconciliation with American Society*. Unpublished dissertation, University of Iowa, 1953.

Wheeler, John, *I've Got News for You*. New York: E. P. Dutton, 1961. Like Grantland Rice's, Wheeler's memoir is almost totally useless to a Lardner biographer.

Wilson, Edmund, *The Shock of Recognition*. New York: Doubleday, 1943.

———, *The Shores of Light*. New York: Vintage, 1961.

———, *The Twenties*. New York: Farrar, Straus and Giroux, 1975.

Wheelock, John Hall, ed., *Editor to Author: The Letters of Maxwell E. Perkins*. New York: Scribner's, 1950.

Wolff, Geoffrey, *Black Sun: The Brief Transit and Violent Eclipse of Harry Crosby*. New York: Random House, 1976.

Woolf, Virginia, *The Moment and Other Essays*. New York: Harcourt Brace, 1948. Contains the essay "American Fiction," first published in the *Dial* in 1925.

Magazine Articles

Anderson, Sherwood, "Four American Impressions." *The New Republic* (October 11, 1922).

———, "Meeting Ring Lardner." *The New Yorker* (November 25, 1933).

Berryman, John, "The Case of Ring Lardner." *Commentary* (November, 1956). A thoughtful but unduly condescending assessment of Lardner contained in a review of the Elder biography.

Fadiman, Clifton, "Ring Lardner and the Triangle of Hate." The *Nation* (March 22, 1933).

Frank, Stanley, "Bible of Baseball." The *Saturday Evening Post* (June 20, 1942). A breezy history of the *Sporting News*.

Fullerton, Hugh S., "Between Games." *American* magazine (July, 1911). Written with Fullerton's characteristically florid style, but a delightful picture of ballplayers on the road in 1911.

Hemingway, Ernest, "Defense of Dirty Words." *Esquire* (September, 1934).

Holland, Gerald, "Taylor Spink Is First-Class." *Sports Illustrated* (February 27, 1961).

Johnstone, Will B, "The 'Big' Time." Published in 1922 in a local magazine for Great Neck residents, this is on file at the Great Neck library, but its exact source is unclear.

Lardner, Ring, Jr., "Ring Lardner & Sons." *Esquire* (March, 1922).

Mizener, Arthur, "Scott and Zelda in Great Neck," *On the Sound* (April, 1974). A most useful article, published in a Long Island magazine.

Pritchett, V. S., "The Talent of Ring Lardner." The *New Statesman* (April 25, 1959).

Rattray, Jeanette Edwards, "East Hampton Literary Group—II." *Long Island Forum* (September, 1962).

Smith, Leverett T., Jr., " 'The Diameter of Frank Chance's Diamond': Ring Lardner and Professional Sports." *Journal of Popular Culture* (Summer, 1972). The best examination available of the relationship between Lardner and the games he covered; I am indebted to its author for his perceptions.

Stewart, Charles D., "The United States of Base-Ball." *Century* magazine (July, 1907). A pioneering (and delightful) piece of serious inquiry into the meaning of the national pastime.

Tiverton, Dana, "Ring Lardner Writes a Story." *Writer* magazine (January, 1933).

Tobin, Richard L., "The Phoenix Nest." The *Saturday Review* (July 20, 1963).

———, "The Phoenix Nest." The *Saturday Review* (January 25, 1964).

Van Doren, Carl, "Beyond Grammar." *Century* magazine (August 9, 1924). The subtitle is, "Ring W. Lardner: Philologist Among the Low-Brows."

Webb, Howard W., "The Meaning of Ring Lardner's Fiction: A Reevaluation." *American Literature* (January, 1960).

Index

About the Author

JONATHAN YARDLEY is the book critic and a columnist for the *Washington Post*. In 1968–1969 he was a Nieman Fellow in Journalism at Harvard University, and in 1981 he was awarded the Pulitzer Prize for Distinguished Criticism. He is the author of six books as well as the editor of a posthumous memoir by H. L. Mencken and a collection of short stories by Ring Lardner. Yardley lives in Washington, D.C., with his wife, Marie Arana. Both of his sons, by a previous marriage, are journalists: Jim at the *New York Times* and William at the *Miami Herald*.